First World War
and Army of Occupation
War Diary
France, Belgium and Germany

46 DIVISION
137 Infantry Brigade
Prince of Wales's (North Staffordshire Regiment)
1/5 Battalion
1 February 1915 - 15 January 1918

WO95/2685/1

The Naval & Military Press Ltd
www.nmarchive.com
Published in association with The National Archives

Published by

The Naval & Military Press Ltd

Unit 10 Ridgewood Industrial Park,

Uckfield, East Sussex,

TN22 5QE England

Tel: +44 (0) 1825 749494

www.naval-military-press.com

www.nmarchive.com

This diary has been reprinted in facsimile from the original. Any imperfections are inevitably reproduced and the quality may fall short of modern type and cartographic standards.

© Crown Copyright
Images reproduced by permission of The National Archives, London, England, 2015.

Contents

Document type	Place/Title	Date From	Date To
Heading	WO95/2685/1		
Heading	46th Division 137th Infy Bde 1-5th Bn Nth Staffs 1915-1918 Jan To 59 Div 176 Bde		
Heading	N.M. Div 1st Happordshire Brigade 1/5th North Haffs Regt Vol I 1-28.2.15		
Heading	War Diary. Of 1/5th North Stafford Regt February 1st To February 28th, 1915		
War Diary	Saffron Walden.	01/02/1915	28/02/1915
Heading	137th Inf. Bde. 46th Div. Battn. Disembarked Havre From England 5.3.15. War Diary 1/5th Battn. The North Staffordshire Regiment. March 1915		
Heading	War Diary of 1/5th N. Staffordshire Regt March 1st To March 31st 1915		
War Diary	Saffron Walden	01/03/1915	01/03/1915
War Diary	Southampton	02/03/1915	04/03/1915
War Diary	Havre	05/03/1915	06/03/1915
War Diary	Arneke	07/03/1915	08/03/1915
War Diary	Borre	09/03/1915	10/03/1915
War Diary	Sailly	11/03/1915	15/03/1915
War Diary	Outtersteene	16/03/1915	19/03/1915
War Diary	Armentieres	20/03/1915	24/03/1915
War Diary	Outtersteene	25/03/1915	30/03/1915
War Diary	Bailleul	31/03/1915	31/03/1915
Heading	137th Inf. Bde. 46th Div. 1/5th Battn. The North Staffordshire Regiment April 1915		
War Diary	Neuve Eglise	01/04/1915	30/04/1915
Heading	137th Inf. Bde. 46th Div. 1/5th Battn. The North Staffordshire Regiment May 1915		
War Diary	Neuve Eglise	01/05/1915	31/05/1915
Heading	137th Inf. Bde. 46th Div. 1/5th Battn. The North Staffordshire Regiment June 1915		
Heading	War Diary of 1/5th North Staffs. Regt June, 1915		
War Diary	Neuve Eglise	01/06/1915	22/06/1915
War Diary	Ouderdom	25/06/1915	30/06/1915
Heading	137th Inf. Bde. 46th Div. 1/5th Battn. The North Staffordshire Regiment. July 1915		
War Diary		01/07/1915	31/07/1915
War Diary	137th Inf. Bde. 46th Div. 1/5th Battn. The North Staffordshire Regiment. August 1915		
Heading	War Diary of 1/5th. Battalion North Stafford Regiment From 1st. August 1915 To 31st. August 1915		
War Diary	Kruistraat.	01/08/1915	31/08/1915
Heading	137th Inf. Bde. 46th Div. 1/5th Battn. The North Staffordshire Regiment September 1915		
Heading	1/5th. North Staffs. Regt. War Diary For Month Of September, 1915		
War Diary	Verbranden Molen	01/09/1915	29/09/1915
Heading	137th Inf. Bde. 46th Div. 1/5th Battn. The North Staffordshire Regiment. October 1915		

Heading	War Diary For October, 1915 Of 1/5th North Staffs Regt		
War Diary	Hill 60	01/10/1915	01/10/1915
War Diary	Dickebusch	02/10/1915	02/10/1915
War Diary	L'Ecleme	03/10/1915	06/10/1915
War Diary	Drouvin	07/10/1915	12/10/1915
War Diary	Trenches E Of Vermelles	13/10/1915	14/10/1915
War Diary	Sailly La Bourse	15/10/1915	19/10/1915
War Diary	Allouagne	25/10/1915	25/10/1915
Miscellaneous	Brigade Operation Orders Nos. 20, 21 & 23		
Operation(al) Order(s)	Operation Orders. No. 20. By Brigadier General E. Feetham. C.B. Commanding 137th Infantry Brigade.	05/10/1915	05/10/1915
Operation(al) Order(s)	Operation Orders No 21. By Brigadier General Feetham. C.B. Commanding 137th. Infantry. Brigade.	11/10/1915	11/10/1915
Operation(al) Order(s)	Operation Order No 22 By Brigadier General E. Feetham. C.B. Commanding 137th Infantry Brigade.	11/10/1915	11/10/1915
Miscellaneous	Issued at 8-30p.m. by D.R. Copy No. 1 War Diary		
Operation(al) Order(s)	Operation Order No 23 By Brigadier General E. Feetham. C.B. Commanding 137th Infantry Brigade.	12/10/1915	12/10/1915
Heading	137th Inf. Bde. 46th Div.1/5th Battn. The North Staffordshire Regiment. November 1915		
Heading	War Diary of 1/5th Battalion North Staff Regt. For Month Of November, 1915		
War Diary	Fouquereuil	01/11/1915	05/11/1915
War Diary	Ni Merville	06/11/1915	07/11/1915
War Diary	Vieille Chapelle	08/11/1915	10/11/1915
War Diary	Croix Barbee	11/11/1915	14/11/1915
War Diary	Neuve Chapelle	15/11/1915	30/11/1915
Heading	137th Inf. Bde 46th Div. 1/5th Battn. The North Staffordshire Regiment. December 1915		
War Diary	Neuve Chapelle (Loretto. Rd Rest. Houses)	01/12/1915	04/12/1915
War Diary	St. Floris	05/12/1915	19/12/1915
War Diary	Mollinghem	20/12/1915	27/12/1915
War Diary	Marseille	28/12/1915	31/12/1915
Heading	War Diary of 1/5th. Battalion North Stafford. Regiment. From 1/1/16 To 31/1/16 Vol 12		
War Diary	Marseilles. Samti Camp	01/01/1916	05/01/1916
War Diary	H. T"Beltana"	06/01/1916	12/01/1916
War Diary	El Shallufa	13/01/1916	29/01/1916
War Diary	Alexandria	30/01/1916	31/01/1916
Heading	War Diary of 1/5th Battalion North Stafford Regiment From February 1st, 1916 To February To 29th, 1916 Vol XIII		
War Diary	Alexandria. Sidi Bishr Camp.	01/02/1916	05/02/1916
War Diary	H.T. "Transylvania"	06/02/1916	14/02/1916
War Diary	Buigny L'Abbe	15/02/1916	21/02/1916
War Diary	Bernaville	22/02/1916	29/02/1916
War Diary	War Diary 1/5th Battalion North Staffordshire Regiment. March 1st To 31st, 1916, Vol XIV		
War Diary	Hem	01/03/1916	01/03/1916
War Diary	Boisbergue	02/03/1916	06/03/1916
War Diary	Rebreuviette	07/03/1916	08/03/1916
War Diary	Penin.	11/03/1916	11/03/1916
War Diary	Acq	12/03/1916	12/03/1916
War Diary	Ecoivres.	13/03/1916	13/03/1916
War Diary	Neuville St. Vaast.	14/03/1916	25/03/1916

War Diary	Ecoivres	26/03/1916	30/03/1916
War Diary	Neuville St. Vaast.	31/03/1916	31/03/1916
Miscellaneous	1/5th Battalion North Stafford Regiment. Appendix To War Diary, March, 1916	28/03/1916	28/03/1916
Miscellaneous	Operation Orders By Lieut-Colonel W. Burnett. Commanding 1/5th Battalion North Staffs. Regt.	12/03/1916	12/03/1916
War Diary	Neuville St Vaast	01/04/1916	16/04/1916
War Diary	Ecoivres	16/04/1916	19/04/1916
War Diary	Chelers.	21/04/1916	21/04/1916
War Diary	Marquay	22/04/1916	30/04/1916
Heading	1/5th Battalion The Prince Of Wales North Staffordshire Regiment. War Diary For The Month Of May. 1916 Vol 16		
War Diary	Marquay	01/05/1916	03/05/1916
War Diary	Rebreuviette.	04/05/1916	04/05/1916
War Diary	St. Amand	05/05/1916	05/05/1916
War Diary	Foncquevillers.	06/05/1916	19/05/1916
War Diary	Bienvillers Au-Bois	20/05/1916	20/05/1916
War Diary	Sus-St-Leger.	21/05/1916	31/05/1916
Heading	War Diary. Of 1/5th Battalion North Staffordshire Regt. For The Month Of June. 1916 Vol 17		
War Diary	Sus-St-Leger	01/06/1916	06/06/1916
War Diary	Bienvillers	07/06/1916	18/06/1916
War Diary	Sus-St-Leger	19/06/1916	21/06/1916
War Diary	Fonque-Villers	22/06/1916	26/06/1916
War Diary	Humber-Camps	27/06/1916	30/07/1916
Miscellaneous	1/5th Battalion North Staffs. Regt.	00/06/1916	00/06/1916
War Diary	War Diary. Of 1/5th Battalion (The Prince Of Wales) North Staffordshire Regiment. July, 1916 Vol 18		
War Diary	Fonque-Villers.	01/07/1916	02/07/1916
War Diary	Bailleul-Mont.	03/07/1916	03/07/1916
War Diary	Ransart	04/07/1916	07/07/1916
War Diary	Bailleul-Val	08/07/1916	15/07/1916
War Diary	Ransart	16/07/1916	21/07/1916
War Diary	Bailleul-Mont.	22/07/1916	28/07/1916
War Diary	Ransart	29/07/1916	31/07/1916
Miscellaneous	Narrative Of Operation On July 1st, 1916	01/07/1916	01/07/1916
Miscellaneous	Summary Of Casualties Officers July 1916	00/07/1916	00/07/1916
Miscellaneous	Working Parties Night Of 8/7/16	08/07/1916	08/07/1916
Miscellaneous	46th Division./1714/G.		
Miscellaneous	Instructions For Carrying Parties.		
Miscellaneous	Notes Re Programme Of Work.		
Miscellaneous	1/5th. Battn. North Staffs Regt.	22/07/1916	22/07/1916
Miscellaneous	O.'s C. Companies & Section.	28/07/1916	28/07/1916
Miscellaneous	Summary Of Casualties For July 1916. 1/5th Battalion North Staffs Regt.	29/07/1916	29/07/1916
Operation(al) Order(s)	Operation Orders By Major A.E.F. Fawcus. Commanding.	30/07/1916	30/07/1916
War Diary	1/5th Battalion (Prince Of Wales's) North Staffordshire Regiment. War Diary For Month Of August, 1916. Vol 19		
War Diary	Ransart.	01/08/1916	02/08/1916
War Diary	Berles-Au-Bois.	03/08/1916	08/08/1916
War Diary	Ransart.	09/08/1916	15/08/1916
War Diary	Bailleulmont	16/08/1916	22/08/1916
War Diary	Ransart	23/08/1916	28/08/1916

War Diary	Berles-Au-Bois.	29/08/1916	31/08/1916
Operation(al) Order(s)	Operation Orders No. 4. By Major, A.H. Fawcus, Commanding 1/5th Battalion North Staffs. Regiment.	03/08/1916	03/08/1916
Miscellaneous	1/5th Battalion North Staffs Regt.	15/08/1916	15/08/1916
Miscellaneous	1/5th Battalion North Staffs. Regt. War Diary. /1916	00/08/1916	00/08/1916
Miscellaneous	1/5th Battalion North Stafford Regiment.		
War Diary	Berles	01/09/1916	03/09/1916
War Diary	Trenches	04/09/1916	09/09/1916
War Diary	Bailleul-Mont	10/09/1916	15/09/1916
War Diary	Trenches	16/09/1916	21/09/1916
War Diary	Berles	22/09/1916	27/09/1916
War Diary	Trenches	28/09/1916	30/09/1916
Operation(al) Order(s)	Operation Orders by Major H.H. Stoney, Commanding 1/5th Battalion North Staffs. Regt.	08/09/1916	08/09/1916
Operation(al) Order(s)	Operation Orders No. 8	08/09/1916	08/09/1916
Miscellaneous	Amendments To Operation Orders No. 8. by Major H.H. Stoney, Commanding 1/5th Bn. North Staffs Regt.	08/09/1916	08/09/1916
Miscellaneous	1/5th Battalion North Staffs Regt.	09/09/1916	09/09/1916
Operation(al) Order(s)	Operation Orders by Major R.H. Stoney. Commanding 1/5th Bn. North Stafford Regiment.	07/09/1916	07/09/1916
Miscellaneous	1/5th Battalion North Staffs Regt.	20/09/1916	20/09/1916
Miscellaneous	Statement Shewing Strength.		
War Diary	Trenches	01/10/1916	03/10/1916
War Diary	Bailleulmont.	04/10/1916	09/10/1916
War Diary	Trenches	10/10/1916	15/10/1916
War Diary	Berbes	16/10/1916	21/10/1916
War Diary	Trenches.	22/10/1916	26/10/1916
War Diary	Bailleulmont	27/10/1916	28/10/1916
War Diary	Humbercourt.	28/10/1916	29/10/1916
War Diary	Lucheux	30/10/1916	31/10/1916
Miscellaneous	1/5th Battalion North Staffs Regt.	03/10/1916	03/10/1916
Miscellaneous	1/5th Battalion North Staffs Regt.	12/10/1916	12/10/1916
Operation(al) Order(s)	1/5th Battalion, North Stafford Report on Operation during night of 25th/26th/Oct/1916	26/10/1916	26/10/1916
Heading	1/5th Battalion North Staffordshire Regiment. War Diary. Month Of November 1916. Vol 22		
War Diary	Lucheux	01/11/1916	01/11/1916
War Diary	Fortel	02/11/1916	03/11/1916
War Diary	Noyelle	04/11/1916	11/11/1916
War Diary	Domvast	12/11/1916	22/11/1916
War Diary	Yvrencheux	23/11/1916	23/11/1916
War Diary	Rougefay.	24/11/1916	25/11/1916
War Diary	Bouquemaison	26/11/1916	30/11/1916
Miscellaneous	1/5th. Battalion North Staffordshire Regiment Programme of Training.	13/11/1916	13/11/1916
Miscellaneous	1/5th Battalion North Staffs Regiment.	00/11/1916	00/11/1916
Miscellaneous	1/5th Battalion North Stafford Regiment.	19/09/1916	19/09/1916
Heading	1/5th Battalion (Prince Of Wales) North Stafford Regiment. War Diary For Month Ending 31st December 1916. Vol 23		
War Diary	Bouquemaison	01/12/1916	04/12/1916
War Diary	St. Amand	05/12/1916	05/12/1916
War Diary	Trenches	06/12/1916	09/12/1916
War Diary	St. Amand.	10/12/1916	15/12/1916
War Diary	Trenches	16/12/1916	19/12/1916
War Diary	Pommier	20/12/1916	23/12/1916

War Diary	Trenches.	24/12/1916	27/12/1916
War Diary	St. Amand.	28/12/1916	31/12/1916
Heading	1/5th Battalion North Stafford Regiment. (Prince Of Wales) War Diary. For Month Of January, 1917. Vol 24		
War Diary	Trenches	01/01/1917	03/01/1917
War Diary	Pommier.	04/01/1917	07/01/1917
War Diary	Bienvillers	08/01/1917	09/01/1917
War Diary	Trenches	10/01/1917	11/01/1917
War Diary	St. Amand	12/01/1917	16/01/1917
War Diary	Trenches	17/01/1917	18/01/1917
War Diary	Bienvillers	19/01/1917	20/01/1917
War Diary	Pommier.	21/01/1917	24/01/1917
War Diary	Bienvillers	25/01/1917	26/01/1917
War Diary	Trenches	27/01/1917	28/01/1917
War Diary	St. Amand	29/01/1917	31/01/1917
Heading	1/5th Battalion North Staffordshire Regiment. (Prince Of Males) War Diary For Month Of February 1917 Vol 25		
War Diary	In The Field	01/02/1917	28/02/1917
Operation(al) Order(s)	Operation Order No. 74. Lieut. Colonel Sir Hill Child Part. D.S.O. M.V.O.	24/02/1917	24/02/1917
Miscellaneous	Operation Orders by Lieut-Colonel A.E. F. Fawcus. M.C. Commanding 1/5th Battalion North Stafford Regiment.	24/02/1917	24/02/1917
Miscellaneous	Report On A Minor Enterprise Carried Out By The 1/5th Battn. North Staffordshire Regiment On The Nigth Of 25th/26th February 1917. Appendix I	25/02/1917	25/02/1917
Miscellaneous	Appendix 1		
Miscellaneous	Programme		
Heading	1/5th. Battalion (Prince Of Wales) North Staffordshire Regiment. War Diary For The Month Of March 1917 Vol 26		
War Diary	Bienvillers & Berles.	01/03/1917	02/03/1917
War Diary	Trenches	03/03/1917	06/03/1917
War Diary	Bienvillers	07/03/1917	07/03/1917
War Diary	Halloy.	08/03/1917	10/03/1917
War Diary	Souastre.	11/03/1917	13/03/1917
War Diary	Biez Wood	14/03/1917	14/03/1917
War Diary	Souastre	15/03/1917	17/03/1917
War Diary	Bayencourt	18/03/1917	18/03/1917
War Diary	Gommecourt	19/03/1917	23/03/1917
War Diary	Bertrancourt	24/03/1917	24/03/1917
War Diary	Harponville	25/03/1917	25/03/1917
War Diary	Cardonette	26/03/1917	26/03/1917
War Diary	Guignemicourt	27/03/1917	29/03/1917
War Diary	Berguette.	30/03/1917	30/03/1917
War Diary	Bourecq	31/03/1917	31/03/1917
Miscellaneous	Casualties.		
Miscellaneous	Report On Operation On Night 13/14th March 1917. By Lieut-Colonel A.E.F. Fawcus. M.C. Commanding 1/5th Battalion North Stafford Regiment.	13/03/1917	13/03/1917
Heading	1/5th Battalion (Prince Of Wales) North Staffordshire Regiment. War Diary For Month Of April 1917 Vol 27		
War Diary	Bourecq.	01/04/1917	12/04/1917
War Diary	Bethune	13/04/1917	20/04/1917
War Diary	Pt. Sains	21/04/1917	30/04/1917

Miscellaneous	137th Infantry Brigade Order No. 129 Appendix 1	11/04/1917	11/04/1917
Operation(al) Order(s)	137th Infantry Brigade Order No. 130 Appendix No 2	16/04/1917	16/04/1917
Operation(al) Order(s)	Operation Orders No. 37. By Lieut-Colonel A.E.F Fawcus M.C. Commanding 1/5th Battalion North Staffs. Regt. Appendix 3	19/04/1917	19/04/1917
Operation(al) Order(s)	Operation Orders No. 39. By Lieut.-Colonel A.E.F Fawcus M.C. Commanding 1/5th Battalion North Staffs. Regt. Appendix 32	27/04/1917	27/04/1917
Operation(al) Order(s)	137th Infantry Brigade Order No. 135. Appendix No. 4	28/04/1917	28/04/1917
Operation(al) Order(s)	Operation Orders No. 39a. by Lieut-Colonel A.E.F Fawcus M.C. Commanding 1/5th Battalion North Staffs. Regt. Appendix 5	29/04/1917	29/04/1917
Miscellaneous	To Accompany War Diary For April. 1917	00/04/1917	00/04/1917
War Diary	1/5th Battalion North Stafford Regt. War Diary. For Month Of May 1917. Vol 28		
War Diary	Lievin	01/05/1917	12/05/1917
War Diary	Pt. Sains	13/05/1917	19/05/1917
War Diary	Trenches (St. Pierre)	20/05/1917	24/05/1917
War Diary	Trenches	25/05/1917	30/05/1917
War Diary	St. Pierre	30/05/1917	31/05/1917
Operation(al) Order(s)	Operation Orders. No. 42. by Lieut-Col. A.E.F. Fawcus. M.C. Commanding Ormond. Appendix I	08/05/1917	08/05/1917
Operation(al) Order(s)	Operation Orders No. 40 by Major C.E.Graham, Cmdg. 1/5th Bn, North Staffs. Regt. Appendix II	17/05/1917	17/05/1917
Operation(al) Order(s)	Operations Orders No. 46 by Major C.E.Graham. Commanding Ormonde. Appendix III	23/05/1917	23/05/1917
Miscellaneous	Copy Of Patrol Report 10/11 May 1917		
Heading	1/5th Battalion North Staffordshire Regiment War Diary For Month Of June 1917 Vol 29		
War Diary	Trenches.	01/06/1917	07/06/1917
War Diary	Lievin	08/06/1917	11/06/1917
War Diary	Trenches	12/06/1917	15/06/1917
War Diary	Pt. Sains	16/06/1917	22/06/1917
War Diary	Trenches	23/06/1917	30/06/1917
Operation(al) Order(s)	Operation Orders. No. 52. by Lieut-Colonel A.E.F. Fawcus F. Commanding 1/5 North Staffs Regiment.	22/06/1917	22/06/1917
Miscellaneous	1/5th Battalion, North Stafford Regiment. Appendix No. 4		
Operation(al) Order(s)	Operation Orders No. 53. by Lieut-Colonel A.E.F. Fawcus M.C. Commanding 1/5th North Stafford. Regt.	25/06/1917	25/06/1917
Miscellaneous	1/5th Battalion North Staffs Regiment. Appendix No. 6	26/06/1917	26/06/1917
Miscellaneous	1/5th Battalion North Stafford Regiment.		
Miscellaneous	1/5th Battalion North Stafford Regiment. Appendix No 1	10/06/1917	10/06/1917
Operation(al) Order(s)	Operation Orders No. 56. by Lieut-Colonel A.E.F Fawcus M.C. Commanding 1/5th North Staffs. Regt.	30/06/1917	30/06/1917
Miscellaneous	Report On Raid Carried Out by the 1/5th Battalion North Stafford Regiment. on the night Of the 14th June 1917		
Miscellaneous	Carrying Parties.		
Miscellaneous	Signals attached to Operation Order No. 56		
Heading	1/5th Battalion North Staffs Rgt War Diary For Month of July 1917 Vol 30		
War Diary	Lens (Trenches)	01/07/1917	01/07/1917
War Diary	Lievin	02/07/1917	02/07/1917
War Diary	Raimbert.	03/07/1917	25/07/1917

Type	Description	From	To
War Diary	Verquin.	26/07/1917	31/07/1917
Miscellaneous	1/5th Battalion North Stafford Regiment.	00/07/1917	00/07/1917
Miscellaneous	1/5th Battalion North Stafford Regiment.	01/07/1917	01/07/1917
Miscellaneous	1/5th Battalion North Stafford Regiment.	00/07/1917	00/07/1917
Miscellaneous	G.O.C. 137th Brigade.	03/07/1917	03/07/1917
Miscellaneous	1/5th Battn. Prince Of Wales's (North Staffordshire Regt.) Operation Order No. 71	25/07/1917	25/07/1917
Operation(al) Order(s)	1/5th North Staffordshire Regiment Operation Orders No. 57	24/07/1917	24/07/1917
Heading	1/5th Battalion North Staffordshire Regiment Vol 31 War Diary For North Of Regiment 1917		
War Diary	Verquin	01/08/1917	03/08/1917
War Diary	Noeux-Les-Mines	04/08/1917	07/08/1917
War Diary	Trenches	08/08/1917	11/08/1917
War Diary	Mazingarbe.	12/08/1917	14/08/1917
War Diary	Trenches.	15/08/1917	17/08/1917
War Diary	Nouex-les-Mines	18/08/1917	21/08/1917
War Diary	Trenches.	22/08/1917	25/08/1917
War Diary	Noeux-Les-Mines	26/08/1917	26/08/1917
War Diary	Verquin	27/08/1917	31/08/1917
Miscellaneous	Casualties.		
Miscellaneous	1/5th Battalion North Stafford Regt. Operation Order No. 58,	01/08/1917	01/08/1917
Miscellaneous	1/5th Battalion North Stafford Regiment.	02/08/1917	02/08/1917
Operation(al) Order(s)	1/5th Battalion North Stafford Regiment. Operation Order No. 59	06/08/1917	06/08/1917
Operation(al) Order(s)	1/5th Bn. North Staffordshire Regt. Operation Order No. 60		
Operation(al) Order(s)	1/5th Battalion North Staffordshire Regiment Operation Order No. 61	13/08/1917	13/08/1917
Miscellaneous	Copies To:-		
Operation(al) Order(s)	1/5th Battalion North Stafford Regiment. Operation Order No. 62		
Miscellaneous	1/5th Battalion North Stafford Regiment.	14/08/1917	14/08/1917
Miscellaneous	1/5th Bn. North Stafford Regiment.	15/08/1917	15/08/1917
Miscellaneous	1/5th Battalion. North Stafford Regiment.	16/08/1917	16/08/1917
Miscellaneous	1/5th Battalion North Stafford Regt. Operation Order No 63		
Miscellaneous	1/5th Battalion North Staffordshire Regiment. Relief. Order No 64	20/08/1917	20/08/1917
Miscellaneous	1/5th Battalion North Stafford Regt. Operation Order No 61	24/08/1917	24/08/1917
Miscellaneous	Appendices		
Miscellaneous	1/5th Battalion North Stafford Regiment. Amendments To Relief Order No. 64	21/08/1917	21/08/1917
Miscellaneous	137th Infantry Brigade-Patrol Report.	24/08/1917	24/08/1917
Miscellaneous	1/5th Battalion North Staffordshire Regiment.	00/08/1917	00/08/1917
Miscellaneous	1/5th Battalion North Staffordshire Regiment. Relief Order. No. 64	25/08/1917	25/08/1917
Miscellaneous			
Miscellaneous	1/5th Battalion North Staffordshire Regiment. Reference Order No. 64	25/08/1917	25/08/1917
Operation(al) Order(s)	1/5th Battalion North Stafford Regiment. Operation Order No. 2	26/08/1917	26/08/1917

Heading	1/5 Battalion Prince Of Wales' (North Stafford Regiment.) War Diary For Mont Of September 1917. Vol 32		
War Diary	Verquin	01/09/1917	02/09/1917
War Diary	Trenches	03/09/1917	06/09/1917
War Diary	Mazingarbe	07/09/1917	10/09/1917
War Diary	Trenches	11/09/1917	14/09/1917
War Diary	Mazingarbe	15/09/1917	18/09/1917
War Diary	Trenches	19/09/1917	24/09/1917
War Diary	Verquin	25/09/1917	30/09/1917
Miscellaneous	Summary Of Casualties And Strength		
Operation(al) Order(s)	1/5th Battalion North Stafford Regiment. Relief Order No. 65	01/09/1917	01/09/1917
Miscellaneous	1/5th Bn.Prince Of Wales's (North Staffordshire) Regt. Relief Order No. 66	05/09/1917	05/09/1917
Operation(al) Order(s)	Operation Order No. 67	19/09/1917	19/09/1917
Miscellaneous	Appendix "A"		
Miscellaneous	1/5th Bn. Prince Of Wales's (North Staffordshire Regiment) Relief Order No. 67	09/09/1917	09/09/1917
Operation(al) Order(s)	Operation Order No. 68		
Operation(al) Order(s)	Relief Order No. 68	13/09/1917	13/09/1917
Operation(al) Order(s)	Operation Order No 69. By	21/09/1917	21/09/1917
Operation(al) Order(s)	Relief Order No. 59		
Operation(al) Order(s)	Operation Order No. 70 By Major H.	23/09/1917	23/09/1917
Operation(al) Order(s)	Ref Operation Order No 70	23/09/1917	23/09/1917
Operation(al) Order(s)	Ref Operation Order No. 70		
Operation(al) Order(s)	Gerald Relief Order No 70 Sheet 36b 1/20,000	24/09/1917	24/09/1917
Miscellaneous	1/5 Battalion North Staffordshire Regiment.	19/09/1917	19/09/1917
Operation(al) Order(s)	1/5th Battalion North Staffordshire Regiment.	20/09/1917	20/09/1917
Miscellaneous	1/5th Battalion North Staffordshire Regiment.	20/09/1917	20/09/1917
Miscellaneous	1/5 Battalion North Staffordshire Regiment.	23/09/1917	23/09/1917
Miscellaneous	1/5 Battalion North Staffordshire Regiment.	26/09/1917	26/09/1917
Miscellaneous	1/5 Battalion North Staffordshire Regiment.	29/09/1917	29/09/1917
Miscellaneous	1/5 Battalion North Staffordshire Regiment.	30/09/1917	30/09/1917
Miscellaneous	1/5th Bn. Prince Of Wales's (North Stafford Regt.)		
Miscellaneous	Copies Issued To		
Heading	1/5th Battalion Prince Of Wales's (North Stafford Regt). War Diary From 1st October 1917 To 31st October 1917. Vol 33		
War Diary	Trenches	01/10/1917	02/10/1917
War Diary	Mazingarbe	03/10/1917	06/10/1917
War Diary	Trenches	07/10/1917	10/10/1917
War Diary	Verquin	11/10/1917	14/10/1917
War Diary	Trenches	15/10/1917	18/10/1917
War Diary	Mazingarbe	19/10/1917	22/10/1917
War Diary	Trenches	23/10/1917	26/10/1917
War Diary	Mazingarbe	27/10/1917	30/10/1917
War Diary	Trenches	31/10/1917	31/10/1917
Miscellaneous	Casualties.		
Miscellaneous	1/5 Battalion North Staffordshire Regt.	01/10/1917	01/10/1917
Operation(al) Order(s)	1/5th Bn. Prince Of Wales's (North Staffordshire Rgt) Relief Order No. 72	01/10/1917	01/10/1917
Miscellaneous	Report On Raid Carried Out By 1/5th Battalion North Stafford Regt. On The Night 15th October 1917	15/10/1917	15/10/1917
Miscellaneous	1/5th Battn. Prince Of Wales's (North Staffordshire Regt)	04/10/1917	04/10/1917

Miscellaneous	1/5th Battalion Prince Of Wales's (North Staffordshire Regt.) Relief Order No. 74	05/10/1917	05/10/1917
Operation(al) Order(s)	1/5th Bn. (Prince Of Wales's) North Staffordshire Rgt. Relief Order No. 73		
Operation(al) Order(s)	1/5th Battalion Prince Of Wales's (North Staffs Regt) Relief Order No. 75	09/10/1917	09/10/1917
Miscellaneous	1/5th Battalion Prince Of Wales's (North Staffordshire Regt.) Relief Order No 76	13/10/1917	13/10/1917
Operation(al) Order(s) Miscellaneous	Operation Order No 77	25/10/1917	25/10/1917
Miscellaneous	46th Division	19/10/1917	19/10/1917
Operation(al) Order(s)	1/5th Battalion Prince Of Wales's (North Staffordshire Regt.) Relief Order No 76	17/10/1917	17/10/1917
Operation(al) Order(s)	1/5th Battalion Prince Of Wales's (North Staffordshire Regt.) Relief Order No 79	19/10/1917	19/10/1917
Operation(al) Order(s)	1/5th Battalion Prince Of Wales's (North Staffordshire Regt.) Relief Order No 80	21/10/1917	21/10/1917
Miscellaneous	1/5th Battalion Prince Of Wales's (March Staffordshire Regt.) Relief Order No 81	26/10/1917	26/10/1917
Operation(al) Order(s)	1/5th Bn. Prince Of Wales's (North Staffordshire Regt.) Relief Order No 82	27/10/1917	27/10/1917
Miscellaneous	1/5th Battalion Prince Of Wales's (North Staffordshire Regt.) Relief Order No83	29/10/1917	29/10/1917
Miscellaneous	1/5th Battalion Prince Of Wales's (North Staffordshire Regt.) Operation Order No. 84		
Operation(al) Order(s)	1/5th Battalion North Stafford Regiment. Notes On Dummy Raid On Left Battalion	31/10/1917	31/10/1917
Miscellaneous	1/5th Battalion North Stafford Regiment. Notes On Dummy Raid On Left Battalion Front. Of Hulluch Section.	31/10/1917	31/10/1917
Heading	1/5th Battalion Prince Of Wales's (North Staffordshire Regiment). War Diary For Month Of November 1917		
War Diary	Trenches.	01/11/1917	03/11/1917
War Diary	Verquin	04/11/1917	07/11/1917
War Diary	Trenches	08/11/1917	11/11/1917
War Diary	Mazingarbe	12/11/1917	15/11/1917
War Diary	Trenches	16/11/1917	19/11/1917
War Diary	Verquin	20/11/1917	23/11/1917
War Diary	Trenches	24/11/1917	27/11/1917
War Diary	Noyelles	28/11/1917	30/11/1917
Miscellaneous	Summary of Strength and Casualties for month of November 1917	00/11/1917	00/11/1917
Miscellaneous	1/5th Battalion Prince Of Wales's (North Stafford Regt) Operation Order No. 85		
Miscellaneous	1/5th Battalion Prince of Wales's (North Staffs. Regt.). Relief Order No. 87	02/11/1917	02/11/1917
Operation(al) Order(s)	1/5th Battalion Prince Of Wales's (North Staffs Regt.) Relief Order No. 88	06/11/1917	06/11/1917
Miscellaneous	1/5th Battalion North Staffordshire Regiment	10/11/1917	10/11/1917
Operation(al) Order(s)	1/5th Battalion Prince Of Wales's (North Staffs. Regiment). Relief Order No. 89	10/11/1917	10/11/1917
Operation(al) Order(s)	1/5th Battalion Prince Of Wales's (North Staffs. Regiment). Relief Order No. 90	12/11/1917	12/11/1917
Miscellaneous	1/5th Battalion Prince Of Wales's (North Staffs. Regiment). Relief Order No. 91	14/11/1917	14/11/1917

Operation(al) Order(s)	1/5th Battalion Prince Of Wales's (North Staffs. Regiment). Relief Order No. 92	18/11/1917	18/11/1917
Operation(al) Order(s)	1/5th Battalion Prince Of Wales's (North Staffs. Regiment). Relief Order No. 93	22/11/1917	22/11/1917
Operation(al) Order(s)	1/5th Battalion Prince Of Wales's (North Staffs. Regiment). Relief Order No. 94	26/11/1917	26/11/1917
Operation(al) Order(s)	1/5th Battalion Prince Of Wales's (North Staffs. Regiment). Relief Order No. 95	28/11/1917	28/11/1917
Operation(al) Order(s)	1/5th Battalion Prince Of Wales's (North Staffs. Regiment). Relief Order No. 96	30/11/1917	30/11/1917
Heading	1/5th Battalion Prince Of Wales's (North Staffordshire Regiment) War Diary For Month Of December 1917 Vol 35		
War Diary	Noyelles	01/12/1917	01/12/1917
War Diary	Trenches	02/12/1917	05/12/1917
War Diary	Noeux-Les-Mines.	06/12/1917	09/12/1917
War Diary	Trenches	10/12/1917	13/12/1917
War Diary	Noyelles	14/12/1917	17/12/1917
War Diary	Trenches	18/12/1917	21/12/1917
War Diary	Noeux-Les-Mines	22/12/1917	25/12/1917
War Diary	Trenches	26/12/1917	29/12/1917
War Diary	Mazingarbe	30/12/1917	31/12/1917
Miscellaneous	Summary Of Casualties And Strength.		
Miscellaneous	1/5th Battalion Prince of Wales's (North Staffordshire Regiment). Order No. 97	04/12/1917	04/12/1917
Operation(al) Order(s)	1/5th Battalion Prince of Wales's (North Staffordshire Regiment). Order No. 98	08/12/1917	08/12/1917
Operation(al) Order(s)	1/5th Battalion Prince of Wales's (North Staffordshire Regiment). Order No. 99	12/12/1917	12/12/1917
Operation(al) Order(s)	1/5th Battalion Prince of Wales's (North Staffordshire Regiment). Order No. 101	16/12/1917	16/12/1917
Operation(al) Order(s)	1/5th Battalion Prince of Wales's (North Staffordshire Regiment). Order No. 100	14/12/1917	14/12/1917
Operation(al) Order(s)	1/5th Battalion Prince of Wales's (North Staffordshire Regiment). Order No. 102	20/12/1917	20/12/1917
Operation(al) Order(s)	1/5th Battalion North Staffordshire Regiment Operation Order No. 103	20/12/1917	20/12/1917
Miscellaneous	Report On an attempt to kill Enemy and secure identification carried cut in daylight by the 1/5 Battalion North Staffordshire Regimen.	21/12/1917	21/12/1917
Operation(al) Order(s)	1/5th Battalion Prince Of Wales's (North Staffordshire Regiment). Order No. 104	24/12/1917	24/12/1917
Operation(al) Order(s)	1/5th Battalion Prince Of Wales's (North Staffordshire Regt). Order No. 105	28/12/1917	28/12/1917
Heading	1/5th Battalion Prince Of Wales's (North Stafford Regiment). War Diary For Month Of January 1918		
War Diary	Mazingarbe	01/01/1918	02/01/1918
War Diary	Trenches	03/01/1918	06/01/1918
War Diary	Noeux-Les-Mines	07/01/1918	10/01/1918
War Diary	Trenches	11/01/1918	14/01/1918
War Diary	Mazingarbe	15/01/1918	18/01/1918
War Diary	Trenches	19/01/1918	22/01/1918
War Diary	Mazingarbe	23/01/1918	24/01/1918
War Diary	Fouquereuil	25/01/1918	30/01/1918
Operation(al) Order(s)	1/5th Bn. Prince Of Wales's (North Staffordshire Regiment). Order No. 106	01/01/1918	01/01/1918

Operation(al) Order(s)	1/5th Bn. Prince Of Wales's (North Staffordshire Regiment). Order No. 108	05/01/1918	05/01/1918
Operation(al) Order(s)	1/5th Bn. Prince Of Wales's (North Staffordshire Regiment). Order No. 109	09/01/1918	09/01/1918
Operation(al) Order(s)	1/5th Bn. Prince Of Wales's (North Staffordshire Regiment). Order No. 110	13/01/1918	13/01/1918
Miscellaneous	First Army Summary of Operations for the 24 hours ending in the early morning of 7/1/18.	07/01/1918	07/01/1918
War Diary	1/5th Bn Prince Of Wales's (North Staffordshire Regiment.). Order No. 111	15/01/1918	15/01/1918
Heading	1/5th Bn. Prince of Wales's (North staffordshire Regiment.) Operation Order No. 112	16/01/1918	16/01/1918
Miscellaneous			
Miscellaneous	1/5th Battalion Prince Of Wales's (North Staffordshire Regiment) Operation Order No. 113	17/01/1918	17/01/1918
Operation(al) Order(s)	Operation Order No. 116	21/01/1918	21/01/1918
Miscellaneous	Summary of Casualties and Strength for month of January 1918	00/01/1918	00/01/1918

Woods/2685/1589/2685/1

46TH DIVISION
137TH INFY. BDE

1-5TH BN NTH STAFFS
MAR 1915 - 1918 JAN

TO 59 DIV 176 BDE

ABSORBED 2/5 BN 1918 FEB

N.M. Div.

1st Staffordshire Brigade

12/4634

1/5th North Staffs. Regt.

Vol I. 1-28.2.15

WAR DIARY.

of

1/5th NORTH STAFFORD REGT.

FEBRUARY 1st to FEBRUARY 28th, 1915.

Army Form C. 2118.

WAR DIARY
or
INTELLIGENCE SUMMARY.
(Erase heading not required.)

Instructions regarding War Diaries and Intelligence Summaries are contained in F. S. Regs., Part II. and the Staff Manual respectively. Title pages will be prepared in manuscript.

Hour, Date, Place	Summary of Events and Information	Remarks and References to Appendices
Monday 1/2/15 Saffron Walden. Tuesday 2/2/15 Saffron Walden.	Company Drill and Musketry.	
Wednesday 3/2/15 Saffron Walden.	General Holiday. Final for the Stuart-Wortley Football Cup. Won by the Battalion. 145 men proceeded to Luton to fire Regular Soldiers' course.	
Thursday 4/2/15 Saffron Walden. Friday 5/2/15 Saffron Walden.	Company Drill and Musketry.	
Saturday 6/2/15 Saffron Walden.	Field Firing at Dunstable.	
Monday 8/2/15 Saffron Walden.	Company Drill. Musketry parties returned from Luton.	
Tuesday 9/2/15 Saffron Walden.	Musketry and Kit Inspections. One Company night-Entrenching.	
Wednesday 10/2/15 Saffron Walden.	Brigade Route March, 15 miles. One Company night-Entrenching.	
Thursday 11/2/15 Saffron Walden.	Battalion training. Fifty men proceeded to Dunstable for Field Firing. Officers' conference.	
Saturday 13/2/15 Saffron Walden.	Re-distribution of Billets on Four-company formation. Practice entrainment of transport at Audley End station. Party returned from Dunstable.	
Monday 15/2/15 Saffron Walden.	Companies in the attack.	
Tuesday 16/2/15 Saffron Walden.	Battalion training "The attack".	

Army Form C. 2118.

WAR DIARY
or
INTELLIGENCE SUMMARY.
(Erase heading not required.)

Instructions regarding War Diaries and Intelligence Summaries are contained in F. S. Regs., Part II. and the Staff Manual respectively. Title pages will be prepared in manuscript.

Hour, Date, Place		Summary of Events and Information	Remarks and References to Appendices
Wednesday 17/2/15	Saffron Walden.	Lecture to Officers by G.O.C. Division. Brigade march-past.	
Thursday 18/2/15	Saffron Walden.	Ceremonial drill.	
Friday 19/2/15.	Saffron Walden.	Inspection of N.M. Division by H.M. The King. at Great Halingbury Park.	
Saturday 20/2/15.	Saffron Walden.	Interior economy.	
Monday 22/2/15.	Saffron Walden.	Battalion drill. Finals of Divisional Boxing Competition at Bishops Stortford (Won by Staffs. Brigade).	
Wednesday 24/2/15 Thursday 25/2/15	Saffron Walden.	Snow - Battalion Route march.	
Friday 26/2/15	Saffron Walden.	Battalion Drill. Officers' conference.	
Saturday 27/2/15.	Saffron Walden.	Entraining and embarkation orders received from S.I.B. at 8 a.m. Order received at 3 p.m. to postpone entrainment for 24 hours.	

Saffron Walden,
28/2/15.

J. Knight
Colonel.
Commanding 1/5th North Staffs. Regt.

137th Inf.Bde.
46th Div.

Battn. disembarked
Havre from England
5.3.15.

WAR DIARY

1/5th BATTN. THE NORTH STAFFORDSHIRE REGIMENT.

M A R C H

1 9 1 5

WAR DIARY

of

1/5th N. Staffordshire Regt

March 1st to March 31st 1915

WAR DIARY
or
INTELLIGENCE SUMMARY

(Erase heading not required.)

Instructions regarding War Diaries and Intelligence Summaries are contained in F.S. Regs., Part II. and the Staff Manual respectively. Title pages will be prepared in manuscript.

Hour, Date, Place	Summary of Events and Information	Remarks and references to Appendices
Monday 1/3/15 SAFFRON WALDEN	Battalion entrained at AUDLEY END Station at 4.10 and 6.10 a.m. arrived at SOUTHAMPTON at 10 a.m. and 12 noon – proceeded to Rest Camp and billets at Princes' Pleasant Schools.	
Tuesday 2/3/15 SOUTHAMPTON	Right half Battalion sailed by S.S. Bridès – Left half Battalion embarked at 4.30 p.m.	
Wednesday 3/3/15 "	Transport Lorries embarked 1.30 p.m. on detachment of 2 Officers and 70 men embarked at 6.30 p.m.	
Thursday 4/3/15	Remainder of Battalion disembarked at 2 p.m.	
Friday 5/3/15 HAVRE	Remainder of Battalion disembarked at 6 a.m.	
Saturday 6/3/15 "	Battalion less detachment entrained at 7 a.m. – detachment embarked at 12.30 p.m.	
Sunday 7/3/15 ARNEKE	Battalion less detachment arrived at ARNEKE at 7 a.m. detachment arrived at 7.30 a.m.	
Monday 8/3/15 "	Spoken to officers by G.O.C. Division & detachment arrived at ARNEKE at 11.30 a.m.	
Tuesday 9/3/15 BORRE	S.I.B. marched at 10 a.m. and billeted at BORRE at 4 p.m.	
Wednesday 10/3/15 "	Battalion stood by in billets ready to move at short notice.	
Thursday 11/3/15 SAILLY	After orders for embarkation Battalion marched at 1.30 p.m. and bivouacked at SAILLY at 10 p.m.	
Friday 12/3/15 "	Battalion stood by ready to move – billeted at SAILLY at 6 p.m.	
Saturday 13/3/15 "	Battalion standing by in billets.	
Sunday 14/3/15 "	Battalion standing by – physical drills and bayonet fighting.	

INTELLIGENCE SUMMARY

(Erase heading not required.)

Instructions regarding War Diaries and Intelligence Summaries are contained in F.S. Regs., Part II. and the Staff Manual respectively. Title pages will be prepared in manuscript.

Hour, Date, Place	Summary of Events and Information	Remarks and references to Appendices
Monday 15/3/15 SAILLY	Battalion paraded ready to march off at 9.45 a.m. Battalion returned to billets at 10.30 a.m. Company training.	
Tuesday 16/3/15 OUTTERSTEENE	S.I.B. moved at 10 a.m. and billeted at OUTTERSTEENE 1 p.m.	
Wednesday 17/3/15 "	Company parades. S.I.B. inspected by Field Marshal Sir John French at 3 p.m.	
Thursday 18/3/15 "	Company training.	
Friday 19/3/15 "	Officers' exams. Company commanders single tent management.	
Saturday 20/3/15 ARMENTIERES	S.I.B. marched at 9.15 a.m. to ARMENTIERES and relieved Battalion attached to 18th Infantry Brigade for instruction.	
Sunday 21/3/15 "	Church parade & inspection by Major Genl Capper Comdg 7th Infantry Bgde. A ½ Coy to trenches at 6.30 p.m.	
Monday 22/3/15 "	B ½ Coy instructed in Louis work at 10 a.m. — relieved A ½ Coy in trenches at 6.30 p.m.	
Tuesday 23/3/15 "	A ½ Coy instructed at 10 a.m. — relieved B ½ Coy in trenches 6.30 p.m.	
Wednesday 24/3/15 "	B ½ Coy billeting parades. A ½ Coy relieves 7.30 p.m.	
Thursday 25/3/15 OUTTERSTEENE	S.I.B. marched at 10 a.m. and returned to billets at OUTTERSTEENE.	
Friday 26/3/15 "	Company training. Meeting of Coln commdrs.	
Saturday 27/3/15 "	"	
Sunday 28/3/15 "	Instruction in estimating & best manipulation of ammg.	
Monday 29/3/15 "	Battalion entrained — church parade and address by Bishop of London 5.30 p.m.	
Tuesday 30/3/15 "	Battalion moved order. Was inspected at 1.30 p.m. to go ready to march at 3 p.m. — marched at 4 p.m. to BAILLEUL and billeted	
Wednesday 31/3/15 BAILLEUL	"	

J.R. Knight
Colonel
Comdg 1/5 R. Staffs. Regt

31/3/15

137th Inf.Bde.
46th Div.

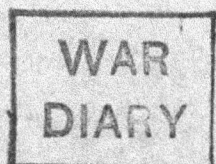

1/5th BATTN. THE NORTH STAFFORDSHIRE REGIMENT.

A P R I L

1 9 1 5

Army Form C. 2118.

WAR DIARY
INTELLIGENCE SUMMARY.
(Erase heading not required.)

Instructions regarding War Diaries and Intelligence Summaries are contained in F. S. Regs., Part II and the Staff Manual respectively. Title pages will be prepared in manuscript.

Hour, Date, Place	Summary of Events and Information	Remarks and References to Appendices
Thursday, 1/4/15. NEUVE EGLISE.	Battalion marched from BAILLEUL at 3 p.m. and took over trenches 11A, 11B, 12 and 13 from the Yorks. & Lancaster Regt. at 8&30 p.m.	
Friday 2/4/15 NEUVE EGLISE) Saturday 3/4/15. ")	Quiet except for enemy's Snipers.	
Sunday 4/4/15. "	Some artillery activity.	
Monday 5/4/15. "	Battn. relieved in trenches by 1/6th North Staffs. Regt. and went into Rest Camp at NEUVE EGLISE.	
Tuesday 6/4/15.) Wednesday 7/4/15.) " Thursday 8/4/15.)	Battn. in rest camp - company inspections.	
Friday 9/4/15. "	Battn. relieved 1/6th North Staffs. Regt. in trenches, 8.30 p.m.	
Saturday 10/4/15. "	Considerable Artillery activity, heavy rifle fire all night, particularly about 11 p.m.	
Sunday 11/4/15) Monday 12/4/15) " Tuesday 13/4/15)	Situation quiet, except for occasional shelling by both sides.	
Wednesday 14/4/15. "	Battn. relieved in trenches by 1/6th North Staffs. Regt.	
Friday 16/4/15 "	Enemy attack expected near YPRES. Orders received about 9 p.m. to be alert.	
Saturday 17/4/15. "	Heavy artillery fire heard from direction of YPRES, 7 p.m.	

COLONEL,
COMMANDING 5th /NORTH STAFFORD REGT.

Army Form C.2118.

WAR DIARY
or
INTELLIGENCE SUMMARY.

(Erase heading not required.)

Instructions regarding War Diaries and Intelligence Summaries are contained in F. S. Regs., Part II. and the Staff Manual respectively. Title pages will be prepared in manuscript.

Hour, Date, Place	Summary of Events and Information	Remarks and References to Appendices
Sunday 18/4/15. NEUVE EGLISE.	Battn. relieved 1/6th North Staffs. Regt. in trenches.	
Monday 19/4/15 "		
Tuesday 20/4/15 "	Battn. in trenches. Situation quiet.	
Wednesday 21/4/15 "		
Thursday 22/4/15. "	Battn. Relieved by 1/6th North Staffs. Regt.	
Saturday 24/4/15. "	Commenced working on 2nd.line trenches.	
Monday 26/4/15. "	Relieved 1/6th North Regt. in trenches.	
Tuesday 27/4/15 "		
Wednesday 28/4/15 "	Battn. in trenches; situation quiet.	
Thursday 29/4/15 "		
Friday 30/4/15. "	Battn. relieved by 1/6th North Staffs. Regt.	

NEUVE EGLISE.
20/5/15.

J. A. Knight
COLONEL
COMMANDING 5th NORTH STAFFS. REGT.

137th Inf.Bde.
46th Div.

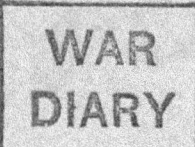

1/5th BATTN. THE NORTH STAFFORDSHIRE REGIMENT.

M A Y

1 9 1 5

Army Form C. 2118.

WAR DIARY
or
INTELLIGENCE SUMMARY.
(Erase heading not required.)

Instructions regarding War Diaries and Intelligence Summaries are contained in F. S. Regs., Part II. and the Staff Manual respectively. Title pages will be prepared in manuscript.

Hour, Date, Place	Summary of Events and Information	Remarks and References to Appendices
Saturday 1/5/15)		
Sunday 2/5/15.) NEUVE		
Monday 3/5/15) EGLISE		
Tuesday 4/5/15. "	Battalion in Rest Camp.	
Wednesday 5/5/15.) "	Relieved 1/6th North Staffs. Regt. in trenches.	
Thursday 6/5/15.) "		
Friday 7/5/15.)	Battalion in trenches.	
Saturday 8/5/15. "	Relieved by 1/6th North Staffs. Regt.	
Sunday 9/5/15.) "	Battalion in Rest Camp.	
Monday 10/5/15)		
Tuesday 11/5/15 "	Rearrangement of trenches and additional trenches taken over. — one Company in reserve to 1/6th North Staffs. Rest.	
Wednesday 12/5/15. "	Relieved 1/6th North Staffs. Regt. in the Trenches.	
Thursday 13/5/15.) "		
Friday 14/5/15.) "	Battalion in trenches.	
Saturday 15/5/15)		
Sunday 16/5/15 "	Relieved the 1/6th North Staffs. Regt. in the trenches. by	
Monday 17/5/15.) "	Battalion in Rest Camp.	
Tuesday 18/5/15.) "		
Wednesday 19/5/15)		
Thursday 20/5/15 "	Relieved the 1/6th North Staffs. Regt.	

Army Form C.2118.

WAR DIARY
or
INTELLIGENCE SUMMARY.
(Erase heading not required.)

Instructions regarding War Diaries and Intelligence Summaries are contained in F. S. Regs., Part II. and the Staff Manual respectively. Title pages will be prepared in manuscript.

Hour, Date, Place	Summary of Events and Information	Remarks and References to Appendices
Friday 21/5/15 } NEUVE Saturday 22/5/15 } EGLISE Sunday 23/5/15 }	Battalion in trenches.	
Monday 24/5/15 "	Relieved by 1/6th North Staffs. Regt.	
Tuesday 25/5/15 " Wednesday 26/5/15 " Thursday 27/5/15 "	Battalion in Rest Camp.	
Friday 28/5/15 "	Relieved 1/6th North Staffs. Regt.	
Saturday 29/5/15 "	Company of 8th R.B. Attached to the Battalion for instruction.	
Sunday 30/5/15 } Monday 31/5/15 } "	Battalion in trenches.	
NEUVE EGLISE. 19/6/15.		J.Knight Commanding 1/5th North Staffs

137th Inf.Bde.
46th Div.

WAR DIARY

1/5th BATTN. THE NORTH STAFFORDSHIRE REGIMENT.

JUNE

1915

WAR DIARY.
of
1/5th NORTH STAFFS. REGT.

JUNE, 1915.

Army Form C. 2118.

WAR DIARY
or
INTELLIGENCE SUMMARY.
(Erase heading not required.)

Instructions regarding War Diaries and Intelligence Summaries are contained in F. S. Regs., Part II and the Staff Manual respectively. Title pages will be prepared in manuscript.

Hour, Date, Place	Summary of Events and Information	Remarks and References to Appendices
Tuesday 1/6/15. NEUVE EGLISE.	Battalion relieved in trenches by 1/6th North Staffs. Regt. and one Coy. 8th Rifle Brigade.	
Saturday 5/6/15. Do.	Battalion relieved 1/6th North Staffs. Regt. in trenches.	
Sunday 6/6/15. Do.	One Coy. of 9th Rifle Brigade attached for instruction.	
Wednesday 9/6/15. Do.	Battalion relieved by 1/6th North Staffs. Regt. and 1 Coy. 9th Rifle Brigade.	
Saturday 12/6/15. Do.	Battalion and one Coy. 6th Somerset L.I. (attached for instruction) relieved 1/6th North Staffs. Regt.	
Tuesday 15/6/15 Do.	Battalion relieved by 1/6th North Staffs. Regt. and one Coy. 6th Somerset L.I.	
Saturday 19/6/15. Do.	Battalion relieved 1/6th North Staffs. Regt.	
Tuesday 22/6/15. Do.	Battalion relieved by 7th Northumberland Fusiliers and 5th Border Regt.	
Friday 25/6/15. OUDERDOM 137. Bn.	Marched at 8=15=p.m. to OUDERDOM. 9=0	
Saturday 26/6/15. Do.	Battalion Bivouacked at OUDERDOM at 1 a.m.	
Sunday 27/6/15. } to } Wednesday 30/6/15 } Do.	Shelter trenches dug, bayonet fighting, etc.	
OUDERDOM. 28/7/15.		

J. K. Knight-
COLONEL,
COMMANDING 6th NORTH STAFFORD REGT.

137th Inf.Bde.
46th Div.

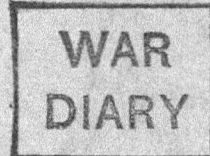

1/5th BATTN. THE NORTH STAFFORDSHIRE REGIMENT.

J U L Y

1 9 1 5

Army Form C.2118.

WAR DIARY
or
INTELLIGENCE SUMMARY.
(Erase heading not required.)

Instructions regarding War Diaries and Intelligence Summaries are contained in F. S. Regs., Part II. and the Staff Manual respectively. Title pages will be prepared in manuscript.

Hour, Date, Place	Summary of Events and Information	Remarks and References to Appendices
1/7/15 to 4/7/15.	Battn in Rest bivouac at Ouderdom.	
5/7/15.	Battalion relieved 1/5th. Lincoln Regt. in trenches A 9 to 12, B 1 to 5. Sanctuary Wood.	
6/7/15.	Local attack near Hooge by 6th. Division, 5-30a.m.	
7/7/15 to 10/7/15.	Quiet time generally, but enemy enemy crumped wood at intervals from direction of Hill 60.	
11/7/15.	Battalion relieved by 1/8th. Sherwoods and returned to bivouac at Ouderdom.	
12/7/15 to 17/7/15.	Battalion in bivouac at Ouderdom.	
18/7/15.	Battalion moved to Railway dug-outs in Brigade Reserve.	
20/7/15.	Heavy shelling by enemy during evening. Our artillery replied. Transport delayed one hour.	
22/7/15.	Battalion relieved 1/6th. South Staffs. Regt. in trenches 38 to 41 opposite Hill 60.	
23/7/15.	Enemy shelled Railway Cutting at short intervals all night. Reason unknown.	
25/7/15.	Hostile aeroplane brought down by one of our own behind our lines afternoon.	

INTELLIGENCE SUMMARY.

(Erase heading not required.)

Hour, Date, Place	Summary of Events and Information	Remarks and References to Appendices
26/7/15.	Our artillery howitzers bombarded enemy trenches 12 - 1-30 p.m. Enemy replied with whizz bangs.	
27/7/15.	Enemy exploded small mine near Railway Bridge. No damage. Battalion relieved by 1/6th. South Staffs., and returned to Hutments *Divisional Reserve*	
30/7/15.	Germans attacked 14th. Division at Hooge with liquid fire. 3-30 a.m. 6p.m. Battalion ordered to proceed to bivouac near Kruistraat.	
31/7/15.	Battalion stood by in bivouac. Artillery of both sides active.	

Hutments, Ouderdom,
Vlamertinghe Road.
26/7/15.

J. H. Knight,
Colonel,
Commanding 1/5th. North Staffs. Regt.

137th Inf.Bde.
46th Div.

WAR DIARY

1/5th BATTN. THE NORTH STAFFORDSHIRE REGIMENT.

AUGUST

1915

CONFIDENTIAL.

W A R   D I A R Y.
----

of

1/5th. BATTALION NORTH STAFFORD REGIMENT.

From 1st. August 1915,............to 31st. August 1915.

INTELLIGENCE SUMMARY

(Erase heading not required.)

Hour, Date, Place	Summary of Events and Information	Remarks and references to Appendices
1/8/15. KRUISTRAAT.	Battalion stood by in bivouac. Considerable artillery activity on both sides.	Casualties Week Ending 7/8/15 Killed 2 Wounded 24 Sick & Gone to Hospital 74
2/8/15.	Battalion relieved 1/6th. South Staffs. Regt. in trenches 58 to 61 opposite Hill 60.	
3/8/15.	Considerable casualties from Whizz bangs and trench mortars.	
6/8/15 to 8/8/15.	Our artillery bombarded enemy trenches at Hooge each day at daybreak.	
9/8/15.	British bombardment at Hooge 2/45 to 3/45 a.m. followed by attack. Attack supported by artillery fire on our front. Enemy replied, but caused no casualties.	
10/8/15.	Battalion relieved by 1/6th. South Staffs. Regt. and went into Brigade Reserve at Railway dug-outs.	
12/8/15.	One Officer killed and one wounded by enemy shell close to Railway Embankment.	

(continued).

INTELLIGENCE SUMMARY

(Erase heading not required.)

Instructions regarding War Diaries and Intelligence Summaries are contained in F. S. Regs., Part II. and the Staff Manual respectively. Title pages will be prepared in manuscript.

Hour, Date, Place	Summary of Events and Information	Remarks and references to Appendices
12/8/15 to 16/8/15.	Digging and Carrying Fatigues.	Casualties Week ending 15/8/15 Killed 5 Wounded 8 Sick & gone to Hospital 26
17/8/15.	Battalion relieved 1/6th. South Staffs. Regt. in trenches.	
18/8/15.	Enemy strong points opposite left of our front and Brigade on our left bombarded by our 9" and 8" howitzers (20 shells) 5 p.m.	
20/8/15.	Enemy commenced retaliation with whizz bangs, trench mortars, and grenades. Lasted almost continuously for 3 days.	
21/8/15.	Enemy sent over 7 aerial torpedoes about 10 a.m. into Railway Cutting. Casualties 2 killed, several wounded.	
22/8/15.	Trenches 41 and 41B. taken over by Lincoln & Leicester Brigade. One Company returned to Rest Huts.	Casualties for Week ending 22/8/15 Killed 4 Wounded 20 Sick & Gone to Hospital 18
23/8/15.	Remainder of Battalion relieved by 1/6th. South Staffs. Regt.	
24/8/15 to 29/8/15.	Battn. in Rest Camp between OUDERDOM and VLAMERTINGHE.	
30/8/15.	Battalion relieved 1/6th. South Staffs. Regt. in trenches 37 to 40.	

(Continued).

INTELLIGENCE SUMMARY

(Erase heading not required.)

Hour, Date, Place	Summary of Events and Information	Remarks and references to Appendices
31/8/15. DICKEBUSCH. 25/8/15.	Officer wounded slightly by fragment of whizz bang in Trench 37. J.W. Knight Colonel, Commanding 1/5th. North Staffs. Regt.	Casualties for Week ending 30/8/15 Killed — Wounded 10 Sick & lame to Hospital 22

137th Inf.Bde.
46th Div.

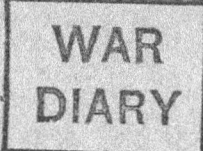

1/5th BATTN. THE NORTH STAFFORDSHIRE REGIMENT.

S E P T E M B E R

1 9 1 5

1/5th. North Staffs. Regt.

~~Wxx~~ War Diary for month of
September, 1915.
---- -----------------

Confidential.
_____

WAR DIARY
or INTELLIGENCE SUMMARY.

September, 1915.

(Erase heading not required.)

Instructions regarding War Diaries and Intelligence Summaries are contained in F. S. Regs., Part II. and the Staff Manual respectively. Title pages will be prepared in manuscript.

Hour, Date, Place	Summary of Events and Information	Remarks and References to Appendices
1/9/15. VERBRANDEN MOLEN 2/9/15.	Enemy trenches opposite 37 shelled by 6" Howitzers. Some whizz bangs in reply.	
3/9/15. – 6/9/15. –	Battalion relieved by 1/6th. S. Staffs. Regt. and went into Brigade Reserve – two Companies in Railway Dug-Outs, one at Bedford House and one in wood behind Trench 33.	
6/9/15. 7/9/15 to 11/9/15. 12/9/15.	Quiet generally. One M.G. Sergeant killed and one wounded by Shrapnel at Railway Dug-Outs. Battalion relieved 1/6th. South Staffs. Regt. in Trenches 37 to 40.	Casualties for Week Ending 10/9/15. Killed 2. Wounded 5 Sick & Gone to Hospital. 8
13/9/15 14/9/15 15/9/15.	Enemy continually annoyed by our R Field Artillery and 5.2 Howitzers on Hill 60.	
16/9/15.	Enemy shelled Battalion Headquarters and dug-outs in Railway Cutting heavily about 6 p.m.	Casualties for Week Ending 17/9/15. Killed 5 Wounded 26 Sick & Gone to Hospital. 8
17/9/15.	Severe bombardment of our Trenches opposite Hill 60 by enemy between 5/15 and 6/30 p.m. 380 Heavy Shells in 45 minutes.	
18/9/15.	Battalion relieved by 1/6th. South Staffs. Regt. and proceeded to Rest Huts at DICKEBUSCH.	
23/9/15.	Battalion ordered to stand by ready to move off at an hour's notice.	Casualties for Week Ending 17/9/15. 24/9/15 Killed 5 Wounded 5 Sick & gone to Hospital. 7.
25/9/15.	Battalion relieved by 1/8th. South Staffs. Regt in trenches. Very wet night.	
26/9/15.	Generally quiet. Very little artillery activity on either side.	

WAR DIARY

or

INTELLIGENCE SUMMARY. for September, 1915.

(Erase heading not required.)

Instructions regarding War Diaries and Intelligence Summaries are contained in F. S. Regs., Part II. and the Staff Manual respectively. Title pages will be prepared in manuscript.

Hour, Date, Place	Summary of Events and Information	Remarks and References to Appendices
29/9/15.	Orders received that 46th. Division would proceed to join 1st. Army.	Casualties for Week-Ending September 30th. 1915. Killed. 10. Wounded 42 Sick & gone to Hospital. 19 William Burnett Major.

137th Inf.Bde.
46th Div.

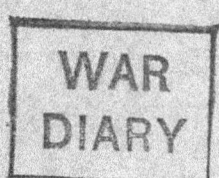

1/5th BATTN. THE NORTH STAFFORDSHIRE REGIMENT.

OCTOBER

1915

Attached:

Brigade Operation Orders Nos. 20, 21, 22 & 23.

Confidential

War Diary
for
October, 1915.
of
1/5th Bn North Staffs. Regt.

WAR DIARY
or
INTELLIGENCE SUMMARY.
(Erase heading not required.)

Army Form C. 2118.

Instructions regarding War Diaries and Intelligence Summaries are contained in F. S. Regs., Part II. and the Staff Manual respectively. Title pages will be prepared in manuscript.

Hour, Date, Place		Summary of Events and Information	Remarks and References to Appendices
HILL 60	1/10/15	Mine exploded in trench no 1 by enemy. Brigade relieved by 17th Division. Relief finished about 11.30 pm. Battalion attached to battalions at DICKEBUSCH	Casualties during month
DICKEBUSCH	2/10/15	Battn. marched to Abeele and entrained for FOUQUERES. Marched to Billets at L'ECLEME near Zillers. Arrived 11.30 pm	Officers K. W. M. Safe
L'ECLEME	3rd 4th 5th /10/15.	In Billets	Period 1-7 5 2 5(See below)
"	6/10/15	Marched at 10.15 a.m. to DROUVIN near BETHUNE. Billets	8-15 5 2 5 1
PROUVIN	7th to 11th /10/15	In billets	Total 5 2 5 1
"	12/10/15	Marched to trenches relieved 3rd Guards Brigade. Line taken over E. of VERMELLES.	Other ranks
TRENCHES E. of VERMELLES	13/10/15	Attacked the German Position.	K. W. M. Sick 1-7 3 7 70
"	14/10/15	Relieved by 2nd Guards Brigade. Marched to Billets at SAILLY LABOURSE	8-15 60 223 196 8 (See below)
SAILLY LA BOURSE	15/10/15	Marched at 2.15 pm to FOUQUIERES.	16-23 1 8
"	19/10/15	Marched to ALLOUAGNE	24-31 11
ALLOUAGNE	25/10/15	Marched to FOUQUEREUIL	Total 69 232 196 37

Brigade operation orders attached. Casualties in the attack.

Officers K. W. M.
5 9 5
Other ranks K. W. M.
66 223 196

Officers missing, Blank, Thistle Wainright, Copstage
J.R.S.Henry

Commission taken over 19/10/15 by Major D. Burnett, 1st 5th Bn. P.B.
Battln 15/5 N. Staff Infantry "Combined"

10/2/15

William Burnett Major
January 1/5 N. Staff. Regt.

BRIGADE OPERATION ORDERS NOS. 20, 21, 22 & 23.

Copy.   Copy No. 2.

OPERATION ORDERS. No. 20.
by
Brigadier General E. Feetham. C.B.
Commanding 137th Infantry Brigade.

                                                                5/10/15.

Brigade will march at 10 a.m. to-morrow to go into new billets at VAUDRICOURT (Square K.4)

Starting Point will be road junction V.o. b. 10. 10.

Order of march will be

        Headquarters 137th Infantry Brigade.
        1/5th North Staffs Regt.
        1/5th South Staffs Regt.
        1/6th South Staffs Regt.

First Line Transport under command of Lieut G.H. Fletcher, 1/6th North Staffs Regt. will march in rear of the 1/6th South Staffs Regt. in the above order.

Brigade Headquarters Transport and that of the 1/5th North and 1/6th South Staffs Regt. will not draw on to the road until the 1/6th South Staffs Regt. has passed their lines. Neither will that of the 1/6th North and 1/5th South Staffs Regt. draw out on to the road until 1/5th South Staffs Regt. has passed. Baggage Wagons will march with First Line Transport.

Blankets and Surplus Stores. Blankets will be rolled in bundles of ten and will be left in charge of a N.C.O. at Battalion Headquarters. All will be ready by 8/30 a.m.

Billeting Parties. of one Officer and four N.C.O's per Battalion will meet the Staff Captain at the Church FOUQUEREIL E 14 c.2.

Medical. Any N.C.O's and men whom the Battalion Medical Officers have reported as unfit to march will be assembled at the Starting Point not later than 9/15 a.m. and will be conveyed by motor ambulance; the number to be reported by 7/30 a.m.

Reports to Head of Column.

                                          R. Abadie,   Major,
5/10/15.   Brigade Major, 137th. Infantry Brigade.

Issued at 11/45 p.m. by Orderly.

        Copy No. 1   War Diary.
                    2   1/5th. South Staffs. Regt.
                    3   1/6th. South Staffs. Regt.
                    4   1/5th. North Staffs. Regt.
                    5   1/6th. North Staffs. Regt.
                    6   No. 3 Coy. 2 46th. Divisional Train.
                    7   1/3rd. N.M. Field Ambulance Train.
                    8   Staff Captain.

Copy No. 2

Operation Orders No 21.
by
Brigadier General E. Feetham. C.B.
Commanding 137th. Infantry. Brigade.

NO ORDERS OR SKETCHES WHICH WOULD BE USEFUL TO THE ENEMY ARE TO BE TAKEN BEYOND BATTALION HEADQUARTERS.

Reference Map. 1/40,000 (Combined Sheet) Bethune.
11/10/15.

The Brigade will assemble in the trenches to-morrow

The Brigaded Machine Guns under Capt Caddick-Adams 1/5th North Staffs Regt. will march from road junction K. 5.a.7. 9. VERQUIN at 10 a.m. via LA BOURSE AND SAILLY LA BOURSE to VERMELLES and will arrive at entrance to GORDON ALLEY at 2-30 p.m. They will then proceed to their position of assembly.

Order of March:-
> 1/5th South Staffs Regt.
> 1/6th South Staffs Regt.
> 1/5th North Staffs Regt.
> 1/6th North Staffs Regt.

The empty limbered wagons will return at once to their transport lines after unloading at VERMELLES.
Machine Gun Sections will draw their rations for the 13th and issue to the men as in para 45.

The 1/5th South Staffs Regt. will march at such time as to be East of and clear of the Cross Roads at SAILLY LA BOURSE at 2-30 p.m. This Battalion will draw rations as detailed in para 45. and halt for teas about L.4.c.90.

The Brigade)(Less 1/5th South Staffs Regt) with units attached will march at 3-45. p.m. in the following order:-
> Headquarters.
> 1/6th South Staffs Regt.
> 100 Bombers 139th Brigade.
> 1/2nd Field Coy R.E.
> 1/5th North Staffs Regt.
> 1/6th North Staffs Regt.

(Separate instructions will be issued to the O.C. Divisional Cyclist Coy.)
Cookers will march with their Battalions.
Other First Line Transport will be marshalled in above order of march That of the 1/5th North Staffs Regt. will not move on to the road in front of the 1/6th North Staffs Regt. and that of the 1/6th South Staffs. Regt. will remain North of Verquin until the 1/6th North Reaches the starting point.
Starting Point. Road Junction S end of VERQUIN.

Dress. Field Service marching order. without packs. Each man will carry three sandbags and 200 rounds of ammunition. - N.C.O's and men of Bombing parties 100 rounds of ammunition.

Battalions will halt to draw and issue rations and to have teas at about L.4.c.90.

Rations for the 13th. Rations for the 13th October will be drawn from the supply dump on the roadside at L.4.c.9.0 and will be issued to the men. An extra ration of bacon will be issued to Units today and will be cooked and issued to the men tomorrow to provide a supper on the night of Wednesday 13th October.

Rations for the 14th. will be issued to Quartermasters or representatives at 6 a.m. on the 13th inst. on track between G.8 a. 8 7 and G.2.d.central. 1 carrying party of 1 officer and 60 men of the 139th Bde. per Battalion will be provided and 1 N.C.O. and

21.

B.O.O. No. 20 contd.   II.

2 for 1/2nd Field Coy. R.E.. The two Sections Cyclists will draw their own rations. Units will detail sufficient guides to conduct Carrying Parties to the Regimental Ration Dump to be selected in the trenches. Guides to be at place of issue at 6 a.m.
Both GORDONS ALLEY and BARTS ALLEY will be used for Rations parties coming up. These rations will at once be issued to the men and carried in the advance.

WATER. Men must be induced to use the water from the petrol tins, keeping their water bottles filled for the advance. All empty petrol tins will be carried down by ration carrying parties of the 139th Infantry Brigade. Carrying parties to be west of Railway by 11-30 a.m. on 13th inst.

Battalions will .... at the following

        1/5th South Staffs. Regt.   5-30 p.m.
        1/6th South Staffs. Regt.)   6-30 p.m.
        100 Bombers 139th Bde.   )
        1/2nd Field Coy. R.E.   )
        1/5th North Staffs. Regt.   7-30 p.m.
        1/6th North Staffs. Regt.   8-30 p.m.

and will then proceed up BARTS ALLEY to their positions of Assembly. Guides, one per Company, will meet Battalions at the Brewery.

Each Battalion will draw the following stores from the Divisional T.E. Dump at the Brewery VERMELLES as they pass through:-

BOMBS. Each Bomber of each Bombing Party - 10 MILLS Bombs.
     Each Carrier   - 15 "   "
Total 285 MILLS Bombs per carrying party.
The Bombers of the 139th Bde. will each carry up 15 Bombs.

WATER.- Petrol Tins.

Vermoral Sprayers and syringes.
Battalions will also carry in with them:-
    Sprayer solution 16 tins.)
    Bombing Flags)   ) Issued today.
    Very lights)   )

The men will be cautioned that they must not shew themselves or move about on the morning of the 13th as it is most important to keep the assembly of troops secret.

All 1st line transport will return to Transport Lines after the march. Baggage Wagons will be loaded up and sent to the train with two men per Battalion in charge. Blankets and packs will be stored at the Transport Lines.

An advance party of one Officer and 10 men per Battalion will report to A Divisional Staff Officer at the R.E. Park, the Brewery, VERMELLES, G.8.a2.1. at 3 p.m. tomorrow, the 12th inst. in order that arrangements may be made for the quick issue of sprayers, grenades, carryers and petrol tins.

.2 S.A.A. Wagons only per Battalion will accompany Battalions. They will be unloaded at Bde. Headquarters at G.7.c.5.3, thus forming a Brigade ammunition reserve.

Brigade Headquarters will be on west of Railway line about G.c.5.3.

/10/15.
                                       R. ABADIE, Major,
                           Brigade Major 137th Infantry Bde.

SECRET   Copy No 12

OPERATION ORDER No 22
by
Brigadier General E. Feetham. C.B.
Commanding 137th Infantry Brigade.

11-10-15.

These orders are issued with reference to 46th Division Operation Order No 20, 6 copies of which have been issued to each Battalion. Map references are the same.

Paras 1, 2, 3 and 4 (i) require no amplification.
As regards 4 (ii) the Brigade will advance without checking on to the second objective; it will only cease its advance at the first objective if it is found impossible to reach the second.
The advance will be in four lines:-
The 1/5th and 1/6th South Staffs Regt with their left directed on the centre of the DUMP will assault the right portion of the objective allotted to the Brigade; the 1/5th and 1/6th North Staffs Regt with their right directed on the centre of the DUMP will assault the left portion of the objective allotted to the Brigade.
The two Companies of the 1/5th North Staffs Regt detailed for the first line will advance at 2.p.m., having previously, under cover of the bombardment, left their trench and passed through the remains of the wire in front of them; the two Companies of the 1/5th South Staffs Regt detailed for the first line will similarly get through the wire in front of their trench and advance in line with the two Companies of the 1/5th North Staffs Regt as they come level with them; the two Companies of the 1/5th South and 1/5th North Staffs Regt detailed for the second line will advance 50 paces in rear of the first line.
The following bombing parties will follow the second line and will bomb trenches as follows, care being taken that any of the enemy secreted in dugouts are bombed:-

I. 1/5th South Staffs Regt - SLAG ALLEY
II.   "   "   "   " - DUMP trench from 5.A.6.0 in a
                              North Westerly direction.
III. 1/5th "   "   "   - FOSSE ALLEY to the South East from
                              G.5.b.39.
IV   "   "   "   "   - trench running to 3 CABARETS from
                              G.5.b.39.
V 1/6th North Staffs Regt. - SOUTH FACE
VI   "   "   "   "   - trench running North from 5.A.6.0.
VII 1/5th "   "   "   - Dugouts, if any, on the DUMP
VIII "   "   "   "   - trench running from G.5.a.53 to the
                              PENTAGON

Nos VI and VIII Bombing parties will then bomb up trench running from PENTAGON to CORONS DE PEKIN.
The two Companies of the 1/5th South and 1/6th North Staffs Regt detailed for the third line will follow the second line at 200 paces distance, and will carry up shovels, picks and sandbags; the shovels, picks and sandbags are being arranged in loads, and must be drawn from the Brigade R.E. Dump early on the morning of the 13th; loose shovels and picks are also being placed in the Assembly trench of the third line and as many as possible must be carried up.
The fourth line will at once follow the third line and occupy DUMP trench on the frontage allotted to the Brigade. They will carry up to it S.A.A. and all available Trench Stores and bombs left in the Assembly trenches of the Brigade and will send up parties with wire, pickets and sandbags for the consolidation of the line forming the objective of the Brigade.
All Officers must take compass bearings of the line of their advance in case the DUMP should be obscured by smoke at the moment of their advance.

3. Reference para 5, the allotment of communication trenches comes into force after the relief is complete on the night 12th/13th.

4. Reference para 6 and Appendix "C", the Brigade R.E. Trench Bump is about G.10.b.4.9 not G.10.b.8.9; additional wire cutters can be drawn there.

5. Reference Appendix "B" para 1, Officers Commanding Battalions will arrange for orders to light up the smoke arrangements to be conveyed to the men of the Guards in charge of them by their own Battalion Officers; the smoke will not be made if the wind is unfavourable.
Reference para 2 of Appendix "B", the Officer of the 139th Brigade in charge of the 139th Brigade Bombers will arrange for parties of bombers to carry up the fumite and lachrymator grenades if they are received, behind the third line and for them to be thrown as necessary during the consolidation. Two 4" Mortars will also be available for this purpose, the personnel being found by R.A.

6. All S.A.A. boxes in the Assembly trenches must be placed in conspicuous positions near, but not actually in the communication trenches.

7. The 6th Btn Sherwood Foresters will come under the command of the G.O.C. 137th Brigade at 12 noon on the 13th inst. The Battalion will be located in the following trenches:-

   1. Trench from JUNCTION KEEP to CENTRAL KEEP - KEEPS exclusive.
   2. The trench from G.9.b.02 to G.9.b.79.
   3. The trench from G.10.a.79 to G.4.c.23.

   The O.C. No 2 Section 46th Divisional Signal Coy will arrange for telephonic communication with Headquarters, 137th Infantry Brigade.

8. One Section of 1/2nd Field Coy R.E. will follow the 3rd Line of the Right Attack, and one section the third line of the Left Attack. Their first duty will be to block trenches leading to the enemy after they have been cleared by the bombers, and secondly, to assist in the consolidation of the position by wiring.

9. The Brigade Machine Gun Officer will arrange to send up eight machine guns to cover the consolidation of the line forming the objective; they will follow the third Line and take advantage of the enemy's trenches where necessary and possible; the remaining eight guns will remain with fourth Line until required elsewhere.

10. The position of Brigade Headquarters will be at G.3.c.5.3 and Officers Commanding Battalions must make every endeavour to get reports sent back by telephone or runners who should be lightly equipped; the extreme importance of timing messages must not be forgotten.

11-10-15

R. ABADIE. Major.
Brigade Major, 137th Infantry Bde.

Issued at 8-30p.m. by D.R.

Copy No.1 War Diary
" " 2 " " "
" " 3 138th Infantry Brigade. D.R.
" " 4 139th Infantry Brigade "
" " 5 1/2nd N.H.Field Coy. R.E."
" " 6 22nd Brigade R.F.A. "
" " 7 to 12 5th South Staffs Regt. D.R.
" " 13 to 18 1/6th South Staffs Regt. "
" " 19 to 24 1/5th North Staffs Regt. "
" " 25 to 30 1/6th North Staffs Regt. "
" " 31. O.C. No.2 Sect. Sig. Coy. "
" " 32. Brigade Bombing Officer
" " 33. Brigade Machine Gun Officer
" " 34. Staff Captain.

Secret

Copy No - 12

OPERATION ORDER No 23
by
Brigadier General E. Feetham. C.B.
Commanding 137th Infantry Brigade.

12-10-15.

1. With reference to para 2 Operation Order No 22, the advance of the first line of the Brigade will be postponed 5 minutes, the two companies of the 1/5th North Staffs Regt will advance at 2.15 p.m. and the two companies of the 1/5th South Staffs Regt will advance as the two companies of the 1/5th North Staffs Regt come level with them.
This postponement does not apply to the Brigades on the right and left or to the 5th Bombing party.
The objective of the 5th Bombing party will be the trench running from G.5.c.1.10 to G.4.b.6.0 starting at 2.p.m; they will then work up SOUTH FACE and must take up their position on the left of the two advanced companies of the 1/5th South Staffs Regt to-night; a bombing party of the 138th Brigade has also been detailed to work up SOUTH FACE.
The undermentioned Bombing party will also be formed.
9th - 1/6th South Staffs Regt to work up and block a new enemy trench running from G.5.b.5.8 towards A.30.c.7.8

BOMBING PARTIES 5 spare carriers with each party will carry three shovels and two picks.

12-10-15
R. ABADIE. Major.
Brigade Major, 137th Infantry Brigade.

Issued at 9.a.m. by D.R.

Copy No 1   War Diary
      2   "   "
      3   138th Infantry Brigade
      4   139th Infantry Brigade
      5   1/2nd Field Coy R.E.
      6   22nd Brigade R.F.A.
      7 to 12 1/5th South Staffs Regt.
     13 to 18 1/6th South Staffs Regt.
     19 to 24 1/5th North Staffs Regt.
     25 to 30 1/6th North Staffs Regt.
     31   O.C No 2 Section 46th Divl Sig. Coy.
     32   Brigade Bombing Officer.
     33   Brigade Machine Gun Officer.
     34   Staff Captain.

137th Inf.Bde.
46th Div.

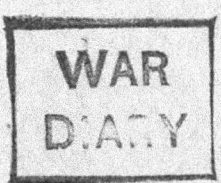

1/5th BATTN. THE NORTH STAFFORDSHIRE REGIMENT.

N O V E M B E R

1 9 1 5

Confidential

War Diary
of
1/5th Battalion North Staffs. Regt.
for
month of November, 1915.

Army Form C. 2118.

WAR DIARY
or
INTELLIGENCE SUMMARY.
(Erase heading not required.)

Instructions regarding War Diaries and Intelligence Summaries are contained in F. S. Regs., Part II. and the Staff Manual respectively. Title pages will be prepared in manuscript.

Hour, Date, Place		Summary of Events and Information	Remarks and References to Appendices
FOUQUEREUIL	1/11/15	Billets	Casualties during however 1/11/05
"	2/11/15	"	Period K W M Sick
"	3/11/15	"	1st – 7th 22
"	4/11/15	Capt. & Adjutant Lamond, 1/5th South Staffs Regt attached temporarily	8th – 15th 14
"	5/11/15	Marched to billets near MERVILLE	16 – 23rd — 7 — 14
Mt MERVILLE	6/11/15	In Billets	24 – 31st — 1 — 50
"	7/11/15	Marched to VIEILLE CHAPELLE	Total 5 8 — 50
VIEILLE CHAPELLE	8/11/15	In Billets	
"	9/11/15	"	Officers
"	10/11/15	"	Period K W M. Sick
CROIX BARBEE	11, 12, 13/11/15	Marched to Reserve Billets at CROIX BARBEE and took over from the 4th Br Suffolk Regt	1 – 7 1
"	14/11/15	In Reserve Billets	24 – 31st 2
NEUVE CHAPELLE	15, 16/11/15	Took over trenches at NEUVE CHAPELLE from 4th London Regt and 4th Suffolk Regt. SIGNPOST LANE (left) to BREWERY ROAD (right) map reference TRENCH MAP S.W.3. Sheet 36 c.N. 36.d. + 6. to S.6.A. 9.4. 6	
"	17/11/15	In trenches. A "crump" fell in one of our dugouts killed 3 men of this Battalion and wounded 6 others (one afterwards died) This shell also killed 3 men and wounded one of other Battalion	17/11/15 Captn & acting Servant Sgt Bostock Wounded by rifle and shrapnel fire within 15 South Staff Regt
NEUVE CHAPELLE	18/11/15	Battalion relieved by the 1/4th Lincoln Regt and proceeded to Reserve Dugouts	
"	19/11/15	MERIDIANA LODGE, LUDHIANA LODGE Dugouts	
"	20/11/15	1/4 LUDHIANA LODGE Dugouts and went to Reserve Billets, LORETTO RD No. 12	
"	21/11/15	Rest House Billets	
"	22/11/15	LORETTO RD	
"	23/11/15	Relieved 1/4 Lincolns in trenches. Line extended and now as follows MAP Reference Sheet 36 S.W.3 M.36. d. + 6. to CHURCH ROAD S.5.a. 9 2 . 2 8.	
"	24/11/15	Trenches all quiet.	
"	24/11/15	Heavy Bombardment of the German trenches in SIGNPOST LANE Battalion relieved by the 1/5th Br South Stafford Regt in the trenches	

Army Form C. 2118.

WAR DIARY
or
INTELLIGENCE SUMMARY.
(Erase heading not required.)

Instructions regarding War Diaries and Intelligence Summaries are contained in F. S. Regs., Part II. and the Staff Manual respectively. Title pages will be prepared in manuscript.

Hour, Date, Place	Summary of Events and Information	Remarks and References to Appendices
NEUVE CHAPELLE 25/11/15	Battn in trenches. Relieved by the 1/5th South Staffs Regt and proceeded to No. 12 Rest Horse Billets, LORETTO ROAD	
" 26, 27/11/15	No. 12 Rest Horse Billets	
" 28/11/15	Battalion relieved the 1/5th South Staffs Regt in the trenches	
" 29/11/15	Battalion in trenches. all quiet.	
" 30/11/15	Battn in trenches. all quiet.	

9/12/15

William Burnett, Major.
Commanding 1/5th North Staffs Regt.

137th Inf.Bde.
46th Div.

WAR DIARY

1/5th BATTN. THE NORTH STAFFORDSHIRE REGIMENT.

DECEMBER

1915

Army Form C. 2118.

WAR DIARY
or
INTELLIGENCE SUMMARY.
(Erase heading not required.)

Instructions regarding War Diaries and Intelligence Summaries are contained in F. S. Regs., Part II. and the Staff Manual respectively. Title pages will be prepared in manuscript.

Hour, Date, Place	Summary of Events and Information	Remarks and References to Appendices
NEUVE CHAPELLE (LIVERPOOL REST HOUSES) 1st December, 1915. 2nd y 3rd Dec. " " 4th Dec. "	Battalion in Brigade Reserve. do. do.	Casualties 1st to 7th To hospital, sick 34 other ranks
ST. FLORIS Dec. 5th to 18th 1915.	Battalion marched to ST FLORIS. Nr Merville. Dinner on the way. Arrived destination abt 5.7pm. Billets. In Billets. Proceeded with disciplinary training; route marches, company and platoon drill. Officers drill orders issued at 10.30 pm on 18th Dec. to move to rest	8th-15th To hospital, sick Officers 1. Other ranks 8. 10th Battalion medically inspected for service in the East. 12 "Other ranks" rejected by A R M S
December 19th 1915	Battalion marched to Billets at MOLLINGHEM Nr BERGUETTE. arriving at 1 pm.	
MOLLINGHEM December 20th 1915	Training proceeded on lines of "Infantry training" guide book with advance guards etc.	16th-23rd To hospital, sick Other ranks 8.
December 21, 1915	Intimation received that Battalion (and Brigade) will entrain on 25 December	24th-31st To hospital, sick Other ranks 1.
December 24, 1915	Christmas Eve festival as Christmas Day. Christmas Dinner for troops provided from home.	
December 25, 1915	Battalion entrained at BERGUETTE. Train left at 9.41 am. Transport, personnel and horses left behind to be temporarily attached to 139th Inf. Brigade. In train.	31st 90 per cent Officers vaccinated 24.8 % of other ranks present (only 6,000) vaccinated
December 26, 1915 December 27, 1915	Battalion arrived at MARSEILLE at 2 pm. Marched to Rest Camp (SANTI CAMP)	
MARSEILLE Dec. 28, 1915. Dec. 29th " " 30th 31st	Rest Camp (SANTI CAMP) Rest and cleaning up. Route March. Bathing. do. Route March. Bathing. Interior Economy.	William Burnett Lt. COLONEL COMMANDING 1/5th NORTH STAFFORD REGT

CONFIDENTIAL.

WAR DIARY

of

1/5th Battalion NORTH STAFFORD. REGIMENT.

From 1/1/16 to 31/1/16.

Army Form C. 2118.

WAR DIARY
or
INTELLIGENCE SUMMARY.
(Erase heading not required.)

Instructions regarding War Diaries and Intelligence Summaries are contained in F. S. Regns., Part II. and the Staff Manual respectively. Title pages will be prepared in manuscript.

Place	Hour, Date	Summary of Events and Information	Remarks and References to Appendices
Marseilles.	Sat. 1/1/16	Route March, Bathing in sea.	1/1/16. 0 officers, 30 other ranks of 1/5th S. Staffs. Regt. attached (to be left behind when 1/5th S.Staffs.Regt. embarks).
Santi Camp.	Sun. 2/1/16	Divine Service.	
Do.	Mon. 3/1/16	Training and interior economy. Orders received 4/1/16 that Battn. will embark on H.T. "Beltana" on 5/1/16 at 2 p.m. (with details of 1/5th South Staffs. Regt. attached).	
Do.	Tue. 4/1/16		
Do.	Wed. 5/1/16	Battalion marched from Camp at 12-30 p.m. Embarked H.T. "Beltana" 2 p.m. Ship sailed about midnight.	4/1/16. Battn Medically Inspected (Venereal). No cases discovered.
H.T."Beltana."	Thur. 6/1/16	Lifeboat Drill, etc.	
	Fri. 7/1/16		
Do.	Sat. 8/1/16	Anchored in harbour at MALTA at 9-30 a.m.	
Do.	Sun. 9/1/16	Left MALTA 7-30 a.m.	
Do.	Mon. 10/1/16		
Do.	Tue. 11/1/16	Medical Inspection. (Venereal) No cases discovered.	12/1/16. Five other ranks transferred to hospital.
Do.	Wed. 12/1/16	Arrived ALEXANDRIA 11 a.m. Disembarked 10 p.m. and entrained for EL SHALLUFA	- taken ill on voyage.
EL SHALUFA	Thur. 13/1/16	Detrained at EL SHALLUFA 10 a.m. Erected tents and encamped on East bank of SUEZ canal.	Casualties. Officers. O.Ranks.
Do.	Fri. 14/1/16 to 28/1/16	Training on lines of Infantry Training", extended order, marching by compass, and stars. Outpost duty. Camp fortified by digging trenches.	Week ending. Sick. Sick.
			8/1/16 1 -
			15/1/16 - 5
			22/1/16 - 3
Do.	Sat. 29/1/16	Orders received to entrain for ALEXANDRIA. Entrained 10 p.m.	29/1/16 1 3
Alexandria.	Sun. 30/1/16	Detrained Alexandria (Sidi Gaber) 10-30 a.m. Marched to SIDI BISHR Camp. Erected tents.	
Do.	Mon. 31/1/16	Bathing in sea. Interior economy.	

William Burnett Lieut Colonel
COMMANDING 5th NORTH STAFFORD REGT.

CONFIDENTIAL.

WAR DIARY.

of

1/5th Battalion NORTH STAFFORD REGIMENT.

From February 1st, 1916 to February 29th, 1916.

Vol XIII

Army Form C. 2118.

WAR DIARY
or
INTELLIGENCE SUMMARY.
(Erase heading not required.)

Instructions regarding War Diaries and Intelligence Summaries are contained in F. S. Regs., Part II. and the Staff Manual respectively. Title pages will be prepared in manuscript.

Hour, Date, Place		Summary of Events and Information	Remarks and References to Appendices
ALEXANDRIA. Sidi Bishr Camp.	1/2/16 to 5/2/16	Orders received on 3/2/16 to embark on 5/2/16. 5/2/16 marched from camp at 8-30 a.m. Embarked at 1-0 p.m. in H.T. "TRANSYLVANIA".	Medical Inspection (venereal) 20/2/16. No cases discovered.
H.T. "TRANSYLVANIA"	6/2/16 to 12/2/16	arrived MARSEILLES 4-30 p.m. 10/2/16. Disembarked 9 a.m. 12/2/16. Half Battalion entrained (with 1/6th S. Staffs. Regt.) at 10-40 a.m. Remainder entrained at 7-0 p.m. with 1/5th S. Staffs. Regt.	Casualties. Sick to Hospital Week ending: Officers. O.R. 5/2/16. Nil. 3. 12/2/16. Nil. 2. 19/2/16. Nil. 7. 26/2/16. Nil. 17.
	14/2/16.	Battalion detrained at PONT REMY, half at 12-30 p.m. half at 4-0 p.m. and marched to billets at EUIGNY L'ABBE	
EUIGNY L'ABBE	15/2/16 to 20/2/16	Training. Orders received 19/2/16 for Brigade to move on 21/2/16.	
Do.	21/2/16	Marched to BERNAVILLE, arrived 2-30 p.m.	
BERNAVILLE	22/2/16 to 28/2/16	Training. Orders received 25/2/16 to march to fresh billets on 29/2/16 and probably march for four consecutive days.	
Do.	29/2/16.	10/30 a.m. Battalion (and Brigade) marched to HEM, arrived 2-30 p.m. Received orders Brigade probably staying in this area four days. Later received Orders for Battalion to march to BOISBERGUE on 1/3/16.	

William Burnett
LIEUT.-COLONEL,
COMMANDING 1/5th NORTH STAFFORD REGT.

Secret.

WAR DIARY.

1/5th Battalion NORTH STAFFORDSHIRE REGIMENT.

March 1st to 31st, 1916.

Vol XIV

Army Form C. 2118.

WAR DIARY
or
INTELLIGENCE SUMMARY.

(Erase heading not required.)

Instructions regarding War Diaries and Intelligence Summaries are contained in F. S. Regs., Part II. and the Staff Manual respectively. Title pages will be prepared in manuscript.

Hour, Date, Place		Summary of Events and Information	Remarks and References to Appendices
HEM	Wednesday, 1/3/16	Battalion marched at 11-30 a.m. to billets at BOISBERGUE, arriving at 1 p.m.	
BOISBERGUE	Thursday 2/3/16) to Sunday, 5/3/16.)	Battalion training, Firing on Range, etc. Draft of 41 other ranks arrived on 3/3/16.	
BOISBERGUE	Monday, 6/3/16	Battalion marched at 10-30 a.m. to Billets at REBREUVIETTE arriving about 2 p.m. 2nd Lieut H.F.Green sent to Third Army Headqrs. for Anti-Gas course.	
REBREUVIETTE.	Tuesday, 7/3/16)	Trenches to be taken over from the French reconnoitred by Commanding Officer, Adjutant, Signalling and Intelligence Officers (from each Battalion in the Brigade). Captain F.E. Wenger taken as Interpreter.	
REBREUVIETTE.	Wed. 8/3/16.	Battalion marched at 11 a.m. to billets at PENIN. One Company re-inoculated on arrival.	
PENIN,	Saturday, 11/3/16	Battalion marched at 10 a.m. to Billets at ACQ (Men billeted in French rest Huts).	
ACQ	Sunday, 12/3/16.	Battalion marched at 5 p.m. to ECOIVRES. Men billeted in French Rest Huts.	
ECOIVRES.	Monday, 13/3/16	Battalion proceeded to the trenches in relief of the Centre Battn. 50th French Regiment. Trenches taken over (approx) A 4 d 1.7 to A 4 a 6.7.(Map Sheet 51b,N.W.1, 1/10,000); on the right, 1/6th Battn. North Staffs. Regt.; on the left- 1/6th Battr. South Staffs. Regt. Relief complete by 11/30p.m.	Battalion Strength in trenches Officers.27 O.R.457. Copy of Battalion Operation Orders attached.
NEUVILLE ST.VAAST.	Tuesday, 14/3/16.	Battalion in trenches. Quiet. No casualties.	
NEUVILLE ST.VAAST.	Wednesday, 15/3/16.	Battalion in trenches. Quiet. No casualties.	
NEUVILLE ST. VAAST.	Thursday, 16/3/16.	1/6th North Staffs. Regt. and 1/6th Bn. South Staffs. Regt. each took over part of Centre Sector and Battalion withdrew into Brigade Reserve, in and about village of NEUVILLE ST. VAAST. Relief completed by 10-30 p.m.	

CONTINUED.

1.

Army Form C. 2118.

WAR DIARY
or
INTELLIGENCE SUMMARY.
(Erase heading not required.)

Instructions regarding War Diaries and Intelligence Summaries are contained in F. S. Regs., Part II. and the Staff Manual respectively. Title pages will be prepared in manuscript.

Hour, Date, Place	Summary of Events and Information	Remarks and References to Appendices
NEUVILLE ST. VAAST. Friday, 17/3/16.	Battalion in Brigade Reserve.	
NEUVILLE ST. VAAST, Saturday, 18/3/16.	Battalion in Brigade Reserve. One man wounded while out with digging party.	
NEUVILLE ST. VAAST. Sunday, 19/3/16.	Battalion relieved 1/6th Battalion North Staffs. Regt. in the Right Sector, taking over trenches (approx) from A 10 b 1½.10 to A 4 a 7.2½, (map. Sheet 51b,N.W.1.,1/10,000). Battalion on left, 1/5th South Staffs. and 51st Division on the right.	
NEUVILLE ST.VAAST, MONDAY, 20/3/16.	Battalion in Trenches. Quiet.	
NEUVILLE ST. VAAST, Tuesday, 21/3/16.	Battalion in trenches. Quiet.	
NEUVILLE ST. VAAST. Wednesday, 22/3/16.	Battalion in trenches. Quiet.	
NEUVILLE ST. VAAST. Thursday, 23/3/16.	Battalion in trenches. Quiet.	
NEUVILLE ST.VAAST. Friday, 24/3/16.	Battalion in trenches. Quiet.	
NEUVILLE ST. VAAST. Saturday, 25/3/16.	Battalion relieved by the 1/6th Battalion North Staffs. Regt. and came into Divisional Reserve at ECOIVRES. Relief complete by 11 p.m. Last Company arrived at Rest Huts about 12/45 a.m. 26th. CONTINUED.	

11.

Army Form C. 2118.

WAR DIARY
or
INTELLIGENCE SUMMARY.
(Erase heading not required.)

Instructions regarding War Diaries and Intelligence Summaries are contained in F. S. Regs., Part II. and the Staff Manual respectively. Title pages will be prepared in manuscript.

Hour, Date, Place	Summary of Events and Information	Remarks and References to Appendices
ECOIVRES. Sunday, 26/3/16.	Battalion in Divisional Reserve. Rest and clean up.	
Do. Monday, 27/3/16.	Battalion in Divisional Reserve. Bathing. Commanding Officer's inspection of two Companies. Fatigue parties found for local work (two parties of one officer and fifty other ranks each). One officer and one N.C.O. sent to Divisional School on general course.	
Do. Tuesday, 28/3/16.	Battalion in Divisional Reserve. Bathing continued. Other two Coys. inspected by Commanding Officer. Four fatigue parties provided, one officer and fifty other ranks each, for local work. Orders received for Battalion to relieve 1/6th Battn. North Staffs. Regt. on night of 30th.	
Do. Wednesday, 29/3/16.	Battalion in Divisional Reserve. Battalion inspected by Commanding Officer, in fatigue dress. Two Fatigue parties for local work provided. Three of 1 officer and fifty other ranks each). At 6-50 p.m. 1/6th South Staffs. Regt. exploded a camouflet in Crater B4 in Right sector. At 7-30 p.m. orders received for two companies to fall in on alarm post and stand by ready if needed. Coys. "stood by" all night but were not called upon.	
Do. Thursday, 30/3/16.	Divine Service in Morning. Battalion marched at 6=30 p.m. to relieve 1/6th Battalion North Staffs. Regt. in the Right Sector. Relief complete at 19-30 p.m.	
NEUVILLE ST. VAAST, Friday, 31/3/16.	Battalion in trenches.	

COMMANDING 1/5th NORTH STAFFORD REGT.

1/5th Battalion North Stafford Regiment.

APPENDIX to WAR DIARY, March, 1916.

Casualties.

Week ending.	OFFICERS. Sick.	OTHER RANKS. Sick.	Wounded.	Time expired.
1/3/16	-	6	-	
11/3/16	-	3	-	
18/3/16	-	6	2	3
25/3/16	-	8	-	10.

3 N.C.O's and 1 men sent to England for Commissions 28/3/16.

COPY.   OPERATION ORDERS
                          by
                 Lieut-Colonel W. Burnett.
          Commanding 1/5th Battalion North Staffs. Regt.
                                          Sunday, 12/3/16

Reference Map.51b,51c,1/40,000.

1. The Battalion will proceed to the trenches in relief of the French
   tomorrow, 13/3/16.

2. The following men will be left behind with the Transport:-

              Transport N.C.O's and men   46

              Quartermaster's Stores   9
                (R.Q.M.S.,Arm.Staff.Sgt.,
                 Shoemaker Sgt. and
                 Assistant.,Tailor,
                 Storeman,Postman,
                 Butcher, Q.M'sOrderly)

              Orderly Room Sgt.   1
              Sgt. Cook and two one
                 cook per Company.   5
              Storeman, 1 per Coy.   4
                                                ──
                                                65
                                                ══

   Pioneers, Spare Signallers and Police will parade with their Coys.

3. The Battalion will parade at 7-0 p.m.; Dress -Field Service Marching
   Order with one blanket. Order of March D.C.B.A.Coys.
   Headquarters party, consisting of Orderly Room Staff and Cyclists
     Orderlies will march at the rear of the Battalion.
   All Coy.Q.M.Sgts. will parade with "B" Coy.
   Companies will march from here with 250 yards distance between Coys.

4. Platoon Guides will meet Platoons at the Cross Roads A.8.a.5.7.

5. A carrying party of the one officer and 32 men of the 1/5th Battalion
   South Staffs. Regt. will parade with both "C" and "D" Coys. to carry
   stores from Brigade Headquarters to the trenches.

6. Lewis Gunners, Telephonists and Bombers (30) will relieve in the
   morning. These will parade at 8-30 a.m. and will go in the trenches
   making use of the BOYAU des TERRITORIAUX from FERME BRUNHAUT,
   F.22.d.6.1. marching via MAROEUIL in small parties at intervals:
   after leaving MAROEUIL, the movements from MAROEUIL will be controlled
   by the O.C. Brigade Machine Gun Company. 2nd Lieut. L.M. Copeland
   will, act as guide to this party.

6. Extracts from Brigade Operation Orders.:-
         52 (4). Cooking for the garrisons of the trenches in front of
   the TRANCHEE de SOUTIEN should be done under cover in rear of that
   trench. There are suitable places such as the cellars of NEUVILLE
   ST. VAAST. Food may be warmed up on the front line on braziers,
   provided these are lit at night and no smoke is visible by day.

         52 (8). No unnecessary movement is to take place E. of the
   line BRAY - MONT ST.ELOY. Vehicles , including motor cars are not
   to proceed by day beyond MOULIN DE BRAY (F.14.d.5.1) and cross-roads
   F.14.b.9.7.

         53 (4). Medical. A collecting station (3rd N.Midland Fld.
   Amb.) is being established in NEUVILLE ST.VAAST on the road to
   MAROEUIL about A.8.b.5.6. Advanced Dressing Station is situated on
   the road about A.8.b.2.6. A motor ambulance will be kept at the
                                                              /latter
                         (Continued.)

Operation Orders, Continued. 12/3/16.

    letter place ready for evacuating serious cases by day or night. Casualties may be sent direct to the latter point or to the collecting station as convenient, under Battalion arrangements.

8. **Returns.** O.C. Coys. and Sections will render the following certificates to Orderly Room previous to moving off:-

    Trench Standing Orders have been read over.
    All tube helmets have been inspected.
    Every man has rubbed his feet with whale oil or Anti-frostbite Grease.

9. **Trench Stores, etc.** The transport will take upto Brigade Headquarters the following:-

    Gum Boots.
    All tools.
    Braziers.
    Periscopes.
    Sniperscopes,
    Vermorel Sprayers.
    Wiping Gloves.
    Telescopic Rifles.
    Dixies and Frying Tins.

12/3/16

                        Sd/ E. A. WILSON,
                        Captain and Adjutant,
              1/5'h Battalion North Staffs. Regt.

Army Form C. 2118.

WAR DIARY
or
INTELLIGENCE SUMMARY.
(Erase heading not required.)

Instructions regarding War Diaries and Intelligence Summaries are contained in F. S. Regs., Part II. and the Staff Manual respectively. Title pages will be prepared in manuscript.

Hour, Date, Place	Summary of Events and Information	Remarks and References to Appendices
NEUVILLE ST VAAST Saturday, 1/4/16	Battalion in trenches. 2nd Lieut. R. H. Wood (Intelligence Officer) killed in action (shot through the head while examining new Sniping Post.	**Casualties.**
NEUVILLE ST VAAST Sunday, 2/4/16	Battalion in trenches. Wire exploded in B4 crater, O 40 trench, in section held by 1/5th Battn. South Staffs. Regt. on our left, at 4.30 p.m. Reinforced lost Country (under arrangements already made) sent by Scots and S.A.F. further Gunners assisted in keeping the enemy from occupying the crater. Eventually 1/5th South Staffs. Regt. held lip of crater on British side. Situation quiet by 11 p.m. One man killed. Several wounded.	Week- ending. Officers. O.Ranks. Sk.K.W.M. Sk.K.W.M. 1/4/16 2.1.1*.- 17.-.-.- 8/4/16 3.-.-.- 6.1.2.- 15/4/16 -.-.-.- 7.7.1*.- 22/4/16 -.-.-.- 12.-.1X.- 29/4/16 -.-.-.- 8.-.-.- Other) *Self-inflicted. Ranks.) XAccidental.
NEUVILLE St. VAAST. 3/4/16.	Battalion in trenches. Quiet.	Offrs. *M.O.Attached. 14 men sent Base, time-expired. During month.
NEUVILLE ST. VAAST.4/4/16	Battalion relieved by the 1/6th North Staffs. Regt. and came into Brigade Reserve.	Draft of 68 other ranks arrived from England, 22/4/16.
NEUVILLE ST VAAST.5/4/16 to 8/4/16.	Battalion in Brigade Reserve.	Draft of 203 other ranks arrived from England 10/4/16.
NEUVILLE St. VAAST. 9/4/16.	Battalion relieved 1/6th Battn. North Staffs. Regt. in right Sector.	
Do. 10/4/16 to 15/4/16	Battalion in trenches. Quiet.	
Do. 16/4/16	Battalion relieved by 1/6th Battn. North Staffs. Regt. and went into Divisional Reserve at ECOIVRES. Last Company arrived at Hutments at 12 midnight.	
ECOIVRES. 17/4/16 to 18/4/16	Battalion in Divisional Reserve. Local/Fatigues. Bathing. Tube Helmet Drill. Inspections by C.O. and trench	
Do. 19/4/16.	Battalion marched at 10 a.m. to Billets at CHELERS, arrived abt. 3-30 p.m.	

Army Form C. 2118.

WAR DIARY
INTELLIGENCE SUMMARY.
(Erase heading not required.)

Instructions regarding War Diaries and Intelligence Summaries are contained in F. S. Regs., Part II. and the Staff Manual respectively. Title pages will be prepared in manuscript.

Hour, Date, Place	Summary of Events and Information	Remarks and References to Appendices
CHELERS. 21/1/16	Battalion marched at 10-0 a.m. to Billets at MARQUAY to go into Corps Reserve. Arrived 12.30 pm.	
MARQUAY 22/1/16 to 25/1/16	Battalion in Corps Reserve. Four days devoted to cleaning up. "D" Coy. proceeded to Third Army Headquarters, ST POL, on 23/1/16, to relieve Detachment of L.R.B.	Draft of 68 other ranks arrived from Base. (see page 1.)
Do. 26/1/16 to 30/1/16.	Battalion in Corps Reserve. Commenced Training on 26/1/16. Musketry, Bombing. Platoon and Company Drill, extended order, etc.	

T. Eustate
Lieut. Major,
Commanding 1/5th Battn. North Staffs. Regt.

S E C R E T.

1/5th Battalion The Prince Of Wales North Staffordshire Regiment.

War Diary

For the month of May. 1916.

Army Form C. 2118.

WAR DIARY
or
INTELLIGENCE SUMMARY.
(Erase heading not required.)

Instructions regarding War Diaries and Intelligence Summaries are contained in F. S. Regs., Part II. and the Staff Manual respectively. Title pages will be prepared in manuscript.

Hour, Date, Place	Summary of Events and Information	Remarks and References to Appendices
MARQUAY. Monday, 1/5/16.	Battalion in Corps Reserve. Orders received to reconnoitre new trenches tomorrow.	
do. Tuesday, 2/5/16.	Commanding Officer, one officer per Company, Intelligence officer, and Bomb Officer reconnoitred trenches at FONCQUEVILLERS.	
do. Wednesday, 3/5/16.	Received orders to commence march to new area tomorrow, 3/5/16. Battalion marched at 10-0 a.m. to billets at REBREUVIETTE, arriving about 1-30.p.m.	
REBREUVIETTE. Thursday, 4/5/16.	Battalion marched at 9-0.a.m. to billets at ST. AMAND. Dinner and tea served on the way. Arrived at about 7-30.p.m.	
ST. AMAND. Friday. 5/5/16.	Battalion marched at 9-30.a.m. to FONCQUEVILLERS in relief of the 1/8th Battalion Royal Warwicks Regiment, and took over trenches E27D.75.05. - E.28. a.70.75. (Map 57D. N.E. Parts of 1.&2. 1/10,000 Edition 2.) (Trench Map) Relief of three Companies complete by about 8-30.p.m. Detachment (D.Coy. & other details) returned from Third Army Headquarters; D.Coy relieved last Coy of 8th Bn. Royal Warwicks. Relief complete 5-0.p.m.	
FONCQUEVILLERS. Saturday. 6/5/16.	Battalion in trenches. Quiet.	
do Sunday, 7/5/16.	Do.	
Do. Monday, 8/5/16.	Do.	
Do. Tuesday, 9/5/16.	Do. Inter-Battalion relief. B.& D. Coys relieved A.&.C. Coys in fire trenches. from Support and Reserve Relief complete 5-0.p.m.	
Do. Wednesday, 10/5/16.	Battalion in trenches. Artillery duel at noon. Enemy artillery shelled our working party, 1 Sgt killed, 4 men wounded.	
Do. Thursday. 11/5/16.	Battalion in trenches. Extended our frontage, taking over trenches 50, & 51, (from E.28.a.70.75. to E.22.d.20.05.)	
Do. Friday, 12/5/16.	Battalion relieved by the 1/6th Battalion South Staffs Regt, and went into Brigade Reserve. Relief complete, 11-45.p.m.	
Do. Saturday, 13/5/16.	Battalion in Brigade Reserve. Working on trenches in and about FONCQUEVILLERS.	

CONTINUED. *William Burnett* LIEUT. COLONEL
COMMANDING 1/5th NORTH STAFFORD REGT.

Army Form C. 2118.

WAR DIARY
or
INTELLIGENCE SUMMARY.
(Erase heading not required.)

Instructions regarding War Diaries and Intelligence Summaries are contained in F. S. Regs., Part II. and the Staff Manual respectively. Title pages will be prepared in manuscript.

Hour, Date, Place		Summary of Events and Information	Remarks and References to Appendices
FONCQUEVILLERS.	Sun. 14/5/16.	Battalion in Brigade Reserve. Working on trenches in and about FONCQUEVILLERS.	
Do.	Monday. 15/5/16.	12-30.a.m. Considerable artillery activity by the enemy until 1-10 a.m. Battalion "Stood to" although no orders were received from Brigade Headquarters	
Do.	Tuesday, 16/5/16.		
Do.	Wednesday, 17/5/16.	Battalion in Brigade Reserve.	
Do.	Thursday, 18/5/16.	Do.	
Do.	Friday. 19/5/16.	Battalion relieved by the 1/8th Battalion Sherwood Foresters Regt. previous to going into Corps Reserve. Relief complete by 12. noon Battalion proceeded to Bienvillers-au-Bois, in billets.	
BIENVILLERS-au-BOIS. Saturday.	20/5/16.	Battalion in reserve to 139th Infantry Brigade, from arrival in village until 9-45.p.m. 20/5/16. Relieved by the 1/5th Battalion Lincolnshire Regiment at 9-45.p.m. and marched to billets at SUS-ST-LEGER, in Corps Reserve. Distance about 12 miles. Arrived at 3-0.a.m. 21/5/16.	
SUS-ST-LEGER. Sunday.	21/5/16.	Battalion in Corps Reserve Rest. Church Service (united) at night.	
Do. Monday.	22/5/16.	Cleaning of Billets. Training: Saluting Drill. Platoon, and Squad Drill, Bombing, Tube Helmet Drill. Route March by Companies. Party of 1 Officer and 32 Other Ranks proceeded to Brigade Bomb School to complete Course of Bombing commenced at MARQUAY.	
Do. Tuesday,	23/5/16.	6 Officers and 260 Other Ranks engaged in making hurdles in LUCHEUX FOREST, under instructions by the R.E. 3 Officers and 132 Other Ranks engaged in digging trenches for practice attack. 1 Company and Specialists training. 1 Officer and 8 Other Ranks proceeded to Third Army School of Mortars for traing as Trench Mortar Battery Reserves.	No.5108. Sgt. R. Downing 1/5th Battalion North Staffs Regt. gazetted to Commission in this Battalion. 23/5/16.
Do.	Wednesday, 24/5/16	Whole Battalion employed all day in digging practice trenches.	

CONTINUED.

William Burnett
LIEUT. COLONEL
COMMANDING 1/5th NORTH STAFFORD REGT.

Army Form C. 2118.

WAR DIARY
or
INTELLIGENCE SUMMARY.
(Erase heading not required.)

Instructions regarding War Diaries and Intelligence Summaries are contained in F. S. Regs., Part II. and the Staff Manual respectively. Title pages will be prepared in manuscript.

Hour, Date, Place		Summary of Events and Information	Remarks and References to Appendices
SUS-ST-LEGER.	Thurs. 25/5/16.	Battalion employed on digging practice trenches.	Summary of Casualties
Do.	Friday. 26/5/16.	Morning. Bayonet Fighting, Physical Drill, Afternoon. Battalion practise attack at practice trenches.	Officers.
Do.	Saturday. 27/5/16.	Employed all day on making hurdles in LUCHEUX FOREST.	Week K. W. M. S.
Do.	Sunday. 28/5/16.	Morning. Battalion practise attack at practice trenches. Afternoon. Physical Drill, Bayonet Fighting.	ending.
Do.	Monday. 29/5/16.	Battalion employed all day on hurdle making in LUCHEUX FOREST. Lewis Gunners and Snipers on range. Bayonet Fighting class of 1 N.C.O per platoon under 2nd Lt. L.T.Wood, and two specially trained N.C.O.s commenced. Two Lewis Gunners proceeded to Machine Gun School. CAMIERS. for course of instruction.	20/5/16. - - - 1.
Do.	Tuesday. 30/5/16.	Battalion employed all day on hurdle making in LUCHEUX FOREST.	Other Ranks.
Do.	Wednesday. 31/5/16	Battalion practised attack at practice trenched. Marched off 4-0.a.m. 10.a.m. to 12. noon. Two Companies practise Bayonet Fighting and Physical Drill. Two Companies Bathing.	Week K. W. M. S.
			Ending.
			6/5/16. 2. 1. - 11.
			13/5/16. 2. 7ˣ - 6.
			20/5/16. - - - 36.
			27/5/16. - - - 20.
			ˣ 2 since died.
			To Base, time-expired.
			Total for month:- 3.

William Bennett
LIEUT. COLONEL.
COMMANDING 1/5th NORTH STAFFORD REGT.

SECRET. ORIGINAL.

WAR DIARY.

of

1/5th BATTALION NORTH STAFFORDSHIRE REGT.

for the Month of

JUNE, 1916.

Army Form C. 2118.

WAR DIARY
or
INTELLIGENCE SUMMARY

(Erase heading not required.)

Instructions regarding War Diaries and Intelligence Summaries are contained in F. S. Regs., Part II. and the Staff Manual respectively. Title Pages will be prepared in manuscript.

Place	Date	Hour	Summary of Events and Information	Remarks and references to Appendices
SUS-ST-LEGER	1/6/16		Battalion in Corps Reserve. Training: Rapid wiring, Bayonet Fighting, Saluting Drill, Physical Drill.	
Do.	2/6/16		Holiday. One party (1 Officer and 80 O.R.) employed on hurdle making at LUCHEUX Forest for two hours. Football match in the afternoon. Battalion played 4th Battalion Leicester Regt. in final for Stuart-Wortley Cup and were "runners-up" thereby winning prize of £5.	
Do.	3/6/16		Battalion practice attack at practice trenches. March off 3-30 a.m.	
Do.	4/6/16		Brigade practice attack at practice trenches.	
Do.	5/6/16		Do.	
Do.	6/6/16		Battalion marched at 6-0 p.m. to billets at BIENVILLERS., arriving at 10-30 p.m., at which hour Battalion came into Divisional Reserve. Draft of 60 other ranks arrived from Base.	
BIENVIL-LERS.	7/6/16 to 17/6/16		Large working parties out on assembly and communication trenches, by day and night. Practically whole Battalion employed on this. Weather very wet practically the whole time. Men returned to billets from these fatigues wet through and in very muddy condition. No blankets to wear while clothes dry so practically wet through all the time.	
Do.	18/6/16.		Conference of Commanding Officers at Brigade Headquarters. Sudden orders to move - received 12-30 p.m. Working parties recalled. Battalion marched to billets at SUS-ST-LEGER (leaving BIENVILLERS by daylight by platoons), arrived SUS-ST-LEGER 10-30 p.m.	
SUS-ST-LEGER.	19/6/16.		Rest. One officer per Company witnessed practice attack at practice trenches at 4-0 p.m.	
Do.	20/6/16.		Brigade practice attack at practice trenches. Once in morning and once in afternoon. Second practice witnessed by the Army Commander. Received orders to march to FONQUEVILLERS tomorrow.	
Do.	21/6/16.		Battalion marched at 2-30 p.m. Arrived FONQUEVILLERS 11 p.m. and relieved 4th Leicesters in centre sector. Relief complete 1-5 a.m. 22nd.	

CONTINUED.

Army Form C. 2118.

WAR DIARY
or
INTELLIGENCE SUMMARY

(Erase heading not required.)

Instructions regarding War Diaries and Intelligence Summaries are contained in F.S. Regs., Part II. and the Staff Manual respectively. Title Pages will be prepared in manuscript.

Place	Date	Hour	Summary of Events and Information	Remarks and references to Appendices
FONQUE- VILLERS.	22/6/16		Battalion in trenches. 1/6th North Staffs Regt., and 1/5th South Staffs Regt., commenced digging assault trench 100 yards in front of our front line. Covering parties, (7 of 1 NC.O. and 10 men each, under four Officers) provided by this Battalion. Work commenced at 10-30 p.m. and parties worked until 2-15 a.m. Trench dug to a depth of about 3. ft. about 350 yards in length.	
do	23/6/16		Battalion in trenches. Heavy rainstorms and trenches flooded. Work on assault trench continued at night (at same time.) Enemy heavily shelled working party about 1-0 a.m. Many casualties. Our covering parties sustained casualties as follows:- Other Ranks Killed.1. Wounded 20. Missing 3. (two bodies since found). 2nd Lieut A.G. Paxton. wounded (in trenches.)	
do	24/6/16		Battalion in trenches. "U" Day. Bombardment commenced 7-45 a.m. Chiefly cutting wire cutting Very wet; trenches in very wet condition. Enemy retaliated very little.	
do	25/6/16		Battalion in trenches. "V" Day. Bombardment proceeded. Very Heavy. Reported on wire cutting several clearances cut or partly cut. More smashing still required. Enemy's retaliation not heavy. Digging of assault trench proceeded with at night (at same time).	
do	26/6/16		Battalion in trenches. "W" Day. Bombardment proceeded. Faked attack at 10-15 a.m. Artillery bombarded heavily enemy front line trenches and then lifted fire. Smoke was let off from Battalion on our left but not from our front. Enemy put up barrage fire and heavily bombarded our trenches. Trenches still in very wet condition. Battalion relieved by 4th Battalion Leicester Regt. and proceeded to Rest Camp at HUMBERCAMPS, marching by platoons, commencing at about 5-0 p.m. "B" Coy. remained behind to bale out and clean assault trench, worked until 2-15 a.m., whole of Battalion in Rest Camp by about 5-0 a.m. 27th. 2 Lieut R.A Varley wounded	
HUMBER-CAMPS.	27/6/16		Battalion in Rest Camp. Rest and clean up. "X" Day.	
do	28/6/16		Battalion in Rest Camp. "Y" Day. Preparation for attack. Part of Battalion marched off at noon., remainder to march off commencing at 7-0 p.m. Orders received about 4-0 p.m. that operations were postponed. Bombs. Wire Cutters, etc., collected from the men.	

CONTINUED.

Army Form C. 2118.

WAR DIARY
INTELLIGENCE SUMMARY
(Erase heading not required.)

Instructions regarding War Diaries and Intelligence Summaries are contained in F. S. Regs., Part II. and the Staff Manual respectively. Title Pages will be prepared in manuscript.

Place	Date	Hour	Summary of Events and Information	Remarks and references to Appendices
RUMBER- CAMP.	29/7/16.		Battalion in Rest Camp. Orders received that attack will take place on 1st July.	
Do.	30/6/16.		Battalion in rest camp. Preparation for attack. One platoon marched off at noon, 14 clearing parties marched off commencing at 4-30 p.m. Main body marched off at 10-30 p.m.	

J.L. Wing
Captain,
Commanding 1/5th Battalion North Staffs. Regiment.

1/5th Battalion North Staffs. Regt.

APPENDIX to War Diary. June, 1916. Summary of Casualties.

Officers:

Week ending:	K.	W.	M.	S.
3/6/16	-	-	-	1.
10/6/16.	-	-	-	-
17/6/16.	-	1	-	2.
24/6/16.	-	1	1	1.
30/6/16.(Friday)				
	-	2	-	4

Other Ranks.

Week ending:	K.	W.	M.	S.	W. to duty.	Accidentally Injured.	Self Inflicted Wd
3/6/16.				10			
10/6/16.				16			
17/6/16.				13	1.		
24/6/16.	3	24	3	16	2	1	
Friday, 30/6/16.	4	16	-	5	4		1
	7	40	3	60	7	1	1

J.P.Wragg
CAPTAIN,
Commanding 1/5th Battalion North Staffs.
Regiment.

WAR DIARY.

of

1/5th Battalion (The Prince of Wales) North Staffordshire Regiment.

JULY, 1916.

Army Form C. 2118.

WAR DIARY
or
INTELLIGENCE SUMMARY
(*Erase heading not required.*)

Instructions regarding War Diaries and Intelligence Summaries are contained in F. S. Regs., Part II. and the Staff Manual respectively. Title Pages will be prepared in manuscript.

Place	Date	Hour	Summary of Events and Information	Remarks and references to Appendices
	1916.			
FONCUR-VILLERS	Jul.1st.	7-30 a.m.	Attack on GOMMECOURT. See copy of "NARRATIVE of Operations" attached. Battalion relieved by 4th Leicesters at 4-30 p.m. and went into Advanced Corps Reserve line. Lieut.Colonel H. Burnett wounded.	Summary of Casualties attached.
FONCUR-VILLERS	Jul.2nd.		In Advanced Corps Reserve line. Received orders about 1-0 p.m. to march to BAILLEULMONT and to be prepared to take over new line of trenches on 3/7/16. C.O.(Captain F.E.Wenger) reconnoitred new line to be taken over (with other C.O's of the Brigade). Battalion marched at 1-30 p.m. to BAILLEULMONT arriving at 4-30 p.m. Lieut. C.J.B. Masefield and draft of 106 other ranks joined from Base.	
BAILLEUL-MONT.	Jul.3rd.		Battalion relieved 13th Battalion Royal Fusiliers in trenches at RANSART. Battalion on right, 1/5th Bn. South Staffs. Regt. on the left, Battalion of 139th Inf.Brigade. Line was X.98.90 to X7.c.5.90 (RANSART, 2.B. 1/10,000).	
RANSART	Jul.4th		Battalion in trenches; quiet.	
Do.	Jul.5th		Battalion in trenches. Quiet. Captain H.H. Stoney, North Staffordshire Regiment, joined from England to take up a second-in-command appointment. 7 other ranks arrived from Base.	
Do.	Jul.6th.		Battalion in trenches. Quiet. 2/Lieut. (now Captain) G. Cavill took over Adjutant Duties (vice Pt. (now Major.) commencing at 8-0 p.m.; orders subsequently issued.	
Do.	Jul 7th.		Battalion relieved by 1/4th Battalion North Staffs. Regt. and went into Divisional Reserve ... Rest and clean up. Provided covering parties at night for ...	

Army Form C. 2118.

WAR DIARY
or
INTELLIGENCE SUMMARY
(Erase heading not required.)

Instructions regarding War Diaries and Intelligence Summaries are contained in F. S. Regs., Part II. and the Staff Manual respectively. Title Pages will be prepared in manuscript.

Place	Date	Hour	Summary of Events and Information	Remarks and references to Appendices
BAILLEUL-VAL.	Jul.9th.		Battalion in Divisional Reserve. Carrying parties for gas cylinders found as on night of 8th.	
Do.	Jul.10th.		Battalion in Divisional Reserve. Carrying parties found for gas cylinders as above.	
Do.	Jul.11th.		Battalion in Divisional Reserve. Carrying parties found for gas pipes, etc. as above.	
Do.	Jul.12th.		Battalion in Divisional Reserve. 1 N.C.O. (Sgt. J. Lodey) proceeded Base to act as Instructor to drafts).	
Do.	July.13th.		Battalion in Divisional Reserve. 2nd Lieuts. C.F.Holton, H.C.Lindop, J.M.Lovatt, T.R.Lewty joined from Base.	
			Owing to fatigues very little opportunity for training during above period in Divisional Reserve. Coys. inspected by Commanding Officer. Rifles of all Four Companies inspected at Brigade Armourer's Shop.	
Do.	Jul.15th.		Battalion relieved 1/6th Battalion North Staffs.Regt. (two Companies of) in trenches 122 to 132 inclusive. 3rd & 6th Battalion Sherwood Foresters (139th Bde.) in trenches 133 to 140 inclusive; line then extended from W.18.a.20.80 to X.14.4.0 (Map: RANSART, sheet 28./10000) Relief complete by 4-30 p.m.	
RANSART	July 16th.		Battalion in trenches. Discharge of gas by 1/5th South Staffs.Regt., Right Sub-Sector, at 11 p.m. No enemy retaliation on our sub-sector. (left). 2nd Lieuts. J.L.Newton, F.S.Ross, A. Malkin joined from Base.	
RANSART	Jul. 17th.		Battalion in trenches. Discharge of gas by 1/5th South Staffs.Regt., Right Sub-sector. at 10 p.m. No retaliation on Left Sub-Sector. by enemy.	
RANSART.	Jul. 18th.		Battalion in trenches. 11-52 p.m. to 1-45 a.m. 19th. bombardment of enemy's rear billets and approaches. over Brigade Sector. Very little retaliation by enemy. Lieut. & Quartermaster G.A.Dewsnap thrown from his horse and severely injured.	

Army Form C. 2118.

WAR DIARY
or
INTELLIGENCE SUMMARY
(*Erase heading not required.*)

Instructions regarding War Diaries and Intelligence Summaries are contained in F.S. Regs., Part II. and the Staff Manual respectively. Title Pages will be prepared in manuscript.

Place	Date	Hour	Summary of Events and Information	Remarks and references to Appendices
	1916.			
RAMSART	Jul.19th.		Battalion in trenches. Quiet.	
RAMSART	Jul.20th.		Battalion in trenches. Enemy heavily bombarded sector of Brigade on left and left Company of our sector from midnight(19th/20th)to 2-15 a.m. Our artillery replied and silenced enemy fire. Casualties very slight (1 man slightly wounded).	
RAMSART	Jul.21st.		Battalion relieved by 1/6th Battalion North Staffs.Regt. and went into Divisional Reserve at BAILLULMONT. Battalion in billets by 8-0p.m. Two platoons proceeded to Divisional School to form part of Company with which Officers are instructed in drilling, etc. Three platoons occupied Forts and Support Points in Divisional Line in rear of Brigade Sector. 2nd Lieuts. J.E.Lowe and H.H.Watson joined from Base with draft of 70 other ranks.	
BAILLUL-MONT.	Jul.22nd.		Battalion in Divisional Reserve. Bathing. C.O's Inspection.	
Do.	Jul.23rd.		Do. Battalion inspected by G.O.C. 46th Division - also Transport. Working Parties of total of 2 Officers and 122 other ranks provided. Divine Service.	Programme of Training during this period attached
Do.	July 24th		Battalion in Divisional Reserve. Major A.E.F. Fawcus, 7th Manchester Regiment, joined and took Command. Working parties of a total of 7 Officers and 304 other ranks provided. Training as per programme except where interfered with by working parties.	
Do.	July 25th) July 26th)		Battalion in Divisional Reserve. Working parties provided as on 23rd. Training as per programme (save for working parties) with addition of Range Practice.	
Do.	July 27th		Battalion relieved 1/6th Battalion North Staffs.Regt in the trenches. Relief complete by 10-30 p.m. Two platoons rejoined from Divisional School.	
Do.	July 28th		Battalion in trenches. Quiet. Captain T.F.Weiger proceeded to PAS to take up appointment of Commandant of VII Corps Concentration Camp (for German Prisoners).	

Army Form C. 2118.

WAR DIARY
or
INTELLIGENCE SUMMARY
(Erase heading not required.)

Instructions regarding War Diaries and Intelligence Summaries are contained in F. S. Regs., Part II. and the Staff Manual respectively. Title Pages will be prepared in manuscript.

Place	Date	Hour	Summary of Events and Information	Remarks and references to Appendices
RENCART	Jul.29th.		Battalion in trenches. Quiet. Proposed operation of two Company to advance our F.B. Covering Parties provided by this Bat'lion.	Copy of special orders re-this operation attached.
	30th		Battalion in trenches. Quiet.	
	31st		Battalion in trenches. Proposed operation postponed until further orders.	

M. Carter
Major
Commanding 1/5th Battalion North Staffs. Regiment.

Narrative of Operations on July 1st, 1916.
----

1. The Battalion moved into position in assembly trenches and was reported all correct about 4-0 a.m.
2. The bombardment commenced at 6-25 a.m.
3. The attack was launched at 7-30 a.m.
4. The first three waves got well away, with few casualties, at proper intervals.

As the 4th wave was reaching the advance trench machine gun fire was opened from the S.W. end of FORD TRENCH and an artillery barrage was opened on our advanced line, support and communication trenches. At this time the 5th wave (consolidating parties) were coming up LINCOLN LANE; many men were hit and dropped their R.E. Material (Chevaux de frise, etc.) causing obstruction which seemed to delay this wave. At the same time a party of Monmouths who were at the head of LINCOLN LANE caught it badly from shell fire, many being killed or wounded which created a further blockage.

When the 5th wave arrived at the advance trench they found the 4th wave had not left this line, although considerably overdue; considerable confusion ensued and in spite of all efforts from the officers the 4th wave could not be persuaded to go forward. The 5th Wave (less 1 party) therefore, went through the 4th Wave and advanced through them towards the German wire; on arriving there this wave had all its officers killed or wounded and a large number of men knocked out. There they were met by a party of the former waves under an officer (unknown Captain who was afterwards killed) who gave the word to retire.- a few men managed to get back to the advance trench where they remained. The 6th Wave (Carrying parties) under Captain Wilton was met by these just about the advance trench.

/Captain

Captain Wilton was wounded in the neck[and had to crawl back]
and Second Lieut. Good put himself in the C.T. leading to the
advance trench - where he was met by returning party and, in
spite of all messages forward, was unable to get his party forward.
2nd Lieut. Gethin who got out of the trench to investigate
was immediately killed. 2nd Lieut. Scrivener's party could
not get further than the front trench owing to the block.
The 4th wave, rainy-taps under 2/Lieut. Deson, got to our
front line and were unable to move forward or backwards owing
to the congestion.

The Support Company and 1 Lewis Gun, under Captain Worthington,
moved up to the support trench allotted to them.

Lieut.-Colonel B. Burnett, on hearing that the attack was not
developing as arranged, personally went forward to the advance
trench and, with 2nd Lieut. Read and Lieut. E. Robinson, tried
to re-organise and push on. Lieut. Robinson's party moved
forward but Lieut. Robinson and most of his men were killed;
Col. Burnett disappeared and was only found about 1 p.m.
seriously wounded in the abdomen alongside a C.T. leading to
the advance trench.

Things then got in utter confusion; At 11-0 a.m. Captain
Wenger was 'phoned for by the Brigade Major to go out to
Adv. Battalion Headquarters and take the situation in hand
pending the return of Lieut.-Colonel Burnett who, up to that
time, could not be traced. At 12 noon Captain Wenger was given
orders to re-organize the remaining 5th North Men into two
waves using a party of 5th Lincs. to form 3rd and 4th waves.
The fresh attack was timed for 1-15 p.m. but as the re-organization
was not complete by 1-0 p.m. the time for attack was altered
to 3-30 p.m. Captain Wenger was given orders to side-slip and
get in touch with 139th Brigade on his left, his left to be
directed on the N.W. corner of GOMMERCOURT WOOD- the 5th South
to side-slip to the top of LINCOLN LANE and the whole to go over
together. At 3-15 p.m. Captain Wenger 'phoned to the Brigade
Major 137th Brigade that the 5th South left had not reached this
point and they were not in touch with his right; he received orders

/to

to attack without them. In the meantime he went to H.Q.
6th Sherwoods and saw Maj. Hall of 6th Sherwoods and/the Brigade
Major, 139th Brigade, who informed him they were not going
to attack unless a smoke barrage was put up - this was 'phoned
to the Brigade Major, 137th Brigade.

At 3.25 p.m. the 4 waves (two 5th North and two 5th Leicesters.)
were ready to attack; the 1st wave was on the parapet, the 2nd
behind in the front trench and the 5th Leics. in Support Trench
behind ready told off. 2nd Lieut. Lemon was on left of 1st
wave, 2nd Lieut. Read in centre, Captain Wenger himself on the
right, Capt. Worthington with 2nd Lieut. Scrivener in command
of the 2nd wave. 2nd Lieut. Lemon was to give the signal when
the 139th Brigade were ready at 3-30 p.m., so as to make the
attack simultaneous. At 3-28 p.m. Captain Wenger received word
from 2nd Lieut. Lemon that the 139th Brigade had made no
preparations and Captain Robinson of the 6th Sherwoods told him
they had no orders to attack and were not going over at the
time mentioned. Captain Wenger immediately despatched an
orderly to Captain Wilson (Adjutant, 5th North) to 'phone the
Brigade Major, 137th Bde, that the 139th Brigade were not going
over and were the 5th North to go by themselves; the Brigade
Major's reply was to sit tight. The 5th North remained in that
position for half an hour under severe artillery barrage on
their front wire and heavy machine gun fire from the right.
About 4-30 p.m orders came through to man the trench and all
6th North and 5th Leics. to file out.

        I have collected the first part of the narrative from
Officers and men who survived as I myself was not then present.

4/7/16.
                    Captain,
        Commanding 1/5th Battalion North Staffs. Regt.

SUMMARY OF CASUALTIES ON 10th July 1916.

KILLED.

Capt. F.G. Fletcher.
2nd.Lt. A.H. [illegible]
 "   [illegible]
 "   [illegible]

DIED.

[illegible] ([illegible] 2/7/16)
[illegible]
 "   [illegible]
 "   [illegible]
 "   D.F.J.Jones.
 "   L.T.Wood.
 "   T.A.Bowers (Died 2/7/16)

WOUNDED & MISSING.

2nd.Lt. A.D.Chapman.

WOUNDED to Duty.

2/Lt.(A/Capt) G.Lemon.

Lt.: [illegible] (Turned [illegible] 12/7/16)

SECRET

WORKING PARTIES Night of 8/7/16.

Designation of party or emplacement to be filled	Officer.	Party.	Coy.	Rendezvous.	Time of Rendezvous.	Time of parade here.
37	2/Lt.G.M.Scott	5 N.C.O's 60 other ranks 2 S.Bearers.	A.	BERLES Dump. W.21.b.70.18	11-10 p.m.	10-10 p.m.
38a.	2/Lt.F.G. Savage.	Do.	B.	Do.	11-30 p.m.	10-30 p.m.
38b.	2/Lt.L.G. Snelling.	Do.	C.	Do.	11-30 p.m.	10-30 p.m.
39.	2/Lt.A.T. Scrivener	Do.	B & C.	Do.	11-30 p.m.	10-30 p.m.
40a.	Lieut.W.H. Robinson.	Do.	D.	Do.	11-50 p.m.	10-50 p.m.

Each Party will report to the Adjutant before moving off and again on return, stating number of accessories carried up in position.

For further instructions see appendices.

46th Division
1714/G.

SECRET.

The attached instructions are issued in regard to tonights carrying operations.

1. Carrying Parties will not wear caps or steel helmets. They will wear gas helmets on their heads rolled up and the top button of their jacket undone.

2. The rifles of men carrying cylinders will be carried by the third man

3. There must be no smoking and absolute silence will be kept up from the dump inclusive till the men have deposited their poles against at the pole dump.

4. Poles must not be raised over the shoulder after the accesory has been dumped at his emplacement.

5. Officers in charge of parties must keep their parties together and prevent any straggling and stop gaps occurring.

6. If men are wounded on the way they must be lifted out of the communication trenches. A block must not be allowed to occur.

7. Should a cylinder be hit and burst, no gas alarm is to be sounded. Men will put their helmets down and the R.E.guide will be infoemed. On no account is the gas alarm to be sounded.

8. On the way back, care must be taken to prevent noise walking along the MONCHY ROAD. Parties must keep on the sides of the road and avoid noise of tramping.

9. Secrecy must be impressed on all men.

DETAIL OF PARTIES. 8/9th July,1916.

Each party will carry 20 accessories, 3 men to each accessory. Each party will be provided with one R. .guide,(not shewn on strength of party) The guide will wear a white brassard on the left arm.

All the accessories carried by any one party will be placed in one recess in the front line and every N.C.O. of the party will be given a docket showing the number of the recess, O.R. being informed of this number. Two spare poles will be carried by the last relief man of each party.

ROUTES and DESTINATIONS OF PARTIES 8/9th July,1916.

Route up :-
(ii) From BERLES dump, up NOBS LANE turning to the right on reaching RAVINE, up NEVERENDING STREET, turning to the right on reaching front line.
Along front line to recess for accessories.
Route down :-

All parties will go down 90 Street, turning to left in Support Line. Along support line a short distance and down by BIENVILLERS-MONCHY ROAD before 2 a.m. by STONEYGATE ROAD after 2 a.m. dumping poles on lorry at BIENVILLERS CHURCH.

INSTRUCTIONS FOR CARRYING PARTIES.

General instructions.

(i) During the nights of 8/9th and 9/10th July, 1916, accessories will be placed in the recesses made for them on the frontage :-
Sectors 85-93 inclusive.
and 109 to 114 "

(ii) Carrying parties will be detailed in accordance with the attached table and will rendezvous at the dumps :-
BERLES W.21.b.70.18.
BIENVILLERS E.9.b.15.40.
at times detailed herewith.
The head of the first party will be halted 50 yards clear of the dump (at the barrier in the case of the BIENVILLERS dump).
The Officer i/c of each party will report on arrival to Officer i/c Dump (An Officer of the Special Brigade R.E.) who will detail an R.E.guide to accompany him. All guides will wear a white armlet on the left arm.
Before moving off to pick up stores each party will be formed up on the right of the road in single file in the order in which it is to proceed through the trenches and each N.C.O i/c sub-party will be given a docket showing the number of the recess into which his sub-party is to place stores.

(iii) All turnings where parties might go wrong will be blocked by sentries
A traffic Officer (with two orderlies) at the head of each of the following streets :-
(i) 85 STREET.
(ii) 90 STREET.
(iii) NEVERENDING STREET.
will control the carrying parties passing these points and note the number of each party passing, informing the Officer i/c Dump by telephone if any serious departure from programme occurs. The trenches in use for carrying parties will be kept clear of other traffic from 9-30 p.m. to 3-30 am. each night.
N.C.O's i/c sub-parties will report on completion of task to the
(iv) Officer i/c Dump for poles at BIENVILLERS CHURCH. Officers i/c Parties will be responsible for the return of all poles to this point.

(v) The same personnel should be used as far as possible on both nights and Officers and N.C.O's on special duties should remain the same.

(vi) The success of these operations depends primarily on the absence of struggling. The efforts of all Officers, N.C.O's and men should therefore be made to attain this end.

Notes re Programme of Work.

(i) Lewis Gunners parade under Lewis Gun Officer. Reserves to be trained.
(ii) Sharpshooters to parade daily under the Intelligence Officer.
(iii) Signallers to parade daily under the Signal Officer.
(iv) Route March for the above details at 9-0 a.m. on Tuesday, under the Lewis Gun Officer.
(v) Lectures on General Smartness and Cleanliness on and off parade during rests on drill parades.
(vi) Smoke helmet drill to be arranged between Companies on Drill parade on Tuesday.
(vii) 6-0 to 7-0 p.m. Daily. Subaltern Officers Class : Map reading, Tactical Schemes.

At 3-0 p.m. on Tuesday "B" Company relieve 1 Platoon "B" Coy. and two Platoons "A" Coy. in Support Points.

1/5th Battn. North Staffs Regt. — PROGRAMME OF WORK During tour in Divisional Reserve.
Commencing 22/7/16.

Saturday			Sunday			Monday			Tuesday			Wednesday			Thursday
Time	Coy.	Detail	Time	Coy.	Detail	Time	Coy.	Detail	Time	Coy.	Detail	Time	Coy.	Detail	
Morning	All	Bathing & Fitting Clothing.	10-15	All	Battalion Parade for G.O.C's Inspection	9-0	B.	Route March	9-0	C.	Route March	9-0	D.	Route March	RETURN TO TRENCHES.
3-0 to 5-0	All	C.O.'s Inspection & Battalion Parade.	2-45	All	Church Parade	9-30 to 10-30	C.	Physical Training & Bayonet Fighting.	8-30 to 9-30	B.	Physical Training & Bayonet Fighting.	9-30 to 10-30	A.	2 platoons	
						10-30	D.	Drill without arms, Carriage, Marching & Saluting	9-30	D.	Drill.		B.	1 Platoon C.O's Inspection	
						10-30 to 11-30	D.	Physical Training etc.	9-30 to 10-30	D.	Physical Training.		C.	Drill with srms.	
						11-30 to 12	C.	Drill without arms	10-30	B.	Drill.	10-30 to 11-30	A.	Musketry. Standard Test.	
							All	Musketry.	10-30 to 12-0	All	Musketry.		B.		
						2-0 to 3-0	All	Coy. Officers Parade. Drill with arms.	11-0 to --	--	Subaltern Officers & N.C.O's		C.		
						3-15	--	Drill parade for Subalterns and N.C.O's	2-30 to 3-0		Drill & Communication Drill. All	12-0		Coy.Officer's Parade. Drill with arms.	
						4-15	--	Lecture to N.C.O's by Sgt.Major.	3-0		Coy.Officer's Parade, Drill.	2-30 to 3-0		Physical Training & Bayonet Fighting.	
									3-15		Sub.Officers Parade. Physical Training & Bayonet Fighting.	3-15 -		Young Officer's and N.C.O's Drill	
									5-0		N.C.O's Parade. Physical training & Bayonet Fighting				

O.'s C.
 Companies & Sections.

A New trench will be thrown out in the near future from the 5th Bay south of L.P.27 to the point where LINCOLN LANE meets the front line. O.C. 1/2nd Field Coy. R.E. will arrange to trace this trench tonight.

A Covering Party under Captain R.A.Stoney, consisting of 1 Officer and 30 other ranks Dorsets, 2 Officers and 1 Sergt. and 30 other ranks [illegible] will take up a position in front of the position [illegible] to cover the tracing and subsequent laying of wire.
 Dress: Skeleton Order without waterbottle, haversack or entrenching tool.
 No firing will take place without orders. If any enemy patrols are encountered the bayonet only will be used.
 Absolute silence will be maintained.

The covering party will rendezvous in fire trench at L.P.27, at 9-30 p.m.
"C" Coy. will provide 1 Officer and "D" Coy. 2 Officers to report to Captain Stoney, at above rendezvous, at 9-30 p.m.

O'S.C. "C" and "D" Coys. will arrange for guides to conduct the R.E. and Covering Party to the point at which they debouch.

The R.O.C. will be at C.Coy. Coy. H.Q. at 9-30 p.m.

The O.C. 1/2nd Field Coy. R.E. will inform O.C. 5th North, through Captain Stoney, when his men are back in our trenches, so that the covering party may be withdrawn.

The covering party will be in position at 10 p.m.

The Headquarters of the 1/2nd Field Coy. R.E. will be at the point where L.P. 27 meets our front line. O.C. Covering Party will make his Headquarters with O.C. 1/2nd Field Coy. R.E. and will arrange for a sufficient number of runners to be at this point.

All ranks of the 1/2nd Field Coy.R.E. will wear white bands on each upper arm as distinguishing badge.

The Brigade Signal Officer will arrange for signal communication from the junction of L.P.27 with the front line, to the nearest Coy.Headquarters.

23/7/16.

SUMMARY OF CASUALTIES FOR JULY 1916. (Not including Officers)
1/5th Battalion North Staffs Regt.

Week ending	Killed	Wounded	Missing	Wounded to Duty	Wounded Missing	Gas	Died	Total
1/7/16	27	127	23					
8/7/16	-	-	-					21
15/7/16	-	-	-					28
22/7/16	-	-	-					
29/7/16	-	-	-	-	-	-	-	14
	27	127	23	8	8	1	1	81

Secret

OPERATION ORDERS
by
Major A.E.F. Fawcus.
Commanding.

1. The line of the new trench, from W.12.c.4.2 to W.12.b.50.25 has now been traced.

2. Wiring will be done under the supervision of O.C. 1/2nd Fld. Coy. R.E. Wire will not be put out parallel to the trace of the new trench. Advantage will be taken of any ground dead to the enemy.

3. The following covering party, under the command of O.C. "C" Coy. will be in position by 10-15 p.m:-

    2nd Lieut. T.E.Lewty and the ASSAULT Detachment (30 men).
    The Support Platoon of "A" and "D" Coys., each platoon consisting of 25 men under and officer.
    One platoon of "C" Coy. (left platoon in the line) consisting of 25 men under an officer.
    One platoon of "D" Coy. (centre platoon in the line). consisting of 25 men under an officer.

    TOTAL 6 Officers and 130 men.

4. The covering parties will take up a position in front of our foremost belt of wire. Dress Skeleton order without haversack, water bottle or entrenching tool.
   There will be no talking, and absolute silence must be maintained.
        No firing will take place without orders from O.C. covering party., and if any hostile patrol is encountered the bayonet will be used.
        this Battalion

5. The O.C. 5th North will be at L.P.29 at 10-15 p.m. until the withdrawal of the covering party.
   O.C. Covering Party, O.C. 1/2nd Field.Coy. R.E. and the F.O.O. will be with the O.C. this Battalion.

6. The Signal Officer will arrange communication from L.P. 29 to Battalion Headquarters.

   6th South
7. The carrying parties from the ~~Battalion in this Battalion Reserve~~ will be moving up RUGBY ROAD and LINCOLN LANE. ~~THESE~~ These Communication trenches must be kept clear.

8. The parties will rendezvous at 9-15 p.m. at the following ppoints:-
    "A" Coy. party.   Junction of LINCOLN LANE & fire trench.
    "C" Coy. party.   L.P.26.
    "D" Coy. party.   L.P.29.
    Assault Detachment. L.P.27.

9. All officers detailed for the above will report to O.C. "C" Coy. at "C" Coy. Headquarters at 8-30 p.m.

10. The platoon of 6th South from ~~Battalion~~ Battalion Reserve will replace the Company Reserve Platoon in LINCOLN LANE.

11. "B" Coy. will send out a standing patrol of 1 Officer and 15 men North of the ALLOUETTE - RANSART Road, about 100 yards in front of our wire, at X.7.a.5.5, for the purpose of watching the flank of the operations.

30/7/16

E.A.WILSON,
Captain & Adjutant.

1/5th BATTALION (PRINCE OF WALES'S) NORTH STAFFORDSHIRE
REGIMENT.

War Diary

for   AUGUST, 1916.

Month of

SECRET.

Army Form C. 2118.

WAR DIARY
or
INTELLIGENCE SUMMARY.
(Erase heading not required.)

Instructions regarding War Diaries and Intelligence
Summaries are contained in F. S. Regs., Part II.
and the Staff Manual respectively. Title pages
will be prepared in manuscript.

Hour, Date, Place	Summary of Events and Information	Remarks and References to Appendices
AUGUST, 1916.		
1st. RANSART.	Battalion in trenches. Quiet. 1 Officer and 30 other ranks attached 1/2nd Fld. Coy. R.E. to form part of DUG-Out Building Party.	
2nd Do.	Battalion relieved by 6th North and went into Brigade Reserve at BERLES-AU-BOIS. Battalion in billets by 10-0 p.m.	
3rd} Berles-au-Bois. 4th}	Battalion in Brigade Reserve. Commenced digging advanced trench (previously marked out and wired) Energy turned heavy Machine Gun fire or party and caused many casualties. Casualties of this Battalion : 2nd Lieut. C.F.Bolton wounded (Died 4/8/16) 2nd Lieut. F.B.Lee wounded. Other ranks, Killed 3 wounded 11.	Operation Orders attached.
5th. BERLES-AU-BOIS	Battalion in Brigade Reserve. Raid by 5th South, 11-5 p.m. 137th Brigade Horse Show. Battalion won highest points in Brigade.	
6th. BERLES-AU-BOIS.	Do. Digging of advanced trench continued. Quiet, No Casualties.	
7th. Do.	Battalion in Brigade Reserve.	
8th. Do.	Do. Battalion relieved 6th North in trenches. Relief Complete by 8-0 p.m.. At 11-45 p.m. orders received to "Stand to Arms". Stood down again at 1-30 a.m. 9th. Nothing happened. 2nd Lieut. H.S READ to hospital, sick.	
9th. RANSART	Battalion in trenches. Work on advanced trench continued. Covering party provided by this Battalion. Major A.E.F.Fawcus, in charge of operations, wounded (by shrapnel) in a Listening Post.	
10th. RANSART.	Battalion in trenches. Covering party as above again provided. Party shelled by enemy, casualties of this Battalion other ranks wounded 7.	
11th to} RANSART. 15th }	Battalion in trenches. Quiet. Digging of advanced trench continued Much activity in patrolling "No Man's Land", chiefly by 2nd Lieut. H.T.TW and men of Assault Detachment.	

Army Form C. 2118.

WAR DIARY
or
INTELLIGENCE SUMMARY.
(Erase heading not required.)

Instructions regarding War Diaries and Intelligence Summaries are contained in F. S. Regs., Part II. and the Staff Manual respectively. Title pages will be prepared in manuscript.

Hour, Date, Place	Summary of Events and Information	Remarks and References to Appendices
AUGUST, 1916.		
15th. RANSART.	Battalion relieved by 6th North and went into Divisional Reserve at BAILLEULMONT. Battalion in billets by 6-0 p.m. One Coy. left in Support Points and Forts in Divisional Line.	
16th. to) BAILLEULMONT 21st RANSART	Battalion in Divisional Reserve. Bathing. Fatigues. Training as per programme attached. Played Cricket Match with 5th Sherwood Forester's at BAILLEUVAL on 21st.	
22nd Do.	Battalion relieved 6th North in Trenches. Relief complete 9-30 p.m. Digging of Advanced trench continued.	
23rd. to) RANSART. 28th.) RANSART	Battalion in trenches. Quiet. Digging of advanced trench continued. Activity in patrolling as in previous tour.	
28th.	Battalion relieved by 6th North and went into Brigade Reserve at BERLESauBOIS. Relief complete by 6-30 p.m. 4 two platoons left in Battalion Reserves to Battalions in line.	
29th BERLES-au-BOIS.	Battalion in Brigade Reserve. Bathing. 2nd Lieut. J.M.Lovatt to Hospital.	
30th. Do.	Battalion in Brigade Reserve.	
31st. Do.	Do. Relieved platoons in Battn.Reserves and took over Forts in Divisional Line from Battalion in Divisional Reserve.	

K M Newey
Major,
Commanding 1/5th Battalion North Staffordshire Regiment.

SECRET.

OPERATION ORDERS No.4.

By

Major, R.E.FFawcus,

Commanding 1/5th Battalion North Staffs. Regiment.

1. An advanced trench will be dug tonight from L.P.26 to the junction of **LINCOLN LANE** with the front line trench.

2. The trench will be dug tonight at least 4'0" deep, 2'6" wide at the top and 1'6" wide at the bottom. Two templets will be issued to each party. The final dimensions of the trench will be 6'0" deep, 5'0" wide at the top and 3'0" wide at the bottom.

3. The trench will be held during the 4th August by 3 posts of 1 Sgt. and 6 men under an Officer of the 5th South, and 3 posts of 1 Sgt. and 6 men 5th North, under an officer. These posts will not be warned before 2-0 a.m on the morning of the 4th August. This will be made known to all ranks. Arrangements will be made for rations and water for these parties by Battalions concerned.

4. Parties will be found as follows :-

   "A" Party. L.P.26 to L.P.27. 5th South - 6 Officers and 260 other ranks, under command of a senior Officer 5th South, and 2 Officers and 50 other ranks 5th North.

   "C" Party. L.P.29 to L.P.30. 5th North - 4 Officers and 155 other ranks under Senior Officer 5th North.

   "D" Party. L.P.30 to junction of LINCOLN LANE with front line. 5th North. 7 officers and 275 other ranks.

Composition of Parties :-

   "A" ------- 2nd Lieut Reid   -------- 30 other ranks Bomb Platoon
                2nd Lieut. Lewty   20   "   " Assault Section.

   "C" ...... Capt. Wood   -------- 100 "   " "B" Company.
                2nd Lieut. Slater -----   32   "   " L.Gun Section.
                2nd Lieut. Malkin   15   "   " "D" Company.
                2nd Lieut. Copeland   11   "   " Signal Section.

   "D" ------- Capt. Worthington ------- 84   "   " "A" Company.
                Lieut. Noke   111 "   " "C"   "
                2nd Lieut. Keeling   80   "   " "D"   "
                "   "   Lee
                "   "   Holtom.
                "   "   Hughes.
                "   "   Masefield.

Each man will draw one pick and one shovel

5. ROUTES. Parties will use following trenches to their rendezvous :-
   "A" RUGBY ROAD to L.P. 26.
   "B" RUGBY ROAD to L.P. 29.
   "D" LINCOLN LANE to L.P. 30.

Routes will be reconnoitred beforehand by officers in charge of parties.

6. The 6th North will arrange for a large Covering Party to be in position by 10-0 p m or as soon after as light permits.

7. The O.C.1/2nd Field Coy. R.E. will arrange to tape the front edge of the cutting line as soon as it sufficiently dark.

8. O.C. 1/2nd Field Coy.R.E. will arrange for working parties to be detailed to tasks - commencing from the right of each section.
Each man will be allotted a task of 5'0" long. This will be dug at least 4'0" deep, at least 2'6" wide at the top, and at least 1'6" wide at the bottom
Work will be continued as late as possible on morning of 4-8-16.
Each man will be placed at the left front corner of his task.
He will insert the point of his pick at this point. Should any men be found to be surplus they will be placed under an officer in the front line trench and will act as a relief when required.

OPERATION ORDERS No.4. Continued. (2).

10. CONTINUED. It will be clearly understood that the Officers in charge of infantry working parties are entirely responsible that the tasks are performed.

11. GUIDES. Guides from R.E. will meet each party at BEERLES at 8-0 p.m. and will remain with them until tasks have been allotted.

12. SILENCE It is most essential that silence is maintained.

13. All earth will be thrown to the front.

14. EQUIPMENT Skeleton order, without haversack, waterbottle or entrenching tool. 50 rounds S.A.A. only to be carried.

15. EVERY MAN MUST KNOW THE NUMBER OF THE PARTY TO WHICH HE BELONGS.

16. Parties must be in position at their rendezvous in the front line by 9-30 p.m.

3-8-15

                         ....NASON.
                         Captain & Adjutant,
                     1/5th Bn.North Staff's Regt.

1/5th Battalion North Staffs Regt.

PROGRAMME OF WORK
For Period in Divisional Army Reserve 15/8/16 – 21/8/16

COMPANY	THURSDAY	FRIDAY	SATURDAY	SUNDAY	MONDAY
"A"	Co. drill:- Rifle. 2–0 to 3–0 p.m. Tube Helmet Drill Phys.Drill Drill without arms & salutes.	7–0 – 9–0 a.m. Range Practice. 2–0 to 3–0 p.m. Phys.Drill & Drill without arms. Tube Helmet Drill & Instructions in pluaces.	Route March 6 miles.		
"B"	On Fatigue.	Route March 6 Miles.			
"C"	Divisional H.Q.	Divisional H.Q.			
"D"	7–0 to 9–0 a.m. Range Practice 5 rounds grouping. 5 " application. 10 " snap Drill. 2–7 to 3–0 p.m. Phys.Drill & Drill without arms Saluting. Tube helmet Drill.	Fatigue.	7–0 to 9–0 a.m. Range Practice. 2–0 to 3–0 p.m. Phys.Drill Drill without arms & salutes. Eating of Tube Helmet Drill. Relieve "C" Coy in Div. HQ.		
Advance Party.	2–0 to 3–0 p.m. Drill Parade.	2–45 to 3–45 p.m. Drill Parade.	2–45 to 3–45 p.m. Drill Parade.		
L.Gunners, Bombers, Scouts Signallers.	2–12 & 2–3 p.m. Training under respective officers.	9–12 & 2–3 p.m. Training under respective officers.	9–12 & 2–3 p.m. Training under respective officers.		

1/5th Battalion North Staffs. Regt. War Diary, August/1916.

SUMMARY OF CASUALTIES.

OFFICERS.

Week Ended.	Killed.	Wounded.	Wd. to duty.	Sick.
5th.	-	2	-	-
12th.	-	1	1	1
19th.	-	-	-	-
26th.	-	1	1	1
Total.	-	ˣ 3	ˣ 1	2

ˣ1 Died of wounds.
ˣ1. wounded by premature burst
of Newton Rifle Grenade. (2nd Lt. J.E.Lowe).

OTHER RANKS.

Week ended.	Killed.	Wounded.	Wounded to duty.	Sick.
5th.	3	11	3	5
12th.	1	7	-	26
19th	-	-	-	13
26th	-	5	-	24
Total	4	ˣ23	3	68

ˣ 2 wounded by premature burst of Newton
Rifle Grenade.

REINFORCEMENTS.

Officers. Joined Battalion in the Field from 5th (Res.) Battalion.

2nd Lt. A.G.Hammersley. 17/8/16. 2nd Lt. C.Edwards. 18/8/16.
2nd Lt. W.G.Forester.   18/8/16. 2nd Lt. C.R.Krell 18/8/16.
2nd Lt. W.Meakin   23/8/16. 2nd Lt. T.H.Billington 21/8/16.

Other Ranks.

4/8/16. 30. from Base. Proceeded Bde. School of Instn. on arrival)
                                           for fortnight's Course.
18/8/16. 30. from 4th Entrenching Battalion. Ditto Ditto.

29/8/16. 9 from Base.

1/5th Battalion North Stafford Regiment.

SPECIAL REPORT.

At 10-15 p.m. last night the sentry in Bay 11, Trench 130, heard a noise in our wire. Sgt.Johnson fired a Verylight and immediately between 20 and 30 men sprung up in our wire, shouted and threw about 6 bombs, one of which fell in the trench and killed Pte.Maydew. Our men 'stood to' and threw 5 or 6 bombs back. By this time the Listening Post on the left had come in and rapid fire was opened on the enemy who was scattering. About half-an-hour later the enemy threw 3 or 4 bombs into his own wire opposite and began to shoot. Our fire was stopped and abot 11-15 p.m. a party of 1 Officer and 2 men went out through our wire. They found one dead German, two German rifles and a bomb and brought them in.
Later another patrol went out and found more bombs in our wire. At 'stand to' this morning and a little later while it was misty two other patrols went out in front of our wire. They brought in more bombs also one German boot riddled with holes and covered with blood, but no more enemy could be found in the immediate neighbourhood. The Corps Intelligence Officer has examined the rifle and has taken all the man's documents.

                                                (Sd) H.H.Stoney, Major,
Commanding 1/5th Bn North Staffs Regt.

Army Form C. 2118.

1/5 North Staffs

Vol 20

WAR DIARY

or

~~INTELLIGENCE SUMMARY~~

(Erase heading not required.)

Instructions regarding War Diaries and Intelligence Summaries are contained in F. S. Regs., Part II. and the Staff Manual respectively. Title Pages will be prepared in manuscript.

Place	Date	Hour	Summary of Events and Information	Remarks and references to Appendices
BERLES.	1-9-16.		Battalion in Brigade Reserve. B.E. Fatigues & Tube Helmet Drill.	
do	2-9-16.		do do R.E. Fatigues. Military Tournament held at BAILLEULMONT. Bayonet fighting was won by 1/5th North Staffs Regt. The Inter-Coy Shooting Competition was won by "D" Coy. 1/5th North Staffs Regt. The Bombing Competition was won by the 1/5th South Staffs.	
do	3-9-16.		The Battalion went to the trenches in relief of the 1/6th North Staffs Regt. Relief complete 7-10.pm.	
Trenches.	4-9-16.		Quiet day.	
do	5-9-16		Quiet day.	
do	6-9-16		Quiet day.	
do	7-9±16.		Quiet day. Lieut Goss, 2nd Lt. J.L.Heath, and 2nd.Lt. S.B.Bridgwood joined the Battn from the Base.	
do	8-9-16		The Battalion raided the enemy's trenches opposite RANSART, as per Operation Orders and report attached.	
do	9-9-16		The Battalion (Less "A" Coy who found the garrisons of the Divisional Line) went into Divisional Reserve at BAILLEULMONT. Relief commenced at 4-30p.m. 2nd.Lieuts C.H.Robinson, H.R.A.Garnett, and J.W. Cook joined the Battalion from the Base.	
BAILLEUL- MONT.	10-9-16		Battalion in Divisional Reserve. Bathing. A Fatigue Party of 2 Officers and 50 Other Ranks worked under the C.R.E. LARBRET. At night a fatigue party of 5 Officers and 282 Other Ranks carried 88 Gas Cylinders to the trenches opposite MONCHY. No casualties.	
do	11-9-16.		Battalion in Divisional Reserve. The Battalion paraded for Commanding Officer's inspection at 3.pm.	

2449 Wt. W14957/M90 750,000 1/16 J.B.C. & A. Forms/C.2118/12.

Army Form C. 2118.

WAR DIARY

Instructions regarding War Diaries and Intelligence Summaries are contained in F. S. Regs., Part II. and the Staff Manual respectively. Title Pages will be prepared in manuscript.

(Erase heading not required.)

Place	Date	Hour	Summary of Events and Information	Remarks and references to Appendices
BAILLEUL-MONT.	Sept.1916. 12th		Battalion in Divisional Reserve. A Fatigue Party of 4 Officers and 100 Other Ranks worked under C.R.E. LARBRET. "B" Coy relieved "A" Coy in the Forts in the Divisional Line. Relief complete 10.am. At night, a Fatigue Party of 4 Officers and 244 Other Ranks carried gas cylinders up to the trenches opposite MONCHY. No casualties.	
do	13th		Battalion in Divisional Reserve. The Battalion paraded in Field Service Marching Order for the Commanding Officer's inspection. Two Platoons went to the 46th Div. Inf. Schools.	
do	14th		Battalion in Divisional Reserve. Battalion paraded in Field Service Marching Order for inspection by the Brigadier General Commanding 137th Inf. Bde.	
do	15th		The Battalion (Less the Raiding Party) went to the trenches in relief of the 1/6th North Staffs. Relief complete 7-15.pm. Two Platoons of the 1/6th North Staffs remained in the trenches until relieved by the two platoons from the 46th Div. Inf. School, about 10-30.pm.	
Trenches.	16th		Quiet day. No. 2069. Pte Hindmarsh. P. was awarded to Medal of St. George, 3rd Class, for gallant conduct on the night of 4/5th September, 1916. 4th April 1916.	
do	17th		Quiet day.	
do	18th		Quiet day.	
do	19th		Quiet day. The Raiding Party came up to the trenches.	
do	20th		A Party from the Battalion carried out a raid at 2. am. on the enemy's trenches opposite RANSART, as per Operation Orders and Report attached.	
do	21st		The Battalion went into Brigade Reserve. Two Platoons of "C" Coy going to FORT 147. Two Platoons to the dug-outs near Left Battn Headquarters, and the remainder of the Battn to BERLES. Relief commencing about 4-30.pm. A Draft of 17 Other Ranks joined the Battalion from the Base, and went to the 137th Inf. Bde School for further instruction.	

Army Form C. 2118.

WAR DIARY

or

~~INTELLIGENCE SUMMARY~~

(Erase heading not required.)

Instructions regarding War Diaries and Intelligence Summaries are contained in F. S. Regs., Part II. and the Staff Manual respectively. Title Pages will be prepared in manuscript.

Place	Date	Hour	Summary of Events and Information	Remarks and references to Appendices
BERLES.	Sept.1916. 22nd		Battalion in Brigade Reserve. 50 percent of the Battalion went to a lecture at BAILLEULMONT at 10-30.am., on Bayonet Fighting by Major Campbell.	
do	23rd.		Battalion in Brigade Reserve. R.E. Fatigues.	
do	24th		Battalion in Brigade Reserve. "B" Coy relieved "D" Coy in the dug-outs near Left Battalion Headquarters. R.E. Fatigues. 6.Officers and 8 Other Ranks went to a lecture at the 46th Divl.Anti-Gas School on the Small Box Respirator.	
do	25th		Battalion in Brigade Reserve. R.E. Fatigues. Captain C. Lister. (Northamptonshire Regt) was attached to the Battalion as Second in Command. The Bishop of Khartoun held a Confirmation Service at BAILLEULMONT, and 12 Other Ranks ~~were~~ of this battalion were confirmed.	
do	26th		Battalion in Brigade Reserve. R.E. Fatigues. A cellar was filled with gas under arrangements made by the Divisional Gas Officer, and 200 men in batches of 30 were in the gas for about 5 minutes. No casualties. Capt. S.B. Wilton and 2nd Lt. T.R. Bland joined the Battalion from the Base.	
do	27th		Battalion in Brigade Reserve. The remainder of the Battalion were in the gas cellar. No. 2308 Sgt Warrilow. and No. 2278 were awarded the Military Medal for gallant conduct on the night of the raid 19/20th September. 1916. The Battalion proceeded to the trenches in relief of the 1/6th North Staffs. Relief complete 6-15.pm. Enemy patrol threw bombs on Trench 130 at 10-15.pm. See report attached.	
Trenches.	28th		Quiet day.	
do	29th		Quiet day. The Raiding Party went back to BAILLEULMONT to train. Two Platoons of the 1/6th North Staffs Regt. came up to replace them. 2nd,Lieut J.W.A. Harke and 2nd.Lieut L.C.Grice joined the Battalion from the Base.	
do	30th		Quiet day.	

Commanding 1/5th North Stafford

SECRET.

OPERATION ORDERS   Copy No. 2
by   8th Sept.1916
Major H.H.Stoney,
Commanding 1/5TH BATTALION NORTH STAFFS.REGT.

Reference Trench Map RAMPART 1/10,000 EDITION 2 C.

1. On the night of the 8th/9th two gaps will be cut in the enemy wire by exploding ammonal tubes :-
    No.1. at W.1.d.2.3.
    No.2. at W.18.b.2.8.

2. OBJECT
    (a) To make gaps in enemy wire.
    (b) To secure identification of enemy troops by rushing through No.2.Gap and taking prisoner any enemy that may be there.

3. PARTIES
    "A" - 1 Officer (2nd.Lieut.J.B.Lowe) and 14 other ranks and 3 sappers, to enter enemy work at W.18.b.2.8.
    "B" - 1 Officer (2nd.Lieut.Edwards) and 4 other ranks and 3 sappers, to place ammonal tubes on wire at W.1.d.2.3.

4. NARRATIVE OF OPERATIONS.

    (a) "A" Party will leave front line at 1-30 a.m. near point where 84th STREET joins New Front Line and will rendezvous in RAVINE near W.18.a.7.5.

    (b) "B" Party will go out at 1-30 a.m. from L.P.39 and rendezvous behind BANK near W.1.d.65.70.

    (c) "A" Party will send on from rendezvous a patrol to cut a gap in outer fence or wire.

    (d) Sappers and Escort of 1 N.C.O. and 2 men from "A" Party and the whole of "B" Party will go forward at 1-50 a.m. and place tubes in position on wire and remainder of "A" Party will get within 50 yards of wire ready to rush in. "B" Party will return as quickly as possible to L.P.39

    (e) The tubes will be exploded at 2-0 a.m.

    (f) "A" Party will rush in immediately on explosion and if wire is sufficiently cut get into enemy work, secure one or two prisoners and then get back to our lines.

    (g) The line from gap in fence opposite W.18.b.2.8. and thence by RAVINE to our lines will be taped out.

5. EQUIPMENT.

    (a) All ranks will remove all marks of identification except a piece of paper stating name and number, to be carried in left breast pocket. Officers will inspect each party before moving to the trenches.

    (b) Bayonet men will take rifle, bayonet and bandolier (50 rounds) and bombs.

    (c) Bombers will wear waistcoats containing 12 bombs and take bayonets but no rifles.

    (d) Gas Helmets - One per man will be taken and carried in the inner coat pocket.

    (e) Flash lamps will be carried.

    (f) Faces will be blackened.

    (g) Four pairs of wire cutters will be carried by "A" Party.

P.T.O.

OPERATION ORDERS No. 8.

SHEET - 2.

6. **COUNTERSIGNS.**

   "A" Party - 'LOWE'.   "B" Party - 'EDWARDS'.

7. **NECESSITY FOR ABSOLUTE SILENCE** and no coughing must be impressed on all ranks.

8. **HEADQUARTERS.** Battalion Headquarters will be at "C" Company H.Qrs.

   Signal Officer will arrange communications direct to the Batteries.

9. **M.O.** will be in dugout in RUGBY ROAD.

10. **F.O.O.** will be at Battalion Trench Headquarters.

11. **ARTILLERY.**

    (a) The artillery will open fire at 2-0 a.m. on enemy Saps in Front Line from W.12.d.95.40 to W.18.b.6.2. and on the following machine gun emplacements :-
    X.8.a.2.2.   X.7.d.15.70   X.7.c.9.2.

    (b) The Medium Trench Mortars will fire on enemy front line in X.7.c.

    (c) Stokes Mortars will fire on Sap at X.7.a.2.1. and enemy Front Line North of ABLOUETTE-RANSART ROAD.

    (d) Machine guns will fire on enemy Front Line in :-
    W.18.b. and d.   X.7.b.   X.1.d.

Issued at :-

```
Copy 1 and 2    -   War Diary.
     3 to 7    -   5 Companies.
     8    9    -   137th Infantry Brigade.
     10       -   1/5th South Staffs Regt.
     11       -   1/5th Sherwood Foresters.
     12       -   O.C. 1/2nd. Field Coy. R.E.
     13       -   2nd. Lieut. Lowe
     14.      -   2nd. Lieut. Edwards.
     15       -   137th Machine Gun Coy.
     16       -   V.48 T.M. Battery.
     17.      -   137th F.M. Battery.
```

8/9/16.

(Sd) E.A. ILSON.
Captain & Adjutant.
1/5th Bn. North Staffs Regt.

SECRET.   Attachment to Operation Order No.5.

                    Commanding 1/5th ………… Battalion …… 8/7/17

1. Gaps will be cut in double wire at …………………… ……………

2. Reference …map…( )
   Para 4.( )
        …………… will leave front line at …… a.m. from trench 117.
   Para 4.( )
        "A" …… will be out at ……………… at 1.45 a.m.
   Para 4 ( )
        The line from ……… ………… opposite …………… to trench 117
        will be taped out.

3. A bouquet of ……… …… will be fired …… ……… ……… a.1235
   in case any of our ……… …… will be …… ……… …… that   All
   direction.

   8/8/16.

1/5th Battalion North Staffs Regt.

To:- Headquarters
         137th Inf. Bde.

Reference Operation Orders No 8.

Two gaps were cut in the enemy's wire by exploding ammonal tubes No. 1. at or about X.1.d.2.3.   No2. at or about W.18.b.2.8.

Party of 1 Officer and 17 Other Ranks entered enemy work at W.18.b.2.8., and found two shell holes, which had been scooped out to give cover to a man lying. An Officer and two men proceeded along path towards enemy lines, but saw no signs of any hostile party. Neither path nor shell holes shewed signs of having been used recently Party returned to our trenches at 117 Trench.   No casualties.

After exploding ammonal tube B Party returned to our trenches and no further action was taken.

                                    (sd) H.H. Stoney. Major,
9-9-16.   Coammanding 1/5th Bn. North Staffs Regt.

Copy No 2

OPERATION ORDERS, No.

by
Major ....
Commanding 1/5th Battalion .... Regt.

Reference trench map HAMMEL 1/10,000 Edition ....

1. The night of the 18th/19th a party from the Battalion will carry out a raid in the enemy line, the trenches between points ..7...2.8. ....
   85.   Point of entry will be at ....

2. OBJECT.
   (A) To secure identification of enemy troops holding line near HAMMEL.
   (B) To kill Germans.
   (C) To obtain articles and information of every kind such as ...
       Gas helmets, Grenades, Documents, etc...

3. WIRE CUTTING. During the afternoon of the 18th Inst. edition .... BATTERY
   will cut two gaps in the enemy wire about 40 yards apart at or near
   H.7.c.15.70.   Both these gaps will be used.
   They will also cut a gap at H.7.a.5.8. which will not be used.
   Centre Group R.A. will cut a gap at U.18.b.0.85. This gap will not be used.

4. STRENGTH OF PARTY AND ROUTE TO BE TAKEN. The Party will consist
   of 5 Officers and about 80 other ranks under the command of Lieut.-.....
   Hawthorn, and will leave by NEW LINCOLN LANE and assemble in No Man's Land
   according to the orders of O.C. Raiding Party.

5. ARTILLERY. The artillery programme consists of the following phases.
   Phase "A"   Zero minus 90 mins to 70 mins.
               Ground in front of objective from H.7...2.8. to ..18.d.6.4.
               will be sprinkled by 18 pounders to drive in any
               Listening Posts or parties working on the wire.
   Phase "B"   Zero to plus 5 mins.
               Intense bombardment of enemy front and support lines
               between H.7.a.9.0. and ..18.1.6...
   Phase "C"   Zero plus 5 min to plus 15 mins.
               Lift off objectives on front line.

   Phase "D"   Zero plus 15 mins. to plus 30 mins.
               Same as phase "C" but other objectives to be covered
               to prevent fire being brought on raiding party during
               withdrawal.
   Phase "E"   Zero plus 30 minutes onwards.
               Fire to be continued till orders to stop given ...
               action on orders of O.C. Battalion.
   When O.C. Raid reports "all clear" fire of 18 pounders will then
   return on to front line objectives.

6. NARRATIVE OF OPERATION.
   After Phase ...... patrols will go out to reconnoitre and lay tapes
   to gaps.   After Phase "B" raid will go in.
                Parties ...

7. WITHDRAWAL. Company will be withdrawn under orders of .... and
   will file up by LINCOLN LANE into LINCOLN LANE and assemble there.
   Head of party at Junction of LINCOLN LANE and ....
   When party is complete they will be marched back to ....
   where the men will be given a hot drink.

8. Trench Battalion Headquarters will be at .... in
   LINCOLN LANE.   Prisoners, loot and documents will be brought there.

   R.M.O. and M.O. will be at these Headquarters.

CONTINUED.

9. COMMUNICATION. Communication will be arranged by the Signalling Officer from Trench Battalion Headquarters to Hollow in 'No Man's Land' which will be the headquarters of O.C.Raiding Party.
   Communication by runners must also be arranged.

10. O.C."D" Coy will detail an Officer and 2 N.C.Os. to prevent blocks occurring in NEW LINCOLN LANE and ensure rapid passage of the party on return. This Officer will be responsible for getting in the tape after the Raiding Party has returned.
    On no account must tapes be left out.

11. Five White Rockets will be fired together from a place between BASTION H and ALLOUETTE in case any of the raiding party should lose their way.

12. Stokes Mortars, 137th Bde.M.G.Coy and Medium T.M.Battery will co-operate as follows from Zero onwards until order to cease fire is given. Stokes Mortars will fire on Gap at A.7.a.2.0. to point where it joins enemy front line trench, on C.T. from A.7.c.2.9. to A.7.c.5.5. and support trench from A.7.a.53.75. to A.7.c.9.3. and on any other points within range North of ALLOUETTE RANSART ROAD.
    137th Bde.M.G.Coy. will fire on RANSART and enemy trenches in A.13.b.&d.
    Medium T.M.Battery will fire on Gap from A.7.a. 0.0 to point where it joins front line and any other objective within range North of ALLOUETTE-RANSART ROAD.

13. All marks of identification (except a piece of paper stating name and number) will be removed and Officers will inspect their parties before leaving billets.

14. The necessity for absolute silence and no coughing while parties are moving out into position must be impressed upon all ranks.

15. Zero will be notified later.

16. Watches will be synchronised at 7-0 p.m.

17-9-16.
                                                            Major,
                                    Commanding 1/5th Bn.North Staffs Regt.

        Issued at   p.m.   16.

        No. 1 & 2.   War Diary.
         " 3 to 7.   5 Companies.
         " 8.   137th Infantry Brigade.
         " 9.   Lieut. J.Hawthorn.
         " 10.   1/5th South Staffs Regt.
         " 11.   1/6th Notts & Derby Regt.
         " 12.   138th Infantry Brigade.
         " 13.   Centre Group R.A.
         " 14.   T.M. I.M.Battery.
         " 15.   137th Bde. T.M.Battery.
         " 16.   137th Bde. M.G.Coy.
         " 17.   O.C. 1/2nd Field Coy.

1/5th Battalion North Staffs Regt.

To:- Headquarters,
    137th Inf. Bde.

I have the honour to report that a party from my Battalion, consisting of 7 Officers and about 80 N.C.O.s and men carried out a raid on the enemy's trenches at about W.18.b.95.65. (S.W. RANSART)

One party(2nd. Lt S.B. Bridgwood's) succeeded in entering the front line trench, and state that they found it unoccupied. The same party bombed a dug-out and killed some Germans (exact number is unknown) but they state that they saw several lying huddled up on floor of dug-out.

Part of the Right Party entered a sap and found noone.

No identification was obtained, as there was delay in getting into trench, and the 15 minutes allowed did not prove sufficient. The enemy appeared to be keeping no look-out, and one of the parties were able to cut a lot of wire, and yet attract no attention.

The casualties consisted of 1 man wounded and 5 men slightly wounded.

The enemy sent up numerous red rockets bursting into two. and their artillery opened 15 to 20 minutes later. After all the party had returned enemy rifle fire started and lasted about 1 hour.

(sd) H.H. Stoney, Major.
20-9-16.   Commanding 1/5th Bn. North Staffs Regt.

Statement shewing Strength.

	Offs.	O.R.s.
Week ending 7-9-16.	39	827
" " 14-9-16	41	797
" " 21-9-16	41	810
" " 28-9-16	43	817

Casualties. (b) Officers.

	Wounded.	Killed.	Hospital.
Week ending 7-9-16.	1	-	-
" " 14-9-16	-	-	2
" " 21-9-16	-	-	2
" " 28-9-16	-	-	2
Two days ending 30-9-16.	-	-	-

Casualties to Other Ranks.

	Wounded.	Killed.	Hospital.
Week ending 7-9-16	1	1	12
" " 14-9-16	2	2 1	29
" " 21-9-16	3	-	10
" " 28-9-16	-	1	30
Two days ending 30-9-16	1	-	5

Army Form C. 2118.

WAR DIARY
or
INTELLIGENCE SUMMARY.
(Erase heading not required.)

5th N. Staff R

Vol 21

Place	Date	Hour	Summary of Events and Information	Remarks and references to Appendices
	1st		Quiet day.	
	2nd		Quiet day.	
	3rd		2 Officers and 3 Other Ranks killed enemy listening post at T.19.b.4.6. Casualties. 1 man wounded. Party raided March 131. See report attached. Battalion relieved by the 1/6th North Staffs Regt. Moved to Divisional Reserve about 4 p.m.	
	4th		Battalion in Divisional Reserve. Refitting and cleaning up. Advised that cases of three men sent to hospital, have been diagnosed as Scarlet Fever. 4 Officers and Men isolated.	
	5th		Battalion in Divisional Reserve. Parades as per programme of Training. Another case of Scarlet Fever. 20 more men isolated.	
	6th		Battalion in Divisional Reserve. Parades as per Programme of Training. 2nd. Lieut. Lowe and Ross recorded with the "Tipperary Times" at the R.O.C. Relief of Forts in Divisional Line.	
	7th		Battalion in Divisional Reserve. Work as for Programme.	
	8th		Battalion in Divisional Reserve. Kit inspection. Church Parades. Training in Plot Operations.	
	9th		Battalion sent to trenches in relief of the 1/6th North Staffs Regt. Relief complete about 4 p.m.	
	10th		Quiet day.	
	11th		Quiet day.	
	12th		Enemy counter burst on enemy trenches to by stokes mortars and 26th Divl. Artillery. No report attached.	
	13th		Quiet day.	

Army Form C. 2118.

WAR DIARY
or
INTELLIGENCE SUMMARY.
(Erase heading not required.)

5th N. Staffs Rgt

Instructions regarding War Diaries and Intelligence Summaries are contained in F. S. Regs., Part II. and the Staff Manual respectively. Title pages will be prepared in manuscript.

Place	Date	Hour	Summary of Events and Information	Remarks and references to Appendices
	OCTOBER 1915			
TRENCHES.	14th.		Quiet day.	
do.	15th.		Battalion relieved by 1/6th North Staffs Regt. Relief complete 4.pm. Battalion went into Brigade Reserve at BERLES.	
BERLES.	16th.		Battalion in Brigade Reserve. R.E. Fatigue Parties.	
do.	17th.		do.	
do.	18th.		do.	
do.	19th.		do.	
do.	20th.		do.	
do.	21st.		Battalion went to the trenches in relief of the 1/6th North Staffs Regiment. Relief complete about 4.pm.	
TRENCHES.	22nd.		Quiet day.	
do.	23rd.		Quiet day.	
do.	24th.		Quiet day.	
do.	25th.		Raid carried out by 1/6th South Staffs Regt. See special report attached.	
do.	26th.		Battalion relieved by 1/6th North Staffs Regt, and went into Divisional Reserve at BAILLEULMONT. 70 Other Ranks and 3 Officers carried gas cylinders to the trenches near BIENVILLERS.	
BAILLEULMONT	27th.		Battalion in Divisional Reserve. Bathing and Cleaning up. 4 Officers and 220 O.Rs carried gas cylinders at night, to the trenches near MONCHY and BIENVILLERS.	
do.	28th.		Battalion relieved by the 2nd Batt Yorks Regt, and marched to HUMBERCOURT, arriving about 2.am. 29th.	
HUMBERCOURT				

T.2134. Wt. W708—776. 500000. 4/15. Sir J. C. & S.

Army Form C. 2118.

WAR DIARY
or
INTELLIGENCE SUMMARY.
(Erase heading not required.)

5th N. Staff R

Place	Date	Hour	Summary of Events and Information	Remarks and references to Appendices
	OCTOBER. 1916.			
	29th		Battalion marched to LUCHEUX, arriving about 2-30.pm., and took over billets from 18th Liverpool Regt.	
	30th		1st day of Training Programme, Platoon Drill, Bayonet Fighting &c.	
	31st		2nd. day of Training Programme. Coy Drill, Bayonet Fighting, Lectures &c.	

Summary of Casualties.

	Officers			Other Ranks		
Week ending	K.	W.	Hosp.	K.	W.	Hosp.
Week ending 7-10-16.	-	-	-	1	3	21
" 14-10-16.	-	-	1	1	2	25
" 21-10-16.	-	-	2	2	2	21
" 28-10-16.	-	-	-	1	2	10
3 days " 31-10-16.	-	-	2	-	-	4
	-	-	5	5	9	81

J M Hey Lieut-Colonel
Commanding 1/5th North Staffs Regt.

1/5th Battalion North Staffs Regt.

To:- Headquarters,

137th Inf. Bde.

SPECIAL REPORT.

At 4-30.am. this morning, a German Patrol (about 8 or 10 men) bombed the Listening Posts and bays at Junction of Trench 130 and NEW LINCOLN LANE. Our right Lewis Gun fired in front of Trench 130 immediately 2nd. Lt. A.T. Scrivenor and a Corporal got up behind the trench with bombs and went along to the corner bombing. By that time there was no enemy in sight. The men in the Listening Post had heard wire-cutting and a Lewis Gun had fired one drum into the wire about 10 minutes previously.

The account of the men in the L.P. is that the enemy suddenly appeared, xxxxxxxxxxxxxxxxx within a few yards of the L.P. and threw bombs. One man in the L.P. was hit on the head with a bomb used as a bludgeon. One man went along the trench to warn the remainder of his platoon, and the third man (Pte. Butcher) appears to have obtained some bombs, mounted our parapet in order to be in a better position to fight the patrol.

Although the enemy were in our trench for less than one minute, they captured Pte Butcher, who apparently struggled, for his Steel Helmet and gas helmet were fond inside our own wire. The following were also found:- two German rifles, 3 Bayonets, 4 pairs of wire-cutters and a number of bombs.

Both the Right and Left Lewis Guns of this Company fired across this corner all the time, but no evidence can be found of any of the enemy having been hit, other than the rifles and bayonets.

The man who was struck on the head was left in our trenches but he only has a very vague notion of what ocurred.

(sd) H.H. STONEY, Major,

3-10-16.

Commanding 1/5th Bn. North Staffs Regt.

1/5th Battalion North Staffs Regt.

To:- All Companies.

1. A combined bombardment with Stokes Mortars and Divisional Artillery (18 prs) will take place on night of 12/13th Oct. 1916.

2. (a) Stokes Mortars Batteries will engage targets as follows:-

    137th Inf. Bde.   X.7.b.33.75.
                        X.1.d.15.10 to X.1.a.45.05.
                        W.24.a.30.30.
    800 Rounds.   T.24.a.15.45.
                        T.24.a.53.58.
                        T.24.a.06.32.
                        T.34.a.14.15.

  (b) Fire will be maintained in four bursts of 3 mins each.
                  10.pm. to 10-3.pm.
                  10-18.pm. to 10-21.pm.
                  12. mid. to 12-3.am.
                  1.am. to 1.3.am.

3. During these periods of Stokes mortar fire, 18 prs will fire on the following targets.
         Communication trenches running back from
     X.3.b.62.75   T.24.a. 00.30.
     X.3.b.75.60.   T.24.a. 25.40
     R.34.c. 22.18.   T.24.c.50.60
     R.34.b.45.33.   T.5.a.30.00. to S.W.
     R.34.b.40.60   T.5.a.15.40.
         R.5.c.16.11.

4. 2 Mortars of Y.46 T.M. Battery will engage enemy dans at W.24.a.40.85. and T.23.d.75.95. during the above periods.

(Sgd) F.A. TINSON.
Capt & Adjt.
1/5th Bn. North Staffs Regt.

12-10-16.

1/5th BATTALION, NORTH STAFFORD REGT.

Special Report
on
Operations during night of 25th/26th/Oct/1916.

From dusk untill 8-20 p.m. patrols of 1 N.C.O. and 3 men frequently patrolled near W.18.b.2.8. and W.18.b.05.30. and reported that these posts were not occupied by the enemy.
At 8-20 p.m. covering parties went out, and reported that they were in position; at 8-45 p.m. Stokes Mortars and ammunition were carried out.
Stokes Mortars opened fire at 10-15 p.m. and were back in our trenches by 10-40 p.m. the covering parties were then withdrawn.
At 11-15 p.m. a patrol went out to reconnoitre W.18.b.4.5. report already submitted.
The feint at X.7.c.15.80. was carried out by the light and medium trench mortars, numerous flares were sent up but there was no retaliation.
Enemy Machine Guns from about X.1. and from opposite this sector were firing over Ridge Road. Machine Guns were very active sweeping 'No Mans Land'.
Feints did not appear to divert the enemy's attention as regards Artillery fire.

26-10-16.   E.A. WILSON.

                        Captain & Adjutant.

1/5th BATTALION NORTH STAFFORDSHIRE REGIMENT.

WAR DIARY.

Month of NOVEMBER 1916.

Army Form C. 2118.

WAR DIARY
or
INTELLIGENCE SUMMARY

5th N. Staff

(Erase heading not required.)

Instructions regarding War Diaries and Intelligence Summaries are contained in F. S. Regs., Part II. and the Staff Manual respectively. Title pages will be prepared in manuscript.

Place	Date	Hour	Summary of Events and Information	Remarks and references to Appendices
	November 1916.			
LUCHEUX.	1st		The Battalion marched to FORTEL, arriving about 11.am.	
FORTEL.	2nd		Training as per programme	
FORTEL.	3rd		The Battalion marched to NOYELLE-en-Chaussee. arriving about 2.p.m.	
NOYELLE.	4th		Training as per programme.	
do	5th		Inspection by the G.O.C. 46th Division. No.4051 Pte T. Johnson decorated with MILITARY MEDAL.	
do	6th		Training as per programme.	
do	7th		Training as per programme as far as weather would permit. (Very wet)	
do	8th		Training as per programme.	
do	9th		do do	
do	10th		do do	
do	11th		The Battalion moved to DOMVAST., arriving about 12-30.pm.	
DOMVAST.	12th		Church Parade.	
do	13th		Training as per programme attached	
do	14th		do do	
do	15th		do do	
do	16th		do do	
do	17th		do do	

H H Hay LIEUT-COLONEL.
COMMANDING 5TH NORTH STAFFORD REGT

Army Form C. 2118.

WAR DIARY
or
INTELLIGENCE SUMMARY
(Erase heading not required.)

5th N. Staff

Instructions regarding War Diaries and Intelligence Summaries are contained in F. S. Regs., Part II. and the Staff Manual respectively. Title pages will be prepared in manuscript.

Place	Date	Hour	Summary of Events and Information	Remarks and references to Appendices
	November 1916.			
DOMVAST.	18th		Training as per programme attached	
do	19th		do do do	
do	20th		do do do	
do	21st		do do do	
do	22nd		2nd. Lt. G.H. Tortoishell joined Battalion from Base. Training as per programme in the morning. The Battalion marched to YVRENCHEUX in the afternoon arriving about 2-30.pm.	
YVRENCHEUX	23rd		The Battalion moved by Brigade to ROUGEFAY, arriving about 1.pm.	
ROUGEFAY.	24th		Resting and Company Inspections.	
do	25th		The Battalion moved with Brigade to BOUQUEMAISON, arriving about 2.pm.	
BOUQUEMAISON	26th		Resting. Wet day and no Church Parade. Capt A.F. Wedgwood joined Battalion from 1/5th Yorkshire Regt.	
do	27th		Training.	
do	28th		Training.	
do	29th		Brigade Parade for Ceremonial Drill. Fatigue Party of 2 Officers and 100 O.R.s went to LE SOUICH	
do	30th		Training. in the morning. Divisional Cross Country Run took place. First. 4th Leicesters. A Fatigue Party of 2 Officers and 100 Other Ranks went to LUCHEUX WOOD to make facines.	

K H Stone
LIEUT-COLONEL,
COMMANDING 1/5th NORTH STAFFORD REGT.

1/5th. Battalion North Staffordshire Regiment.

PROGRAMME OF TRAINING.
13th. to 18th. November 1916.

Nov. 13th.	8.30 a.m.	Coy. Drill, Bayonet fighting & Bombing, Musketry and J.D.	
	5.30 p.m.	Lectures-(for Officers-Infantry in the attack) (for N.C.O's.-Musketry)	
" 14th.	8.30 a.m.	Battalion drill. Bayonet fighting. Musketry and J.D.	
	5.30 p.m.	Lectures(for Officers-Writing reports (for N.C.O's. - by R.S.M.)	
" 15th.	9.0 a.m.	Company Drill. Bombing, J.D. 2 Coys. Range practice.	
	5.30 p.m.	Lectures(for Officers-Bombing.) (for N.C.O's. - by R.S.M..)	
" 16th.	8.30 a.m.	Battalion in the attack.	
	2.0 p.m.	Lecture for Officers-Night Operations	
	5.30 p.m.	Lecture for Officers and N.C.O's. on Anti-gas.	
" 17th.	8.30 a.m.	Companies in attack and defence.	
	p.m.	Night Operations.	
" 18th.	8.30 a.m.	Battalion in the attack. Practice in consolidation and Rapid Wiring.	

On the 13th. and 17th. Scouts, Lewis Gunners and Signallers will train under their own Officers.

12/11/16.

F... H.C.,
Captain & Adjutant.

1/5th BATTALION NORTH STAFFS REGIMENT.

SUMMARY OF CASUALTIES.

MONTH OF NOVEMBER 1916.

	OFFICERS				OTHER RANKS			
	Killed.	Wounded.	Missing.	Hospital.	Killed.	Wounded.	Missing.	Hospital.
Week ending 7th November 1916.	-	-	-	1	-	-	-	13
" " 14th " 1916.	-	-	-	-	-	-	-	15
" " 21st " "	-	-	-	-	-	-	-	16
" " 28th " "	-	-	-	-	-	-	-	14
2 days " 30th " "	-	-	-	-	-	-	-	9
	-	-	-	1	-	-	-	67

SECRET.   1/5th Battalion North Stafford Regiment.   War Diary

REFERENCE OPERATION ORDERS No.11

Z E R O. will be at 11-5 p.m. tonight.

19-9-16.

Please acknowledge

F.W.SLATER, 2nd.Lieut.
A/Adjutant.

Vol 23

1/5th Battalion (Prince of Wales) NORTH STAFFORD REGIMENT.

------ W A R   D I A R Y. ------

for month ending 31st December 1916.

Army Form C. 2118.

WAR DIARY
or
INTELLIGENCE SUMMARY
(Erase heading not required.)

5th N. Staff 46 Div

Place	Date	Hour	Summary of Events and Information	Remarks and references to Appendices
	December 1916.			
BOUQUEMAISON.	1st		137th Inf. Bde was inspected by the G.O.C. Third Army. The Semi-final of the Divl. Football Competition took place, 5th North beating 1/3rd Field Ambulance by two goals to one.	
do	2nd		The 46th Divl Cross Country Run took place. The fitting of Box Respirators was carried on in the morning.	
do	3rd		Church Parades. The final of the 46th Divl Football Competition took place at LUCHEUX. 5th North beating 4th Leicesters by three goals to one.	
do	4th		The Battalion moved to ST. AMAND, arriving about 12-30.pm. Relieved the 1/4th Yorks & Lancs Regt in Divisional Reserve.	
ST. AMAND	5th		The Battalion took over trenches from 1/5th Yorks & Lancs Regt in Sector. Z. Subsector. 1. (opposite MONCHY) Relief complete about 12 noon.	
TRENCHES.	6th		Quiet day.	
do	7th		Quiet day. 1. O.Rank wounded.	
do	8th		Quiet day.	
do	9th		The Battalion relieved by the 6th North Staffs Regt., and went into Divisional Reserve at ST. AMAND. Relief complete at 12-30.pm. Lt-Col. A.E.F. Fawcus (7th Manchester Regt) took over command of the Battalion.	
ST. AMAND.	10th		Battalion in Divl. Reserve. Bathing and cleaning up. 150 men on fatigue.	
do	11th		do do Training. 150 men on fatigue.	
do	12th		do do do do	
do	13th		do do Route march by Companies in Field Service Marching Order, distance about 6 miles. 150 men on fatigue.	

Army Form C. 2118.

WAR DIARY
or
INTELLIGENCE SUMMARY

(Erase heading not required.)

5th A.J.Staffs. 46 Div.

Place	Date	Hour	Summary of Events and Information	Remarks and references to Appendices
	December	1916.		
ST. AMAND.	14th		Battalion in Divisional Reserve. Training. 150 men on fatigue.	
do	15th		Battalion proceeded to the trenches in relief of the 6th North. relief complete 4-30.pm. Quiet night.	
TRENCHES.	16th		Quiet day.	
do	17th		Quiet day.	
do	18th		Quiet day.	
do	19th		Battalion relieved in the trenches by the 6th North. Relief complete 3-30.pm. Battalion went into Brigade Reserve at POMMIER.	
POMMIER.	20th		Bathing, Cleaning up. 100 men on fatigue.	
do.	21st		Battalion in Brigade Reserve. Bathing. Training. 100 men on fatigue.	
do	22nd		do do do do	
do	23rd		do do Proceeded to the trenches to relieve the 6th North. Relief complete at 3-30.pm.	
TRENCHES.	24th		Quiet day.	
do	25th		Quiet day.	
do	26th		Quiet day.	
do	27th		Battalion relieved in the trenches by 6th North. Relief complete 3-30.pm. Battalion went into Divisional Reserve at ST. AMAND.	
ST. AMAND.	28th		Bathing and cleaning up. Battalion celebrated Christmas.	

Army Form C. 2118.

WAR DIARY
or
~~INTELLIGENCE SUMMARY~~

(Erase heading not required.)

Instructions regarding War Diaries and Intelligence Summaries are contained in F. S. Regs., Part II. and the Staff Manual respectively. Title pages will be prepared in manuscript.

5th N Staffs 46 Div

Place	Date	Hour	Summary of Events and Information	Remarks and references to Appendices
	December 1916.			
ST. AMAND.	29th		Battalion in Divisional Reserve. Bathing. Fatigues (100 men). Training.	
do	30th		do do do do	
do	31st		Battalion proceeded to the trenches to relieve to 6th North Staffs Regt. Relief complete at 12.30 p.m. First Company had to relieve over the top before day-break, owing to waterlogged state of trenches.	

ANALYSIS OF CASUALTIES. month ending 31st December 1916.

	Officers.				Other Ranks.			
	Killed.	Wounded.	Missing.	To Hospital.	Killed.	Wounded.	Missing	To Hospital.
Week ending 7-12-16.	-	-	-	-	-	1	-	14
Week ending 14-12-16.	-	-	-	1	-	-	-	5
Week ending 21-12-16.	-	-	-	-	-	-	-	5
Week ending 28-12-16.	-	-	-	1	-	-	-	10
3 days. " 31-12-16.	-	-	-	-	-	-	-	4
	-	-	-	2	-	1	-	38

LIEUT. COLONEL.
COMMANDING 1/5th NORTH STAFFORD REGT.

Vol 24

1/5th BATTALION NORTH STAFFORD REGIMENT.
(Prince of Wales)

W A R   D I A R Y.

for

month of

J A N U A R Y, 1917.

Army Form C. 2118.

WAR DIARY
or
INTELLIGENCE SUMMARY.
(Erase heading not required.)

Instructions regarding War Diaries and Intelligence Summaries are contained in F. S. Regs., Part II. and the Staff Manual respectively. Title pages will be prepared in manuscript.

Place	Date	Hour	Summary of Events and Information	Remarks and references to Appendices
	January, 1917.			
TRENCHES.	1st		Quiet day, Enemy shelled front line for about one minute at midnight. 2 men killed.	
do	2nd		Quiet day.	
do	3rd		The Battalion was relieved by the 1/6th North Staffs Regt, and went into Brigade Reserve at POMMIER. Relief complete at 4-30.am 4th Jany. 1917.	
POMMIER.	4th		Battalion in Brigade Reserve. Bathing and cleaning up. 300. O.R.s on Fatigue.	
do	5th		do do Bathing &c. 300 O.R.s on Fatigue.	
do	6th		do do 300 O.R.s on Fatigue.	
do	7th		The Battalion proceeded to BIENVILLERS (Battalion Reserve) and relieved two Companies of 1/5th North Staffs Regt and two Companies of 1/6th South Staffs Regt.	
BIENVILLERS.	8th		Battalion Reserve. Quiet day. Provided carrying Parties for 1/5th South Staffs Regt.	
do	9th		Battalion proceeded to the trenches and took over from the 1/5th South Staffs Regt in Z Sector trenches 76 to 92 inclusive (Opposite MONCHY) relief complete 7-15 pm.	
TRENCHES.	10th		Quiet day. 2 O.R.s wounded.	
do	11th		Battalion relieved by the 1/6th North Staffs Regt. Relief complete at 8.pm. Battalion went into Divisional Reserve at ST. AMAND.	
ST. AMAND.	12th		Battalion in Divisional Reserve. Bathing and cleaning up. 70 men on Fatigue. 6 Officers joined from the Base.	
do	13th		Battalion in Divisional Reserve. Bathing, &C. 70 men on Fatigue.	
do	14th		do do 70 men on Fatigue. Commanding Officers inspection by Coys.	

T.2134. Wt. W708—776. 500000. 4/15. Sir J. C. & S.

Army Form C. 2118.

WAR DIARY
or
INTELLIGENCE SUMMARY

(Erase heading not required.)

Instructions regarding War Diaries and Intelligence Summaries are contained in F. S. Regs., Part II. and the Staff Manual respectively. Title pages will be prepared in manuscript.

Place	Date	Hour	Summary of Events and Information	Remarks and references to Appendices
	January, 1917.			
ST. AMAND.	15th		Battalion in Divisional Reserve. 70 men on Fatigue. Revolver Practice for Lewis Gunners Box Respirator Drill under Coy arrangements.	
do	16th		The Battalion proceeded to the trenches and relieved the 1/6th South Staffs Regt. Relief complete at 8.pm.	
TRENCHES.	17th		Quiet day.	
do	18th		Battalion relieved by the 1/5th South Staffs Regt and went into Battalion Reserve at BIENVILLERS. Relief complete at 4-20.pm. 60 men on carrying parties.	
BIENVILLERS	19th		Battalion in local reserve. 170 men on carrying parties and 50 men on working parties.	
do	20th		Battalion relieved by the 1/6th North Staffs Regt and went into Brigade Reserve at POMMIER Relief complete about 4-30.pm.	
POMMIER.	21st		Battalion in Brigade Reserve. 7. Offs and 330 men on Fatigue. 2 Officers joined from Base.	
do	22nd		do do do	
do	23rd		do do do	
do	24th		Battalion relieved the 1/6th South Staffs Regt in BIENVILLERS. Relief complete 3.pm.	
BIENVILLERS	25th		Battalion in Local Support. Provided carrying parties for Battalion in the line.	
do	26th		Battalion proceeded to the trenches and relieved the 1/5th South Staffs Regt. Relief complete at 4.pm. Quiet night. 3 Officers joined from base	
TRENCHES	27th		Quiet day. One man killed and one man wounded.	
do	28th		Battalion relieved by the 1/6th North Staffs Regt. relief complete at 6-15 p.m. Battalion went into Divisional Reserve at ST. AMAND.	

T.2134. Wt. W.708—776. 500000. 4/15. Sir J. C. & S.

Army Form C. 2118.

WAR DIARY
or
INTELLIGENCE SUMMARY.
(Erase heading not required.)

Instructions regarding War Diaries and Intelligence Summaries are contained in F. S. Regs., Part II. and the Staff Manual respectively. Title pages will be prepared in manuscript.

Place	Date	Hour	Summary of Events and Information	Remarks and references to Appendices
ST. AMAND	January, 1917. 29th		Battalion in Divisional Reserve. Training under Company arrangements. Inspections and cleaning up	map
do	30th		do do do	
do	31st		Medical Inspection of the Battalion by the Medical Officer.	

Analysis of Casualties

	Officers.			Other Ranks.				Strength.	
	K.	W.	M. Hosp¹	K.	W.	M.	Hosp¹	Offs.	O.R.s
4 days ending 4-1-17.	-	-	-	2	-	-	12	26	951
week ending 11-1-17.	-	-	-	-	2	-	36	26	936
week ending 18-1-17.	-	-	-	-	-	-	18	32	917
week ending 25-1-18.	-	-	-	2	2	-	14	37	955
							80		

3-2-17.

Austen Lieut-Colonel,
Commanding 1/5th Battalion North Staffs Regt.

Vol 25

1/5th Battalion North Staffordshire Regiment
(Prince of Wales)

War Diary
for month of
February 1917.

Army Form C. 2118.

5th North Staffs Regt
46 Div

WAR DIARY
or
INTELLIGENCE SUMMARY
(Erase heading not required.)

Instructions regarding War Diaries and Intelligence Summaries are contained in F.S. Regs., Part II. and the Staff Manual respectively. Title pages will be prepared in manuscript.

Place	Date	Hour	Summary of Events and Information	Remarks and references to Appendices
IN THE FIELD				
February	1st	----	The Battalion relieved the 6th South Staffords in the trenches. Relief complete about 6-15 p.m. Quiet night.	
	2nd.		Trenches. There was a partial change in the Brigade Front today. the 5th Leicesters relieved the Right & Right Centre Companies who went into BIENVILLERS. Relief complete at 2-0 p.m.	
	3rd		The Left and Left Centre Companies were relieved by the 6th North Staffords and went into Brigade Reserve at BERLES. Headquarters at BERLES. The other two Companies remain in Brigade Reserve at BIENVILLERS. Relief was complete by 2-0 p.m.	
	4th.		"A" and "B" Companies in Brigade Reserve in BIENVILLERS. "C" and "D" Companies and Headquarters in BERLES. 500 men on working Parties.	
	5th		"A" and "B" Companies in BIENVILLERS. "C" & "D" Coys and H.Q. in BERLES. 220 men on working parties.	
	6th.		The Battalion relieves the 6th North Staffords in the trenches. "B" Company two over new trenches. Relief complete about 4-0 p.m. Line now held with a three Company front.	
	7th.		Trenches. Enemy drop about 15 Medium Trench Mortars on Centre Company's front line cutting a gap in the wire. Special precautions against a raid taken, day quiet otherwise.	
	8th.		Trenches. Quiet day. Enemy continued to Trench Mortar Centre Company. Two Companies of the 2/7th Londons join us in the line for instruction.	
	9th.		Trenches. Battalion relieved in the trenches by the 6th North Staffords and goes into Divisional Reserve at POMMIER. Relief complete about 1-0 p.m. All Companies bathe.	
	10th.		Battalion training for offensive action.	

T.J.134. W.t W.708-776. 500000. 4/15. Sir J.C. & S.

Army Form C. 2118.

5th North Staffs Regt
46 Division

WAR DIARY
or
INTELLIGENCE SUMMARY.
(Erase heading not required.)

Instructions regarding War Diaries and Intelligence Summaries are contained in F. S. Regs., Part II. and the Staff Manual respectively. Title pages will be prepared in manuscript.

Place	Date	Hour	Summary of Events and Information	Remarks and references to Appendices
IN THE FIELD.				
February	11th.		Battalion continues training for offensive action, practising the Assault Formation.	
	12th.		The Battalion relieves the 6th North Staffords in the trenches. Relief complete about noon. Only one Company in the line as the other two Company fronts are held by the 2/7th Londons attached for instruction. Two Officer reinforcements joined from Base.	
	13th		Trenches. "A" and "C" Companies relieve the 2/7th Londons. Relief complete about 10-30 a.m. Two Companies of the 2/9th Londons (Q.V.R) are attached for instruction. Enemy continues to Trench Mortar Centre Company. Casualties two killed and two wounded.	
	14th.		Trenches. Quiet day. Casualty, one wounded.	
	15th.		Trenches. The Battalion is relieved in the trenches by the 6th North Staffords. Relief complete about 4-0 p.m. The Battalion goes into Brigade Reserve in BERLES and BIENVILLERS.	
	16th.		BERLES and BIENVILLERS. Half Battalion in each. At 9-0 p.m. the G.s Alarm is received from the Brigade on right and 'stands to' at the Alarm Posts. Instructions to 'stand down' received about 10-0 p.m. 210 men on working parties.	
	17th.		BERLES and BIENVILLERS, half Battalion in each. 210 men on working parties.	
	18th.		A change of Brigade front takes place. The Battalion relieves the 6th North Staffords (except one Company) in the trenches. Relief complete about 3-30 p.m. The Battalion also relieves the 5th Leicesters in the trenches. Relief complete about 4-0 p.m. One Officer reinforcement, joins from the 5th Royal Berkshires.	
	19th.		Unusually quiet day. Four patrols out.	
	20th.		Trenches. Unusually quiet day. One large fighting patrol and three patrols sent out. Enemy's sentries very vigilant.	

Army Form C. 2118.

WAR DIARY
or
INTELLIGENCE SUMMARY.
(Erase heading not required.)

5th North Staffs Regt.
46 Division

Place	Date	Hour	Summary of Events and Information	Remarks and references to Appendices
IN THE FIELD				
February	21st.		The Battalion is relieved in the trenches by the 6th North Staffords and goes into Divisional Reserve at POMMIER. Relief complete about noon. All companies bathe.	
	22nd.		POMMIER. Battalion continues training in Assault Formation.	
	23rd.		POMMIER. The Battalion continues training in Assault Formation.	
	24th.		The Battalion relieves the 6th North Staffords in the trenches. Relief complete about 1-30 p.m. One large fighting patrol and four other patrols sent out. One Company practices for raid on enemy trenches.	
	25th.		Trenches. Quiet day. One Company practising for raid.	
	26th.		Trenches. Two Officers and 40 Other Ranks of "D" Company raid the enemy trenches at 2-0 a.m. and capture two prisoners. Our casualties one slightly wounded. During the day enemy retaliated by shelling our lines heavily.	See Report attached Appendix 1.
	27th.		The Battalion is relieved in the trenches by the 6th North Staffords. Relief complete about 6-0 p.m. Quiet morning. Enemy shell trenches heavily in the afternoon.	
	28th.		Two Companies Brigade Reserve at BIENVILLERS, two Companies in Brigade-Reserve in BERLES. About 250 men on working parties. One man wounded to duty.	

R.K. Austin
LIEUT COLONEL,
COMMANDING 1/5th NORTH STAFFORD REGT.

COPY.

OPERATION ORDERS No.74.
by
Lieut.Colonel Sir Hill Child Bart.D.S.O. M.V.O.
Commanding Left Group 46th Divisional Artillery
24th February 1917.

Reference FONQUEVILLERS)
         RANSART   ) 1/10,000.

1. Left Group Operation Order No.73 is cancelled and the following substituted.

2. During the night 25th/26th Feby.1917 the 137th Infantry Brigade will raid the enemy's trenches, the point of entry will be E.S.a.21.01. At the same time a small patrol will entry the enemy's trenches immediately North of the sap E.5.d.05.40.

3. The Left Group will assist in this operation according to the attached programme.

4. At 8-0 p.m. 10-0 p.m.,and 12 midnight A/231,B/231 and C/231 Batteries will fire two rounds gun fire on the targets detailed for them for the zero hour.

5. 2/lieut.O.S.WINDEMAR will act as Liason Officer with the Battalion Commander at "B" Coy. Headqrs., SERGEANTS PARADE.

6. The following code words have been arranged by the Infantry.

    UNDEROUT   Gap completed.
    RAINING   Patrol starting to return.
    RAIN STOPPED   All are back.
    BUCKETS   Prisoners.

   In addition the following rockets will be used.
    Single Red Rocket (if communications are out). All are back.
    Single white Rockets (at five minutes intervals will be sent after zero plus 30 to guide party in.

7. 18 Pdrs will fire 75% Shrapnel and 25% H.E.

8. Zero hour will be 2-0 a.m.

9. Watches will be synchronised from this office at 7-30 p.m. and 1-0 a.m. on the night of the 25th/26th.

10. Acknowledge.

                                                F.W.ADSHEAD
                                                Lieut.& Adjutant
                                                231st Brigade R.F.A.

OPERATION ORDERS   Copy
by
Lieut-Colonel A.E.F.Fawcus.M.C.
Commanding 1/5th Battalion North Stafford Regiment.
                                                    24th February 1917.

Map Reference 57D N.E.Sheets 1 & 2 (Part of) 1/10,000
         and 51C Sheets 3 & 4   "   "   1/10,000.

1. On the night of the 25th/26th Feb.1917 this Battalion will carry out a small raid on the enemy's trenches at point of salient E.5.a.20.00 with a view to obtaining identification.

2. The Raiding Party will be composed as follows :- ~~Right Blocking Party~~
   "A" Right Blocking Party. One N.C.O. and 3 other ranks from "D" Coy 2 Other Ranks from Battn.Bombing Platoon.
   "B" Left Blocking Party. One N.C.O. and 3 O.Rs.from "D" Coy, 2 O.Rs from Battn.Bombing Platoon.
   "C" Mopping Party. 1 Officer and 5 O.Rs. "D" Coy, 4 O.Rs.Battn.Bombing Platoon, 2 O.Rs of 137th Trench Mortar Battery.
   "D" Parapet Covering Party 1 Officer and 6 O.Rs "D"Coy.
   "E" Left Flank Guard. 1 Lewis Gun and 3 Lewis Gunners from "D" Coy, 3 Rifle Grenadiers "D"Coy.
       Right Flank Guard. 1 Lewis Gun and 3 Lewis Gunners "C" Coy and 3 Rifle Grenadiers "D" Coy.
   "F" Wirecutting Party. 1 N.C.O. and 1 Sapper from 1st Field Coy. R.E's.
   "G" Telephone Party. 2 Signallers from "D" Coy.

3. O.C."D" Coy (Capt WILTON) will be in command of the raid with Headquarters in 85 Trench near Junction with 85 STREET.

4. 2nd.Lieut.LOWE M.C. will be in command of Raiding Party and will be with "D" Party.

5. 2nd Lieut.G.E.E.WILLIAMS will be O.C. "C" Party.

6. The northern limit to be exploited by Raiding Party will be E.5.a.20.00 and the eastern limit E.5.a.30.00.

7. At zero minus 20 minutes Raiding Party will be clear of our wire and at zero minus 5 minutes "F" Party will be ready to place ammonal tubes in enemys wire. Ammonal tubes will cut enemys wire at zero.

8. Zero time will be 2-0 a.m. 26th Feby.,and the Raiding Party will leave enemy's trenches when task has been completed but not later than 2-20 a.m. 20 minutes after zero.

9. ARTILLERY   At zero minus 5 minutes single rounds from 18 pdrs will be fired on E.5.a.20.15 and E.5.a.30.00. At zero the rate of fire will be increased and a box barrage will be made round,but avoiding,E.5.a.20.00 to E.5.a.20.35. At the same time points about W.29.c.30. & E.5.c.80.65 will be shelled. The rate of fire will be increased from zero plus ten minutes to zero plus 20 minutes.

10. TRENCH MORTARS. Stokes Mortars (a) at head of 79 STREET (b) 85 STREET (c) 90 STREET (d) 92 STREET.
    (a) From zero to zero plus 20 minutes will bombard points about E.5.d.15.50 and E.5.c.80.60.
    (b) will be ready at call of O.C.raid to barrage E.5.a.45.00 to E.5.a.35.50.
    (c) will bombard from zero to zero plus 20 minutes E.5.a.20.25 to E.5.a.15.70.
    (d) will bombard from zero to zero plus 20 minutes W.29.c.29.30.

11. MACHINE GUNS. O.C.137th Bde.Machine Gun Coy. will arrange for one of his Machine Guns and also of one of 138th Bde.M.G's to fire at roads and tracks in MONCHY at zero minus 5 minutes (1-55 a.m.) to zero (2-0 a.m. so as to cover noise made by Wiring Party.

12. Stores as shown in Appendix 1. will be carried by Raiding Party.

---- 2 ----

13. All watches will be synchronised at 6-0 p.m. on the 25th.

14. Details of Raid will be arranged by O.C.Raid.

15. Very's Lights will be sent up singly at 3 minutes intervals from following points.
    (1) Junction of 78 STREET and Firing Line.
    (2) Junction of 90 STREET and Firing Line.
    from zero minus ten minutes (1-50 a.m.) to zero (2-0 a.m.) O.C. "B" and "C" Coys respectively will each detail an Officer for this work.

16. Regtl.Medical Officer will arrange for stretcher bearers to be with O.C. Raid and will himself be at Aid Post at the Old Battn.Headqrs SHELL STREET.

17. Advance Battn.Headqrs will be at "B" Coy Headqrs SERGEANTS BAR-DE.

18. At Zero a patrol of 1 Officer and 9 Other Ranks from "B" Coy will assist in diverting enemys attention from Raiding Party by blowing a gap in enemys wire with amonal tubes at N.5.c.95.45.

19. All marks of Identification will be removed.

24-2-17.

                                                 C.C.CHICP, 2nd.Lieut.
                                                 a/Adjutant.
                                              1/5th Bn. North Staffs Regt.

Appendix 1.

Report on a Minor Enterprise carried out by the 1/5th Battn. North Staffordshire Regiment on the night of 25th/26th February 1917.

1. OBJECT. To enter enemys trenches and
   (a) To find out if enemy were still holding the line opposite Z.1.SubSector.
   (b) If they were, to obtain identification.
   (c) If found unoccupied, to push out strong patrols into enemys lines and reconnoitre.

2. OBJECTIVE.
   The tip of salient at E.5.a.20.00. As smoke had been observed in the early morning rising from this point and from the study of aeroplane maps I considered this a probable position of a dugout.

3. RAIDING PARTY.
   As shown in my Operation Orders dated 24-2-17 attached herewith

4. OPERATIONS.
   Artillery, Machine Guns and Stokes Mortars opened according to programme. An amonal tube 15 feet long and 2" diameter was exploded on the thick belt of wire on cheveux de frises at 2-2- a.m. and a good gap about 12 feet wide was immediately reported. "A" "B" "C" and "D" Parties then advanced from position they had taken up (about 25 yards from wire) "A" Party moving to the right, "B" to the Left and "C" in the Centre into enemys trench. "D" Party remained on parapet as Covering Party. Enemys trench was found to be deep well revetted and floor boarded with three steps leading up to fire-step. There was a covered sentry post near point of entry where a steel helmet and rifle were found.
   The entrance to a dugout was found a few yards to the right of point of entry and two more entrances to the same dugout were found at a few yards interval in the trench. As no one would come out, No.5 Grenades were thrown down two of the entrances. A German then appeared at the third entrance and was at once taken prisoner. A second German appeared at the same entrance just as a Stokes bomb was about to be thrown down, he was also taken prisoner. No enemy were seen to the right of dugout by "A" Party, "B" Party moving to the Left saw two men jump down from the fire-step and enter a shelter in the trench. Bombs were thrown into the shelter and burst among the men. A further shower of bombs was then thrown over next traverse. "B" Party started to advance to the shelter into which they had dropped the bombs but the signal for retirement was then given by O.C. Raiding Party and they withdrew. Before leaving the trench two Stokes bombs were thrown down each of the two entrances to the dugout. Groans and cries were heard after the first bomb had been thrown. These entrances were blown in. Raiding Party withdrew at 2-17 a.m in good order with their two prisoners.
   Spare amonal tube, telephone, tape and all stores except trench ladder were brought in. The telephone had been brought out into No Man's Land near enemys wire and proved of great use for keeping in touch with Headqrs.

Meanwhile a Party of 1 Officer and 10 Other Ranks were creating a diversion by blowing a gap in enemys wire at E.5.c.90.45. This patrol successfully blew up 15 feet amonal tube but found depth of wire belt was at least 30 feet deep and very dense and only half was cut by explosion of amonal. Patrol then returned in accordance with their instructions, as they were unable to get through enemy wire at any adjacent point.
This patrol reported that a Machine Gun opened fire from E.5.c.80.60 but as a Machine Gun position was suspected at this point I had arranged for a Stokes Mortar to bombard it.
This was most effectively done and almost immediately the Machine Gun that had been firing was silenced. The Stokes Mortar appeared to have obtained directs hits with a shower of bombs.
A bomb was thrown at patrol but thrower was also silenced when Stokes Mortar opened fire.
Another diversion was created by artillery and Stokes Mortar bombarding enemys gap in wire at W.29.c.80.30.
A fighting patrol of 3 sections and one Lewis Gunteam reconnoitred No Man's Land and enemy wire from the HANNESCAMPS-MONCHY Road to a point about 400 yards South. This patrol reported that enemy were very alert and line appeared to be well held.
These diversions were most useful in making it almost impossible for enemy to know at which point the raid was taking place.

— 2 —

There was no retaliation by enemy artillery.

5. RESULTS.
   (a) By the numbers and positions of Very's Lights sent up and by positions of enemy's posts and Machine Guns it appears that they still held normally.
   A notable feature was that as soon as barrage commenced numbers of Very's Lights thrown considerably decreased.
   In addition to obtaining prisoners casualties were undoubtedly inflicted on the enemy in dugout and shelter.

   (b) 2 N.C.Os of 108th Regiment were captured thus providing identification

6. ARTILLERY
   Left Group. The support given by artillery was excellent and contributed largely to the success of the raid.
   The shooting was very accurate.

7. 137th Brigade Trench Mortar Battery.
   I cannot praise the work of the Stokes Mortars too highly.
   Their accuracy was wonderful and they were successful in certainly keeping two Machine Guns silent as well as probably destroying one of these.

8. 1/1st Field Coy (N.M.) R.E's
   The N.C.O. and Sapper lent me for this raid worked admirably and were of great assistance in exploding ammonal tubes.

9. CASUALTIES.
   One man slightly wounded.

10. GENERAL.
    The conduct of all ranks concerned in the raid was splendid, and the whole programme was carried through without a hitch.
    The spirits and morale of the whole party both before and after the raid could not have been better.
    I am sending special recommendations as soon as possible.
    The training and arrangements of details were carried out by Capt.WILTON O.C. "I" Coy and I consider that the success of the raid was very largely due to the excellence with which he performed these duties.
    The Raiding Party was commanded by 2nd Lieut J.E.LOWE M.C. who showed great coolness and good leadership.

    Sgd. A. E. T. Lawson.

26-2-17

Lieut-Colonel.
Commanding 1/5th Battn. North Staffs Regt.

APPENDIX 1.

Amonal Tubes------ 2,15 feet with 12 seconds fuses and igniters
Spool, with 350 yards of white tape.

    Wire cutters, short   9
       "   "   long   4
       "   "   rifle   10
    Electric torches   4
    Rifle Grenades   60
    Wiring Gloves   2 pairs.
    Bomb waistcoats   16
    Cudgels.   10
    Ladder   1
    Smoke bombs   8
    Stokes bombs   4
    Petrol   1 tin

P R O G R A M M E

Battery.	Task.	Ammunition.	Remark.
	Zero minus 5 to zero		
A/231 (1 Gun)	Engage M.G.emplacements F.5.a.20.21.		
231			
B/231x (2 guns Main position) Engage front line & supports N.29.c.15.25 to N. 35.a.25.37		1 round per gun per minute	
C/231 (Flank gun)	Enfilade front line F.5.a.47.00 to F.5.c.76.80.		
D/231. (1 gun)	engage junction of sap and trench at F.5.d.05.40.		
	Zero plus 10		
A/231 (Flank gun)	engage communication trench F.5.a.44.23 to F.5.a. 56.24.	)	
"/231 (1 gun)	engage M.G.emplacement F.5.a.20.21.	) 1 round	
A/231 (2 guns)	enfilade communication trench F.5.a.23.23. to F.5.a.40.22	) per	
B/231. (5 guns)	engage front line N.29.c.15.46. to N.29.c.85.37.	) gun	
C/231 (Flank gun)	enfilade front line F.5.a.47.00 to F.5.c.75.80	) per	
C/231 (4 guns)	engage communication trench F.5.a.50.20. to F.5.a.42.01.	) minute.	
D/231 (4 guns)	engage trench junctions F.5.a.17.43., F.5.a.73.05.,F.5.a.59.30.,and F.5.d.55.85.	)	
D/231 (2 guns)	engage M.G.emplacements N.29.c.	)	
	Zero plus 10 until all clear		
	All batteries same targets - 2 rounds per gun every 3 minutes.		

1/5th. BATTALION (PRINCE OF WALES) NORTH STAFFORDSHIRE REGIMENT.

WAR DIARY.

for the Month of MARCH 1917.

Army Form C. 2118.

WAR DIARY
INTELLIGENCE SUMMARY.

(Erase heading not required.)

Instructions regarding War Diaries and Intelligence Summaries are contained in F. S. Regs., Part II. and the Staff Manual respectively. Title pages will be prepared in manuscript.

Place	Date	Hour	Summary of Events and Information	Remarks and references to Appendices
	March 1917.			
BIENVILLERS & BERLES.	1st.		Battalion in Brigade Reserve. 2 Coys in BIENVILLERS, 2 Coys and Headquarters in BERLES. "B" Coy (from BIENVILLERS) relieved a Coy of the 1/6th North Staffs Regt. in the trenches 7 men slightly gassed by gas shells in BERLES.	
do	2nd		The remainder of the battalion relieved the remainder of the 1/6th North Staffs Regt in the trenches. Relief complete about 1-30.pm. Enemy quiet but vigilant. Draft of 6 O.Rs joined Divisional Depot and taken on the strength of this Battalion.	
TRENCHES.	3rd	4-30 a.m.	One of our patrols engaged an enemy patrol, and after a sharp fight the enemy retired to his own trenches. Our casualties were 3 O.Rs slightly wounded. Enemy's casualties unknown.	
do	4th		Quiet day, snipers active. 2 Officer reinforcements joined Battalion from the Base.	
do	5th		Fairly quiet day. Enemy trench-mortared Left Coy. Casualties.1 O.R. wounded.	
do	6th		The Battalion was relieved in the trenches by the 1/6th North Staffs Regt, and went into support at BIENVILLERS. Relief complete at 2-15 pm. Enemy shelled BIENVILLERS between 4.pm. & 8.pm. with shells of various calibres including gas shells. Casualties 2 O.R.s wounded.	
BIENVILLERS	7th		The Battalion marched to HALLOY by Companies. Last Coy arrived at 2-30.pm. A draft of 16 O.Rs joined the Divisional Depot, and were taken on the strength of this Battalion.	
HALLOY.	8th		Company kit inspections, and inspection by the Commanding Officer.	
do	9th		General Training and medical inspection.	
do	10th		The Battalion marched to SOUASTRE, arriving about 1.pm.	
SOUASTRE.	11th		Parades under Company arrangements. A draft of 5 O.R.s joined the Divl Depot from the Base, and were taken on the strength of this Battalion.	

Army Form C. 2118.

1/5 North Staff Regt

WAR DIARY

Instructions regarding War Diaries and Intelligence Summaries are contained in F.S. Regs., Part II. and the Staff Manual respectively. Title pages will be prepared in manuscript.

(Erase heading not required.)

Place	Date	Hour	Summary of Events and Information	Remarks and references to Appendices
	March 1917.			
SOUASTRE.	12th		Battalion engaged in practising the attack on enemy line in the neighbourhood of BUCQUOY.	
do	13th		Battalion again practised the attack in the morning.	
		2-15 p.m.	Battalion received instructions to attack at midnight.	
		6-0. p.m.	Battalion marched to ROSSIGNAL WOOD, arriving about 10. pm.	
		11. pm.	Battalion moved off for BIEZ WOOD. Hour of attack postponed to 1. am. 12th March 1917.	
BIEZ WOOD.	14th	1. am.	Battalion attacked enemy front line. See report attached. Our casualties 10 Officers and 134 O.Rs wounded, killed, & missing. The Battalion was relieved by the 1/6th South Staffs Regt, and marched to billets at SOUASTRE.	Appendix marked 1.
		9. am		
SOUASTRE.	15th		Company inspections. G.O.C. congratulated this Battalion and 1/5th South Staffs Regt. on the good work they did on the night of the 13/14th March 1917. Brigadier also congratulated these Battalions.	
SOUASTRE.	16th		Inspection by the Commanding Officer.	
do	17th		Battalion moved by Companies to BAYENCOURT arriving about 2.pm.	
BAYENCOURT	18th		Battalion moved by Companies to GOMMECOURT, arriving about 3.pm. Worked on salvaging stores &c.	
GOMMECOURT	19th		Battalion engaged on road mending	
do	20th		Battalion engaged on salvaging in old German trenches and No man's land.	
do	21st		Battalion engaged on road-mending in and near BUCQUOY.	
do	22nd		Battalion continued road mending on BUCQUOY - ESSARTS Rd.	
do	23rd		Battalion marched to BERTRANCOURT, arriving about 4.pm. and was billeted in huts at LYNDURST CAMP.	

Army Form C. 2118.

WAR DIARY

1/5 North Staffs Regt

(Erase heading not required.)

Instructions regarding War Diaries and Intelligence Summaries are contained in F. S. Regs., Part II. and the Staff Manual respectively. Title pages will be prepared in manuscript.

Place	Date	Hour	Summary of Events and Information	Remarks and references to Appendices
	March 1917.			
BERTRANCOURT	24th		Battalion moved by Companies to HARPONVILLE. arriving about 4-30.pm. A Draft of 36 O.R.s joined the Battalion from the Base.	
HARPONVILLE.	25th		Battalion moved by Companies to CARDONETTE, arriving about 5.pm.	
CARDONETTE	26th		Battalion moved to GUIGNEMICOURT, part of the journey being done in Motor Lorries. Arrived about 3.pm.	
GUIGNEMICOURT	27th		Company Inspections.	
do	28th		Company Inspections and Parades in the morning. Billeting party of 1. Officer and 10 O.R.s entrained at BACouel at 11.16.pm.	
do	29th		The Battalion (less "B" Coy) entrained at BACOUEL at 7-15.a.m. "B" Coy entrained at 3.pm.	
BERGUETTE.	30th		The Battalion less "B" Coy arrived at BERGUETTE at about 2.am. Battalion march to BOURECQ, arriving about 5.am. "B" Coy arrived at BERGUETTE at 6.am and marched to BOURECQ, arriving at 8-30.am.	
BOURECQ.	31st		Battalion paraded under Coy Commanders. The Corps Commander 2nd.Corps (Lt-Genl Sir Claude Jacob. K.C.B.) gave an address to all Officers of the 137th Inf. Bde at ST. HILAIRE at 10. am.	

LIEUT. COLONL.
COMMANDING 1/5th NORTH STAFFORD REGT.

Army Form C. 2118.

1/5th Staff Regt.

WAR DIARY
or
~~INTELLIGENCE SUMMARY~~
(Erase heading not required.)

Instructions regarding War Diaries and Intelligence Summaries are contained in F. S. Regs., Part II. and the Staff Manual respectively. Title pages will be prepared in manuscript.

Summary of Events and Information

MARCH 1917

Place	Date	Hour		OFFICERS				OTHER RANKS			Battalion Strength		Remarks and references to Appendices
			K.	W.	M.	Hosp.	K.	W.	M.	Hosp.	Offs.	O. Ranks.	
For week ending 8-3-17.			-	-	-	2	1	10	-	17	43	944	
do	15-3-17.		5	4	1	1	27	90	22	15	33	819	
do	22-3-17.		-	-	-	1	-	-	-	18	33	815	
do	29-3-17		-	-	-	-	-	-	-	15	33	833	
			5	4	1	4	28	100	22	65			

LIEUT.-COLONEL,
COMMANDING 1/5th NORTH STAFFORD REGT.

T.2134. Wt. W708—776. 500000. 4/15. Sir J. C. & S.

REPORT ON OPERATIONS ON NIGHT 13/14th MARCH 1917.
by
Lieut-Colonel A.E.F. Fawcus. M.C.
Commanding 1/5th Battalion North Stafford Regiment.

Map reference. 57.d. 1 & 2 (Parts of)

At 2-15.pm. on the 13th inst, I received orders to attack the enemy's
trenches from F.26.d.4.5 to F.26.a.2.3. in accordance with
previously arranged plans as given in 137 Bde Preliminary Order No.1.
dated 11-3-17.
Zero time was to be at 11-50.pm.
Owing to the shortness of time, and the distance to move up to the
starting point, I ordered Companies to move to ROSSIGNAL WOOD from
SOUASTRE at 6.pm. where they would receive a hot meal.
Arrangements were made for Cookers and Lewis Gun Limbers to move off
from SOUASTRE as soon as possible so as to clear the track between GOMMECOURT
and the CRUCIFIX before the arrival of the Infantry. Companies were to
move from ROSSIGNAL Wood to their starting off line North East of BIEZ Wood
at 9.pm. Owing however to the extremely bad state of the track between
GOMMECOURT and ROSSIGNAL WOOD the transport was held up by some Artillery
Limbers which were bemired. Considerable delay was caused and my
battalion did not reach its rendezvous at ROSSIGNAL WOOD until 9.pm.
At this time the Cookers were about 1000 yards behind.
At Brigade Headquarters I was informed that ZERO hour had been postponed
until 1. am. I immediately sent back parties to bring up the hot meal
from the Cookers.
At 11.pm. I commenced to move off for our starting off line which had
been taped by a party under Major Lister and 2nd. Lt. L.C. Grice, in the
meantime. Owing however to the extremely bad condition of the ground
and the fact that it had been necessary to disperse the battalion during
the halt owing to shell fire, it was not until 11.25 pm. that the whole
battalion was on the move.
The path from ROSSIGNOL WOOD to the junction of REDFEHRER Trench and the
Eastern Side of BIEZ WOOD had been taped. This track was very bad and
going was very slow, and, in order to be on my line by 12-30 am. I had to
push the men very hard, and was not able to wait for ammonal tubes (which
were being fitted together), Machine guns, Stokes mortars, or picks and
shovels.
Guides were waiting to meet Companies at the junction of RADFEHRER trench
and the Eastern side of BIEZ WOOD, and to guide them to their places on the
taped line.

My plan of Attack was as follows :-
"A" Coy. on the Right with 230 yards frontage, "C" Coy. in the Centre with
240 yards frontage, "D" Coy. on the Left with 230 yards frontage. This
Company had also to make a strong point to cover our Left flank at
F.26.a.20.25.
2 Platoons were detailed (from "B" Coy.) to hold and consolidate
Communication trench from Junction with RETTEMOY GRABEN F.25.d.15.85 to
Junction with BUCQUOY GRABEN at F.26.a.00.12., and to push out bombing
posts and make barrier at F.25.b.9.2.,
"A","C" and "D" Coys. and one platoon of "B" Coy. were to advance under
our barrage in two waves of four lines, one platoon of "B"Coy. was to
move straight from its starting point to work along Communication trench
and establish posts therein, the remaining two platoons I kept as my
Reserve.

The Barrage opened punctually at 1 am. and my Battalion immediately advanced
as if on parade up to within 20 or 30 yards of the enemy's wire. All reports
say the barrage was very accurate.
Enemy barrage descended at 1-4 am. but by this time all my men except
Battn.Headqrs. were clear of the enemy's barrage lines.
At a few minutes past 1-0 am. heavy enemy machine gun fire opened from my
Right and Left flanks and also from enemy second line trench.

I received my first news as to the situation at 1-45 am. 2nd.Lt.Cliff
reported to me that "C" Coy. in the centre had failed to enter the enemy's
trench owing to the wire being uncut and that many of the Company including
Capt. Wedgwood, the Coy. Commander and 2nd.Lt.Hammersley had been killed
on the enemy's wire. This Officer informed me that he had collected some
30 or 40 men in RETTEMOY GRABEN on my Left.

At about 2-15 am. 2nd.Lt.Goss, O.C."B"Coy. arrived at my Headqrs. with three German prisoners : he, himself, was badly wounded. He informed me "D" and "B" Coys. had reached their objective on the Left, but that "D" Coy. had been driven back from the enemy's second line to their first line, and that they were badly in need of reinforcements.

As my reserve of 2 platoons could not be found I ordered 2nd. Lt. Cliff with the men he had collected to advance and reinforce Capt. Wilton at once.

About 3 am. I heard very heavy bombing from the direction of my Left and shortly afterwards learnt that "D" Coy. and the one platoon from "B" Coy. had been driven back by a very strong bombing counter attack to the Road at the North-east corner F.25.d.

2nd.Lt.Cliff returned with only about 12 of his men and informed me that he had been unable to get into touch with Capt. Wilton.

I thereupon ordered him to make three posts in RETTEMOY GRABEN between F.25.d.80.50 and F.25.d.15.85. and to consolidate these posts.

(He remained there until after dark on the night of the 14th./15th. insts. when he reports that considerable numbers of the enemy advanced in lines of platoons towrads RETTEMOY GRABEN and on nearing the trench extended into lines of groups of three.

He was unable to resist the attack as his rifles were too full of mud : He therefore retired to BIEZ WOOD and informed a machine gun post there.)

Later reports informed me that "D" Coy. and the one platoon of "B" Coy. had entered the enemy's trench with but little opposition and had captured 7 prisoners and killed many of the enemy as they came out of dugouts, and had also entered enemy dugouts and bombed several of the enemy who would not come out, and that we were able to hold our position there until our supply of bombs gave out. The O.C."D" Coy.(Capt.Wilton) although shot through the stomach remained with his Coy. and held back the enemy for three quarters of an hour.

The bombing attack was made by the enemy across the open from their second line trench and also from the flanks in BUCQUOY trench, a notice board in the trench was marked BISMARCK GRABEN.

The remaining platoon of "B" Coy. had established their posts on their objective, the road at F.25.d.75.97. to RETTEMOY trench and after the retirement of "D" Coy.from BUCQUOY trench were reinforced by the platoon of "B" Coy.from BUCQUOY trench.

They report that the communication trench between the road and it's junction with BUCQUOY trench has been filled in with earth except for a few places which have been covered over with sticks and grass with large pools of water underneath.

These posts remained out until 1-30 pm. on the 14th. when they were withdrawn to BIEZ WOOD.

They report that the trench where they had made their posts was on the whole in good condition, with trench gratings.

Early on in the operations 2nd.Lt.Cowlishaw, my signalling officer had gone forward to find out what was happening. He collected about 70 men who had been unable to penetrate the enemy wire in the centre and was holding the road from about F.26.c.20.60. to F.26.c.00.75.

In the meantime my Right Company under 2nd.Lt.Keeling was in touch with the 5th.S.Staffs. on my Right and had succeeded in reaching enemy's first line trench on the right of their objective at F.26.d.25.30. whilst a small party under 2nd/Lewty had reached enemy's second line trench about F.26.d.25.45. Lt.

They were held up here by the wire and 2nd.Lt.Lewty and some of his men were killed whilst bombing an enemy machine gun at close quarters.

2nd.Lt.Keeling reports that the enemy's first line trench from the point where he reached it about F.26.d.20.35. for some considerable distance to the Left was filled with wire. He tried to cut a way through this but did not succeed.

Heavy fire from machine guns and a considerable counter attack by the enemy with bombs and light trench mortars compelled the 5th.S.Staffs. and his men to fall back from this corner to RETTEMOY GRABEN which they started to consolidate.

At about 3-30 am. an officer from the 5th.S.Staffs. informed me that his battalion had been driven back from their objective and later had retired to BIEZ WOOD.

As the condition of RETTEMOY GRABEN was extremely bad I did not consider it advisable to keep many men therein, as in most places it was deep with mud and water and was very wide and practically impossible to hold.

I gave orders for six posts to be left in this trench and for the remainder to withdraw to BIEZZ WOOD. This was about 4 am.

During the attack my Bn.Headqrs. were in ROTTEMOY GRABEN at F.25.d.90.47

and when I gave the order to withdraw to BIEZ WOOD I removed my Headquarters to the junction of RADFEHRER and East side of BIEZ WOOD.
At 4 am. my Northernmost post at F.25.d.75.97 saw a large number of Germans standing up on their parapet about F.25.b.85.20.
The post opened Lewis gun fire at once and inflicted considerable loss on the enemy as several were seen to fall.
Reports from these posts and also from the posts at RETTEMOY GRABEN show that the enemy was relieved on the morning of the 14th. inst.
Shortly after daybreak on the 14th. inst. large bodies of Germans were seen out in front of their own wire. I ordered a Lewis gun to open fire upon a party of about 20 of them, but no damage appeared to have been done, they, however, dispersed and entered their trench.
As many others appeared and commenced to collect our wounded and dead I gave orders to cease firing.

At 5-30 am. 2 platoons of the 6th. South reported to reinforce me, as there were now considerably more men than were necessary to hold our line in BIEZ WOOD I ordered my men to withdraw to suitable dugouts and trenches in the rear of the wood.
My own Headqrs. were moved to a dugout on the ROSSIGNOL WOOD-BIEZ WOOD Road about 300 yards South-west of BIEZ WOOD, in a deep dugout there.

I was relieved by the 6th. South at 9 am.

GENERAL.
The enemy's main line of barrage appeared to be on the line of RETTEMOY GRABEN and was particularly heavy from about F.26.c.40.40. to F.25.d.30.75.
This barrage consisted chiefly of 75 mm. and 105 mm.H.E. and shrapnel and a few 105 and 150 mm. Howitzers.
A barrage was also put on the North-eastern side of BIEZ WOOD and the ground immediately in front of it and a third line on the South-western edge of BIEZ WOOD. This latter consisted mostly of shells of heavy calibre.

BATTN.HEADQRS.
I could not well have chosen a more unsuitable place for Battn. Headqrs. than in RETTEMOY GRABEN as there is no cover in this trench, it is deep in mud and was well barraged by the enemy.
My Headqrs. in BIEZ WOOD were also extremely unsuitable. There is a good dugout at L.1.b.50.80. and in case of future operations I should certainly recommend that this place be used as Battn. Headqrs. during attack on the objectives we attempted to take.
The enemy shelled this section of the WOOD considerably but it appears to be the only point from which it is at all possible to control operations, the enemy barrage the South-western edge of BIEZ WOOD, it is not advisable to have many troops in this neighbourhood.

We were unable to use any ammonal tubes for making gaps in the enemy's wire owing to the fact that, although these tubes were up at the Southern corner of BIEZ WOOD in plenty of time they had not been put together, and the sappers who had charge of them could not get them ready in time to advance with us.
I would suggest that in any future operations where these tubes may be necessary that they should be absolutely complete. with detonators and lighters and carried as far forwrad as possible some time before the advance is to commence.

All reports show that our barrage was extremely accurate, and that during the period that it was on the enemy's trench, enemy were very quiet in their trenches. However, in a remarkably short space of time after it had lifted their machine guns were extremely busy.
Considerable numbers of twin red lights and twin green lights were sent up from their second line and from BUCQUOY.
The enemy appeared to collect our wounded and in one case bandaged a man and sent him back to our lines.
The ground between BIEZ WOOD and RETTEMOY GRABEN is badly broken with shell holes. The heavy rain and mud hampered operations very much.

(Sgd.) A.E.F.Fawcus, Lieut.-Col.
Cmmdg. 1/5th. Bn. North Stafford Regt.

1/5th Battalion
(Prince of Wales)
North Staffordshire Regiment.

W A R   D I A R Y .
- for month of -
A P R I L
1917.

Army Form C. 2118.

WAR DIARY
or
INTELLIGENCE SUMMARY
(Erase heading not required.)

Instructions regarding War Diaries and Intelligence Summaries are contained in F. S. Regs., Part II. and the Staff Manual respectively. Title pages will be prepared in manuscript.

Place	Date	Hour	Summary of Events and Information	Remarks and references to Appendices
	APRIL, 1917.			
BOURECQ.	1st		Church Parades.	
do	2nd		Training, Section, Platoon & Company Drill. Lectures by Coy Commanders. Instruction for Specialists. Bayonet Fighting. Musketry. Physical Training.	
do	3rd		General Training. do	
do	4th		do do	
do	5th		Brigade Route March. Route:-(Ref. 36.a. 1/40,000) Main road through NORRENT-FONTES Cross Roads 200 yds West of MAZINGGHEM Church - Road running through N.22. and the H in LINGHEM - LINGHEM - thence South via Road running through N.26.c. &c. - LA COUTURE - Cross Roads marked 96.1. - Cross Roads just North of T.14 - ST. HILAIRE.	
do	6th		General Training.	
do	7th		General Training.	
do	8th		Church Parades. Lectures by Platoon Commanders to Platoons on "Outposts"	
do	9th		Divisional Route March. Route:- (Ref. HAZEBROUCK. 5.a.) Cross Roads 450 yds South of M E in COTTES. - AUCHY-au-BOIS. - ESTREE-BLANCHE. - LONGHEM - LINGHEM. - ST. HILAIRE. Distance approx. 12 miles. *Divisional Staff Ride*	
do	10th		General Training. Outpost Scheme under 2nd in Command. Battalion Commanders Conference. Draft of 25 Other Ranks arrived from Base.	
do	11th		General Training. Assault Formation. Musketry & Bayonet Fighting.	
do	12th		Battalion moved to BETHUNE, starting at 10.am. Before moving off the G.O.C. presented MILITARY MEDALS to Sergt. Copestake, L/cpl.Challiner, Ptes Fishwick & Cusby. Recommendations are attached. Battalion arrived in BETHUNE at 2-30.pm., and billetted in FEUILLARDE BARRACKS.	Schedule No. 1.

Army Form C. 2118.

WAR DIARY
or
INTELLIGENCE SUMMARY.
(Erase heading not required.)

Instructions regarding War Diaries and Intelligence Summaries are contained in F. S. Regs., Part II. and the Staff Manual respectively. Title pages will be prepared in manuscript.

Place	Date	Hour	Summary of Events and Information	Remarks and references to Appendices
	APRIL. 1917.			
BETHUNE.	13th		General Training. Commanding Officer, 2nd. in Command & Company Commanders visit right (CAMBRIN) Sector. See Brigade Operation Orders No. 130 attached.	Schedule No. 2.
do	14th		General Training. Commanding Officer. 2nd in Command & Company Commanders visit left. (GIVENCHY) Sector. "D" Coy acted as Escort Party at the funeral of Brig-Genl Matthews C.B. C.M.G. Comdg a brigade of 66th Division. Battalion also found a firing party and bugle band for this. The Battalion was congratulated by the G.O.C. 66th Division on the manner in which it carried out its duties at the funeral.	do
do	15th		General Training under 2nd in Command (Major C.E.Graham) Commanding Officer, Adjutant, and 2nds in Command of Companies visited Centre (CANAL) Sector of the line. 2nd. Lieut J. SWALES was awarded the MILITARY CROSS for conspicuous gallantry in action at BUCQUOY on the night of the 13/14th March 1917. 2nd. Lieut. A.W. Boulton joined Battalion from the Base.	do
do	16th		General Training. The Battalion in readiness to move at 6 hours notice to support either the 49th or 66th Divisions. See Brigade Operation Orders No. 130 attached.	do
do	17th		General Training. Companies in the Attack. Lectures by Platoon Commanders.	
do	18th		do Section, Platoon & Company Drill. Bayonet Fighting and Musketry. Lectures.	
do	19th		do 2nd. Lieuts, L.T. Wood, J. Oulton. H. Gregory, W.N. Doley Joined Battalion from the Base. 5. Other Ranks Joined Battalion from Base.	
do	20th		Battalion moved at 10.am to Ft.SAINS (FOSSE 10) arriving about 1-30.pm. Battn. Operation Orders attched. Battalion in Divisional Reserve.	Appendice No.3.
FT. SAINS.	21st		Training. Special attention to Platoons and Companies in the Attack.	
do	22nd		Training. Scheme:- Attack through Village including taking of village and consolidating position afterwards. Some intermittent shelling of Ft SAINS by enemy long-range guns 2nd. Lieuts B. Green and J. Greeves joined Battalion from the Base.	

Army Form C. 2118.

WAR DIARY
or
INTELLIGENCE SUMMARY.
(Erase heading not required.)

Instructions regarding War Diaries and Intelligence Summaries are contained in F. S. Regs., Part II. and the Staff Manual respectively. Title pages will be prepared in manuscript.

Place	Date	Hour	Summary of Events and Information	Remarks and references to Appendices
	APRIL.1917.			
PT.SAINS.	23rd		Battalion moved by Sections at intervals of 100 yards to relieve 1/6th South Stafford Regt. at LIEVIN. Whilst on the march, the relief was cancelled, and Battalion returned to Billets at PT. SAINS. "B" Coy bathed at BULLY GRENAY in the afternoon.	
do	24th		General Training. Special attention being given to Fire Orders and Discipline, also Platoons in the Attack. "C" Coy bathed.	
do	25th		General Training. Special attention being given to Fire Control under Section Commanders, and Platoons in the Attack.	
do	26th		Training. Musketry and Fire Control. Specialists under Specialists Officers.	
do	27th		Training. Platoons in the Attack. Musketry, Visual Training for "A" & "B" Coys. Two carrying parties, consisting of 2 Officers, two N.C.O. and 80 men, engaged on carrying projectiles for Special R.E. Coy during night 27/28th, commencing at 10-30.pm.	Appendice 3.a.
do	28th		General Training. Specialists under Specialists Officers.	
do	29th		General Training. Draft of 25 Other Ranks joined Depot Battalion from the Base and taken on the strength of this Unit. Commanding Officer and Company Commanders go up to trenches to reconnoitre new line to be taken over. For particulars of new line see Bde Operation Orders No. 135. copy attached.	Appendice No.4.
do	30th		Battalion proceed to the trenches to take over from 7th Sherwood Foresters. See Battalion Operation Orders No. 139 attached. Relief completed at 12.20 a.m. 1/5/17.	Appendice No.5.

1-5-17.

C.H.Anson.
Lieut-Colonel,
Commanding 1/5th Battalion North Stafford Regiment.

Copy:-   *Appendix No 1.*

SECRET.

137th Infantry Brigade Order No.129.

Wednesday - 11th April 1917.

HAZEBROUCK 5A, 1/100,000.

1. The 137th Brigade will move to billets in BETHUNE tomorrow 12th April, Head of column to pass starting point just South of B in BOURECQ at 10. a.m., Route Main ST. HILAIRE - LILLERS - CHOCQUES Road.

2. An interval of 500 yards is to be maintained between Battalions.

3. Transport will accompany Units.

4. Billeting parties will report to the Staff Captain at 10.30 a.m. at point where Railway crosses Main CHOCQUES - BETHUNE Road just S. of the HU in VENDIN-LEZ-BETHUNE.

5. Blankets and stores will be stacked by 9.0 a.m. at Headquarters of the Units or at a suitable place where they can be loaded on to lorries.

6. Brigade Headquarters will close at ST. HILAIRE at 10. a.m. and re-open at the same hour at BETHUNE.

7. Acknowledge.

C.S.A. FULLBROOK-LEGGATT,
Captain,
Brigade Major, 137th Inf. Bde.

Issued at 6. p.m.

Copy:-

SECRET.

Appendix No 2.

137th Infantry Brigade Order No. 150.

16th April 1917.

Reference : Trench Maps, LOOS
LA BASSEE & RICHEBOURG, 1/10,000
Bethune (Combined Sheet) 1/40,000.

1. The 137th Infantry Brigade will be prepared to move in support of either the 49th Division or 66th Division (XI Corps), priority being given to the 66th Division. All units will be ready to move at six hours notice.

2. RECONNAISSANCE.
The most probable action on the part of the enemy is an attempt to sieze the GIVENCHY RIDGE. Reconnaissance of the ground and trenches between WINDY CORNER, LE PLANTIN SOUTH and the GIVENCHY RIDGE will therefore be necessary.

3. The 66th Divisional Front extends from CLIFFORD STREET G.5.c.05.05. to CANADIAN ORCHARD S.28.a.6.9. (inclusive).
The 49th Divisional Front extends from CANADIAN ORCHARD (exclusive) to East of LAVENTIE.
The 66th Divisional front is divided into:-
  (a) Right, or CAMBRIN Sector, held by 199th Inf. Bde.
  (b) Centre, or CANAL Sector,   " " 198th " "
  (c) Left, or GIVENCHY Sector, " " 197th " "

4. ACTION. On receipt of the Orders:-
  (a) "Move CAMBRIN"
    Units will move in the following order and concentrate at F.21.c. :-

Order of March.	Route.
1/6th North Staffs. Regt	
137th Machine Gun Coy.	
1/6th South Staffs. Regt.	via: BEUVRY.
1/5th South Staffs. Regt.	
1/5th North Staffs. Regt.	
137th Trench Mortar Battery.	

  (b) "Move CANAL"
    Units will move as under and concentrate at LE PREOL F.15.d. :-

Order of march.	Route.
1/6th North Staffs. Regt.	direct.
1/6th South Staffs. Regt.	via: BEUVRY.
1/5th South Staffs. Regt.	via: BEUVRY.
137th Machine Gun Coy.	via: LE QUESNOY.
1/5th North Staffs. Regt.	via: LE QUESNOY.
137th Trench Mortar Batty.	via: LE QUESNOY.

  (c) "Move GIVENCHY"
    Units will move as under and assemble WEST of WINDY Corner and LE PLANTIN:-

Order of march.	Route.	Position of assembly.
1/6th North Staffs.	LE PREOL CANAL BR. at F.10.d.8.9. LONE FARM.	A.8.a.20.- A.8.a.0.6.
1/6th South Staffs.	BEUVRY. LE PREOL. CANAL BR. at F.10.d.8.9.	A.8.c.3.4. A.8.a.2.0.

P.T.O.

(continued).

Order of March.	Route.	Position of assembly.
1/5th South Staffs.	LE QUESNOY. CANAL BR. at F.10.a.7.4. thence by track along BREEZY WALK.	A.7.b.0.0. A.7.B.7.7.
137th M.G.Coy.	By road S. of LA BASSEE Canal to GORRE Southern Branch of Tuning Fork.	STEWART ROAD A.7.b.7.7.
1/5th North Staffs.	By road S. of LA BASSEE Canal to GORRE Southern Branch of Tuning Fork.	N. of ESTAMINET DUMP F.6.c.4.9.
137th T.M.Btty.	By road S. of LA BASSEE Canal to GORRE Southern Branch of Tuning Fork.	ditto.

5. COUNTER ATTACK ON GIVENCHY.
1/6th North Staffs. will move into the defences of LE PLANTIN SOUTH and CHESHIRE ROAD. They will attack with their right directing on GIVENCHY CH. and will re-capture PICCADILLY and PARK LANE.
1/6th South Staffs. will move into position between WINDY CORNER and LE PLANTIN South. They will attack with their Left directing on GIVENCHY CH: they will capture CAMBRIDGE TERRACE and form a defensive flank on the Right.
1/5th South Staffs. will move into the defences of LE PLANTIN SOUTH and will await orders.
1/5th North will remain in Brigade Reserve,
137th Machine Gun Coy. will co-operate and support the attack from position in the "B" line N. of the attacking troops.
137th Trench Mortar Batty. will await orders.

6. Units must take the necessary reconnaissance of the 66th Div. area, so that the approaches to the positions of concentration or assembly in each section are familiar.

7. In the event of the Brigade being ordered in support of the 49th Div. the Routes and Order of march will be issued.

8. Acknowledge.

C. S. A. FULLBROOK-LEGGATT,
Captain,
Brigade Major, 137th Infantry Brigade.

154.17.

Copy:-

SECRET.

Appendice No 2

O P E R A T I O N   O R D E R S   No. 37.
by
Lieut.-Colonel A.L.F.Fawcus M.C.
Commanding 1/5th Battalion North Staffs. Regt..

Thursday - 19.4.17.

Reference:-   Maps 36B & 36C.   1/40,000.

1. The Battalion will move tomorrow into Divisional Reserve at PT.SAINS, R.3.c.3.3.
   Route:-   BETHUNE, - NOUEX les MINES, - PT SAINS Road.

2. The Battalion will parade in the road, head of column at cross roads E.11.c.70.55 at 9.50 a.m. (Battalion will move off at 10.0 a.m.
   Order of march:- Signallers, "C" "D" Band "A" "B" & Transport.

3. All movement East of NOUEX les MINES and SAILLY LA BOURSE will be by parties not larger than a Company, and forward of the AIX - NOULETTE - BULLY GRENAY - MAROC road will be by parties not larger than platoons.

4. Barracks and billets must be left clean.

5. Dinners will be cooked on the march.

6. Waterbottles must be filled.

7. Strict march discipline will be observed.

8. Blankets, valises etc., must be at the Q.M.Stores by 8.30 a.m.. Mess boxes by 9.15 a.m.. Blankets must be rolled & tied in bundles of ten.

E. A. WILSON, Captain & Adjutant,
1/5th Bn. North Staffs. Regt..

Copy.-   Appendix 39
SECRET.

OPERATION ORDERS   No. 39.
by
Lieut.-Colonel A.E.F.Fawcus M.C.
Commanding 1/5th Bn. North Staffs. Regt..

Friday - 27.4.17.

Map Reference:- LENS 36O. S.W.1;
1/10,000.

1. List below shows carrying parties required for placing Projectors in position, with rendezvous and times on night of 27th/28TH April 1917.

2. During these operations silence is to be maintained - no smoking will be allowed.

3. Box respirators will be carried in the alert position.

4. If a drum is injured, no alarm will be sounded, the burst one will be put aside, and the remainder of the party lead on.

5. Guides for each party will be found by B Special Coy. R.E. The route has been marked out by boards with paper and a black arrow.

6. The parties will proceed with guides to the place where limbers will deliver the stores. Carrying parties will report to the Special Company Officer at this dump, and then be directed to forward dumps, guides accompanying them.

7. Company Scouts must be sent out to reconnoitre the way to the rendezvous.

8. On the return of parties to billets the Officer in charge will report to Orderly Room the number of projectors carried and any casualties which have occurred.

Index.	Numbers.	Found by.	Time of rendezvous.	Time of parade here.
Night 27th/28th.				
"F"	1 Officer 2 N.C.Os. & 80 men.	"C" Coy.	Road junction M.8.b.8.0. 10.30 p.m.	8.30 p.m.
"G"	do.	"D" Coy.	do. 11.10 p.m.	9.10 p.m.

E.A.WILSON,
Captain & Adjutant,
1/5th Bn. North Staffs. Regt..

Copy:-   APPENDIX No.4.

SECRET.

137th INFANTRY BRIGADE ORDER No. 135.

28th April 1917.

Reference:- Maps LENS 36C. S.W.1. 1/10,000.
36B & 36C. 1/40,000.

---

1. The 137th Infantry Brigade will relieve the 139th Infantry Brigade in the line on the 30th April. Relief to be complete by 4 a.m. on the 1st May.

2. The 1/5th North Staffords will move from FOSSE 10 to LEFT SECTOR in relief of 7th SHERWOODS.

3. Battalions will move by platoons at five minutes interval East of the line BULLY GRENAY - AIX -LA- NOULETTE.

4. The 231st Brigade will be in support of the Brigade Sector. The 10th Canadian Infantry Brigade will be on the right of the 137th Infantry Brigade, the 138th Infantry Brigade on the left.

5. Brigade boundaries will be :-

   Right - The SOUCHEZ RIVER.
   Left - The LIEVIN - CITE ST. THEODORE Railway.

   The Brigade Sector will be held as follows:-

   Right Sector.   1/6th North Staffs. Regt., from SOUCHEZ RIVER to M.24.c.6.4.
   1/5th North Staffs. Regt. M.24.c.6.4. to Railway.
   Dividing Line between Battalions - ALIEN TRENCH - along N.W. edge of BOIS de RIAUMONT - N.W. of row of houses M.24.c.3.2., M.24.c.6.4. - D of AHEAD (all inclusive to Right Battalion).

   Support. 1/5th South Staffs. Regt. H.Q. at M.22.d.8.2.
                                       Battalion about M.28. Central.

   Reserve. 1/6th South Staffs. Regt.. H.Q. at RED MILL.
                                       Battalion about M.27.b. and M.27. c & d.

6. BRIGADE STORES. Bde. S.A.A. Store. Left Battalion H.Q. M.28.b.70.05.

   Bde. Grenade Stores.   M.29.c.05.65.
                          M.28.b.95.35.

   R.E.Store.   M.29.c.05.65.
                          M.29.a.00.45.

   T.M.Ammunition.   At Battery H.Q.

   Rockets, Very Pistol
   Ammunition & flares.   At M.29.a.00.45.

7. Brigade Headquarters will close at BULLY GRENAY at 10. p.m. Advanced Brigade Headquarters will re-open at M.27.c.6.0. at 12 midnight. Rear Brigade Headquarters will open at AIX NOULETTE R.22.b.5.3. at 6. p.m.

8. Relief complete to be reported to Advanced Brigade Headquarters M.27.c.6 C. by B.A.B. Code.

9. Acknowledge.

Captain,
Brigade Major, 137th Infantry Brigade.

Appendix 5.

SECRET.   OPERATION ORDERS No. 39A
                      by   Copy No.
          Lieut.-Colonel A.E.F.Fawcus M.C.
          Commanding 1/5th Battalion North Staffs. Regt.

     Reference 36.b. and 36.c. 1/40,000 LENS.36.c.S.W.L. 1/10,000.

1. The Battalion will relieve the 7th Battalion Sherwood Foresters in the line tomorrow night - 30th/1st.

2. Boundaries. Right Boundary - ALIEN TRENCH along N.W. edge of BOIS DE RIAUMONT - N.W. of row of houses M.24.c.3.2. - M.24.c.6.4. - D of AHEAD (all exclusive). Left Boundary - the LIEVIN - Cite St. THEODORE Railway.

3. "A" Company will relieve "B" Company 7th Sherwoods in the line.
   "B"   "   "   "   "D"   "   "   "   "   "
   "C"   "   "   "   "C"   "   "   "   "   in support.
   "D"   "   "   "   "A"   "   "   "   "   in reserve.

4. Order of march:- Headquarters Details under 2nd Lt. J.Swales, A. B. C. D. Coys.

5. Headquarters Details will move off from house at R.9 Central at 7.30 p.m. by following route:- Road Junction at R.29.d.65.50. E. of NOULETTE and thence E. to road Junction at M.26.d.80.20. where platoons will be met by guides. The remaining Platoons will follow at 5 minutes interval between platoons, and 15 minutes interval between B. & C. Coys. H.Qrs. A & B Coys will observe a 10 minutes halt at 8.20 p.m., and C. & D. Coys. at 9.15 p.m.

6. Signallers under the Signal Officer will move off at 11.0 a.m.

7. The Battalion Scouts will move off with their Companies, but on arrival at their destination will report to Battalion Headquarters.

8. One guide per platoon from 7th Sherwoods will meet Platoons at Road Junction M.26d.8.2. at 9.0 p.m.

9. Packs, Blankets and valises will be ready at Coy. H.Qrs. at 3.0 p.m. Rations for the 1st May will be carried on the man, also greatcoats and oilsheets. Mess boxes will be ready at Coy. H.Qrs. at 7.30 p.m.

10. Lewis Guns and Magazines will be ready packed at transport lines at 1.0 p.m. and will move at 1.30 p.m. These will be deposited in Gun Emplacements at M.28.b.85.35. and will be collected by Lewis Gun Sections on arrival. Lewis Gun Officer and two men per Section will accompany them. The Scout Officer will detail a Scout to lead this party.

11. One Officer per Company, One N.C.O. per Platoon and the R.S.M. will move off at 2.0 p.m. from Railway Crossing R.9.a.6.7. and will proceed to the trenches to take over from the 7th Sherwoods. Scout Officer will detail one Scout to Guide this party.

12. Battalion Headquarters will be at CHATEAU at M.28.b.70.05.

13. Relief complete will be reported by B.A.B.Code and by runner.

14. Companies will report their dispositions and that they are in touch with troops on either flanks as soon as possible after relief.

15. Strong reconnoitring patrols will be sent out during the night by O.C. "A" & O.C. "B" Companies.

16. Divisional Trench Standing Orders will be strictly observed.

17. Transport & Q.M.Stores will remain in their present billets.

                                      E.A.WILSON, Capt. & Adjutant,
                                      1/5th Bn. North Staffs. Regt..
29.4.17.

To accompany WAR DIARY for APRIL. 1917.

N.C.O.s and men awarded MILITARY MEDALS for conspicuous gallantry at BUCQUOY on night of 13/14th March 1917.

No. 2667. Sergeant. S.B. Copestake.   awarded MILITARY MEDAL.

"For conspicuous gallantry and devotion to duty at BUCQUOY, during the action on the night 13/14th March 1917. He led his men and bombed the enemy out of a strong position. He held his post in face of heavy counter-attacks for over two hours, until he was compelled to retire, as the rest of the line had withdrawn, and he had no more bombs."

No. 3466. L/Cpl. H. Challinor.   awarded MILITARY MEDAL.

"For conspicuous gallantry and devotion to duty during the action at BUCQUOY, on the night of the 13/14th March 1917. He led a party into an enemy dug-out, and although fired on by the occupants, he bombed them, inflicting casualties upon them so that they were compelled to retire to a further recess, and finally ceased resisting."

No. 2264. Private William Fishwick.   awarded MILITARY MEDAL.

"For conspicuous gallantry and devotion to duty during the action at BUCQUOY on the night of the 13/14th March 1917. Although slightly wounded in several places, this man with Pte Busby continued to bomb an enemy machine gun which was holding up the advance, until compelled to retire, as they were the only two left alive on their flank that had succeeded in penetrating the enemy's wire."

No. 3532. Pte. G.F. Busby.   awarded MILITARY MEDAL.

"For conspicuous gallantry and devotion to duty during the action at BUCQUOY, on the night of the 13/14th March 1917. This man with Private Fishwick continued to bomb an enemy machine gun which was holding up the advance, until compelled to retire, as they were the only two left alive on their flank that had succeeded in penetrating the enemy's wire."

No. 5913. L/Cpl. T.B. Swain.   awarded MILITARY Medal.   Wounded 14/4/17.

"For conspicuous gallantry and devotion to duty during the action at BUCQUOY on the night of the 13/14th March 1917. This N.C.O. was in charge of a Lewis Gun. His No.2 was wounded, and he himself was shot through the throat. The remaining two men of his team were lost in the darkness. Although he was the only man left with the gun, and unable to get through the enemy's wire, he carried on. Later when compelled to retire, he was again hit in the thigh, but he still stuck to his gun and brought it safely out of action."

No. 3782. L/Sgt. F. Foster.   awarded MILITARY MEDAL   Wounded 14-4-17.

"For conspicuous gallantry and devotion to duty during the action at BUCQUOY, on the night of the 13/14th March 1917. Although wounded he rallied his men together, and repeatedly resisted enemy bombing attacks until his supply of bombs had given out and he was ordered to withdraw."

To accompany WAR DIARY. for April. 1917.

Weekly Casualties and Strength. for month of April. 1917.

CASUALTIES.

	Officers.			Other Ranks.			STRENGTH.	
	K.	W.	M.	Inv. to England.	K.	W.	M.	Evac. from Field Amb.	Officers.	Other Ranks.
Week ending 5-4-17.	-	-	-	2	-	-	-	11	29	890
do 12-4-17.	-	-	-	-	-	-	-	6	29	913
do 19-4-17.	-	-	-	-	-	-	1.	7	31	905
do 26-4-17.	-	-	-	-	-	-	-	6	35	910
	-	-	-	2	-	-	1	30		

ORIGINAL

Army Form C. 2118.

WAR DIARY
or
INTELLIGENCE SUMMARY.
(Erase heading not required.)

Instructions regarding War Diaries and Intelligence Summaries are contained in F. S. Regs., Part II. and the Staff Manual respectively. Title pages will be prepared in manuscript.

Place	Date	Hour	Summary of Events and Information	Remarks and references to Appendices
			1/5th BATTALION NORTH STAFFORD REGT. WAR DIARY. for month of MAY 1917.	

Army Form C. 2118.

1/5 North Staff Sheet 1

WAR DIARY
or
INTELLIGENCE SUMMARY.
(Erase heading not required.)

Instructions regarding War Diaries and Intelligence Summaries are contained in F. S. Regs., Part II. and the Staff Manual respectively. Title pages will be prepared in manuscript.

Place	Date	Hour	Summary of Events and Information	Remarks and references to Appendices
	MAY. 1917.		Reference Map:- 36.c. S.W.1. 1/10,000.	
LIEVIN.	1st.		Battalion moved on 30-4-17, to take over Sector occupied by 7th Notts & Derby Regt. Boundaries:- Right. ALLEN Trench along N.W. of row of houses M.24.c.3.8. - M.26.c.6.4. all exclusive. Left. LIEVIN- CITE ST THEODORE Railway. "A" Coy & "B" Coy in the line, "C" Coy in support, & "D" Coy in Reserve. Relief complete at 12-40.am. on 1/5/17. Quiet day. Battalion moved to take over line held by 138 Bde from LIEVIN - CITE ST THEODORE Railway to GRENAY - LENS Railway. "A" Coy moved after being relieved by the 1/5th North Staffs Regt., at 10.pm. into cellars at M.22.b.7.7. as Battalion Reserve. "B" Coy remained in present billets. "C" Coy relieved 1/5th Lincoln Regt in the line and posts from LIEVIN - CITE ST THEODORE Railway to GRENAY - LENS Railway. One platoon of "D" Coy remained as support to "B" Coy, and remaining three platoons moved into cellars at M.22.b.95.90. as Battalion Support. Relief complete 1.am. 2-5-17. This Sector was Brigade Left Sector.	
do	2nd.		Normal amount of shelling of trenches and supports. Patrols were sent out, but no special information to report.	
do	3rd.		Normal amount of shelling except in neighbourhood of Battalion Head-qrs, where about 300 shells (5.9.s) fell during the afternoon. Trench Mortars active "near FOSSE 9. Company relief in the evening. "C" Coy being relieved by "D" Coy, with one platoon of "C" Coy to garrison CROOK REDOUBT. (M.17.d.) "A" Coy relieved "B" Coy, but one platoon of "B" Coy remained at the disposal of "A" Coy and billetted in cellars at M.23.d.3.7. Patrols were sent out on whole Battalion front, but no special information was gained.	
do	4th.		Heavy shelling and bombardment of Battalion Head-qrs and neighbourhood, including "B" Coys H.Qrs. from 5.pm. to 8.pm. about 350 to 400 shells (5-9s) Battalion relieved by 1/5th South Staffs Regt., moving into billets in cellars at LIEVIN Headquarters :- M.22.d.80.25. Relief commenced at 10.pm. and completed at 2-30.am. 5-5-17.	
do	6th.		Battalion in Brigade Support: in cellars XX in LIEVIN. Quiet day, some intermittent shelling towards evening.	

Army Form C. 2118.

1/5th North Staff Regt

WAR DIARY
or
INTELLIGENCE SUMMARY.
(Erase heading not required.)

Instructions regarding War Diaries and Intelligence Summaries are contained in F. S. Regs., Part II. and the Staff Manual respectively. Title pages will be prepared in manuscript.

Place	Date	Hour	Summary of Events and Information	Remarks and references to Appendices
LIEVIN.	6th.		Battalion in Brigade Support. Working Parties provided (130.O.R.s) to carry up wire &c to the line.	
do	7th.		Battalion in Brigade Support. Quiet during day. Towards At 9-30.pm. enemy commenced an extremely heavy gas shell bombardment, which continued until 5.am. next morning. Casualties caused by gas were 2 Officers, 2nd.Lts Williams and Cook, also 40 O.R.s, 26 of whom were sent to Hospital. Estimated that 8.000 gas shells were fired: at times, as many as 8 or 9 per minute at one spot being counted.	Appendix No.1.
do	8th.		Battalion relieved 1/5th South Stafford Regt, in the Left sub-sector. Relief complete at 1. am. on 9-5-17. Relief orders attached.	
do	9th.		Normal amount of shelling during the day. Between 5.pm. and 8.pm. enemy shelled Battn H.qrs and neighbourhood. During the night, CROOK & CRIMSON Trenches were heavily trench mortared by the enemy from the direction of N.13.c.85.50. Enemy have apparently got the exact range of all dug outs in LIEVIN, which are used as Battalion or Company Head-qrs, as their shelling is very accurate. All these dug-outs were formerly used by the enemy themselves as Headquarters. Dug-outs are generally good, deep, and well protected by cement, but the entrances of course face the wrong way.	
do	10th.		Usual shelling of front line and back areas. Patrol under 2nd. Lieut C.W.Butterfield went out towards midnight. 2nd. Lt. Butterfield when advancing towards German wire was blown up by a small mine or bomb at 2.am. 11-5-17. Reported Wounded and Missing. Believed Killed on 11-5-17. (see attached patrol report) "A" & "D" Coys relieved "B" & "C" Coys respectively in the line. Relief complete 12-30.am.	
do	11th.		Normal amount of shelling on front line and LIEVIN.	
do	12th.		Situation normal in front line. Heavy shelling in vicinity of Battn Head-qrs from 5.pm. to 9.pm. Battalion relieved in the line by 1/4th Lincoln Regt. Relief complete at 1-35.am. 13-5-17. Battalion moved to billets in PT.SAINS.	
PT. SAINS.	13th.		Battalion in Divisional Reserve. Day spent in cleaning up.	

Army Form C. 2118.

1/5th North Staffs Regt Sheet 3

WAR DIARY
or
INTELLIGENCE SUMMARY.
(Erase heading not required.)

Instructions regarding War Diaries and Intelligence Summaries are contained in F.S. Regs., Part II. and the Staff Manual respectively. Title pages will be prepared in manuscript.

Place	Date	Hour	Summary of Events and Information	Remarks and references to Appendices
	MAY. 1917.			
FT. SAINS.	14th.		Battalion in Divisional Reserve. Battn bathed at SAINS-EN-GOHELLE. One hours training under Platoon Commanders.	
do	15th.		Battalion in Divisional Reserve. General Training. Special attention to patrols and duties of sentries.	
do	16th.		Battalion in Divisional Reserve. "Platoon in Attack"	
do	17th.		Battalion in Divisional Reserve. Training. Rapid Wiring. Box Respirator Drills in the dark.	
do	18th.		Battalion ordered to relieve 1/6th Sherwood Foresters. Orders cancelled at 3.pm. and postponed for 24 hours.	
do	19th.		Battalion moved off at 9-15.am. to relieve the 1/6th Sherwood Foresters as per Operation Orders attached. Relief complete at 12-45.am. 20-5-17.	Appendix II
TRENCHES. (ST. PIERRE)	20th.		Quiet day. Battalion provided working parties during day and night for 3rd Australian Tunnelling Coy. also Working parties for burying cables and for R.E.s	
do	21st.		Quiet day. Working parties as per yesterday. 2nd. Lieut. A.M. Jones joined Battn from Base.	
do	22nd.		Quiet day. Working parties as before. 2nd. Lieut. F.B. Ross joined Battn from Base.	
do	23rd.		Quiet day. Battalion relieved 1/5th South Stafford Regt. in the line. Relief complete 1-40.am. 24-5-17. Operation Orders attached. No Patrolling possible; preparations for sending over gas prevented patrols going out.	Appendix III
do	24th.		Quiet day. Gas Shells sent off during night 24/25th into CITE ST EDOUARD and CITE ST LAURENT. by special R.E.s. 2nd. Lieut C.J.B. Masefield joined this Battalion from 2/5th Br, North Stafford Regt. The following Officers were "Mentioned in Dispatches" in the London Gazette of 23-5-17. Major C. LISTER. M.C. (North Staffs Regt) attached 1/5th North Staffs Regt. Capt. E.A. WILSON. Lieutenants F.E. TAYLOR, H.D. GIBSON, & H.F. GREEN.	

Army Form C. 2118.

WAR DIARY
or
INTELLIGENCE SUMMARY.
(Erase heading not required.)

Instructions regarding War Diaries and Intelligence
Summaries are contained in F. S. Regs., Part II.
and the Staff Manual respectively. Title pages
will be prepared in manuscript.

Place	Date	Hour	Summary of Events and Information	Remarks and references to Appendices
TRNCHES	Ap. 25th 1917		Quiet day. Inter Company relief, commencing at 10.pm. "D" Coy & "A" Coy relieved "C" & "B" Coy in the left and right subsectors respectively.	
do.	26th		Quiet day. During previous night, several patrols were sent out, one under command of 2nd. Lieut R.C.Mate., to reconnoitre COMBAT Trench from N.13.b.9.1. to N.13.b.25.85. Where COMBAT Trench crosses enemy front line. Here the patrolling party was left, and 2nd. Lt. R.C.Mate and one man went along a short distance of the German trench, until sounds of the enemy were heard. They then returned to post, and patrol retraced its way back to our line. The G.O.C. Division complimented 2nd. Lt. Mate on the good work done on this patrol.	
do	27th		Twice the early hours of the morning a few bombs were thrown at the post at COMBAT Trench at N.13.b.9.1. by an enemy patrol. They were fired on and withdrew; casualties unknown.	
do	28th		Situation normal; somewhere at 9-40.pm. enemy fired 6 trench mortar bombs containing gas, at junction of COOPER & CORAL Trenches. N.7.a.55.70. This is the first time that the enemy has fired gas T.M. Bombs, in this Sector, but from information received this is now becoming a regular practice. 2nd. Lieuts D.E. Bridgwood and C.W. Broadhurst joined Battalion from the Base.	
do	29th		Inter Company relief. "A" & "C" Coys relieved "B" & "D" Coys in the right and left sub-sectors respectively. 1/6th South Stafford Regt., provided working parties of one Coy strength for wiring in front of CORAL Trench and deepening COTTAGE Trench.	
do.	30th		Battalior relieved in the line by 1/6th South Stafford Regt. relief complete at 1.am. 1-6-17. Went into support of right Battalion. On night 29/30th 2nd. Lieut. F.G. Moss took out a patrol of 4 O.R.s. They left our line at N.12.5.80.85. and proceeded along Railway embankment until in line with wall at N.7.c. Scouts examined gaps in walls and houses at N.7.c.4.5, the South side of max north house being loopholed. There were signs of a recently trod path to the North. Patrol advanced through gaps in the wall, and crossed main LENS - CITE ST PIERRE Rd, then crossed COMBAT Trench, and found the enemy's wire on far side very weak. Patrol examined roads and houses at about N.7.c.7.6, then advanced across fields to houses at N.7.c.95.85. Here patrol changed direction N.W. and	

Army Form C. 2118.

1/5th N/Staffs WAR DIARY or INTELLIGENCE SUMMARY. Sheet 5

(Erase heading not required.)

Instructions regarding War Diaries and Intelligence Summaries are contained in F.S. Regs., Part II. and the Staff Manual respectively. Title pages will be prepared in manuscript.

Place	Date	Hour	Summary of Events and Information	Remarks and references to Appendices
ST. PIERRE.	MAY. 1917. 30th		and returned to our lines and posts, past South side of CHURCH, entering at N.7.a.2.5. Patrol started at 10-30.pm. and returned at 1-30.am. 1-6-17. No enemy patrols were met. 2nd. Lieut F.S. Moss was congratulated by the G.O.C. Division on this patrol.	
ST PIERRE.	31st.		Quiet day. "B" & "C" Coys supplied working parties for the 1/6th South Staffs Regt during the night.	

		CASUALTIES.						STRENGTH.	
		Officers.			Other Ranks.			Officers.	Other Ranks.
		K.	W.	M. Hosp.	K.	W.	M. Hosp.		
Week ending	3-5-17.	-	-	-	1	2	9	34	943
"	10-5-17.	-	1 2(Gas)	-	2	13 - 24(Gas)	12	32	889
"	17-5-17.	1	-	-	-	4	14	32	916
"	24-5-17.	-	-	-	-	1	15	32	908
"	31-5-17.	-	-	2	-	5	5	34	899
		1	3	2	3	49	55		

Austin Lieut-Colonel,
Commanding 1/5th Batn North Stafford Regt.

SECRET.   Append I

OPERATION ORDERS. No. 42.
by
Lieut-Col. A.E.P.Fawcus. M.C.   8-5-17.
Commanding Ormonde.

1. The Battalion will relieve the 1/5th South Stafford Regt. in the Left Subsector to-night, the 8th/9th May, 1917.

2. Disposition.- B Coy. will take over the outpost line of the Right Coy. from LIEVIN-LENS Road exclusive to post at M 18 c.90.30. inclusive and Support line from LIEVIN-LENS Road to CITE St.ANI-CITE St. THEODORE RLY. inclusive. One platoon of A Coy. will report to O.C.B Coy. and will be at his disposal in cellars near Right Coy. H.Qrs.
   C Coy. will take over outpost line of Left Coy. from post at M 18 b.90.30. exclusive to M 18 d.55.55. to RAILWAY at M 18 b.40.55. to M 13 c.50.10. and Support line from RAILWAY at M 17 c.70.00. CRIMSON TRENCH to M 12 c.50.10. O.C.D Coy will detail one platoon to garrison CROOK REDOUBT; this platoon will report to and be under the orders of O.C.C Coy.
   A Coy., less one platoon, will be in Support in cellars at M 33s. 25.90. D Coy., less one platoon, will be in Reserve in cellars at M 22b.70.70.

3. Details will be arranged between Company Commanders.

4. Times of moving from present area:-
   B Coy. move at 9.30p.m. from billets.
   C Coy.   "   " 9.30p.m.   "   "
   A Coy.   "   " 9.30p.m.   "   "
   D Coy.   "   " 10. 0p.m.
   One Officer per Coy. and one N.C.O. per platoon will move off at one hour before above times to take over from Coys. of 1/5th South Staffs.
   Battalion H.Qrs. will close at M 22d.80.20. at 9.30p.m. and will open at M 22b.25.35. at 9.45p.m.

5. Lewis gun drums will be taken over in the line from 1/5th South Stafford Regt. and those at present with the Battalion will be handed over to 1/5th South Stafford Regt.

6. Water bottles will be filled prior to leaving billets.

7. Rations for the 9th May will carried on the man.

8. All dixies to be returned to Battalion Dump by 6.0p.m. Transport Officer arrange to collect them at 6.0p.m.

9. Relief complete will be reported by BAB Code and runner and will be notified by the word "Daffodil".

C.R.Krell. 2nd Lt.
for Capt. & Adjutant,
1/5th Bn.North Stafford Regiment.

Appendix II

SECRET.

Copy No. 13

OPERATION ORDERS No. 4.
by
Major C.E.Graham,
Cmdg. 1/5th Bn. North Staffs. Regt.

Thursday - 17.5.17.

Reference:- Maps LENS 36C. SW1. 1/10,000.
36B. 1/40,000.

1. The 137th Infantry Brigade will relieve the 139th Inf. bde. in the Left (PIERRE) Sector on the night of the 18/19th May.

2. The Battalion will relieve the 6th Sherwood Foresters in Support of the Right Battalion, and Coys and Platoons will relieve the corresponding Coys and platoons of that Battalion.

3. Order of march:- Hdqr. details under 2/Lieut. J.Swales M.C., "A" "B" "C" & "D" Companies.

4. H.Qr. details will move off from Cross Roads at R.3.c.3.3. at 8.15 pm. via BULLY GRENAY to GRENAY BRIDGE M.1.d.6.3. Coys. will move off by Platoons in the order above stated, No.1 Platn moving off at 8.20 pm. followed by the remaining Platoons at 5 minutes interval.

5. Arrangements have been made for guides (2 for H.Qrs. and 1 per platoon) to be at GRENAY BRIDGE at 9.45 pm. to guide platoons to their billets.

6. Battalion Scouts will move off with their Coys. but on arrival at the destination will report to Hd.Qrs.

7. The Signallers under Signal Officer will move off at 3.0 pm. The R.S.M. will accompany this party to take over Hd.Qr. Stores &c.

8. Packs, blankets and valises will be ready at Coy. Hqrs. at 3.0 pm.

9. Rations for the 19th will be carried on the man, also great-coats & oilsheets.

10. Waterbottles must be filled.

11. Mess-boxes will be ready at Coy.Hdqrs. at 8.pm. Lewis Guns and magazines will be ready packed at the Transport Lines at 6.0 pm. Quartermaster will arrange with the Transport Officer for Conveyance of Cooking Utensils.

12. All Limbers including Lewis Gun Limbers will move off 10 minutes in the rear of Battalion under the supervision of the Transport Officer and will be unloaded at the dump near Battn. Hdqrs. Coys. will arrange for parties to be at the dump to unload Lewis Guns, panniers and Cooking utensils.

13. Battalion Headquarters will be at M.16.b.55.20.

14. Relief Complete will be reported to Orderly Room by Runner.

C.F. TRELL,
2nd Lieut.& A/Adjutant.
1/5th Bn. North Staffs. Regt.

SECRET.

Append III

OPERATION ORDERS No.46
by
Major C.R.Graham.
Commanding Ormonde.   Wednesday, 23-5-17.

Reference:- Trench Map LENS 36 S.W.1., 1/100,000.

1. Battalion will relieve BENDOR in the line to-night, relief to commence at 10.0p.m.

2. Coys. will move off by platoons at 9.45p.m. at 200yds. interval by the main road from the village to new Battalion H.Qrs.-M 11 c.55.45.,in the following order - B?C,A,D. They will relieve the undermentioned Coys. of BENDOR -
   B Coy. will relieve C Coy.BENDOR in the right front line.
   C Coy.   "   " D Coy.BENDOR in the left front line.
   A Coy.   "   " A Coy.BENDOR in the Right Support.
   D Coy.   "   " B Coy.BENDOR in the Left Support.
   One guide per platoon will be at new Bn. H.Qrs. to meet incoming platoons.

3. Coy. Q.M.Sgts. and one N.C.O. per platoon, also H.Q. Signallers will move off at 4.30p.m. under the Signalling Officer. They will assemble in the trench near Battalion Dump; the R.S.M. will accompany the party. Pioneers(with the exception of the Pioneer Corporal) and Battalion Scouts will assemble in the trench near Battalion Dump at 4.45p.m., and will move off under 2/Lt. Swales.

4. Guides will be provided at Bn.H.Qrs. at 5p.m. to show the platoon representatives their posts.

5. S.A.A. for Lewis Guns will be handed over upon relief. The Battalion will take over the Lewis Gun Ammunition of the Right Front Battalion.

6. BENDOR are sending Coy.Q.M.Sgts. and one representative per platoon and two for H.Qrs. to report at 6p.m. Coys. will arrange for guides to be there in the trench to meet them.

7. The remaining H.Q.Details will move off in rear of the Battalion.

8. Water bottles must be filled.

9. Relief complete will be reported to Orderly Room by wire by the word "CHOCOLATE".

10. The Password arranged for to-noght with BENDOR is "GODSALL".

C.R.Krell. 2nd Lt.
for Capt. & Adjutant,
1/5th Bn. North Stafford Regiment.

Copy of Patrol Report 10/11 May 1917

Patrol consisting of 2/Lt. C. W. BUTTERFIELD & 10. O. R. left Head Quarters of double platoon M. 18. b. 15. 10. at 11.30 pm on night of 10/5/17, proceeded to Railway on left of triangle & searched house at M. 13. a 18.12. but found no enemy. On proceeding further ~~soon~~ the patrol saw a belt of wire some 20-30 yds to E of house searched & running N & S.

2nd Lt BUTTERFIELD then went forward with L. Cpl FRYER to investigate & found a gap in the wire. He proceeded to go through the gap & according to the L Cpl who accompanied him there was a flash & an explosion & immediately a M G fired on them. 2/Lt BUTTERFIELD shouted "Ox" & fell, and the enemy then rushed. L Cpl FRYER lay down beside 2/L BUTTERFIELD

& fired at the enemy. The patrol, of which 3 O.R. were wounded, ~~returned~~ retired but Sgt HOLLAND & L/Cpl FRYER returned to search for 2Lt BUTTERFIELD only to find that the body had been taken away.

Patrol then returned to place of departure.

Map Reference LENS 36C S.W.1 $\frac{1}{10000}$.

No. 29

1/5th Battalion North Staffordshire
Regiment

War Diary

1.9.17.
June to ypres

ORIGINAL

1/5th South Staff Regt. Sheet I

Army Form C. 2118.

WAR DIARY
or
INTELLIGENCE SUMMARY.
(Erase heading not required.)

Instructions regarding War Diaries and Intelligence Summaries are contained in F. S. Regs., Part II. and the Staff Manual respectively. Title pages will be prepared in manuscript.

Place	Date	Hour	Summary of Events and Information	Remarks and references to Appendices
	June, 1917.			
TRENCHES.	1st.		Quiet day, "A" Coy found working party for the 1/6th South Stafford Regiment, in the line during the night 31/1st June, 1917.	
do	2nd.		Quiet day, "D" Coy found working party for the 1/6th South Stafford Regt in the line during the night 2/3rd June 1917.	
do	3rd.		Battalion relieved 1/6th South Stafford Regt in F.1. Subsector. "A" Coy Right Support Coy, "B" Coy Right Coy in the line, "C" Coy Left Coy in the line, "D" Coy Left Support Coy, Relief commenced at 10.pm. complete at 11.45.pm.	
do	4th.		Situation normal, usual amount of enemy activity - shells and trench mortars. Work on deepening COOPER & COLLEGE trenches. Patrols at night as usual. 2nd. Lieut. J. Staniforth and two Sections of "B" Coy patrolled from Post M.12.d.85.60. along COLLEGE trench. observed enemy near road at N.7.c.E50.10., party was putting out wire. Two enemy were observed approaching patrol from Rear along Railway embankment. Four of our men endeavoured to cut these men off, but the enemy ran to a trench running N.E. from N.7.c.30.20. & disappeared. Rapid fire was opened on our patrol, and as it was getting light, patrol returned at 341.15.am. 5th inst. 2nd. Lieut. J. Staniforth was complimented by G.O.C. Division on this patrol.	
do	5th.		Enemy artillery fairly active. Continual patrolling was carried out during the night, in order to keep in touch with the enemy. Capt. S.B. WILTON. (Killed in Action 14-3-17) was awarded MILITARY CROSS for good work in connection with a raid on 26-2-17.	
do	6th.		Considerable amount of shelling (5.9s. & 4.2s.) and trench mortars on both Left and Right Companies during the afternoon, about 2-30 to 4.pm. Our artillery retaliated afterwards. Between 6.30. & 8.pm. enemy shelled about Battalion H.Qrs at M.11.b.5.4. Usual patrols patrols were sent out at night. 2nd. Lieut. W.C. Toyser joined Battalion from the Base. Information received from his relatives that 2nd.Lt. G.F.E. WILLIAMS, previously reported Wounded and Missing at BUCQUOY on 14-3-17, is a prisoner of war in German hands.	

Army Form C. 2118.

1/5 North Staff Reg
Sheet 2

WAR DIARY
or
INTELLIGENCE SUMMARY.
(Erase heading not required.)

Instructions regarding War Diaries and Intelligence Summaries are contained in F. S. Regs., Part II. and the Staff Manual respectively. Title pages will be prepared in manuscript.

Place	Date	Hour	Summary of Events and Information	Remarks and references to Appendices
	June.	1917		
TRENCHES.	7th.		Active patrolling during night of 6/7th by all Companies, to keep in touch with enemy. The enemy was located by all patrols. The Battalion was relieved by 1/6th South Staffs Regt and moved into support of Battalion in Right Sector. Relief commenced at 10.pm. and was complete at 12.30.am. 8th June 1917. 2/Lt. E.S. MOSS and 2/Lt. A.C. MATE, Sgt Twyman, and Sgt. Watson, took out patrols on the night 6/7th, with the object of reconnoitring, and keeping touch with the enemy, in case of his having evacuated any positions. All patrols were successful in getting into touch with the enemy. G.O.C. Division wired "consider all patrols did excellent work"	
LIEVEN.	8th.		Quiet day. Capt R.H. Rayner and 2/Lieut A.E. Cockayne joined Battalion from the Base.	
do	9th.		Quiet day. Information received that Tommy RSM Haythurst had been awarded the Croix de Guerre for gallant conduct & devotion to duty during the action at BUCQUOY on the night 18/19 August 1917	1
do	10th.		Quiet day. Brigade Horse Show. see Appendix attached.	
do	11th.		Quiet day. Battalion relieved 1/6th South Stafford Regiment, in the line commencing at 10.pm. Relief complete about 12.midnight. Battalion takes over line previously held. As two Companies ("A" & "C") were to make a raid in a few days, relief orders were altered and only two Companies ("B" & "D") went into the line. 1/6th South Staffs Regt left two Companies in the line to act as Support Coys. "A" & "C" Coys went into billets at BULLY GRENAY to train for raid. 2nd. Lieut H.F. Smith joined from Base. One of our posts at junction of COCK & COCKER Trenches was raided by the enemy. Enemy were driven off, two casualties being inflicted on them.	
TRENCHES.	12th.		"A" & "C" Coys continue training for raid, and moved up into the evening in support into cellars in the line. Quiet day. Enemy fired Trench Mortars and Rifle Grenades into our front line at night.	
do	13th.		"A" & "C" Coys complete their training, and move up in the evening in support into cellars in the line.	
do	14th.		The raid on the enemy's trenches by "A" & "C" Coys was carried out. See attached report. The two Companies of the 1/5th South Staffs Regt. were withdrawn before the raid and	2

Army Form C. 2118.

WAR DIARY
or
INTELLIGENCE SUMMARY.
(Erase heading not required.)

1/5th North Staff Reg. Vol 3

Place	Date	Hour	Summary of Events and Information	Remarks and references to Appendices
	June. 1917.			
TRENCHES.	15th.		"C" Coy held on to Left Coy front, and "A" Coy went into Support. The Battalion was relieved by 1/5th Sherwood Foresters. Relief complete at 1-35.am. 16th. The Commanding Officer - Lt.-Col. A.E.F. Fawcus, M.C. - Went to 137 Bde H.Q.Ps., in temporary command, during the absence of the Brigadier-General.	
FT.SAING.	16th.		Battalion in Divisional Reserve. Resting and cleaning up.	
do.	17th.		do Bathing and cleaning up. Voluntary Church Parades.	
do	18th.		do Battalion parade at 11.am. for address by Divl.Commander and march past.	
do	19th.		Battalion in Divisional Reserve. Training Special attention being paid to Rapid wiring. Commanding Officer Lt.-Col. A.E.F.Fawcus returned to command the Battalion.	
do	20th.		Battalion in Divisional Reserve. Training. Rapid wiring by day and night.	
vdo.	21st.		Battalion in Divisional Reserve. Training. "Platoon & Company in the Attack." Fire Control.	
do	22nd.		Battalion in Divisional Reserve. Training until 9.am. Battalion movedoff at 9-30.pm. for the trenches. Operation Orders attached.	
TRENCHES.	23rd.		Quiet day. Battalion in Brigade Reserve. Bathing & Swimming in Path at RED MILL.	
do	24th.		Quiet day. Sgt. Gater, Ptes Clarke & Bird awarded MILITARY MEDALS for gallantry on night of 14-6-17. Recommendations attached.	
do.	25th.		Quiet day. Battalion moved up to take over line occupied by 1/6th Month Staffs Regt. Operation Orders No. 53 attached. Relief complete	
do	26th.		Quiet day. Usual patrols sent out. A Special patrol under 2/Lt. J.E. LOWE M.C. & 2/Lt. R.C. WATT went out to reconnoitre ABODE & ADULT trenches. See Patrol report attached.	

Army Form C. 2118.

5th North Staff Regt
Sheet H

WAR DIARY
or
INTELLIGENCE SUMMARY.

(Erase heading not required.)

Instructions regarding War Diaries and Intelligence Summaries are contained in F. S. Regs., Part II. and the Staff Manual respectively. Title pages will be prepared in manuscript.

Place	Date	Hour	Summary of Events and Information	Remarks and references to Appendices
	June, 1917.			
TRENCHES.	26th		continued. 2nd. Lieut. J. Keeling slightly wounded. 2/Lt. R.C. Mate wounded to duty. 2/Lts J.E. Lowe and R.C. Mate congratulated by G.O.C. 46th Division on good patrols on night 25/26th.	
do.	27th.		Quiet day. Battalion moved to new billets in LIEVIN, at act as Reserve Battalion during the operations on the 28th inst. Battn H.Q. M.22.b.40.35. and Companies in cellars in neighbourhood. 2nd.Lieuts R.F. Johnson. & W. Smith joined Battalion from Base.	
do	28th		Quiet day. Battalion "stood to" at 7.10pm. until 2-30.am.(28th) in readiness to move at any moment, Battalion being in reserve for the operations taking place. Brigade Orders atteched to copy for Records. Battalion not required as attack was successful.	
do	29th.		Quiet day. Battalion in Brigade Reserve.	
do	30th.		Quiet day. Battalion relieved 1/6th North Staffs Regt & 1/5th South Staffs Regt in the line. in order to attack a position - objective:- N.20.a.00.02. to N.19.d.60.85 on July 1st. See July War Diary.	

3-7-17.

Lawrence Lieut-Colonel,
Commanding 1/5th Battalion North Stafford Regiment.

SECRET.   OPERATION ORDERS. No. 52.

Copy. No. 14.   by
               Lieut-Colonel A.L.F. Fawcus M.C.
                 Commanding 1/5 North Staffs   22-6-17.
                 ----------Regiment.

          Reference Maps 36b. 1/40,000
                        LENS. 36.c.S.W.L. 1/10,000.

1.   The 137th Brigade will relieve the 138th Brigade in the LIEVIN Sector, on the night of the 22/23rd inst.

2.   The 1/5th Bn. North Stafford Regt will relieve the 1/5th Bn. Lincoln Regt, in reserve in LIEVIN, on the night 22/23rd inst. Relief to be complete by 4.a.m.

3.   The Battalion will move off by platoons at 200 yards distance commencing at 9-30.pm. from R.9.a.75.40. via AIX NOULETTE, "E" Track, to BOIS d ROLLENCOURT, - ANGRES - LIEVIN Rd. in the following order, "C" "B" "A" "D" Coys H.and D tails. Strict march discipline will be maintained, and the customary 10 minutes halt at 10 minutes to the hour will be observed.

4.   Guides One per platoon will be at M.27.d.05.55. at 11-30.pm.

5.   Billetting Area. "A" Coy will be billetted in houses between M.27.b.90.30. and M.28.a.10.40. "B" Coy in houses about M.27.b.50.45. "C" Coy in houses about M.27.b.30.80. and "D" Coy in houses about M.27.d.55.95. and M.27.d.20.70.

6.   O.C. Companies will detail one officer per Company and one N.C.O per Company to report to Orderly Room 1/5th Lincolns at the RED MILL at 9-30.pm. 22nd. to reconnoitre billetting areas and take over Stores. The R.S.M. will accompany this party to take over.

7.   Lewis Gun Officer will arrange to have Lewis Guns and Magazines loaded at Tramway Sidings at BULLY GRENAY at 3.pm. 22nd inst. Two men per Lewis Gun Team will accompany the guns on the train. Lewis Guns and Magazines will be unloaded at Tramway Sidings at M.28.a.2.4, and the Lewis Gun Officer will arrange for a guard. Companies will send Lewis Gun Teams to fetch Lewis Guns from this point after arrival of the Company.

8.   Officers valises, Surplus Stores and mens packs will be packed ready by 5.pm. and Mess Boxes (required in the trenches) will be packed ready to be called for by 9.pm.

9.   Rations for the 23rd inst will be carried on the men, and water bottles will be filled.

10.   Battalion Headquarters will be at the RED MILL M.27.d.7.8. and relief complete will be notified by runner by Code word GINGER.

11.
   Copy No.1.   1/5th Lincolns.
    "   2 to 5. 4 Companies.
    "   6.   Headquarters,
    "   7   2nd in Command.
    "   8   T.O. & G.M.
    "   9   L.G.O.
    "   10   Signalling Offr.   C.R. KRELL.
    "   11   M.O.   2nd. Lieut & A/Adjutant.
    "   12   R.S.M.
    "   13   Filing Copy.   1/5th Bn. North Staffs Regt.
    "   14/15. War Diary.

1/5th Battalion, North Stafford Regiment.

Appendix No. 4.

MILITARY MEDALS

No. 242360 Sgt. John Thomas GATER.

"For conspicuous gallantry and devotion to duty during a raid on the enemy's trenches on 14th June, 1917 at CITE ST LAURENT near LENS.

Sgt. Gater was on the left flank of his Company in the hostile trenches, when the enemy made a strong bombing counter-attack down the trench. He organised a defensive flank and drove the enemy back, though they were greatly superior in numbers. He succeeded in holding the flank throughout the raid."

No. 200133 Pte. Sydney John CLARKE.

"For conspicuous gallantry and devotion to duty during a raid on the enemy's trenches, on 14th June, 1917, at CITE ST LAURENT, near LENS.

Pte. Clarke, who is a Signaller, went out under very heavy Trench Mortar Barrage and considerable shelling, and remained out for over an hour, mending the telephone wires between Advanced Battn. Headquarters and O.C.Raid's Headquarters in the front line trenches. The wires were broken in several places, and communication could not have been kept up except for Pte. Clarke's very gallant behaviour.

No. 203138 Pte. Charles Henry BIRD.

"For conspicuous gallantry and devotion to duty during the raid on the enemy's trenches on 14th June, 1917, at CITE ST LAURENT near LENS.

Pte. Bird was foremost in entering a number of enemy dugouts; he displayed great courage and set a fine example to his comrades. He made three prisoners in one dugout.

Strength of Raiding Party:- 8 Officers and 160 Other Ranks.

HONOURS & AWARDS. cont.

No. 263029 Pte. James SARGEANT.   -   MILITARY MEDAL.

"For conspicuous bravery and devotion to duty during a raid on the enemy's trenches at CITE ST. LAURENT near LENS on the night of the 14th June, 1917.

This man, together with Pte. Swain, preceded the first wave carrying an ammonal tube to blow a gap in the enemy's wire. In the face of heavy Trench Mortar fire this man and his comrade succeeded in reaching the enemy's wire and in placing the ammonal tube in position. They succeeded in firing this in spite of the enemy, who had by now discovered them, and was standing on his parapet bombing them.

This man shewed great determination and by his utter disregard for personal safety set a fine example to his comrades, and contributed largely to the success of the raid."

202936 Pte. Herbert SWAIN.   -   MILITARY MEDAL.

"For conspicuous bravery and devotion to duty during a raid on the enemy's trenches at CITE ST. LAURENT near LENS on the night of the 14th June, 1917.

This man, together with a comrade, preceded the first wave carrying an ammonal tube to blow a gap in the enemy's wire. In the face of heavy Trench Mortar fire this man and his comrade succeeded in reaching the enemy's wire and in placing the ammonal tube in position. They succeeded in firing this in spite of the enemy, who had by now discovered them, and was standing on his parapet bombing them.

This man shewed great determination and by his utter disregard for personal safety set a fine example to his comrades, and contributed largely to the success of the raid."

COPY No 11

Operation Orders No 53
by
Lieut Colonel C. R. F. Fawcus M.C.
Commanding 1/6th North Stafford Regt.

Monday 25.6.17

1. The Battalion will relieve the 1/6th North Stafford Regt. in the Left Sub-sector tonight – 25/26th June.

2. Positions of Companies will be as arranged yesterday, namely:-
   "D" Company – Right front line
   "B" " – Left " "
   "A and C Coys. – in Support.

3. Companies will move off by platoons at 200 yards distance at the following times:- Headquarters at 10 p.m. under Scout Officer. "B" and "C" Companies at 10.10 p.m. "D" and "A" Companies at 10.25 p.m. Coys. Somewhere moving off at the same time will arrange to go by different routes.

4. Guides of "D" and "B" Companies will be at the Headquarters of the Right and Left front Companies of the 1/6th North Staffs. respectively, to meet incoming relief and guide platoons to their respective posts.

5. O.C. "D" and "B" Companies will send one officer to be at Headquarters of the Right and Left front Companies 1/6 North Staffs. at 9.30 p.m.

6. Lewis Gun Officer will make all necessary arrangements with the Lewis Gun Officer of the 1/6 North Staffs. re Lewis guns and magazines.

7. Waterbottles must be filled. Rations for front line Coys. will be carried up by platoon Companies. O.C. Support Coys. will detail a party of 20 O.R.s to report to R.S.M. at Battalion Dump as soon as relief complete for this purpose.

8. When relief complete will be reported to Battalion Headquarters 28.b.0.15 (Mentil Church) by code-word NETTLES.

9. The password for this battalion tonight will be THRILL and the counterword TOP.

C. R. KRELL
Lieut & Adjutant
1/6 North Staffs Regt.

Copies to:-
1 & 6. O.C. Coys.
2 & 5. B & C Companies
3. Scouting Off.
4. Lewis gun "
5. Coys.
9. R.S.M.
10. File
11/12. War Diary

Appendix. No.6.

1/5th Battalion North Staffs Regiment.

SPECIAL PATROL REPORT.
Ref. 36.c.S.W.1. 1/10,000.

Composition of Party.

2nd. Lieut. J.E. LOWE M.C. & 2nd. Lieut. R.C. MATE, Two Platoons, & 6 Battalion Scouts.

Task.

(1) To enter ABSALOM Trench, from M.24.d.60.75. to M.24.b.70.30.
(2). To reconnoitre ABODE & ADULT Trenches, and if found empty of the enemy, to occupy and hold them.
(3). To get into touch with the enemy.

Time and Place of Departure.

M.24.c.85.80.   2.10.am.   Note:- Owing to reliefs, patrols could not be sent out earlier.

Patrol Report.

The patrol advanced on Compass bearing due E. of point of departure, in diamond formation, with a Lewis Gun on each flank, and protected by Scouts.
ABSALOM Trench was found to be unoccupied about M.24.d.65.90, and this information was signalled back by lamp. This was then held by main body of patrol, whilst 2Lt.Mate and 6 Scouts advanced to reconnoitre ABODE Trench. After some difficulty, Scouts succeeded in penetrating enemy's wire (which was thick and good) in front of ABODE, and nearly reaching the enemy's trench. They were then seen by the enemy, and heavily attacked from various quarters by Machine Guns, rifle fire and bombs, and were compelled to withdraw.
After returning the fire for some little time, the enemy sent up their S.O.S. red rocket and a barrage was put across NO MANS LAND.
Patrol returned via ABSALOM Trench at 4.am.
Patrol had four casualties near enemy's wire which could not be brought in. In addition 2/Lt.Mate and One O.Rank were Wounded.
I regret to report that in addiation to being unable to bring in our casualties, a Lewis Gun team which had been pushed forward from ABSALOM Trench to protect the Scouts Left flank, was heavily bombed and compelled to retire without its gun.
ABODE Trench appeared to be held in strength, as rifle fire was seen at various points, as well as machine gun fire. A considerable number of Very Lights wer also sent up.

Time and Place of return.

M.24.c.85.70.   4.am.

26-6-17.

(sd) A.F.Fawous, Lt-Col,
Commanding 1/5th Bn. North Stafford Regiment.

1/5th Battalion North Stafford Regiment.

SUMMARY OF CASUALTIES AND WEEKLY STRENGTH.

	CASUALTIES.							WEEKLY STRENGTH.	
	Officers.			Other Ranks.					
	K.	W.	Hosp.	K.	W.	M.	Hosp.	Offs.	O.Ranks.
For week ending 7-6-17.	-	-	1.	-	14.	-	12.	36.	885.
" " " 14-6-17.	-	-	1	1	10.	-	15.	42	866.
" " " 21-6-17.	-	2	1	3	35	8	38.	41	794.
" " " 28-6-17.	-	2	-	2	2	1	7	42	787.
	-	4	3	6	61	9	72		
		X	Z		Y				

Note. X. Includes 2 Died of wounds.   Y. Includes 6 Died of Wounds.
          and One Wounded to duty.

       Z. Missing believed Killed.

Appendix. No. 1

1/5th Battalion North Stafford Regiment.

RESULTS OF HORSE SHOWS.

137 BRIGADE HORSE SHOW.   Held on 10-6-17.

    Transport Turn out.   First Prize.
    Tug of War.   First Prize.
    Officers' Chargers.   First Prize. (C.O's Charger)
    Jumping.   First Prize. (Ridden by Lt.F.E.Taylor.)
    Cross Country Running.   First, Third & ~~Fifth~~. Fourth.

46th Divisional Horse Show.   Held on 13-6-17.

    Transport Turnout.   First Prize & G.O.C's Special Prize.
    Officers' Chargers.   Second Prize.

I Corps Horse Show.   Held on 18-6-17.

    Officer's Chargers.   First Prize.

First Army Horse Show.   Held on 25-6-17.

    Officers' Chargers.   First Prize.

SECRET.   O P E R A T I O N   O R D E R S   No. 56.
by
Lieut.-Colonel A.E.P.Fawcus M.C.
Commanding 1/5th North Staffs. Regt.

REFERENCE:-   LENS 36C.SW1. 1/10,000.   Saturday-30th June 1917.

1. INTENTION. The enemy's position from N.25.b.85.60 to
N.20.c.0.2, ACONITE trench, Aloof at N.13.a.95.60 will be
attacked tonight.

2. OBJECTIVE. ACONITE trench from N.20.a.15.10 inclusive of
the road running N.N.E from the "A" in AGUE to N.19.b.55.83
inclusive of the LENS-LIEVIN road will be attacked by the
137th Infantry Brigade. The attack will be carried out by
the 1/5th North Staffs. Regt. The 1/6th South Staffs. Regt.
will be distributed as follows:- One Company as Moppers-up
one Company carrying and two Companies in immediate support.

3. DISTRIBUTION. The attack will be made on a four Company
front -   "D" Company N.20.a.15.10 to N.19.b.83.16
             "C"   "   N.19.b.83.16 to N.19.b.70.40
             "A"   "   N.19.b.70.40 to N.19.b.60.65
             "B"   "   N.19.b.60.65 to N.19.b.55.83.
The 138th Infantry Brigade will be on our Right and the 139th
Infantry Brigade on our left.

4. PLAN of ATTACK. The attack will be made in two waves. The
first wave in line of sections in column. The second wave in
line of half platoons in column. Half a platoon of moppers-
up 30 yards behind each Company's front wave. Half a platoon
carrying party, 100 yards behind each Company's second
wave. 75 yards between waves. Companies will advance parallel
to the road running towards objective.

5. ASSEMBLY. The 1/5th North Staffs. Regt. will relieve the
1/6th North Staffs. Regt and the 1/5th South Staffs. Regt.
in the Sector allotted to the Brigade for the attack. The
remainder of the Brigade front at present held by the 1/5th
South Staffs. Regt. will be relieved by the 138th Infantry
Brigade. Companies will take over the line opposite their
battle sectors. The front wave and moppers-up in AGUE trench.
The second wave in ADULT trench, carrying parties in ABSALOM
trench.
Relief will be complete by 12 midnight and will be notified
to Battalion Headqrs. by sending the code-word LUCKY.
The leading front wave will assemble on taped line running
from N.19.c.87.92. to N.19.a.60.50. Moppers-up will line up
immediately behind these parties. The second wave will line
up in AGUE trench directly behind the first wave. Carrying
parties ready loaded with the stores shewn on attached list
will be lined up behind AGUE trench.
The two support Companies of the 1/6 th South Staffs. Regt.
will move into their positions when evacuated by attacking
troops.   All parties will be in their battle positions
one hour before Zero.   Runners will be sent back reporting as
soon as Companies are in position by the word "SETTLED".

6. GUIDES. Two guides per platoon for "D" Company will be
provided by the 1/5th South Staffs. Regt. and will be at
SHRAPNEL PLATZ at 10.15 pm. Two guides per platoon for "C"
"A" and "B" Companies will be provided by the 1/6th North
Staffs. Regt. and will be at barrier by Junction of CYCLIST
trench and the LENS-LIEVIN road at 10.30 pm.

7. ZERO TIME will be notified later.

8. PRECAUTION. Great care must be taken that no empty dugouts
or cellars are entered by any troops until explored by
authorised experts, as it is certain that there will be a lot
of booby traps.
No water must be drunk from wells until passed by Medical Officer.

P.T.O.

9. REGIMENTAL AID POST will be at M.24.c.70.35.

10. Battalion Headquarters will be at M.24.c.50.70.

11. Signals as per attached list will be used.

12. Artillery Barrage will commence at Zero 200 yards in advance of AGUE trench and will creep forward at the rate of 100 yards every 3 minutes.

13. Watches will be synchronised at old Battlion Headquarters at 6. pm. today.

14. Water-bottles will be filled before starting and tomorrows rations will be carried on the man.

                                          C.R.KRELL, 2nd Lieut. &
                                              A/Adjutant.
                                      1/5th North Staffs. Regt.

Copies to :-

No. 1 - O.C. 1/6th South Staffs. Regt.
    2 - " 1/5th "   "   "
    3 - " 1/6th North "   "
4/7 - " 4 Companies
8/9 - War Diary
 10.- File.

REPORT ON A RAID

carried out by the 1/5th Battalion North Stafford Regiment.
on the night of the 14th June 1917.

---

1. **OBJECT.**
   (1) To obtain identification.
   (2) To kill or capture enemy.
   (3) To contain and harass enemy.

2. **OBJECTIVES.**
   N.7.a.97.50 to N.1.d.15.00 and houses within a line running 100 yards E. of enemy's front line trench.

3. The RAIDING PARTY consisted of two Companies.
   "A" company on the right - N.7.a.97.50 to N.7.a.97.75.

   Two O.Rs. from the 137th Trench Mortar Battery accompanied this Coy. with Stokes bombs for the purpose of destroying hostile T.Ms.

   "C" Company on the left - N.7.a.97.75 to N.1.d.15.00.

   Each party was accompanied by 4 sappers from the 465th Coy R.Es.

4. **ASSEMBLY.** The Right Company assembled in COST TRENCH and were in position at Zero - 2 (One platoon at Zero + 2).
   The left Company assembled in COOPer TRENCH at 10.15 p.m. and commenced crawling out into position on to line running parallel to and 150 yards away from enemy's trench. They were unobserved and were in position at Zero.
   A most unfortunate accident occurred as the Coy were having hot tea in their callars preparatory to moving to assembly trenches. An experienced bomber whilst seeing that his bombs were in working order detonated one, he tried to clear it from the group of men and rushed up the steps with it, but it exploded before he could get it clear. The result was 13 men wounded and several others severely shaken (2 of the wounded died later) It was then too late to replace these men.

5. **OPERATIONS.** The attack advanced in four parties (2 Right Coy, 2 Left Coy), each party in two waves of two lines each. Distance between lines 10 yards and 20 yards between waves. The four parties each consisted of two platoons and one sapper attached to each platoon. Artillery had previously attempted to cut gaps in wire at points:-
   (1). N.7.a.05.50.
   (2). N.7.a.80.60.
   (3). N.7.b.90.75.
   (4). N.7.b.15.95.
   with good success.
   On the right gaps were completed in enemy's wire by 20' ammonal tubes at points (1) and (2) at Zero + 4 mins and Zero + 3½ mins.
   On attempting to get through these gaps these parties were heavily bombed and light Trench Mortar bombs commenced falling amongst the men. At the same time our own artillery (18 pdrs) were dropping shells short behind our parties.
   Platoon Commanders and one or two men succeeded in reaching enemy's parapet but were too few to withstand the enemy's bombing and machine gun attacks. Capt. Rayner went back and rallied the men who had been scattered by the T.M. fire and again advanced through No.1 gap but as he was in the gap a T.M. bomb landed near him and apparently killed him. His platoon were again scattered by the hostile fire. 2nd Lieuts. Moss and Jones also made repeated attempts to rally their platoons and get through the gaps but were each time dispersed by the enemy fire, and finally the T.M. barrage became so heavy on NO MAN'S LAND that the raiders on this flank were compelled to withdraw to COST TRENCH.
   On the Left. As the barrage commenced the two parties on the left advanced slowly. A party of 12 Germans were lying outside their wire on the raiders left front. These were fired on and one or two fell. The remainder ran into their wire and were caught by our barrage and apparently most of them were killed.
   No. 3 gap was completed by ammonal tube and party entered the enemy's trench.

CONTINUED.-

-2-

The party for No.4 gap found wire well cut and did not need ammonal tube (both sappers with this party had been wounded).

The platoon commanders were unfortunately wounded almost immediately the advance started although there was but little firing on the part of the enemy.

The 1st wave of both parties crossed enemy's trench and pushed on to their second objectives.

2nd Lieut. Green put out a strong covering party and systematically and thoroughly examined the houses in or about which four of the enemy were killed.

A Lewis Gun Section silenced and destroyed an enemy's Machine gun in a house.

The part examined about 12 more houses to the S.E. of their objective but found them unoccupied.

The 2nd wave meanwhile commenced clearing the enemy's trench. Opposition was met with on the right at N.7.a.89.65. and a block was established here and the enemy's fire silenced. Three dug-outs were examined and three prisoners obtained from one, one of them was killed on the way back to our trenches. Another dug-out was entered and after some firing, four or five Germans were left dead at the bottom of the dug-out. In the listening post at N.7.a.80.70 three Germans were found and killed. 2nd Lieut. Poyser in charge of this platoon reports that there were 15 to 20 dead Germans in the trench on his platoon's right. He himself killed one as he was leaving the trench.

A blocking party was also established on the left about N.7.a N.1.d.15.00. Two dugouts were searched here but were quite empty. A severe fight took place with a party of enemy bombers who counter-attacked along the trench. They were however kept back and when our men were withdrawing from the trench at the appointed signal, were dealt with by the parapet L.G.section. *About 50 Germans were killed and many shoulder straps were brought in. Three prisoners were brought in.*

The Parapet Parties on the whole front consisted of 3 L.G.Sections and one Rifle section. These acted as rearguards and effectively covered the withdrawal.

Very fine work was done by the O.C. this Comapny (2nd Lieut. MASEFIELD). He commanded his men splendidly and set a great example. In a hand to hand encounter with a party of Germans he succeeded in killing his opponent.

6. **ARTILLERY.**

The barrage was exceedingly good except on the right of the raiding party. Here it was short and some 18 pdr shells are reported to have fallen behind COST TRENCH. It was also apparently late in lifting at this point. The wire on the whole had been well cut by the 6" Hows. on the day and the day before the raid.

7. **TRENCH MORTARS.**

Effective Support was given by the 2' T.Ms. and the 137th Bde. T.M.Btty who kept up fire on their appointed targets.

8. **MACHINE GUN COY.**

The 137th Machine Gun Coy. covered our left flank by almost continuous M.G.fire.

9. **DIVERSIONS.**

A patrol of one platoon created a demonstration by attacking enemy's post at N.7.a.60.05. The post was found strongly held and well covered by M.G.fire from CORNWALL TRENCH. The post was bombarded with Stokes Mortars and Rifle Grenades.

Various small patrols were also sent out to Houses in N.7.c. and twin red rockets were fired from these points to try and draw the enemy's barrage as this appears to be the enemy's barrage call in this sector. The effect was good as a heavy barrage came down accross NO MANS LAND in this area. COMBAT AND COLLEGE TRENCHES were heavily shelled.

A barrier which appeared to contain a booby trench trap in COMBAT trench was blown up by an ammonal tube. Two other ammonal tubes were blown up under enemy's wire near post at N.7a.60.05.

CONTINUED.-

The Dummy Raid On NASH ALLEY and thw twin red and green rockets sent up from this sector by the Battalion on our left appeared to draw a very considerable amount of fire from the enemy's artillery.

10. HOSTILE ARTILLERY.

The enemy replied very feebly to our barrage on the front being raided. On the flanks however, he put down a considerable barrage of 5.9's and 4.2's '77mm shells. On the front being raided a Heavy T.M. barrage was put down very shortly after Zero and remained so during the entire operations.
It consisted of Heavy and Medium T.M.bombs and Priester Bombs.

11. LIGHT SIGNALS.

Our rocket and light signals were a great success and informed bothe the raiders and the artillery how the situation stood.

12. ENEMY LIGHT SIGNALS.

Twin red rockets followed by white were sent up by the enemy opposite COWDEN TRENCH.

13. MEDICAL ARRANGEMENTS. were good and our wounded were quickly evacuated by relays and stretcher bearers.

14. CASUALTIES.

Our casualties for the raid itself were :-

	Officers	O.Rs.
Killed.....................		1
Missing....................	1	10
Wounded....................	2(one	21 (including 3 R.Es. since died)
	3	29

Accidental casualties before raid :-

	O.Rs.
Killed	1
Wounded.................	12 (one since died)
	13

Diversions and carrying parties :-

	O.Rs.
Wounded.................	5

T O T A L	Officers.	O.Rs.
	3	47

CARRYING PARTIES.

There will be four carrying parties, each consisting of half a platoon from "A" Company, 1/6th Bn. South Staffs. Regt.

In each Party:-

    6 men will carry   S.A.A.
    4 " "   "   water.
   10. "   "   bombs.

Each man will carry a pick or a shovel.

The platoons of the second wave of the attacking force will each carry 10 shovels and 5 picks.

SECRET.

S I G N A L S   attached to
Operation Orders No. 56.

GOLD and SILVER RAIN ROCKETS will be fired from objective when objective is reached.

RED FLARES will be lit at the bottom of trench at foremost posts in trench when Contact Aeroplane signals with KLAXON horn or Very Lights.

ORIGINAL

1/5th Battalion NORTH STAFFS Rgt. 137/46

WAR DIARY FOR MONTH OF JULY 1917

Army Form C. 2118.

WAR DIARY
or
INTELLIGENCE SUMMARY.
(Erase heading not required.)

Instructions regarding War Diaries and Intelligence Summaries are contained in F. S. Regs., Part II. and the Staff Manual respectively. Title pages will be prepared in manuscript.

Place	Date	Hour	Summary of Events and Information	Remarks and references to Appendices
	July. 1917		Ref. 36.b. 1/40,000.	
LENS. (Trenches)	1st.		The Battalion carried out an attack on a portion of LENS. See Operation Orders and Report.	1.
LIEVIN.	2nd.		Battalion moved to BULLY GRENAY. Bathing. Battalion left by Bus on night 2/3rd July. 1917.	
RAIMBERT.	3rd,		Battalion arrived at RAIMBERT at 2.am.	
do	4th		Reorganising sections and platoons. Military Medals awarded to Ptes Sargeant and Swain for conspicuous bravery during the raid on CITE ST LAURENT. Near LENS. Lieut Col A.E.Fawcus M.C. commanded the Bn 16th from 4 of 10 the July 1917.	2.
do	5th		General Training. Musketry. Platoon Drill. "Platoon in the Attack" Special Classes for Lewis Gunners, Scouts and Signallers. Capt. H. POCHIN. M.C. attached to this Battalion as Second in Command.	
do	6th		General Training. G.O.C. Division issued a complimentary message for good work performed on operations of 1st July. 1917. Copy attached.	3.
do	7th		Battalion Route March in the morning. Firing on Range in afternoon.	
do	8th.		Brigade Church Parade ordered for 10 am. but cancelled owing to rain.	
do	9th.		General Training. Special Classes for Lewis Gunners, Signallers and Scouts.	
do	10th.		Inspection of Companies by Commanding Officer in the morning. Battalion marched to No.4. Training Area, in the afternoon.	
do	11th.		General Training. Battalion bathing and had clothes put through "Thresh" Disinfector.	
do	12th.		Battalion marched to BOIS de DAMES D.26.d.2.3 for training and shooting on range.	
do	13th.		Battalion marched to FOSSE 4, RAIMBERT, for training of Platoons and Companies in the attack. Military Medals awarded to Sgt. Hayes, Corps Wain. L/Cpl. J.H. Webb. Ptes Bailey, Allman and Pedley.	2.

Army Form C. 2118.

WAR DIARY
or
INTELLIGENCE SUMMARY.
(Erase heading not required.)

Instructions regarding War Diaries and Intelligence Summaries are contained in F. S. Regs., Part II. and the Staff Manual respectively. Title pages will be prepared in manuscript.

Place	Date	Hour	Summary of Events and Information	Remarks and references to Appendices
	July. 1917.			
RAIMBERT.	14th.		Battalion Sports in the afternoon. Concert in the evening. 2nd. Lt. Keeling joined from Hospital.	4.
do	15th.		Brigade Church Parade, at 11.am. at BURBURE. Distribution of Medals by First Army Commander, General, Sir. H.S. Horne. K.C.B.	
do	16th.		Battalion Rifle Meeting, commenced, Bar to MILITARY CROSS. awarded to Capt. F.E. WENGER. M.C. and MILITARY MEDAL to Pte. A.E. Worthington, by Field Marshall C.I.C. Ceremonial Drill n No. 4. Training Area at ALLOUAGNE. Battalion Rifle Meeting completed.	2, 5
do	17th.		Inspection of the 137th Infantry Brigade by the G.O.C. 46th Division, at BURBURE at 10-30.am.	
do	18th.		General Training. Special Classes for Lewis Gunners. Signallers and Scouts. 100 O.R.s and 4 Lewis Gun Teams shooting in Divisional Rifle Meeting at ROCOURT.	
do	19th.		General Training. 2nd. day of Divisional Rifle Meeting. Capt. E.A. Wilson rejoined from Hospital.	6
do	20th.		Inspection of the Battalion by the Commanding Officer. Box Respirator Drill.	
do	21st.		Church Services.	
do	22nd.		General Training, including Physical Drill Bayonet Fighting, & Bombing.	
do	23rd		do. B. & D" Coys on the Range at Fosse 4. "C" & "D" Coys. Bayonet Fighting Bombing, and Tactical Schemes.	
do	24th.		The 46th Division relieved the 6th Division in the Line. Battalion marched to VERQUIN, and was in Divisional Reserve. Arrived in Billets at 12 noon. Operation Orders attached.	
VERQUIN.	25th.		"B" & "D" Coys worked on Range at K.5.b.4.7. "A" & "C" Coys - General Training including Physical Drill. Musketry, and Platoons & Companies in the Attack.	7

Army Form C. 2118.

WAR DIARY
or
INTELLIGENCE SUMMARY.
(Erase heading not required.)

Instructions regarding War Diaries and Intelligence Summaries are contained in F.S. Regs., Part II. and the Staff Manual respectively. Title pages will be prepared in manuscript.

Place	Date	Hour	Summary of Events and Information	Remarks and references to Appendices
	July. 1917.			
VERQUIN.	27th.		"A" & "C" Coys worked on making range at K.5.b.4.7. "B" & "D" Coys - General Training, including Lectures on "Platoon in the Attack". Battalion - Bathing.	
do.	28th.		General Training, including Fire Control. Platoons and Companies in the Attack. Lectures by Company Commanders. B. & D. Coys Range working at K.4.b.4.7. Shooting Pool.	
do.	29th.		Church Parades. Range Range Shooting Pool	
do.	30th.		Firing Practices. Physical Drill. Platoon and Company Drills. N.C.O.s Classes under R.S.M. and P. & B.T. instructor.	
do.	31st.		General Training. Firing Practices. N.C.O.s classes under .R.S.M. and P. & B.T. instructor.	
FOOTBALL.				
22-7-17.		V. 1/6th South Staffs Regt. Result. Lost. 0. 3.		
23-7-17.		V. 1/5th South Staffs Regt. " Won. 1. 0		
30-7-17.		V. 1/6th North Staffs Regt. " Won. 5. 0		
31-7-17.		V. 31st Corps R.F.S. " Lost. 1. 2.		
CRICKET.				
23-7-17.		V. 1/5th South Staffs Regt. Result. Won. 5. Runs. Battalion Shooting Pool.		
28-7-17.		1st Prize. C.S.M. Maguire, "D" Coy. 2nd. " Pte. Wilkes. J. "B" Coy. 3rd Prize. L/Cpl. A. Peake. "B" "		

Lieut-Colonel
COMMANDING 1/6th NORTH STAFFORD REGT.

1/5th Battalion North Stafford Regiment.

SUMMARY of CASUALTIES & STRENGTH. for month of JULY, 1917.

	Officers.			Other Ranks.			Strength.	
	K.	W.	H.	Hosp.	K.	W.	M.	Hosp.	Officers.	Other Ranks.
For week ending 5-7-17.	2	6	6	1	16	42	116	4	25	614.
" " 12-7-17.	-	-	-	-	-	-	-	15	25	595
" " 19-7-17.	-	-	-	-	-	-	-	9	25	588
" " 26-7-17.	-	-	-	1	-	-	-	5	26	594
	2	6	3	2	16	42	116	33		

CONFIDENTIAL.

1/5th Battalion North Stafford Regiment.

To :- Headquarters,
      137th Infantry Brigade.

R E P O R T   O N   O P E R A T I O N S
of 1st JULY 1917.

Reference :- Trench Map LENS,36 C S.W.1 1/10,000
and 1st Field Survey Coy.R.E's LENS (2) No.2380.

1. At 9-30 p.m. on June 29th I received orders to prepare to attack and consolidate ACONITE Trench on the early morning of July 1st.

2. The frontage allotted to this Battalion was from road running E.N.E.from M.24.d.7.4. to the LIEVIN-LENS Road both inclusive. In addition to this Battalion I was allotted the following troops :- One company as 'moppers up', one company as carrying party and two companies in support (these were all found by the 1/6th South Staffs.Regt). Also one section of the 137th Brigade Machine Gun Coy. and one section of the 137th Brigade Trench Mortar Battery.
Owing to the low strengths in numbers companies were amalgamated into two platoons throughout both battalions.

3. ASSEMBLY. Owing to the enemy barrage on the night of the 28th having come down within 10 seconds of our barrage opening, it was decided to tape out a line 40 yards West and parallel to AGUE trench so as to have the waves well clear of our trench before the enemy barrage opened. This line was partially taped out under very difficult circumstances by LIEUT.THOMPSON of the 466th Field Coy.R.E's. Owing to the enemy still holding the northern end of AGUE Trench and houses in that vicinity it was not possible to complete the line in front of this section.
Company Commanders and Officers from the Attacking Battalion reconnoitred the ground on June 30th.
At 10-0 p.m. on the 29th the Battalion with its 'mopping up' parties moved from the cellars in LIEVIN to relieve the 6th SOUTH and 6th NORTH Battalions who were then holding the line.
The relief was arranged so that the companies moved in to battle formations with the first wave in AGUE Trench so that they could easily move out to the taped position one hour before zero.
Guides were to meet the Right company at SHRAPNEL PLATZ in LIEVIN and the three remaining companies at the CYCLIST BARRIER on the LIEVIN-LENS Road.
Owing to the following reasons great difficulty was experienced in (a) Carrying out the relief (b) Getting into the position of assembly :-
   (1) Heavy shelling of ABSALOM Trench and LENS-LIEVIN Road.
   (2) Intense darkness of the night.
   (3) The trenches ABCDE,ADULT & AGUE in which the Battalion was being placed before moving to the tape line were so destroyed by our artillery fire as to be unrecognisable in the dark.
   (4) Heavy rifle and machine-gun fire from the houses 40 yards west of the tape line and northern end of AGUE trench.
   (5) Casualties to guides.

I ordered CAPT.WENGER,M.C, was detailed to remain in Report Centre at N.19.a.10.30 and at 1-14 a.m. he informed me that my Right Company was completely lost and was down behind him on the left flank.
I ordered MAJOR GRAHAM to go forward at once and to get this company into position as quickly as possible. He came back shortly before zero and informed me that he had succeeded in doing so and that the whole line was in position with the exception of the Left Company

CONTINUED.

Left Company (continued)
who had not been able to get into AGUE Trench as this was found to be held by the enemy.

Owing to the delay in getting the companies into position the guides for the carrying parties did not reach their rendezvous until too late but CAPT. The HON. W. B. WROTTESLEY commanding this company, realising that unless he pushed forward he would be too late to advance, decided to push on without guides but unfortunately his company only reached the assembly point after the attack had had been launched

4. **PLAN OF ATTACK.** The frontage to be attacked was divided into four company sectors and each company was in two waves

   First Wave - in line of sections, in column, followed at 40 yards by 'moppers up' (half platoons per company in line of sections).
   Second Wave - Line of half platoons, in column, at 40 yards in rear of 'moppers up'.

This formation was adopted as the area to be attacked consisted of rows of houses and streets and it had not been possible in any way to reconnoitre by patrols the wire in front of our objective and it was considered advisable to keep the waves close up to each other so as to clear the enemy barrage at once. Also it had been reported on the previous evening that the enemy were shelling ACONITE Trench and as a hostile barrage might be expected during the advance forward small columns would have a better chance of threading their way amongst the houses.

Carrying parties (of half platoons per company) were ordered to follow 100 yards behind the second wave

5. **SIGNALLING ARRANGEMENTS.** A Report Centre with a telephone was *and two pigeons* established in a dugout at R.18.a.10.30. Companies were instructed to send reports by runners to this point and relays of signallers and runners were kept at this post. Except for a short period continuous telephonic communication was maintained with Battalion Headqrs. Signallers accompanied their companies but no chance was found for visual signalling.

Golden rain rockets were carried by the front wave to light as soon as the objective was gained and flares were carried to signal to contact aeroplanes

6. **MEDICAL ARRANGEMENTS.**
A Regimental Aid-post was established at N.24.c.70.60.
Evacuation of the wounded was carried out satisfactorily & expeditiously.

7. **NARRATIVE.**

At zero (3-47 a.m.) the attack was launched under cover of a creeping barrage.

The leading waves of the two Right Companies (with their 'moppers up') succeeded in reaching their objective. Some parties of their second wave were held up in severe house to house fighting and did not reach ACONITE Trench. This was due to the 'moppers up' losing their Officer and senior N.C.Os and the men, instead of clearing the houses, had evidently gone forward with the attacking wave. The attacking wave had gone close up to the Church and immediately they had passed the enemy commenced to come forth from the cellars.

The Left-centre company was held up almost immediately by machine-gun and rifle fire from the houses close to their starting point.

The Left company after after a severe fight captured AGUE Trench and a small trench running paralled to AGUE about 50 yards in front of it. They were held up for some time by machine guns in the houses in front and also by machine guns which fired from their left flank from about N.19.b.00.95.

At 3-15 a.m. golden rain rockets went up from ACONITE and showed that

CONTINUED.

showed that (continued)
objective had been gained..

At 4-45 a.m. a written message was brought down by a wounded man signed by the commanding Officers of the two Right companies saying that they had secured their ibjective and had pushed out patrols to houses about 100 yards to their front.

No news was received for some considerable time as to what had happened to our Left companies.

Information was slow in coming through but about 7-0 a.m. I realised that the Battalions on each of out flanks had failed to advance and in consequence our companies in ACONITE Trench were in a dangerous position. I telephoned to Brigade Headqrs and asked if these Battalions could not push forward and if so I would give them assistance by pushing in flank attacks with my support companies.

At about 7-0 a.m I saw considerable numbers of men firing at each other about CORNWALL Trench and a few minutes later our men in this area commenced to retire across the 'race course'. There was no artillery bombardment on either side and commenced with nothing but desultory rifle fire. When our men were in the open the enemy machine guns were turned upon them and many were seen to fall. The enemy appeared to follow our troops into 'No Man's Land' and then to return to their trenches.

Shortly after this I learnt that my two Left Companies were considerably dis-organised and were engaged in house to house fighting a short distance in front of AGUE Trench.

All the Officers of the Left-centre company had become casualties and only one Officer remained with the Left company. I then ordered CAPT.WENGER to go forward to re-organise the companies and to push forward to attack and get in touch with our companies in ACONITE Trench and to make a defensive line of posts on our left flank from the Church in N.19.b.20.30 to N.19.a.95.60. This Officer at once went forward and succeeded in driving the enemy into cellars around the Church. He left the 'mopping party' to clear these up. They were eventually cleared and eight prisoners & three machine guns captured (these brought our total prisoners up to 13 as 5 had been captured in house to house fighting previous to this.) CAPT.WENGER then pushed forward towards the Left of our objective and found the cellars about N.19.C.Central full of the enemy. These were driven out and large numbers of casualties were inflicted by Lewis-guns mounted to cover the exits. CAPT.WENGER was then wounded and command devolved upon LT.JONES of the 1/6th South Staffs.Regt.

CAPT.WENGER reported to me on his way down to the aid post and informed me how the situation stood When I had ordered CAPT.WENGER to go forward I had been compelled to send MAJOR GRAHAM to replace him at the report centre.

About 8-15 a.m. I ordered two platoons from the companies in support to push out along the houses on each of our flanks, one platoon to each flank, to reinforce our posts and take up a position to protect these flanks.

In the meantime my Left Company had advanced and reached a line N.19.b.25.50 to N.19.b.05.70 and had sent out a patrol along trench running N.W.from the latter point. This was found to be unoccupied as far as its junction with AMALGAM Trench but AMALGAM trench was held by the enemy and after some severe bombing encounters our patrol was forced to withdraw to post at N.19.b.05.70. Patrols were also sent forward but owing to the houses on this flank being levelled to the ground they were exposed to machine-gun fire from the left and were unable to advance owing to casualties being inflicted on them whenever an attempt was made. These posts were held until shortly after 1-0 a.m.2nd.Lieut STANIFORTH (the only remaining Officer on this flank) found that large numbers of the enemy were cutting in behind him from about the railway at N.19.a.73.60 and that they were also counter-attacking on his front, he thought it was necessary to withdraw to AGUE Trench and did so followed closely by the enemy

At 11-45 MAJOR GRAHAM informed me that we had a line of posts well established in the houses around the Church, from this stronghold to our left flank at N.19.b.05.70 and that on the right we had a post at N.19.c.90.70 and that patrols had been pushed out in front of

CONTINUED.

in front of (continued)

these to get forward as far as possible and try to get into touch with our right but no news could be received of these patrols. They appeared to have reached about N.19.d.50.90.

At 1-15 p.m. the enemy commenced barraging ACONITE, AGUE and ADULT trenches and counter-attacked in considerable force on our right flank from which large numbers of the enemy appeared from cellars in CITE DE MOULON and on our left from AMALGAM trench and railway at N.19.a.17.60. and also from our front trench by exits up to at 2-30 p.m. our posts had been driven back to AGUE trench and after severe fighting and repeated efforts on the part of our men to withstand their attack. I immediately ordered MAJOR GRAHAM to organise and send forward the remainder of the support companies and our men he could collect in AGUE and ADULT trenches to reinstate our line of posts and get into touch with my right companies in ACONITE. This counter-attack was launched about 3-30 p.m. but was not successful as the enemy brought up considerable forces and several machine-guns. The line made two attempts to get forward but was driven back on each occasion. On the last occasion MAJOR GRAHAM had apparently himself gone forward on the left flank to attempt to drive the enemy back and I regret to report that from this time there is no further news of this gallant Officer. Shortly after this and before I knew that MAJOR GRAHAM had gone forward I heard from MAJOR EVANS of the 1/6th South Staffs Regt who had gone to the forward report post to assist MAJOR GRAHAM in organising the support companies. He told me that "C" Coy of the 6th South could not be found but this company was shortly afterwards discovered near the junction of ABODE & AGNUS trenches. Owing to the broken nature of the ground and general confusion in the forward trenches it is evident that when this counter-attack was organised it was thought that this company had been included. As it was now too late to get this company up to MAJOR GRAHAM in time for the counter-attack which was at this time actually being launched and as by this time my troops were in a very tired condition, having mostly been fighting throughout the day in house to house fights and owing to the fact that my casualties of Officers had been very heavy I considered it advisable to wait for reinforcements before attacking again.

Owing to the situation on my flanks I did not deem it advisable to throw forward my whole supports earlier in the day.

Information took a considerable time to come through and by the time it reached the report centre the situation had changed. It was never the same for more than half-an-hour at a time as houses were continually changing hands. My flanks were considerably exposed and I thought it necessary to keep a small striking force in hand.

The cellars through many of the houses appeared to be connected and, notwithstanding careful observation having been kept, the enemy came through from both flanks. Our exposed flanks were from 500 to 600 yards in length and at right angles to our main line and had these been secured, I do not think there is any doubt we should have had little difficulty in holding ACONITE Trench with but few casualties.

All ranks fought with the greatest determination and large numbers of the enemy were killed. 13 prisoners of the 23rd Regiment and 3 machine-guns were captured. Although a large majority of the Officers employed became casualties the attack was carried on by the N.C.Os and in many cases Lance/Cpls took forward their part of the line with great dash. A series of house to house fights continued throughout the day, and I cannot speak too highly of the splendid spirit shown by the men in these attacks.

8. **BARRAGE.** The barrage was put down on a line parallel to AGUE trench and about 200 yards in advance of it. This was too far from our starting point and in consequence the enemy posts in the houses between the line and our starting point held part of our line up from at the commencement. The pace was 100 yards in 3 minutes and this appeared to be good. It appears to me that 13 pounders are not sufficiently heavy for house to house work as the enemy appeared in several places to remain ground in the houses during the barrage.

CONTINUED.

the barrage (continued). 5

9. GENERAL. I was relieved by Lieut-Colonel LAMOND 1/5th South Staffs Regt who was preparing with fresh troops to recapture the ground which we had won and lost and relieve our companies which were still holding out in ACONITE Trench.

1/5th Battalion North Stafford Regiment.

Appendix No.
July, 1917.

HONOURS AND AWARDS.

2nd Lieut. Charles John Beech MASEFIELD - MILITARY CROSS.

"For conspicuous gallantry and devotion to duty during a raid made on the enemy's trenches on 14th June, 1917, at CITE ST. LAURENT, near LENS.

2nd Lieut. Masefield led his Company with great dash and skill under a heavy Trench Mortar barrage. On entering the enemy's trenches 2nd Lieut. Masefield himself attacked a party of Germans, and succeeded in killing two at close quarters. Later, he successfully withdrew his Company, after inflicting heavy casualties on the enemy. 2nd Lieut. Masefield showed conspicuous gallantry throughout, and his leadership was splendid."

2nd Lieut. Basil GREEN - MILITARY CROSS.

"For conspicuous gallantry and devotion to duty during a raid made on the enemy's trenches on 14th June, 1917, at CITE ST. LAURENT, near LENS.

2nd Lieut. Green led his men into the enemy trenches and inflicted casualties, after which he penetrated into some cellars and dugouts on the far side of the trench, and inflicted further casualties.

On returning to our trenches 2nd Lieut. Green went out into No Mans Land with one man, and spent above one hour searching for wounded near the enemy's wire. He set a splendid example of courage to his men."

Capt. Felix Edward WENGER - BAR TO MILITARY CROSS.

"For conspicuous gallantry during the operations in LENS on the morning of July 1st, 1917.

This Officer was sent forward to rally a company which had come under heavy machine gun fire and in consequence had been held up. He re-organised the attack in this area and after some very severe hand-to-hand fighting from house to house succeeded in driving a large number of enemy and machine guns into a cellar where they were subsequently all killed, with the exception of eight, who were captured. Three machine guns were also taken.

Captain WENGER pushed forward his attack and succeeded in driving large numbers of the enemy from cellars and these were cut down as they ran by Lewis Guns which he had posted."

No. 200511 Sergt. William Austin HAYES - MILITARY MEDAL.

"For conspicuous gallantry during the operations in LENS on July 1st, 1917.

During the attack this N.C.O. displayed great bravery in leading a party forward to endeavour to silence a machine gun which was holding up his Company. This party was practically wiped out when he reached a point 15 yards from the gun and he was compelled to withdraw.

Later, he led a patrol forward in face of heavy fire from enemy snipers. He captured one sniper and silenced the others and despite severe casualties established a forward post. He was largely instrumental in the capture of eight of the enemy and three machine guns in a cellar. During the whole day of incessant house-to-house fighting he displayed the utmost courage and disregard for personal safety and set a splendid example to his men."

No. 201722 Pte. William Bailey - MILITARY MEDAL

"For conspicuous gallantry and devotion to duty during the operations in LENS on July 1st, 1917.

In house-to-house fighting this man did very valuable work on the morning of the 1st July, 1917. Notwithstanding heavy fire from snipers at close range he continued to work forward and personally accounted for three of the enemy.

He set a fine example of courage and determination to the rest of the men."

HONOURS & AWARDS. cont.

No.200390 Pte. Albert Edward WORTHINGTON   -   MILITARY MEDAL.

"For conspicuous gallantry and devotion to duty, during the operations in LENS on July 1st. 1917.

This man, a Stretcher Bearer, though wounded early in the attack, on the morning of the 1st July, refused to go to the aid post and remained with his Company attending to wounded under heavy fire.

Though unable, on account of his wound, to carry a stretcher, he carried men down on his back, and where possible, compelled enemy prisoners to assist him.

He was on duty continuously for twenty hours and rendered invaluable assistance and set a wonderful example of high courage and determination."

202055 Lance-Corporal Joseph Henry WEBB   -   MILITARY MEDAL.

"For conspicuous gallantry and good leadership during the operations in LENS on July 1st, 1917.

This N.C.O. was with a group of men which met with heavy opposition from the enemy; they were cut off from the rest of their Company and were left without Officer or senior N.C.Os. He re-organised them and again advanced. This party was then surrounded by the enemy but they succeeded in cutting their way through and back to the trench. He re-organised again and for the third time attacked and this time was able to assist in driving some of the enemy into a cellar where they were eventually captured or killed. In the evening he again advanced with a party under an officer. This Officer was killed and L/Cpl. Webb again assumed command."

No. 201156 Pte. Jack ALLMAN   -   MILITARY MEDAL.

"For conspicuous gallantry and devotion to duty during the operations in LENS on July 1st, 1917.

When the enemy heavily counter-attacked in the afternoon of the 1st July, 1917, he kept his Lewis Gun in action in the open for a considerable time, thereby drawing upon himself the fire of a large number of snipers and kept in action until the gun jammed and when, owing to largely superior numbers of the enemy he was compelled to withdraw, although shot through the leg, he brought his gun safely back to the trench."

No. 201545 Lance-Corporal Gilbert Clarence WAIN   -   MILITARY MEDAL.

"For conspicuous gallantry and devotion to duty during the operations in LENS on July 1st, 1917.

In the early morning of July 1st this N.C.O. collected a party of stragglers and cleared a row of houses and cellars, driving the enemy out into fire from our Lewis Guns. He afterwards twice went forward with patrols in endeavour to get into touch with a company which was cut off in ACONITE TRENCH.

Later, in the afternoon he controlled covering fire for a counter-attack and greatly assisted in keeping men together throughout the attack."

No. 1730 Pte. Harry PEDLEY   -   MILITARY MEDAL

"For conspicuous gallantry and devotion to duty during the operations in LENS on July 1st, 1917.

This man shewed great bravery and devotion to duty as a runner. He repeatedly carried messages through sniping and heavy shell-fire."

G.O.C. 137TH BRIGADE.
_____

Congratulate all ranks under your command
on their spirit and determination during the
operations of 28th June - 1st July.
The magnificent manner in which the 5TH NORTH
STAFFORDS reached their objective is beyond
all praise. Lieut-Colonel FAWCUS should be
specially congratulated on the efforts made.
I am proud of the STAFFORD BRIGADE.

                         (Sgd.) W.THWAITE,
3rd July 1917.   Major General.
                 Commdg. 46TH DIVISION.

The above letter which has been received
by the G.O.C. 137th Infantry Brigade is to be
communicated to all ranks of the Brigade.
The Brigadier directs me to add his very great
appreciation of the splendid fighting spirit
shown by all ranks during the recent operations.

                        (Sgd) C.ST.G.FULLBROOK LEGGATT.
7th July 1917.   Capt. Brigade Major
                        137TH INFANTRY BRIGADE.

SECRET.   COPY NO. _____

1/5TH BATTN. PRINCE OF WALES'S (NORTH STAFFORDSHIRE REGT).

OPERATION   ORDER   No.71.

Reference :- Sheets :-   36C.N.W. 1/20,000
                         36B.N.E. 1/20,000
----

1. Gas cylinders will be installed in the HULLUCH front between
   Boyaus 66 and 72, commencing night of 25/26th inst., and to be
   completed on the night of 1st/2nd prox.

2. Carrying parties will be found tonight as per table attached.

3. Lorries will be provided as per attached table.

4. Two copies of 'Standing orders for the carrying of gas cylinders'
   are issued to each company. A copy of this is to be handed
   to the Officer in charge of each party.

5. Acknowledge.

                                              E.A.WILSON,
                                         Captain & Adjutant
                                      1/5th Battn.North Staffs.Regt.

                   ----- ooOoo -------

Copies issued to :-
    No. 1. --------- Commanding Officer.
        2 --------- 2nd. in Command.
        3 --------- H.Q., 137 Infantry Brigade.
        4/7 -------- Os.C.Companies.
        8. --------- Quartermaster.
        9. --------- File.
        10. -------- War Diary.

SECRET.   COPY NO 11

1/5TH NORTH STAFFORDSHIRE REGIMENT

OPERATION ORDERS. No.57. 24-7-17.

Reference :- FRANCE, Sheet 36B, 1/40,000

1. **INFORMATION.** The 46th Division will relieve the 6th Division in the line tomorrow. The 137th Infantry Brigade will be in Divisional Reserve in the VAUDRICOURT Area.

2. **INTENTION.** The Battalion will march to VERQUIN tomorrow.

3. **INSTRUCTIONS.**

    (a) The Battalion will parade on the parade ground.
    Time :- 7-0 a.m.
    Route :- RAIMBERT, AUCHEL, C.28.d.7.6., C.30.d.2.4., J.2.a.95.95., BOIS-DES-DAMES, HESDIGNEUL and VERQUIN.

    (b) Dress :- Field Service Marching Order, water-bottles full. Haversack rations will be carried also box respirators and P.H.Helmets. Steel helmets to be strapped to the valises.

    (c) Transport. The transport will march independently under the Transport Officer.
    Starting point :- Transport Lines. Time :- 8-0 a.m.
    Route :- AUCHEL, LOZINGHEM, MARLES-LES-MINES, LAPUGNOY, LABEUVRIERE, E.7.c.65.40., FOUQUEREUIL, HESDIGNEUL and VERQUIN

    (D). The Billeting Party will meet the Battalion at K.4.b.25.65.

    (e) Mess boxes and valises will be collected from Company Headqrs., at 6-15 a.m.

    (f) All billets must be left scrupulously clean.

    (g) Strict march discipline will be maintained.

    (h) One sanitary man per company will stay behind to ensure that latrines are left clean. These men will march with the Transport and will report to the Transport Officer at 7-45 a.m.

                                                E.A.WILSON,
                                                Captain & Adjutant.

Copies issued as under :-
    Copy No.1 .... Commanding Officer.
    "   " 2 .... Major H.Pochin.
    " Nos. 3 to 6 .. O.C.Companies.
    " No.7 .... Transport Officer.
    "   " 8 .... Medical Officer.
    "   " 9 .... R.S.M.
    "   " 10 .... File.
    " Nos 11 & 12 . War Diary.

1631

1. Original.

1/5th Battalion North Staffordshire Regiment

War Diary

For

the month of August

1917.

ORIGINAL

1/5th North Staffs Regt
Sheet 1

Army Form C. 2118.

WAR DIARY
or
INTELLIGENCE SUMMARY.
(Erase heading not required.)

Instructions regarding War Diaries and Intelligence Summaries are contained in F. S. Regs., Part II. and the Staff Manual respectively. Title pages will be prepared in manuscript.

Place	Date	Hour	Summary of Events and Information	Remarks and references to Appendices
	August 1917.		(Map. ref. Sheet. 36.b. 1/40,000 and 36.c. N.W. 1/20,000)	
VIGNETTE.	1st.		General Training. Including Range Practices, Bombing, Bayonet Fighting, and Musketry.	
do	2nd.		do	
do	3rd.		Battalion Paraded in fighting order at 10 HOPPY-les-HUIT. Batt'n in Brigade Reserve, under orders to be ready to move at two hours notice.	No. 1.
HOPPY-les-PRES.	4th.		General Training. Including Special Classes for Lewis Gunners, Scouts, Signallers &c. Results of Rifle Competition: C.S.M. Maguire. T. 145 Pts. L/Cpl. Creed. 126 Pts.	
do	5th.		Pte. Kelly 126 Pts. "B" Company received a holiday on 6-8-17, for being best Company at Shooting. Captain R.W. Harris joins Battalion from the Base.	
do	6th.		Voluntary Church Parades. Lectures to Officers on Patrols and Intelligence.	
do	7th.		Battalion Bathing. Route marches by "A" "B" & "C" Coys.	
do	8th.		Battalion relieved 1/5th Bn. North Stafford Regiment., in the FRENCH Sector (Left Brigade Subsector). Relief complete 12-30 a.m. 9th August 1917. During relief between 11-20 p.m. and 12-20 a.m., about 50 casualties to 5th last Support Coys N.St.R. - No casualties.	No. 2
TRENCHES.	9th.		Situation Normal. "C" Coy v/Dborne Pos. Spent hrs during day, owing to our Heavy Artillery cutting wire, in front of enemy trenches between H.19.a.3.7. and H.19.c.5.5. "A" Coy. reports front line trench again at dusk. Enemy sent out a very few recognoitring patrols in front of posts, and by "A" Coy. to locate pipe which had been put down during the day. Hostile Artillery active intervals during the day.	
	10th.		Inter-Company relief. "C" & "D" Coy relieved "A" & "B" respectively. Wire cutting carried out as on previous day. Considerable aerial activity on both sides. Enemy Artillery fairly active, especially at 7-15 p.m.	

Army Form C. 2118.

1/5 North Staff Regt
Sheet 2.

WAR DIARY
or
INTELLIGENCE SUMMARY.
(Erase heading not required.)

Instructions regarding War Diaries and Intelligence Summaries are contained in F. S. Regs., Part II. and the Staff Manual respectively. Title pages will be prepared in manuscript.

Place	Date	Hour	Summary of Events and Information	Remarks and references to Appendices
TRENCHES.	10th.	4-0 a.m.	Battalion on our left (5th Sherwoods) called for Artillery Support, from Group covering this Sector, owing to heavy enemy barrage. Enemy's barrage did not affect our left Companies. Enemy Artillery fairly active over subsector, especially between 11-15.a.m. and 12-30.p.m. 2nd. Lieut. R.C. Wood and 2nd. Lt. T.J.H. Malone joined Battalion from Base.	No 3
do	11th		Situation normal. The Battalion was relieved by the 1/6th Bn. North Stafford Regt. Relief complete about 2-30.a.m. 12th August. Battalion marched to MAZINGARBE, and was in Brigade Support, leaving one Company in TENTH AVENUE in close Support.	
MAZINGARBE.	12th.		Battalion in Brigade Support. Bathing and Cleaning up.	No 4
do	13th.		2 hours parade under Company Commanders. "A" Company relieved "B" Coy in close support.	
do	14th.		"B" Coy Bathing. Battalion moved at 8.p.m. to the trenches in relief of the 1/6th Bn. North Stafford Regiment. Relief complete at 12. midnight.	No 5
TRENCHES.	15th.	4-25.am.	Canadian Attack. No. 4 Coy Special R.E. projected Smoke for one hour on Battalion front. Retaliation fairly heavy. Battalion Headquarters shelled, and H.Q. moved into dug out. Intermittent shelling on front of Right Coy from 8-30.pm to 9-30.pm. Large parties of the enemy were seen advancing across the open to form up for counter-attack on Canadian front. Machine & Lewis Gun, and Rifle fire were opened on them, causing them many casualties. Quiet night.	No 5a
do	16th		Raid carried out by 1/5th Leics ter Regiment on our Battalion front. Enemy retaliated on our front line from about midnight 16th/17th to 1.am. 17th August 1917. 2nd. Lieut. Feeston & Oulton joined Battalion from the Base.	5 b
do	17th		Situation normal. Battalion relieved by 1/6th North Stafford Regiment and Proceeded by Companies independantly to billets in NOEUX-les-MINES. arriving about 3.am. 18th. Aug. 1917.	No 6
NOEUX-les-MINES.	18th		Battalion in Brigade Reserve.— Cleaning up.	
do	19th		do do Voluntary Church Parades and Bathing.	

Army Form C.2118.

1/5 North Staff Regt   Sheet 3

WAR DIARY
or
INTELLIGENCE SUMMARY.
(Erase heading not required.)

Instructions regarding War Diaries and Intelligence
Summaries are contained in F.S. Regs., Part II.
and the Staff Manual respectively. Title pages
will be prepared in manuscript.

Place	Date	Hour	Summary of Events and Information	Remarks and references to Appendices
PHILO-LES-MINES.	20th.		General Training, including Physical Drill, Bayonet Fighting, Bombing, & Musketry. 2nd. Lieut. G.M. Humphrey joined Battalion from the Base.	
do	21st.		Battalion relieved the 1/6th Bn. North Stafford Regiment in the Left Subsector. Relief complete about 1.a.m. 22nd. Aug. 1917.	No. 1
TRENCHES.	22nd.		Situation normal. Enemy shelled intermittently during morning on Right Coy Front. 2nd. Lieuts. J.W. Profitt and A. Hill, joined Battalion from the Base.	
do	23rd.		Situation normal. Quiet Day.	
do	24th.		Raids on the enemy's trenches carried out by the Battalion. See attached report.	No. 2
do	25th.		Battalion was relieved in the trenches by 1/6th Bn. North Stafford Regiment, and marched to billets in FOUQUIERES-LES-BÉTHUNE, arriving about 5.a.m. 26th August. 1917.	No. 3
NOEUX-LES-MINES.	26th.		Battalion in Divisional Reserve. Battalion marched to VERQUIN, arriving about 3.p.m. 2nd. Lieuts. A. Beard, R. Hough, and J.H. Garbett, joined the Battalion from the Base.	No. 4
VERQUIN.	27th.		Bathing and Cleaning up.	
do	28th.		General Training, including Physical Drill, Bayonet Fighting, Bombing, Musketry, Platoon and Company Drill.	
do	29th.		Battalion parade for Range Practices. Capt. F.L. Yeagen joined Battn from Base (Wd. 1-7-17)	
do	30th.		General Training, including "Platoons in the Attack"	
do	31st.		General Training, Commanding Officers Inspection of the Battalion in Field Service Marching Order	

H. Parker Major

by Lieut-Colonel,
Commanding 1/5th Bn. North Stafford Regiment.

Army Form C. 2118.

WAR DIARY
or
INTELLIGENCE SUMMARY.

1/5 North Staff Regt Sheet 4.

(Erase heading not required.)

Instructions regarding War Diaries and Intelligence Summaries are contained in F. S. Regs., Part II. and the Staff Manual respectively. Title pages will be prepared in manuscript.

Place	Date	Hour	Summary of Events and Information	Remarks and references to Appendices

CASUALTIES.

	Officers.			Other Ranks.				STRENGTH.	
	Killed.	Wounded.	Missg.	Hosp.	K.	W.	M.	Hosp.	Officers.	O.Ranks
For week ending 2nd. Aug.'17.	-	-	-	-	-	-	-	7	26	597
do 9th " "	-	-	-	1	-	-	-	6	28	596
do 16th " "	-	-	-	1	-	2	-	5	31	604
do 23rd " "	-	-	-	-	-	-	-	6	35	608
do 30th " "	-	-	-	1	-	2	-	1	39	622
	-	-	-	3	-	4	-	25		

SECRET   COPY No. 13

                1/5th Battalion North Stafford Regt.

                O P E R A T I O N   O R D E R S   No. 58.   1-6-17.
                ===

Reference :- SHEET , Sheet 36 N. 1, 2, 3

1. INFORMATION
                        The 137th Infantry Brigade will relieve
                the 138th Brigade in the Right Brigade (EPEHY) Sector
                on the 2/3rd August. The Battalion will be in
                Divisional Reserve at ROUX AU MINEU.

2. INTENTION
                        The Battalion will march to ROUX AU
                MINEU to-morrow. Transport and Quartermaster's Stores
                will move to LABOURSE.

3. INSTRUCTIONS
                (a) The Battalion will parade on the Parade Ground.
                    Time 10.0.a.m.
                (b) Dress Field Service Marching Order. Steel Helmets
                    to be strapped to valises.
                (c) Transport. The transport (less Cookers and S.A.A.
                    Limbers, which will go with the Battalion) and
                    Quartermaster Stores will move independently under
                    the Transport Officer.
                    Time to be notified later.
                (d) A Billeting party of 1 N.C.O. per Company, 1 per
                    Signal Section and 1 cyclist will report to Lieut-
                    J.Keeling at Orderly Room at 7.0.a.m.
                (e) Valises must be sent to Q.M.Stores by 8.0.a.m.,
                    Mess Boxes by 9.0.a.m.
                (f) All billets must be left scrupulously clean.
                (g) Clearance Certificates for all billets must be sent
                    to Orderly Room by 8.30.a.m.
                (h) Strict march discipline will be maintained

                                        E.A.SILSON,
                                            Captain & Adjutant.

Copies issued by runner at   a.m. -
            Copy No.1   Commanding Officer
                 "   2   Major H.Pochin, D.S.O.
                 "   3 & 6   O.C. Companies
                 "   7   Transport Officer
                 "   8   Quartermaster
                 "   9   Medical Officer
                 " 10   R.S.M.
                 " 11   File
                 " 12 & 13   War Diary.

SECRET.
                                                                            COPY No. 13

1/5th Battalion North Stafford Regiment.

                                                                            2-8-17.

AMENDMENT TO OPERATION ORDER No.58.

Para 1.   Line 3   for 2nd/3rd August
                             read 3rd/4th August.

Para 3.   (a)   Time should read 10-30 a.m.

do   (d)   The Billeting Party will report to 2nd.Lt.C.R.KRELL
                             at Orderly Room at 8-30 a.m.

                                                                    E.A.WILSON,
                                                         Captain & Adjutant.

Copies issued by runner as under :-
    Copy No.1.   Commanding Officer.
     "   " 2.   Major R.Rochin, M.C.
     " Nos.3 to 6.   Os.C.Companies.
     " No.7.   Transport Officer.
     "   " 8.   Quartermaster.
     "   " 9.   Medical Officer.
     "   " 10.

SECRET.   (2)   NOT TO BE TAKEN INTO
                THE FRONT LINE TRENCHES.

1/5th Battalion NORTH STAFFORD REGIMENT.

OPERATION ORDER NO. 59.

(Reference Sheet 36.b. 1/40,000 and 36.c.N.E. 1/20,000)

---

1. **INTENTION.** (a). The Battalion will relieve the 1/6th North Staffs Regiment in the Left Subsector on the night of 7th August 1917.

   (b). Dispositions.
   "A" Company. - Right Coy. In Trenches 70 -72.
   "B" Coy & ½ Platoon
   & 1. Lewis Gun "D" Coy. Left Company.
   In trenches 73 - VERMELLES - HULLUCH Rd (excl

   "C" Company. - Right Support Company.

   "D" Company (Less ½ Platoon & 1. L.G.) - Left Support Coy.

   [margin notes: Bn. subsects / H.19.a.35-60 / to G.12.d.75.08]

2. **INSTRUCTIONS.** (a). The Battalion will move off by Platoons at 200 yds distance.
   (b). Time :- 5.pm.
   (c). Route :- Camp. - Cross Roads L.15.c.15.85. - Cross Rds. L.22.d.8.6. - MAZINGARBE CHURCH - Cross Roads L.23.b.3.7. - Road Junction L.24.a.8.8. - to billets in houses about G.20.c.
   (d). Meal. A hot meal will be served in billets.
   (e). Battalion will move from billets at G.20.c. by Platoons at 200 yds distance
   (f). Time :- 9.pm.
   (g). Route.:- Staked line from Railway Crossing at PUITS No.3. to LONE TRENCH.
   (h) Guides from 1/6th North Staffs Regt will be waiting for Platoons in LONE TRENCH, 50 yds EAST of junction of Staked line and Trench at 9-30.pm.
   (i) Order of march :- "A", "B", "C", "D" Coys, H.Qrs. on leaving PHILOSOPHE, the half Platoon of "D" Coy, detailed for post in CARDIFF SAP, will march with "B" Company.
   (j) Dress :- Fighting Order, waterproof sheets, Mess Tins, Water-bottles full, and rations for the 8th.
   (k) Packs. Packs will be left at the Q.M.Stores in camp, labelled with No. Rank, Name, & Company. Time :- 3.pm. The Transport Officer will arrange to collect these Packs and take them to LABOURSE.
   (l) Advance Party. One officer per Company, One N.C.O per Platoon, Signal Section, Lewis Gun Officer, One Lewis Gun N.C.O.per Company, R.S.M. and Pioneer Sergeant will proceed to the trenches to take over. To commence leaving here at 3.pm. Guides will meet this party at 50 yds EAST of the junction of LONE TRENCH & Staked line, at 5-30.pm.
   (m). EAST of PHILOSOPHE, parties must not be more than 2 at 100 yds distance.
   (n). Officers valises and Mess Boxes will be at Q.M.Stores at 5.pm. The Transport Officer will arrange to take up Officers' Trench Mess Boxes (to be as small as possible) these to be at Q.M. Stores at 5.pm.
   (o). Cooking Utensils will be taken over from 1/6th North Stafford Regiment.
   (p). The Transport Officer will detail two water-duty men to go up with Headquarters, and remain there for tour.

continued.

(q). Lewis Gun Magazines and five panniers per gun will be carried by Lewis Gunners from PHILOSOPHE to trenches. Transport Officer will arrange for transport of these to PHILOSOPHE.
The remaining magazines will be handed over to the 6th North Stafford Regt. by Transport Officer, they will be at Quartermasters Stores by 3. p.m.

(r). WORKING PARTIES. During the tour in the trenches the following parties will report to R.E.Officer at Battalion Advanced Headquarters in tunnel :-

  Left Support Company - 1 N.C.O. & 7 men - 1.30 pm. to 9.30pm.

  Right " " 1 N.C.O. & 7 men - 9.30 pm. to 5.30 am.

  Right " " 1 N.C.O. & 7 men - 5.30 am. to 1.30 pm.

(s) TUNNEL WARDENS. A party of 1 N.C.O and 6 men will be appointed to act as tunnel wardens, this party will consist of the Pioneer Corporal , two men each from "A" and "B" Companies and one man each from "C" and "D" Companies, they will be billeted in dugout at   . Standing Orders for Tunnels have been issued to N.C.O. i/c.

(u). Relief complete to be wired to Battalion Headquarters by word "NASTY".

(v). WHALE OIL is to be used by all ranks before proceeding to the trenches.

6th August 1917.   (sd) E.A.WILSON,
              Captain & Adjutant,
           1/5th Bn. North Staffs. Regiment.

SECRET.   Copy No.

1/5th Bn. North Staffordshire Regt.

OPERATION ORDER No.60.

Reference :- 36a. 1/40,000 and 36C. N.E. 1/20,000.

1. **INTENTION.**
   (a) The Battalion will be relieved by the 1/6th North Staffs. Regt. on the night of the 11/12th August.
   (b) The Battalion, less "B" Company will be in Brigade reserve Support in MAZINGARBE and must be prepared to move at half-an-hours notice.
   (c) "B" Company will be in BULLOCH TUNNEL, Hqrs. in Advanced Battalion Headquarters.
   "B" Company will be under orders of Bde. H.Q. for work and tactically for the defence of the QUADRILATERAL under O.C. 6th North.

2. **INSTRUCTIONS.**
   (a) On relief the Battalion, less "B" Company will proceed by platoons to billets in MAZINGARBE and "B" Company to dugouts in BULLOCH TUNNEL.
   (b) ADVANCE PARTY. 2nd Lieut. V.E.Hammersley, 1 N.C.O. 1 Cook & 1 Servant per Company, less "B" Company, will report to H.Q. at 2.30 pm. to proceed to H.Q. 6th South to take over billets.
   2nd Lieut. V.E.Hammersley will report to Town Major.
   "A" Company will also send Bde. Guard & Quarter Guard each 1 N.C.O. and 3 men.
   (c) Mess boxes, stores etc. will be sent down to HAY DUMP by 9.0 p.m.
   (d) Rations for "B" Company will be brought upon 6th North truck. O.C."B" Company will detail a N.C.O. to meet same at HAY DUMP at 9.15 p.m.
   Transport Officer will detail a man to come up with these rations and hand them over to the N.C.O. of "B" Company.
   (e) A party consisting of :-
       1 Cook per Company (less "B" Company)
       1 Servant per Coy. (do.)
       2 Servants - Hdqrs.
   will report to the Provo Sergt. at HAY DUMP at 9.15 p.m to push trucks back to PHILOSOPHE.
   (f) Lewis Gun Magazine Boxes will be sent to Advanced Bn. Headqrs. and handed to a N.C.O. who will be detailed by O.C. "B" Company. This N.C.O. will be at Adv. Bn. H.Q. before 3.0 p.m.
   (g) Lewis Gun Magazines. Eight magazines per gun of "A" "C" "D" Companies will be handed over as per para (f). Twelve magazines per gun will be carried out by the teams. The remainder will be handed over to the incoming companies of the 6th North, separate receipts being taken for these.
   (h) Transport Officer will arrange to collect stores from KINGSBRIDGE STATION.
   (j) List of Stores to be handed over will be sent to Orderly Room by 9.0 p.m.
   (k) After relief Os.C. "A" "C" & "D" Companies will report to Headquarters on the way down.
   O.C. "B" Company will 'phone word APPLE for relief complete.
   (l) Os.C. Companies will report as soon as their Coys. are in billets.

                                      E.A.WILSON,
                                      Captain & Adjutant,
                                      1/5th North Staffs.Regt..

Copies issued by runner at

S E C R E T.   (µ)   Copy No. 11

1/5th Battalion North Staffordshire Regiment.

OPERATION ORDER. No.61.
13th August 1917.

1. "A" Company will relieve "B" Company in CLOSE SUPPORT in TENTH AVENUE tonight.
   Company Headquarters at G.17.b.80.70.

2. Lewis Gun Drums will be taken over but not Lewis Guns.

3. Other details to be arranged between Company Commanders.

4. Relief must be complete by 9-45 p.m. "B" Coy. will report to Orderly Room on arrival in the huts.

5. Rations for the 14th inst will be carried by "A" Coy.

F.A.WILSON,
Captain & Adjutant,
1/5th Bn.North Staffs.Regt.

Issued at 11-30 a.m. to :-
```
Copy No.1.   ----------  Commanding Officer.
  "  No.2.   ----------  Major H.Jochim. .C.
  "  Nos. 3-6 ---------  O's.C.Companies.
  "  No. 7.  ----------  Quartermaster.
  "  No. 8.  ----------  137th Infantry Brigade.
  "  No. 9.  ----------  1/6th Bn.North Staffs.Regt.
  "  Nos. 10-11 -------  War Diary.
  "  No.12.  ----------  File.
  "  No.13.  ----------  Lewis Gun Officer.
  "  No.14.  ----------  R.S.M.
```

Copies to :-

No. 1. Commanding Officer.
" 2. Major H.Joshir V.C.
" 3/6. O.C. Companies
" 7. Transport Officer & Quartermaster.
" 8. Lewis Gun Officer.
" 9. N.C.O. i/c. Signals.
" 10. R.S.M.
" 11/12. War Diary.
" 13. File.
" 14. 137th Infantry Bde.
" 15. 1/5th North Staffs.Regt..

SECRET (5) NOT TO BE TAKEN INTO THE
                FRONT LINE TRENCHES.

Copy No. 14

1/5th Battalion North Stafford Regiment.

OPERATION ORDER No.62

Reference :- Sheet 36B, 1/40,000 and 36C, N.E. 1/20,000

1. **INTENTION.** (a) The Battalion will relieve the 1/6th North Staffs.Regt
   in the Left Subsector on the night of 14th August 1917
   (b) Dispositions.
   "C" Coy. - Right Coy.
   "D" Coy (and ½ Platoon & 1 L.G. of "B") - Left Coy.
   "A" Coy - Right Support Coy.
   "B" Coy.(less ½ Pltn.& 1 L.G.) - Left Support Coy.
   The Northern Post of "D" Company in CARDIFF C.P
   will be found by the half platoon and one Lewis Gun
   of "B" Coy. attached to "D" Company.

2. **INSTRUCTIONS.**
   (a). The Battalion will move off by platoons at 100 yards
        distance.
   (b) Time :- 8-0 p.m.
   (c). Order of march :- "C","D", "H.Qrs" and "B".
   (d). Meal :- A hot meal will be served in billets at 7-0 p
   (e). Route.
        "C" Coy :- LONE TRENCH & ESSEX LANE to front line.
        "D" Coy :- LONE TRENCH, TENTH AVENUE and HAY DUMP
                   entrance to TUNNEL.
        "B" Coy :- LONE TRENCH, TENTH AVENUE, HAY LANE to
                   Reserve trench.
        "A" Coy :- HAY LANE & Reserve Trench.
   (f). Dress
        Fighting order, waterproof sheets, mess tins,
        water bottles filled and rations for the 15th.
   (g). Packs will be left at the Q.M.Stores in the Camp
        labelled with Regtl.No, rank & name and Company., by
        12-0 noon.
        Transport Officer will arrange to collect these and
        take them to LAPOURSE.
   (h). Advance Party consisting of one Officer per Company.
        Lewis Gun Officer, one N.C.O. per platoon. R.S.M.,
        PIONEER Sergt and Battn.Signal Section will proceed to
        the trenches to take over, commencing to leave the
        Camp at 5-0 p.m.
        East of PHILOSOPHE parties will not be larger than
        two at 100 yards distance during daylight.
   (j). Officers valises and mess-boxes will be at the
        Q.M.Stores by 6-0 p.m.
        Mess boxes etc., for the trenches will be at the
        Stores by ~~6-30 p.m.~~ 7-30 PM.
   (l). Cooking utensils will be taken over from the 6th NORTH
        STAFFS.Regt.
   (m). The Transport Officer will detail two water-duty men
        to go up to the trenches and remain there for the tour
   (n). **WORKING PARTIES.**
        During the tour in the trenches the following parties
        will report to R.E.Officer at Battalion Advanced
        Headquarters in tunnel :-
        Left Support Coy. - 1 N.C.O. & 7 men - 1-30 p.m. to
                                               9-30 p.m.
        Right   "   " - 1 N.C.O. & 7 men - 9-30 p.m. to
                                               5-30 am
        Right   "   " - 1 N.C.O. & 7 men - 5-30 am to
                                               1-30 p.m.

CONTINUED.

(o). TUNNEL WARDENS. A party of 1 N.C.O. and 6 men will be appointed to act as tunnel wardens, this party will consist of the Pioneer Corporal, two men each from "A" and "B" Companies, and one each from C & D Coys. Standing orders for Tunnels have been issued to N.C.O. in charge.

(p). WHALE OIL. is to be used by all ranks before proceeding to the trenches.

(r). Relief Complete to be wired to Battalion Headquarters in BAB Code.

(s). LEWIS GUN MAGAZINES.
"B", "C" & "D" Companies take up 12 magazines per gun and take over the remainder from the 6th NORTH STAFFS.REGT. "A" Company will take all the magazines they have with them to their positions in the Reserve Line.

                                                  (sd) E.A.WILSON,
                                                  Captain & Adjutant,
                                        1/5th Bn.North Staffs.Regiment.

Copies issued at 9.30 p.m. to :-

    Copy No. 1. --------- Commanding Officer
    "   " 2. --------- Major H.Pochin, M.C.
    " Nos 3-6. --------- Os.C.Companies.
    " No. 7. --------- T.O. and Q.M.
    "   " 8. --------- Lewis Gun Officer.
    "   " 9. --------- Medical Officer.
    "   " 10. --------- 137th Infantry Brigade.
    "   " 11. --------- O.C. 1/6th North Staffs.Regt.
    "   " 12. --------- N.C.O. i/c Signals.
    "   " 13. --------- File.
    "   " 14. --------- R.S.M.
    "   " 15-16 ------- War Diary.

1/5th Battalion North Stafford Regiment.

(S.a)

To. O.C. "C" Coy.

Other Companies for information.

ZERO Hour 4-25.am. tomorrow, 15th inst.

Withdraw your whole Company to RESERVE LINE, so as to be under cover by above hour.

Your Headquarters will be with "A" Coy.

You will leave your Company Signallers in your H.Qrs in SUPPORT LINE for use of T.M. Battery. Special Coy R.E. are sending off smoke by BOYAU 67 - 71 and 78.

You will remain in Reserve Line until after the 5th Leicesters raid on the night of 15/16th, but as soon as raid is over, and raiders are clear of communication trenches on their way back here, you will reoccupy normal positions.

You will have one Platoon ready to move forward, as a battle patrol, in case enemy returns. In case patrol moves its first objective will be enemy's front line, between HICKS ALLEY & HEMLOCK ALLEY, and second objective, enemy's support line between above C.T.s. The First Patrol will be supported by your remaining Platoons.

"A" Coy will move off behind you.

(sd).A.E.F. Fawcus.
Lt-Col,
Commanding 1/5th Bn. North Stafford Regt.

14-8-17.

1/5th Bn. North Stafford Regiment.

To. Officers Commanding.

All Companies.

The following tunnels and communication trenches are to be clear of all troops, by 9.pm. to allow the 1/5th Leicester Regt's raiding party to move to their positions.

Dump. Drive and BULLOCK TUNNELS, SOUTH EXIT, ESSEX LANE. TENTH AVENUE and SUPPORT LINE.

Zero hour will be 11-45.pm. 15th inst. Raiders will be recalled at Zero plus 40 minutes.

Companies will assist in every way possible the raiders both on their inwards and outward journeys. "A" "B" & "D" Coy's posts will be normal. "C" Coy will remain in the RESERVE LINE until Raiders are all clear, when they will resume their normal positions in the line.

O.C. "C" Coy will detail a party of 1. N.C.O. and 12 O.R.s to report to 2/Lieut. Brooks 5th Leicester Regt. at 8-30.pm. at the Headquarters in the Reserve Line.

O.C. "D" Coy will provide 4 bombers as escort to Machine Guns which are covering the Left flank of the raiders in CRATER at H.13.c.40.65. time and place will be notified later.

Pass-word will be PEPPER.
Acknowledge.

(sd). T.A. WILSON.
Captain & Adjutant.
1/5th Bn. North Staffs Regt.

15-8-17.

1/5th Battalion North Stafford Regiment.

To:- Officers Commanding

ALL COMPANIES.
----

1. No. 4 Special Company will in addition to the THERMITE BOMBS, fire GAS BOMBS on to HULLUCH TRENCH, between HEMLOCK and HALIFAX ALLEYS. Position of Mortar about H.13.a.05.10.

2. About half these bombs will be fired at ZERO, and the others at ZERO plus 30. minutes.

3. From ZERO minus 5, until the ALL CLEAR, the following precautions will be taken:-
   (a). Gas Blankets at exits of HULLUCH TUNNEL, east of Coy H.Qrs G.18.b.9.0, except at Southern Exit H.13.c.15.75. will be lowered.
   (b). All men East of old SUPPORT LINE, and between Southern shaft, HULLUCH TUNNEL and BOYAU 76 will wear Box Respirators from ZERO minus 5 to ALL CLEAR.
   (c). Lieut. J.T. Macnamee O.C. "F" Section in charge of the operation will detail an Officer to report to Left Coy H.Qrs Left Subsector, HULLUCH section, G. 18.b.9.0, when ALL CLEAR.
   O.C. "B" Coy will send the ALL CLEAR to Battalion Headquarters by runner.

4. ZERO will be 11-45.p. tonight. 16th inst.
5. Counter sign will be PEPPER.
6. Instructions contained in my A.F. 30 dated 14-8-17, will hold good for tonight, with the following exceptions:-
   (a) O.C. "C" Coy will not detail party to report to 2/Lt. Brooke
   (b) O.C. "B" Coy will provide the four Bombers as escort to the Machine Guns.

7. Acknowledge.

(sd). E.A. WILSON.

Capt. and Adjutant.

16-8-17.

1/5th Br. North Stafford Regt.

SECRET.

1/6TH BN. NORTH STAFFORD REGT.

INFORMATION.

(a) [illegible]

(b) [illegible]

INSTRUCTIONS.

[illegible]

P.T.O.

SECRET.

Copy No. 16

NOT TO BE TAKEN INTO THE
FRONT LINE TRENCHES.

1/5TH BATTALION NORTH STAFFORDSHIRE REGIMENT.

RELIEF ORDER No.64.

(Reference Sheet 36B,1/40,000 and 36C N.E. 1/20,000)

1. **INTENTION.** (a). The Battalion will relieve the 1/6th NORTH STAFFS Regt., in the Left Subsector on the night of 21st/22nd August.
   (b). Dispositions:-
   "A" Company --- Right Company.
   "B" Company (and ½ platoon & 1 Lewis Gun of "D" Coy)--
   --- Left Company.
   "C" Company --- Right Support Company.
   "D" Company (less ½ platoon and 1 Lewis Gun) -----
   --- Left Support Company.

2. **INSTRUCTIONS.** (a). The Battalion will move off by Companies at 300 yards distance to Brigade Headqrs. grounds.
   (b). Time :- 4-45 p.m.
   (c). Meal. A hot meal will be served on arrival at Brigade Headquarters.
   (d). The Battalion will move off from Brigade H.Q by platoons at 200 yards distance.
   Time :- 8-0 p.m.
   (e). Order of march :- "A", "B", "B.H.Q" "C" & "D".
   The ½ platoon of "D" Coy.,will report to O.C "B" Coy at 8-0 p.m.
   (f). Dress :- Fighting order, waterproof sheets, mess-tins, waterbottles full and rations for the 22nd inst.
   (g). Packs will be left at the Q.M.Stores in the camp, labelled with No.,Rank, Name & Company.
   Time :- 2-30 p.m.
   (h). Advance Party. One Officer per Company, Lewis Gun Officer one N.C.O. per platoon., R.S.M., Pioneer Sergt and Battalion Signal Section will proceed to the trenches to take over early commencing to leave here at 3-0 p.m.
   (j). EAST of PHILOSOPHE parties must not be of more than two at 100 yards distance in daylight.
   (k). Officers valises and messboxes must be at the Q.M.Stores by 4-30 p.m.
   All stores for the trenches will be at Q.M.Stores by 4-0 p.m.
   (l). Transport Officer will detail two water-duty men to go up with R..., and remain there for the tour.
   (m). Lewis Guns and 20 Magazines per gun will be taken to PHILOSOPHE by the Transport and carried from there by the Lewis Gun teams to the line.
   (n). Lewis Gun Limbers to follow the Battalion
   (o). Working Parties. During the tour in the trenches the following parties will report to R.E.Officer at Battn., Advanced Headqrs. in tunnel :-
   Left Support Coy. -- 1 N.C.O. & 7 men - 1-30 pm to 9-30
   Right   "   "   -- 1 N.C.O. & 7 men - 9-30pm to 5-30 a
   Right   "   "   -- 1 N.C.O. & 7 men - 5-30am to 1-30 p
   (p). Tunnel Wardens. A party of 1 N.C.O. and 6 men will be appointed to act as tunnel wardens. This party will consist of the Pioneer Corpl., two men each from "A" & "B" Coys and one man each from "C" & "D" Coys.
   Standing Orders for Tunnels have been issued to N.C.O. in charge.
   (q). Whale Oil is to be used by all ranks before proceeding to the trenches.
   (r) Relief complete to be sent to Battalion Headquarters by B.A.B.code.

CONTINUED.

(s). **Return.** A return giving dispositions of posts etc., (with map references) must be rendered to Orderly Room as soon as possible after relief.

20-8-17.
                                                      (Sd.) E.A.WILSON,
                                                     Captain & Adjutant,
                                            1/5th Bn. North Stafford Regt.

Copies issued by runner at   pm. as under :-

Copy	No.		Recipient
"	No.1.	------------	Commanding Officer.
"	2.	------------	Major H. Pochin, M.C.
"	Nos. 3 - 6.	----	Os.C. Companies.
"	No.7.	------------	O.C. 1/6th North Stafford Regt.
"	8.	------------	137th Infantry Brigade.
"	10.	------------	Transport Officer.
"	9.	------------	Quartermaster.
"	11.	------------	Lewis Gun Officer
"	12.	------------	Medical Officer.
"	13.	------------	R.S.M.
"	14.	------------	N.C.O. i/c Signals.
"	15.	------------	File.
"	16 & 17.	--------	War Diary.

(8)

Secret.

1st Bn. North Staffs. Regt.

Operation Order No. 1.

1. INTENTION.
Battn. will enter enemy's trench tonight for the purpose of removing wire entanglements.

2. INSTRUCTIONS.
(a) Patrol from C Coy will attack post at H.12.b.7.9.
Patrol from D Coy will attack post at H.13.a.3.3.

(b) There will be cut by ... command Lewis guns
(c) There will be no artillery support.
(d) ZERO time will be 10.45 pm.
(e) ... complete wire breaking party.
... as far all others Officers
(f) One officer from the 146th Field Coy R.E.
will be attached to C Coy and one officer
from 146th Field Coy R.E. attached to D Coy
for purpose of conducting command Lewis...
(g) The Corps to be [illegible] and bridges will be
used for communication ... Lieut. B.C.
(h) Patrol must be all clear by 11-10 pm.

24/8/19

Signed A.E.H. MALONE
2/Lieutenant
1st Bn. North Staffs Regt.

Appendices

Appendix A. Machine Guns

The 179th Field Machine Gun Coy will fire on enemy roads and trenches from ZERO minus 20 mins to ZERO plus 20 mins to keep sound of movement of [illegible]

Appendix B. Trench Mortars

The 59th Trench Mortar Battery will fire on [illegible]

ZERO minus 20 mins to ZERO minus 10 mins
[illegible lines]

ZERO minus 10 mins to ZERO plus 20 mins
[illegible lines]

The 8/X Trench Mortar Battery will [illegible]

Appendix C. Code

Patrol left	WATCH WORKING
Patrol [illegible]	[illegible]
Prisoner	[illegible]
Casualties	SOME
[illegible]	DATE
Wounded	[illegible]
Killed	

SECRET.   NOT TO BE TAKEN
                                                          in FRONT LINE TRENCHES.

1/5th Battalion North Stafford Regiment.

AMENDMENTS TO RELIEF ORDER No. 64.

2. INSTRUCTIONS.

    (m). <u>Lewis Guns.</u> Delete figure "20" and substitute "12".

    (o). <u>Working Parties.</u> These will be found as under and not as previously stated.

Right Support Coy.	1. N.C.O.& 7 men.	1-30.pm. to 9-30.pm.
Right " "	do	9-30.pm. to 5-30.am.
Left Support Coy.	do	5-30.am. to 1-30.pm.

                                              (sd).   E.A. WILSON.
                                                      Captain & Adjutant.
21-8-17.   1/5th Bn. North Stafford Regiment.

(8)   137th INFANTRY BRIGADE - PATROL REPORT.   24/25th August 1917.

Composition of party giving unit and name of leader.	T A S K.	Time and place of departure.	Report showing route traversed, intelligence gained and offensive action taken.	Time & place of return.
1/5th North Staffs Regt. Sgt Morrall,15 O.Rs & 2 R.E.sappers	(1) To enter enemy's trench at H.13 c 58.10 & obtain identification. (2). To enter enemy's trench at H.13.c.58.10 (a)Get into touch with the enemy. (b). To obtain identification.	Zero time 10-25 p.m. 71 Trench. and 3-30 a.m.	Patrol was well carried out in the manner of a small raid. Planking parties were left in No Man's Land at H.13.c.50.25 & H.13.c.45.00. A Lewis Gun was posted at the head of sap 70 to deal with enemy M.G at H.19.a.65.70 (this had been located on the previous night). Parapet parties and blocking parties were told off. An 18 ft. Ammonal tube was carried out and successfully placed in enemy's wire. Machine gun fire was used to cover any noise made by the patrol. Stokes' & 2" mortars were occasionally fired on previously appointed targets so as to make the noise of the explosion of ammonal tube less noticeable. At zero the tube was exploded and a gap made. The raiding party of Sgt.Morrall and 4 O.R. entered enemy's front line but although this was patrolled for some distance on either side of the gap no enemy were found. A red very light was sent up from about H.13.c.60.60 and a few green lights from enemy support line, no apparent action followed, except for a few heavy T.M's fired on to ESSEX LANE and fire from the M.G. at H.19.a.65.70. The latter was very promptly silenced by our Lewis Gun posted to deal with it. Owing to Gas Bombs being discharged at 11-30 p.m. a re-call signal had to be settled upon, and this prevented patrol from pushing on to find an enemy post and compelled them to return to their own line. As the enemy had been located near the place where we entered this trench on the two previous nights, it seems probable that a patrol comes to this place every night to make it appear as if it is held as a post.	(4-15 a.m. (71 Trench 11 pm. 71 Trench.
		3-30 am.	On account of the gas, no further action could be taken until this hour, and this meant that only one hour of darkness was available. The patrol again went out with orders (a) get into touch with the enemy (b) obtain identification. The Raiding Party was to enter trench at gap and to move Northward as far as H.13.c.60.60. If no enemy were found here, it was to work along HENDON and SUPPORT LINE. A party under 2nd.Lieut PROFFITT was to move parallel to raiding party whilst they were working along front line trench to attract the attention of an enemy	

PATROL REPORT   (Continued)

post so as to enable Raiding Party in trench to take them in flank by surprise. When Raiding Party (1 N.C.O. and four men) reached gap and started to file through twin red lights were at once fired from the enemy front line trench near this point and almost immediately afterwards a barrage of 4.2's and T.M.Bombs fell in No Man's Land behind them and the patrol itself was bombed from the trench. Sgt.Morrall withdrew his patrol carefully, one party covering another, until they were back in our trench

1/5th North Staffs.Regt:
2/Lt.Hammersley
1 C.Rs.& 2 R.E.
Sappers.

(1) To enter enemy's trench at E.13.a.3.4. and obtain identification H.13.a.0.2.

10-5 p.m. Patrol was carried out in the manner of a small raid. Flanking parties were left in No Man's Land. Parapet and blocking parties were told off and a Lewis Gun was posted to deal with M.G.fire from about H.13.a.40.05. M.G. fire was arranged for, to cover noise Zero time 10.25 pm. of patrol, and Stokes' and 2" Mortars were arranged at various times to make the explosion of the ammonal tube less noticeable.

(2) -ditto-

3.50.a.m. Unfortunately the enemy sent up red lights when the barrage opened at 10.10. P.M. on the Canadian front and our own batteries fired on enemy's trenches near our objective. This held up patrol for 15 minutes. Patrol then put ammonal tube in place and a gap was successfully cut in enemy's wire. Owing to gas bombs being discharged at 11.30.pm., a recall signal had been arranged, and this was now given and patrol were compelled to return to their own trenches.

3.30.a.m. Raiding patrol again went out to enter gap out in enemy's wire earlier in the night. On nearing gap, our scouts discovered that enemy were waiting M.& S. of the gap with large patrols, evidently hoping to cut off our men as they got through the gap. Scouts returned to inform O.C. patrol who was with covering party, and he prepared to attack the enemy. By this time however the enemy had returned to his trench, and as the element of surprise was done away with, O.C. patrol returned to our trenches.

1/5th Battalion North Staffordshire Regiment.   War Diary, Aug, 191

Note re Courses.

Numerous Courses attended by Officers and Other Ranks
throughout the month.

including:-

    Brigade and Divisional Bomb Courses.
    Brigade Courses for Officers.
    Brigade Courses for N.C.O's.
    Divisional Courses in:-

        Anti-gas duties.
        Stretcher Bearer duties.
        Water Duties.
        Sanitary Duties.

    Brigade Courses for: Lewis Gunners.
                         Range Finders.

    Two Officers and 2 N.C.O's. to
        Third Army Infantry Training School.

SECRET.   1/5th Battalion North Staffordshire Regiment.   Copy No. 15

(9)

R E L I E F   O R D E R.   No. 64.

1. INTENTION.
(a) The Battalion will be relieved by the 1/6th Bn. North Staffordshire Regiment on the night of the 25/26th August 1917. Time to be notified later.
(b) The Battalion (Less "C" Company) will be in Brigade Reserve Support in MAZINGARBE and must be prepared to move at half-an-hours notice.
(c) "C" Company will be in TENTH AVENUE, Coy. Headqrs in KINGS'WAY. "C" Company will be under orders of Brigade H.Q. for work and tactically for the defence of the QUADRILATERAL under O.C. 6th NORTH.

2. INSTRUCTIONS.
(a) On relief the Battalion (less "C" Coy.) will proceed by platoons independently to billets in MAZINGARBE and "C" Coy to dugouts in KINGS WAY, TENTH AVENUE.
(b) Advance Party :- 2nd. Lieut Hammersley, 1 N.C.O, 1 cook and 1 Officers servant per Company (less "C" Coy) will report to Battalion H.Q. at 2-30 p.m. to proceed to H.Q. of 6th SOUTH to take over billets.
"A" Company will also send Brigade and Quarter Guards each of 1 N.C.O and 3 men.
(c) Mess boxes, stores etc will be sent down to HAY DUMP by 9-0 p.m.
(d) Rations for "C" Company will be brought up on the 6th NORTH truck and O.C. "C" Coy will detail a N.C.O. to meet same at HAY DUMP at 9-15 p.m.
Transport Officer will arrange for a man to be in charge of these rations and hand them over to the N.C.O. of "C" Coy.
(e) A party consisting of :-
 1 cook per Company (less "C" Coy).
 1 servant per Company (less "C"
 2 servants from H.Q
will report to the Pioneer Sergt at HAY DUMP at 9-15 p m to push trucks back to PHILOSOPHE.
(f) Lewis Gun Magazines. 12 per gun will be carried out by Lewis Gun Sections. "C" Company will take 12 per gun into TENTH AVENUE. Remainder will be handed over to the incoming companies of the 6th NORTH, separate receipts being taken for these.
(g) Transport Officer will arrange to collect these stores from KINGSBRIDGE STATION.
(h) "Lists of Stores to be handed over" will be sent to H.Q. by 9-0 a.m.
(i) On relief Os.C. "A", "B" & "D" Companies will report to Battn. H.Q. on the way down.
O.C. "C" Coy. will phone the word "MAFEKING" for relief complete.
(j) Os.C. Companies will report as soon as their Companies are in billets.
(k) Working Party :- The Company in TENTH AVENUE will detail a party of 5 men to report daily to a representative of Trench Mortar Battery at 9-0 p.m. at H.Q of Left Front Company of Battalion in Right Subsection.
(l) Acknowledge.

(Sgd.) I.J.H.MALONE,
A/Adjutant,
1/5th Bn. North Stafford Regt.

Copies issued at   to :-
 Copy No 1. ---------------- Commanding Officer.
 " " 2. ---------------- 137th Infantry Brigade.
 " " 3. ---------------- O.C. 1/6th Bn. North Staffs. Regt.
 " " 4. ---------------- Major H. Cochin, C.
 " Nos. 5-8. ---------------- Os.C.Companies.
 " No. 9. ---------------- Medical Officer.
 " " 10. ---------------- Lewis Gun Officer.
 " " 11. ---------------- Regtl. Sergt.Mjr.
 " " 12. ---------------- Transport Officer & Quartermaster.
 " " 13. ---------------- O i/c Signals.
 " " 14. ---------------- File.
 "   15 & 16 ---------------- War Diary

DISPOSITIONS continued :-

       (b) The Northern Post of "B" Company in CARDIFF SAP will be found by the half platoon and one Lewis Gun of "D" Company attached to "B" Company.

       Battalion Headquarters will be at G.17.b.90.15.

SECRET.

1/5th Battalion North Staffordshire Regiment.

Reference RELIEF ORDER No.64.

1. **INTENTION.**   for (b) read :-
   The Battalion will be in Brigade Reserve at NOEUX-LES-MINES and must be prepared to move at two hours notice.

   (c). delete.

2. **INSTRUCTIONS.**
   - (a) On relief the Battalion will proceed by platoons independently to billets in NOEUX-LES-MINES.
   - (b). Advance Party :- delete.
   - (d). delete.
   - (f). Lewis Guns and Magazines :- Transport Officer will arrange for limbers and lewis-gun boxes to meet Battn at Railway Crossing PHILOSOPHE (G.26.a.35.30) at 12 midnight.
     Two lewis-gunners per Company will march behind limbers to NOEUX-LES-MINES.
     12 magazines per gun will be carried out by lewis-gun sections and put on limbers at PHILOSOPHE.
     Lewis guns will be carried also by lewis-gun sections and put on limbers there.
   - (h). After relief companies will send an Officer to report 'relief complete' to Battn H.Q. in tunnel.
   - (k) Working party - delete.
   - (l) Acknowledge.

25-8-17.

(Sgd.) I.J.K.MALONE,
A/Adjutant,
1/5th Bn.North Staffs.Regiment

SECRET.   COPY NO.

1/5TH BATTALION NORTH STAFFORD REGIMENT.

OPERATION ORDER No. 62.

1. **INTENTION.**
   (a). The Battalion (less Transport & Q.M.Stores) will march to VERQUIN this afternoon.

2. **INSTRUCTIONS.**
   (a). The Battalion will move by Companies at 200 yards distance.
   Time :- 5-0 p.m.
   Order of march :- Signallers, "A", "B" Band, "C" & "D".

   (b). Dress :- Field Service Marching Order.

   (c). Transport :- Lewis gun limber, cookers, mess cart, Medical cart, one water cart & G.S.wagon will proceed with the Battalion. (On arrival at VERQUIN Mess cart, Medical cart and G.S.wagon will return).

   (d). Mess boxes and valises will be at Q.M.Stores in the Camp by 4-30 p.m.

26-8-17.
(Sgd)E.A.WILSON,
Captain & Adjutant,
1/5th Bn.North Staffs.Regt.

Copies issued by runner at   p.m. as under :-

Copy No.1. --------------- Commanding Officer.
"   " 2. --------------- 137th Infantry Brigade.
"   " 3. --------------- Major H.Pochin,M.C.
"   Nos. 4 - 7. ---------- Os.C.Companies.
"   No.8. --------------- Medical Officer.
"   " 9. ---------------
"   " 10. --------------- Lewis Gun Officer.
"   " 11 --------------- Transport Officer & Quartermaster.
"   " 12. --------------- R.S.M.
"   " 13. --------------- N.C.O. i/c Signals.
"   " 14. --------------- File.
"   Nos 15-18. ---------- War Diary.

1/5th Battalion PRINCE of WALES' (NORTH STAFFORD REGIMENT.)

WAR DIARY.

for

month of

SEPTEMBER 1917.

Army Form C. 2118.

5th NORTH STAFFS REGT.

Vol No 1

WAR DIARY
or
INTELLIGENCE SUMMARY.
(Erase heading not required.)

Instructions regarding War Diaries and Intelligence Summaries are contained in F. S. Regs., Part II. and the Staff Manual respectively. Title pages will be prepared in manuscript.

Place	Date	Hour	Summary of Events and Information	Remarks and references to Appendices
			Reference Map 36.c. N.E. 1/20,000.	
	SEPTEMBER 1917.			
VERDUN.	1st.		Battalion in Divisional Reserve. General Training, including Firing on Range. 2nd. Lt. W.O? FORSER accidentally injured.	
do	2nd.		Battalion in Divisional Reserve. Divine Services. Battalion moved off by Companies at 4-50.p.m. to relieve the 1/5th South Stafford Regiment in the HUTLUCH SECTOR. See Relief Order No. 35 attached. Relief complete 12-25.a.m. 3rd inst.	
TRENCHES.	3rd.		Artillery very quiet, but intermittent Fire from Heavy Trench Mortars on Front and Support Lines.	
do	4th.		Quiet day. Patrolling during the night on whole Battalion front.	
do	5th.		Hostile Heavy Trench Mortar Fire very lively. Our Heavy artillery retaliated with apparently good results.	
do	6th.		Quiet day. Battalion relieved in the line by 1/8th South Stafford Regiment, and arrived back in billets in HUTTRATRE at 11-30.p.m.	
BATTN HDQ.	7th.		Battalion in Brigade Reserve. Cleaning up, and bathing.	
do	8th.		do General Training during the morning, and Specialists during the afternoon. Kit Inspections under Company Commanders.	
do	9th.		Battalion in Brigade Reserve. One hours' Parade. Divine Services. Football match in afternoon - 1/5 Sth Stafford v. 1/5 North Staffs N.C.O.s and N.C.O.s. Result Offrs:- 3 N.C.O.s 2.	
do	10th		Battalion in Brigade Reserve. General Training including Gas Drill. Battalion proceeded to the trenches in relief of the 1/5th Bn. North Stafford Regiment. Relief complete 10-15 p.m. 11th inst.	

WAR DIARY

5th NORTH STAFFS REGT.

Army Form C. 2118.

Sht No 2

Place	Date	Hour	Summary of Events and Information	Remarks and references to Appendices
	September 1917.			
TRENCHES.	11th.		Artillery quiet. H. & M. Trench Mortars fired at intervals during the day. Increased activity with transport in HULLUCH during night.	
do	12th.		Artillery and Trench Mortars very active. A direct hit was obtained on a trench mortar by our Heavy artillery (9.2). Enemy very quiet during the night. 2nd. Lieut. STANIFORTH received a congratulatory note from G.O.C. Division, for good work done whilst patrolling the Craters.	
do	13th.		Quiet during day, Trench Mortars active during night.	
do	14th.		Quiet day. Battalion relieved in the trenches by 1/5th South Stafford Regiment. Relief complete at 11.pm. Battalion marched to billets in MAZINGARBE.	
MAZINGARBE.	15th.		Battalion in Brigade Reserve. Bathing and Cleaning up.	
do	16th.		do do Companies under Company Commanders for training.	
do	17th.		do do General Training and Kit Inspections.	
do	18th.		do do Bathing in morning and afternoon. Battalion relieved the 1/5th South Stafford Regt. in the HULLUCH LEFT Subsector. Relief complete 10-20.pm.	
TRENCHES.	19th.		Quiet day. Patrolling as per report attached. 2nd. LT. H.St.J.B. Watson joined Battn from Base.	
do	20th.		Quiet day. Patrols sent out to examine 2 Northern Craters and examine/wire between enemy H.19a.8.2. and H.19.a.65.60.	
do	21st.		Quiet day. Intercompany relief "D" & "C" Coys relieved "B" & "A" Coy. Patrolling as per reports attached. G.O.C. Division congratulated 2nd. Lt. Wint and his patrol on the good work performed during this night.	

5th NORTH STAFFS REGT. Abel No 3

Army Form C. 2118.

WAR DIARY
INTELLIGENCE SUMMARY.
(Erase heading not required.)

Instructions regarding War Diaries and Intelligence Summaries are contained in F. S. Regs., Part II. and the Staff Manual respectively. Title pages will be prepared in manuscript.

Place	Date	Hour	Summary of Events and Information	Remarks and references to Appendices
	September 1917.			
TRENCHES.	22nd.		Quiet day. Usual patrols sent out to examine wire and patrol NOMANS LAND on Battalion front.	
do	23rd.		Quiet day. 2nd. Lt. Malone and 2nd. Lt. Lockett patrolled as per report attached.	
do	24th.		Battalion relieved by 1/5th South Stafford Regiment and proceeded to billets at VERQUIN. Relief complete, 11.pm. Battalion arrived in billets 2.am. 25th inst.	
VERQUIN.	25th.		Battalion in Divisional Reserve. Bathing and Cleaning up. Congratulatory message received from G.O.C. Division on patrol by 2nd. Lieuts Malone and Lockett on night 23/24th inst.	
do	26th.		Battalion in Divisional Reserve. One hours training. Battn carried "GERTIE" Orders attached.	
do	27th.		Battalion in Divisional Reserve. 1½ hours training.	
do	28th.		do do Bathing. Battalion relieved 1/5th South Stafford Regiment in the line. Relief complete 10-30.pm. Quiet night.	
do	29th.		Quiet day. Patrols sent out under 2nd. Lieuts Humphrey and Beard. One prisoner captured. reports attached.	
do	30th.		Quiet day. Patrols under 2nd. Lts. Malone and Jones. reports attached. Part of Battalion front i.e. BROADWAY to VENDIN ALLEY, handed over to 1/6th Bn. North Stafford Regt. VENDIN inclusive is now Southern Boundary of Battalion front.	

Lieut-Colonel,
Commanding 1/5th Bn. North Stafford Regiment.

5th NORTH STAFFS REGT.

Army Form C. 2118.

Sheet No 1.

WAR DIARY
or
~~INTELLIGENCE SUMMARY~~

(Erase heading not required.)

Instructions regarding War Diaries and Intelligence Summaries are contained in F. S. Regs., Part II. and the Staff Manual respectively. Title pages will be prepared in manuscript.

Place	Date	Hour	Summary of Events and Information	Remarks and references to Appendices
			SUMMARY OF CASUALTIES and STRENGTH.	
			CASUALTIES.	
			Officers. Other Ranks. K. W. M. Hosp. K. W. M. Hosp.	
	For week ending 6-9-17.		- - - 2 - 1 - 7	
	do 13-9-17.		- - - 2 - - - 12	
	do 20-9-17.		1 1 - - - 4 - 8	
	do 27-9-17.		- - - - - - - 12	
			1 1 - 4 - 5 - 39	

Strenght.

	Officers.	Other Ranks.
	39	620.
	40	615.
	40	612.
	39	692.

[signature] LIEUT.-COLONEL,
COMMANDING 1/5th NORTH STAFFORD REGT

SECRET.   Copy No......

1/5th Battalion North Stafford Regiment.

RELIEF ORDER No. 65.

(Reference Sheet 36.b. 1/40,000 and 36.c.N.W. 1/20,000)

1. **INTENTION.** (a) The Battalion will relieve the 1/5th Battalion South Stafford Regiment in the HULLUCH Sector, on the night 2/3rd September 1917.
   (b) **Dispositions.**
       "A" Coy.   Right Company.
       "B" "   Left Centre Coy.
       "C" "   Right Centre Coy.
       "D" "   Left Company.

2. **INSTRUCTIONS.**
   (a). The Battalion will move off by Companies, at 300 yds distance to Brigade H.Q. Ground.
   (b) Time. 4-50.pm.
   (c) Meal. A hot meal will be served, on arrival at Brigade H.Q. Grounds, about 7.pm.
   (d) The Battalion will move off from Brigade H.Q. by Platoons at 200 yds distance.
       Time:- 8-45.pm.
   (e). Order of march:- "A" "C" "B" H.Qrs. "D" Coy.
   (f). Dress:- Fighting Order, waterproff sheet, mess tin, water-bottle full, and rations for the 3rd inst.
   (g). Packs will be collected from Coy. H.Qrs, at 2.pm. These must be labelled will No. Rank & Name, & Coy.
   (h). Advance Party. One officer per Company . L.G.Officer One N.C.O, per Platoon . R.S.M. Pioneer Sgt, and Battalion Signal Section, will proceed to the trenches to take over, leaving here at 4.pm. (Haversack rations will be taken.)
   (j). East of PHILOSOPHE, parties will not be larger than two at 100 yds distance during daylight.
   (k). Officers valises will be collected from Coy H.Qrs at 2.pm. Mess Boxes &c for the trenches, will be collected from Coy H.Qrs at 4-30.pm.
   (l). Transport Officer will detail two water-duty men to go with Battn H.Qrs, and remain for the tour.
   (m). Lewis Guns and 12 Magazines per gun, will be taken on the transport to PHILOSOPHE, and will be carried from there by the Lewis Gun Teams. 80 magazines per Company will be taken over from 1/5th South Stafford Regiment.
   (n). Whale oil will be used by all ranks before proceeding to the trenches.
   (o). Three guides from 1/5th South Stafford Regt, for "A" Coy will be at VICTORIA STATION at 8-45.
   (p). Relief complete will be sent to Battn H.Qrs. by B.A.B. Code
   (q). Returns. A return giving dispositions of posts(with Map. ref.) will be rendered to Orderly Room, as soon as possible after relief: also List of Stores taken over.

                                (sd)   E.A. WILSON. Capt.
                                Adjutant. 1/5th Bn. North Stafford Regt.

Copies issued at......pm. 1st September 1917.
Copy No. 1.   Officer Comdg.   No. 12. R.S.M.
   " No. 2.   2nd. in Command.   13. 1/5th South Staffs Regt.
      Nos 3/6. 4 Companies.   14. 137th Inf. Bde.
      No. 7.   Medical Officer.   15. File.
      No. 8.   Lewis Gun Officer.   16. War Diary.
      No. 9.   Transport Officer.   17.   do.
      No.10.   Quartermaster.
      No.11.   N.C.O. i/c. Signals.

SECRET   1/5th BN.PRINCE OF WALES'S (NORTH STAFFORDSHIRE REGIMENT)   Copy No. 17

RELIEF ORDER No. 67

Reference Sheet 36.b. 1/40,000 and 36.c.N.. 1/20,000.

1. **INTENTION.** (a) The Battalion will relieve the 1/6th Battalion North Stafford Regt. in the HULLUCH Sector, on the night 10/11th September, 1917.
   (b) Dispositions.
   "A" Coy.   -   Right Company
   "D" "   -   Left Centre Company
   "C" "   -   Right Centre Company
   "B" "   -   Left Company.

2. **INSTRUCTIONS.**
   (a) The Battalion will move off by Platoons, at 300 yds distance.
   Time - 7.30.p.m.
   (b) A hot meal will be served in Camp at 6.0.p.m.
   (c) Order of March - "A" "D" H.Q. "B" "C" Coy.
   (d) Dress - Fighting Order, waterproof sheet, mess tin, water-bottle full and rations for the 11th inst.
   (e) Packs will be collected from Q.M.Stores at 3.0.p.m. These must be labelled with No., Rank & Name and Coy.
   (f) Advance Party. One Officer per company, L.G.Officer, One N.C.O. per platoon, R.S.M., Pioneer Sergeant and Battalion Signal Section will proceed to the trenches to take over, leaving here at 4.0.p.m..
   (Haversack rations will be taken).
   (g) East of PHILOSOPHE, parties will not be larger than two at 100yds. distance during daylight.
   (h) Officers' valises will be collected from Coy.H.Qrs. at 3.0.p.m. Mess boxes etc. for the trenches will be collected from Coy. H.Qrs. at 7.0.p.m.
   (j) Transport Officer will detail two water-duty men to go with Battalion H.Qrs. and remain there for the tour.
   (k) Lewis Guns and 12 magazines per gun will be carried by the Lewis Gun Teams.
   80 magazines per gun will be taken over from 1/6th Battalion North Stafford Regt.
   (l) Whale Oil will be used by all ranks before proceeding to the trenches.
   (m) Relief Complete will be sent to Battalion H.Qrs. in B.A.B. Code.
   (n) Returns. A Return giving dispositions of posts (with Map ref.) will be rendered to Orderly Room as soon as possible after relief: also list of Stores taken over.

             D.A.WILSON,
             Captain & Adjutant.
             1/5th Bn.Prince of Wales's
             (North Staffordshire Regt.)

Copies issued at. 5. pm. 9th September, as under -
Copy No.1   Commanding Officer
     2   2nd in Command.
   3/C 4 Companies
     7   Medical Officer.
     8   Lewis Gun Officer
     9   Transport Officer
   10   Quartermaster.
   11   R.S.M.
   12   N.C.O. i/c Signals.
   13   1/6th North Staffs.Regt
   14   137th Infantry Brigade
   15   File
   16/17   War Diary.

SECRET   **GERALD**   Copy No _____

RELIEF ORDER No. 60.   13-9-17

Reference Sheet 36B 1/40,000 and C.R.W. 1/20,000.

1. **INTENTION.**

   (a) The Battalion will be relieved by RUY on the night of the 13/14th September 1917 at about 10 p.m.

   (b) On relief the Battalion will be in Brigade Support at MAZINGARBE and will be available at one and a half hours notice.

2. **INSTRUCTIONS.**

   (a) Companies *[illegible]* will move independently to the *[illegible]* on relief *[illegible]*.

   (b) A hot meal will be served on arrival at MAZINGARBE.

   (c) All stores [of] B.C. and D Coys will be dumped at *[illegible]*. Stores in A Coy at *[illegible]* will at the same time.

   (d) *[illegible]*

   [remainder illegible]

9

Acknowledge.

INSTRUCTIONS

Acknowledge.

SECRET   Copy No. 15

BATTALION ORDER No. 84

Reference Sheet 36.N.E. 1/40,000 and 36.N.W. 1/40,000

1. **INTENTION** (a) The Battalion will relieve ??? in the ??????? Sector,
   on the night, 13/14th September, 1917.
   (b) Dispositions:
   "A" Coy.   -   Right Company
   "B" "   -   Left Company
   "C" "   -   Centre Company
   "D" "   -   Outpost Company

2. **INSTRUCTIONS**
   (a) The Battalion will move off by Platoons, at 100 yards distance.
       Time - 7.30 p.m.
   (b) Hot meal will be served in camp at 5.00 p.m.
   (c) Order of March - "A", "B" Coy., "C", "D" Coy.
   (d) Dress - Fighting Order, waterproof sheet, mess tin,
       water-bottle full and rations for the 14th instant.
   (e) Packs will be collected from Coy. Stores at 5.0 p.m.
       These must be labelled with Coy., Battn. & Name and Coy.
   (f) Advance Party. One Officer per Company, L.G. Officer, Gas n.c.o.
       one N.C.O. per Platoon, R.S.M., Pioneer Sergeant and
       Battalion Signal Section will proceed by motor lorries to
       take over, leaving Camp at 4.30 p.m.
       (Haversack rations will be taken.)
   (g) East of ???????, parties will not be larger than
       two at 100 yards distance during daylight.
   (h) Officers' valises will be collected from Coy.H.Q. at
       5.0 p.m. Mess boxes etc., for the transport will be
       collected from Coy.H.Q. at 7.0 p.m.
   (i) Transport Officer will detail two water duty men to go
       with Battalion ???? and remain there for the tour.
   (j) Lewis Guns and 12 magazines per gun will be carried by
       the Lewis Gun Teams.
   (k) 20 magazines per Company will be taken over from ???.
       Whale Oil will be used by all ranks before proceeding
       to the trenches.
   (m) Relief Complete will be sent to Bn.H.Q. by R.S.M./Coy.
   (n) Returns. A return, giving disposition of ??? (with
       map ref.) will be rendered as quickly as possible on
       completion of ???? relief; also list of stores taken over.

                                        J. ????????
                                        Captain & Adjutant,
                                        ? Bn. ????????

Issued by runner at ? 8.9.17 4-15
Copy No. 1. Commanding Officer
        2   2nd ?
        3   Staff
        4   2nd in Command
        5,6 Companies
        7   Transport Officer
        8   Quartermaster
        9   Medical Officer
        10   L.G. Officer
        11   ????
        12   R.M.O./Signals
        13   File
        14/17 War Diary

Ref. OPERATION ORDER
           No 70.

Delete para 3(c) and substitute
Immediately after the explosion of the oil drum
tube one Stokes Mortar will fire at H.13.a.30.30, one
round every 30 seconds for a period of 20 minutes.
   Another Stokes Mortar will fire bursts of five
rounds at two minute intervals from 10.45 p.m.
until "all clear". The target for this gun
will be H.14.a.50.40.

A 4·5 howitzer will fire on the German front
line at H.7.c.10.05 commencing at 11.0 p.m., firing
one round every five minutes. On the firing
of the oil drum tube the rate of fire will be
increased to four rounds per minute
for two minutes after which one round per minute
will be fired until "all clear".

23·9·17   CRENSHAW
                                          Capt and A

SECRET.

GERM...
RELIEF ORDER NO. 10

Reference: Sheet 26B 1/40,000

INTENTION.

(a) The Battalion will be relieved by A Coy on the night of the 24th/25th Sept. 1917 at about 10 pm

(b) On relief the Batt. will be in Divl. Reserve at VERQUIN and will be in readiness to move at short notice.

INSTRUCTIONS

(a) [illegible] platoon will move independently to [illegible] and report to Coy HQrs from that point.

(b) All stores for A, B and D Coys will be at railhead at 8.0 am [illegible]

(c) [illegible]

(d) Advance Party for billets consisting of [illegible]
and the Quarter party as detailed in B.O. will report to DHQ at [illegible] pm.

(e) [illegible] at VERQUIN.

(f) Transport [illegible]
Relief complete will be reported to [illegible] the Bn. and also arrival in VERQUIN [illegible] reported by [illegible] to Orderly Room.

(g) List of Stores [illegible] Stores [illegible]
[illegible] make of [illegible] to Orderly Room by 10 am.

(h) ACKNOWLEDGE.

[signature illegible]
5 am 24/9/17

[distribution list:]
M/G Inf Bde
O.C. B Coy
O.C. C Coy
O.C. D Coy
[illegible]
Medical Officer

1/5th Battalion North Staffordshire Regiment   Appendix

PATROL REPORT   19/20th Sept: 1917

Composition of Party   2/Lt. [illegible] and 13 Other Ranks.

Task   To enter enemy's trench and if possible to secure identification.

Time and place of departure.   11.30.p.m.
                        N.19.c.55.62.

REPORT

The patrol left our trench at N.19.c.55.62. at 11.30.p.m., and proceeded to the enemy lines with the intention of entering same at N.19.a.65.70. An aerial tube was taken to blow a gap in the enemy's wire, but on arrival there it was found possible to get through the wire a little to the south of point intended. Whilst getting through the wire, patrol was fired on by a machine gun from N.19.a.65.70. and also by one from N.19.a.78.63. The patrol thus lay down in shell holes for 20 minutes until the firing had subsided. They then entered the trench and made their way towards the M.G. emplacement and found it empty. The emplacement itself was a small organised shell hole connected to the front line by a shallow trench. Empty S.A.A. cartridges were found in the emplacement. The party then split up into two, one party going to the right and one to the left. They report that the trench itself was badly knocked about, and in places practically indiscernable. There are enormous shell holes especially just in front of the trench and only a few broken pieces of trench boards in places where the shells had missed, were found; there were no dug-outs to be seen. The enemy wire is badly shattered, but a quantity of stakes remain with wire fastened to them. The patrol remained in enemy trench for two hours and no enemy were encountered.

Stokes Mortars co-operated with the patrol and placed bombs every 10 minutes into the enemy's trench; they also fired several rapid bursts on enemy line North of the craters. Machine guns fired spasmodically on rear positions until 11.30.p.m., they switched on to F.15.b. to create a diversion which was successful as, owing to the wire-cutting which was carried on during the day at N.19.c.6.7., the enemy appeared very nervous at that point. A red light was sent up by the enemy at 1.10.a.m., upon which a short burst was opened from his line opposite this spot. At 1.45.a.m. twin green lights were sent up and burning rockets. The overhead M.G. fire was very useful in deluding the enemy and so our patrol getting through the wire.

A tape was laid across No Man's Land and reeled in on return by the patrol.

Appendix No. _____

1/5th Battalion North Staffordshire Regiment

PATROL REPORT   20/21st Sept: 1917

Composition of Patrol   2/Lt. Wint and 11 Other Ranks

TASK   To enter enemy trench and lie in wait to secure identification.

Time and point of   9.30.p.m.
Departure   H.19.a.35.65.

REPORT   The patrol proceeded to enemy wire at H.19.a. 68.66. and came to the conclusion that new wire had been put out since the night of 19/20th. They then got through the wire and entered his front trench. The wire was more difficult to get through than on the night of 19/20th even though a smaller party got through. They then moved southward into the M.G. emplacement where the enemy was firing from on 19/20th. This happened to be unoccupied so the patrol waited for 2½ hours but no attempt was made by the enemy to man this post neither did anyone come along the front line. The patrol then proceeded to find where the enemy goes when he evacuates this post, and found a very small trench which led into HICKS ALLEY at about 15 yards from junction of HICKS ALLEY and front line, where it is badly knocked about. The patrol then started to return, bringing with them a bomb and knobkerry, the only things to be found. These were brought from the M.G. emplacement. When patrol was about to leave, the only very light from the vicinity came from about 100 yards away (probably in support line) and dropped in the front line near the patrol. Everywhere was quiet and not even a rifle shot was fired. A noise of motor engines was heard behind his lines in the direction of HULLUCH. The patrol then returned.

Time and point of   12.30.a.m.
Return   H.19.a.35.65.

1/5th Battalion North Staffordshire Regiment.

PATROL REPORT 23/24th Sept: 1917

Composition of Patrol 2/Lt.Malone, 2/Lt.Lockett and 10 Other Ranks.
2 Sappers with ammonal tubes.

Task To attack enemy post at H.13.a.20.70. and obtain identification.

Time and point of Departure 10.0.p.m.
No.4 Post

REPORT In pursuance of Operation Order No.70 patrol proceeded from CARDIFF SAP to a point about H.13.a.1.7. Here 2/Lt. Malone and Sgt.Wilshaw went forward to reconnoitre the wire and decide on a suitable point for the insertion of the ammonal tube. A suitable point was found at about H.13.a.20.78. A tape was run back to the main body of the patrol and the ammonal tube was then taken forward and inserted under the wire at the spot selected. The fuses were lit but failed to explode the detonators. A message was then sent back to the R.Es. for more detonators but they had not any. A search was then made for a suitable gap in the wire. None being found and the belt being too wide to get through the patrol had to withdraw, bringing with it the tube, tape, etc., The patrol was exposed to occasional prawn and rifle fire but suffered no casualties. On examination of the tube on return to the trench, it was found that the fuze had burnt right through to the detonators but both had failed to explode.

As far as the patrol was able to judge the enemy front line between the QUARRY and the VERMELLES-HULLUCH ROAD was not held. All very lights except two (one from sap from behind northern crater and one from front line on HULLUCH ROAD) were fired from Support trenches. The enemy were unusually quiet.

Time and point of Return 1.0.am.
No.4 Post.

Appendix No. _____

1/5th Battalion North Staffordshire Regiment.

PATROL REPORT 23/24th Sept: 1917

Composition of Patrol 2/Lt Malone, 2/Lt. Lockett and 8 Other Ranks

Task To inspect enemy wire between saps at H.13.c.60.50. and H.13.c.60.35. and verify the position of enemy posts.

Time and point of Departure 11.45.p.m.
Front line at H.13.c.25.40.

REPORT On leaving the trench, the patrol went due East on a bearing of 92 degrees and struck the enemy wire in front of sap at H.13.c.42.47. There is a belt of wire about 20 ft. thick in front of this sap, and in addition sap appears to be wired across. Sap is not held. Patrol then proceeded South to the road junction here there is a large grass-covered mound on the enemy side of which is a dip of seven or eight feet, which is dead ground from our front line and cannot be seen. The ground enclosed by this mound, the two saps and the ~~army~~ enemy front line, is pitted with deep shell holes, which are filled with wire and pegged down with short iron stakes, making a belt about 50 yards wide. Several members of the patrol penetrated the trip wire on the fringe of this belt, in several places for about 10 feet, to get a better view of the wire. Trip wires are hidden by the grass and weeds, which have grown up amongst them. The lower sap (at H.13.c.60.35.) is also thickly wired and not held. There were no sounds whatever from the post reported on previous occasions at H.13.c.60.55., and the machine gun did not fire. The enemy was unusually quiet during the whole time the patrol was out and gave the patrol no assistance with Very Lights.

Time and point of Return 2.30.a.m.
H.13.c.25.50.

1/5th Battalion North Staffordshire Regiment.

Ref:- 36C.N.W. 1/20,000
36B. N.E. do

CARRYING PARTIES for 26th/27th Sept.1917.

No. of Party.	Detail of Party	Coy	Rendezvous	Time of Rendezvous.	Route. In.	Route. Out.	Reserve.
1.	1 Officer, 4 N.C.Os and 40 men - 1 S.B.	"A"	QUARRY DUMP. (Vendin Alley).	8-30 p.m.	VENDIN.	BROADWAY - VENDIN.	RESERVE.
2.	1 Officer, 4 N.C.Os 1 S.B. & 36 men 4 men	"A" "B"	-do-	8-40 pm	-do-	-do-	-do-
3.	1 Officer, 4 N.C.Os 40 men & 1 S.B.	"B"	-do-	8-50 pm	-do-	-do-	-do-
4.	1 Officer, 4 N.C.Os 40 men & 1 S.B.	"B"	-do-	9-0 p.m.	-do-	-do-	-do-
5.	1 Officer, 4 N.C.Os 40 men & 1 S.B.	"C"	-do-	9-10 pm	-do-	-do-	-do-
6.	1 Officer, 4 N.C.Os 31 men & 1 S.B. 9 men	"C" "B"	-do-	9-20 p.m.	-do-	-do-	-do-
7.	1 Officer, 4 N.C.Os 40 men & 1 S.B.	"D"	-do-	9-30 pm	-do-	-do-	-do-
8.	1 Officer, 4 N.C.Os 37 men & 1 S.B. 3 men	"D" "B"	-do-	9-40 pm	-do-	-do-	-do-

26th Sept. 1917.

C. A. Wilson.
Captain & Adjutant,
1/5th Bn. North Stafford Regt.

1/5th Battalion North Stafford Regiment.

L O R R I E S for Carrying Parties 26th/27th/1917.

f:-m Sheets 36.C.N.W.1/20,000
26 B N.E. 1/20,000.

No. of Lorry.	Rendezvous.	Time.	For Party.	Destination.
2.	VERCUIN - road junction E.29.c.6.4.	6-30 p.m.	1.	PHILOSOPHE, Railway Crossing. G.20.a.3.3.
2.	-do-	6-40 p.m.	2.	-do-.
2.	-do-	6-50 p.m.	3.	-do-.
2.	-do-	7-0 p.m.	4.	-do-.
2.	-do-	7-10 p.m	5.	-do-.
2.	-do-	7-20 p.m.	6.	-do-.
2.	-do-	7-30 p.m	7.	-do-.
2.	-do-	7-40 p.m.	8.	-do-.

Lorries for the return journey will be at PHILOSOPHE BRIDGE (over stream) L.18.c.4.8. at 12.30 a.m. They will be brought up to PHILOSOPHE Railway Crossing by the Traffic Control Officer.

If it is considered advisable, parties will march back to the lorries at the Western end of PHILOSOPHE.

Appendix No. _____

1/5th Battalion North Staffordshire Regiment

PATROL REPORT   29/30th Sept: 1917

Composition of Patrol   2/Lt.Malone and 10 Other Ranks

Task   To find gap in enemy wire, enter trench and secure prisoners.

Time and point of Departure   2.45.a.m.
No. 4 Post

REPORT   The patrol left our trench at G.18.b.60.85. and moved to H.13.a.08.70. The main body of the patrol was left here whilst the leader and a N.C.O. reconnoitred to find the gap. They had proceeded about 20 yards when the covering party reported an enemy patrol advancing from the S.E. The leader at once came back to the right flank of his covering party but owing to the intense fog could see nothing of the enemy patrol. He thereupon disposed his patrol to try and surround the enemy but the latter had apparently turned back and disappeared. The patrol had apparently moved between our No.4 Post and the Western lip of the Northern crater, and was immediately chased by a patrol of Cpl.Pepper and 5 Other Ranks from this post. The enemy patrol disappeared into the Northern craters, and although the craters were well searched and ground behind the craters well examined, the patrol had disappeared. A daylight patrol examined the Southern craters this morning and found it would be an extremely easy matter for a patrol to quickly dodge away in the craters as the ground is so broken.

Time and point of Return   4.0.a.m.
No.4 Post

Appendix No.

1/5th Battalion North Staffordshire Regiment.

P A T R O L   R E P O R T   29/30th Sept: 1917

Composition of Patrol   2/Lt.Jones and 8 Other Ranks.

Task   (1) To destroy enemy wire
                         (2) To enter enemy trench and capture prisoners
Time and point of   1.30.a.m.
Departure   BOYAU 70

REPORT   Owing to the moonlight and active hostile M.G. fire patrol was not able to get away before 3.15.a.m. and the attempt at 1.30.a.m. had to be abandoned. At the later hour patrol reached enemy wire at H.19.a.60.73. Sgt.Hayes and 2 O.Rs. penetrated the enemy's wire at this point and took up a position on the enemy's parapet. In the meantime L/C.Smith and 3 men went 50 yds. N. with an ammonal tube and blew a gap with it at that point. During this time patrol came under heavy M.G.fire from about H.19.a.85.75., one of the patrol was killed. The parapet party was ordered to withdraw and fire the second ammonal tube about 30 yds. S.of gap The igniter worked satisfactorily but the detonator did not explode. The patrol then withdrew half way across No Man's Land and on account of the continued M.G.fire, returned to

Appendix No._____

1/5th Battalion North Staffordshire Regiment.

PATROL REPORT   29/30th Sept: 1917

Composition of Patrol   2/Lt. Jones and 8 Other Ranks

Task
(1) To destroy enemy wire
(2) To enter enemy trench and capture prisoners

Time and point of Departure
1.30.a.m.
BOYAU 70

REPORT   Owing to the moonlight and active hostile machine gun fire patrol was not able to get away before 3.15.a.m and the attempt at 1.30.a.m. had to be abandoned. At the later hour patrol reached enemy wire at H.19.a.60.73 Sgt. Hayes and 2 men penetrated the enemy's wire at this point and took up a position on the enemy's parapet. In the meantime L/C.Smith and 3 men went 50 yards North with an ammonal tube and blew a gap with it at that point. During this time patrol came under heavy machine gun fire from about H.19.a.85.75. and one of the patrol was killed. The parapet party was ordered to withdraw and fire the second ammonal tube about 30 yards South of the gap. The igniter worked satisfactorily but the detonator did not explode. The patrol then withdrew half way across No Man's Land and on account of the continued machine gun fire, returned to our trench. Two of the patrol returned to enemy wire and brought in the body of the man killed. Enemy were very much on the alert, probably owing to the considerable amount of noise made by the special R.Es.

Time and point of Return
4.15.a.m.
BOYAU 70

Appendix No._____

1/5th Battalion North Staffordshire Regiment

PATROL REPORT   28/29th Sept: 1917

Composition of Patrol   2/Lt. Humphrey and 10 Other Ranks.

Task   To reconnoitre and search for gaps in enemy wire near CARDIFF SAP and locate enemy posts.

Time and point of Departure
3.0.a.m.
No.4 Post

REPORT   Patrol proceeded along front line to 20 yards North of CARDIFF SAP and then struck due East. The leader and two men went forward leaving remaindre of patrol in shell holes at H.13.a.10.70. The wire here was thick and undamaged. No gaps were discovered. There was an enemy post at H.13.a.30.55. Our No.1 Post at H.13.c.20.65. succeeded in capturing a prisoner of the 165th Regt. He was one of an enemy wiring party and had lost his bearings. He approached our line and was promptly seen and captured by the post.

Time and point of Return
5.30.a.m.
No.3 Post.

Appendix No. _____

1/5th Battalion North Staffordshire Regiment

PATROL REPORT   30th Sept: 1917

Composition of Patrol   2/Lt. Lockett and 9 Other Ranks.

Task   To make gaps in enemy wire N. of CARDIFF SAP between H.13.a.20.70. and H.13.a.15.80. using ammonal tubes.

Time and point of Departure   4.15.a.m.
No.4 Post

REPORT   The patrol entered the old front line and proceeded to a point about 50 yards North of CARDIFF SAP. Two men were detailed to each of the three tubes. The tubes were then carried across No Man's Land, and interval of 15 to 20 yards being maintained. The tubes were placed in position and one man remained with each one while the remainder of the patrol withdrew to our front line. On a given signal the tubes were exploded simultaneously, gaps being made at H.13.a.20.70. and H.13.a.20.75.
   Three enemy machine guns swept No Man's Land North of CARDIFF SAP for about 20 minutes after the tubes had been exploded.

Time and point of Return   5.45.a.m.
No.4 Post.

Appendix No. _____

1/5th Battalion North Staffordshire Regiment.

PATROL REPORT   30th Sept: 1917

Composition of Patrol   2/LT. Oswell and 18 Other Ranks

Task   To explode 6 ammonal tubes under enemy wire and to destroy as much enemy wire as possible.

Time and point of Departure.   4.45.a.m.
Between BOYAU 70 and BOYAU 71.

REPORT   6 ammonal tubes were blown up under enemy wire and gaps were made at various points between H.13.a.65.65. and H.13.c.60.05. Enemy were not occupying front line in this sector but machine gun was traversing No Man's Land from HICKS ALLEY at H.19.a.85.75.

Time and point of Return   5.45.a.m.
Between BOYAU 70 and BOYAU 71.

1/5th Bn Prince of Wales's (North Staffordshire Regt.)

ADMINISTRATIVE ORDERS.

1. RATIONS & STORES.
   Rations and Stores for H.Qrs., will be brought up each night to POSEN DUMP and for Companies to CHALK PIT on SOUTHERN RAILWAY.

2. WATER.
   Supplies of water are at the following places :-
   In the Reserve Line near the Left Support Coy.H.Q. and near CHALK PIT DUMP.

3. R.E.MATERIAL.
   As there is no special R.E.dump in the Sector, R.E.Indents will be sent to "H.Q" by Fuller by 6-0 am daily.

4. COOKING UTENSILS.
   The Quartermaster will arrange for two cooking boilers to be taken in for each company and one for "H.Q".

E.A.WILSON.
Captain & Adjutant,
1/5th Bn.North Staffs Regt.

Copies issued to :-
    No.1 --------------Commanding Officer
    Nos.2/3 -----------O.C.Companies
    No.4 --------------1/Str'th.South Staffs.Regt.
    No.5 --------------1/Str'th.Southe'tons.Regt.
    No.6 --------------File
    No.7/10 -----------Brigade

CONFIDENTIAL.

1/5th Battalion PRINCE OF WALES'S (NORTH STAFFORD REGT).

WAR DIARY

from 1st October 1917 to 31st October 1917.

WAR DIARY 1/5th Bn. North Stafford Regiment Army Form C. 2118.
or
INTELLIGENCE SUMMARY.

Page 1.

(Erase heading not required.)

Instructions regarding War Diaries and Intelligence Summaries are contained in F. S. Regs., Part II. and the Staff Manual respectively. Title pages will be prepared in manuscript.

Place	Date	Hour	Summary of Events and Information	Remarks and references to Appendices
	October 1917.		Reference Maps. 36.c.N.W. 1/20,000 and 36.b. 1/40,000.	
TRENCHES.	1st.		Quiet day.	
do	2nd.		Battalion relieved by 1/5th Bn. South Stafford Regiment, and went into Close Support. Relief complete about 10-30.pm.	1
MAZINGARBE.	3rd.		Battalion in close Support. Working and Carrying parties. One Coy Bathed.	
do	4th.		do do do Gas discharged on Brigade front.	2
do	5th.		Battalion in Close Support. Working and Carrying Parties. One Company bathed.	
do	6th.		do do do Battalion relieved 1/5th Bn. South Stafford Regiment in HULLUCH Right Subsection. Relief complete 9-45.pm. Quiet night.	3
TRENCHES.	7th.		Quiet day.	
do	8th.		Quiet day.	
do	9th.		Quiet day.	
do	10th.		Quiet day. Lt.-Colonel. A.E.F. Fawcus. M.C. took command of 137th Infantry Brigade. Capt. G.J. Worthington took command of Battalion. Battalion relieved in the trenches by 1/5th South Stafford Regiment. Relief complete about 9-30.pm. Battalion marched to VERQUIN (Divisional Reserve) arriving about 12-30.pm. 11th inst.	4
VERQUIN.	11th		Battalion in Divisional Reserve. Cleaning up and bathing. Major H. Pochin. M.C. rejoined Battalion from Leave, and took command of Battalion.	
do	12th.		Battalion played 138th Inf. Bde H.Qrs at Football, beating them 2. 0. General Training, and Firing on Range.	

Army Form C. 2118.

WAR DIARY

1/5th Battalion North Stafford Regt.   Page. 11.

INTELLIGENCE SUMMARY.

(Erase heading not required.)

Place	Date	Hour	Summary of Events and Information	Remarks and references to Appendices
	October 1917.			
VERQUIN.	13th.		Battalion in Divisional Reserve. General Training in morning. Battalion paraded with 1/4th Bn. Leicester Regt., in the afternoon, as a Guard of Honour for Medal Ribbon Presentation, by G.O.C. 13th 46th Division. Corpl. Staley.C.S. and Corpl. Johnson. T. presented with MILITARY MEDALS.	5
do.	14th.		Battalion relieved the 1/6th South Stafford Regiment in the HULLUCH Left Subsection, relief complete about 8.pm. Battalion played 1/5th Bn. Lincoln Regt at Football, beating them 3. 1.	
TRENCHES.	15th		Quiet day. Staniforth 2nd. Lieut. Staniforth and 2nd. Lieut. J. Oulton and 11 Other Ranks raided the enemy's trenches, and took a prisoner. See report attached, and congratulatory message from Corps Commander.	6
do	16th.		Trench Mortars fairly active. One man killed.	
do	17th.		Quiet day.	
do	18th.		Battalion relieved by 1/5th South Stafford Regt. Relief complete about 8.pm. "A" & "C" Coys and H.Qrd marched to MAZINGARBE. "B" & "D" Coys to TENTH AVENUE.	
MAZINGARBE.	19th.		Battalion in Close Support. Bathing and Cleaning up. Battalion played the Divl. Amm. Column at Football, beating them 3. 1.	
do	20th.		Battalion in Close Support. 2 hours Training. "A" & "C" Coys relieved "B" & "D" Coys.	
do	21st.		do do. Cleaning up and bathing. Lt-Col A.E.F. Fawcus M.C. rejoined from 137th Inf. Bde, and assumed Command.	
do	22nd.		Battalion played 1/6th Bn. North Stafford Regt at Football, beating them 2. 1. Capt. Taylor injured during the match, and sent to Hospital. Battalion relieved 1/5th South Stafford Regiment in HULLUCH Left Subsection. Relief complete at 7-30.pm. Sgt. Shuker awarded MILITARY MEDAL for gallantry during raid on 15-10-17.	

WAR DIARY 1/5th Battn. North Stafford Rgt. Army Form C. 2118.

or

INTELLIGENCE SUMMARY.   Page 111.

(Erase heading not required.)

Instructions regarding War Diaries and Intelligence Summaries are contained in F. S. Regs., Part II. and the Staff Manual respectively. Title pages will be prepared in manuscript.

Place	Date	Hour	Summary of Events and Information	Remarks and references to Appendices
	October 1917.			
TRENCHES.	23rd.		Quiet day.	
do	24th.		Quiet day. Unexpired portion of Pte G. Flint's sentence (48 days) remitted by Corps Commander for gallantry on raid, night of 15th October 1917.	
do	25th.		Quiet day.	
do	26th.		Quiet day. Two practice Gas Alarm carried out. Battalion relieved by 1/6th South Stafford Regt, and proceeded to Close Support. Relief complete about 7-30.pm. "B" & "D" Coys in MAZINGARBE. "A" & "C" Coys in TENTH AVENUE.	11.
MAZINGARBE.	27th.		Battalion in Close Support. Bathing and Cleaning up.	
- do	28th.		do do. Two hours parade under Company's arrangements. "B" & "D" Coys relieved "A" & "C" Coys.	12
do	29th.		Battalion in Close Support. Bathing and Cleaning up.	
do	30th.		do do One hours parade. Battalion relieved 1/6th South Stafford Regt in HULLUCH Left Subsection. Relief complete 7-30.pm. Quiet night.	13
TRENCHES.	31st.		Quiet day. Raid carried out by 1/6th Bn. North Stafford Regt on our right. See Operation Orders attached ard report. Enemy opened heavy fire on our Left Company about 6-20.pm. On the call "ATTACK HULLUCH" our artillery effectively replied. Afterwards quiet night.	14

Lt-Colonel,
Commanding 1/5th Bn. North Stafford Regiment.

Army Form C. 2118.

WAR DIARY
1/5th Bn. North Stafford Regt.

or

INTELLIGENCE SUMMARY.

Page 1v.

(Erase heading not required.)

Instructions regarding War Diaries and Intelligence Summaries are contained in F. S. Regs., Part II. and the Staff Manual respectively. Title pages will be prepared in manuscript.

Place	Date	Hour	Summary of Events and Information										Remarks and references to Appendices
				CASUALTIES.						STRENGTH.			
				OFFICERS.			OTHER RANKS.						
				K.	W.	M.	Hosp.	K.	W.	M.	Hosp.	Officers.	O.Ranks.	
	For week ending 5-10-17.			-	-	-	1	2	3	-	20.	37	685	
	do do 12-10-17.			-	-	-	-	-	-	-	3	41	681	
	do do 19-10-17.			-	-	-	-	1	1	-	11	41	680	
	do do 26-10-17.			-	-	-	3	-	-	-	10	41	826	
				-	-	-	4	3	4	-	44			

[signature]
Lt-Colonel,
Comdg 1/5th Bn. North Stafford Regiment.

SECRET.
                    1/5TH Bn. NORTH STAFFORDSHIRE REGT.

To:- O.C. Companies, T.O. and Q.M.
     and Signal Officer

1. **RATIONS** for the 3rd Battn. will be brought up
   night of the 2nd as under.

   C and D. Coys to HAY DUMP
   (O.C. "C" and "D" Coys will arrange for a N.C.O. to be
   at HAY DUMP at 8-pm to take over their rations).
   "A" Coy to QUARRY DUMP
   (O.C "A" Coy will arrange for a N.C.O to be at QUARRY
   DUMP at 7-45 pm to take over these rations).

2. No **COOKING UTENSILS** will be taken over from
   the 6TH SOUTH.
   Q.M. will arrange for the necessary utensils to be
   brought up with rations on night of 2nd Oct.

3. **SIGNAL STATIONS**.

   The Signal Officer will arrange for Signal Stations
   for C and D Coys. (These stations will not have
   Fuller 'phones).
   A Coy will use the Signal Station of the 137TH M.G.
   Coy. — position cal. X.2.

   Fuller 'phone messages to or from "C" Coy will
   be sent to Battn. exchange - position cal. B.12.
   Fuller 'phone messages to or from D Coy will
   be sent to Bde. exchange - position cal. P.A.2.

   On relief the Signallers of A Coy return to
   MAZINGARBE with the H.Q. signallers.

4. **BATTN CANTEEN** will be open from 2 to 5 PM
   in TENTH AVENUE.

5. Cols. A, C and D Coys will report by quickest route to Coy.
   they have taken over their relief positions.
   O.C "D" Coy will report by runner on arrival in
   MAZINGARBE.

1st Oct.
1st Oct. 1917.
                                    C.A. WILSON
                                Captain & Adjt.

SECRET. COPY No. 17.

1/5TH Bn. Prince of Wales's (North Staffordshire Regt)

RELIEF ORDER No. 72.

Reference Sheet 36 C. N.W. 1/20,000.

1. INTENTION.

(a) The Battn will be relieved by the 1/5TH SOUTH STAFFS. REGT on the night of the 2nd/3rd October at about 10 pm.

(b) On relief the Battn. will be in close support HQ and B Coy in MAZINGARBE.
A, C and D Coys. in TENTH AVENUE.

2. INSTRUCTIONS.

(a) On relief "A" Coy will move into dugouts in TENTH AVENUE. taking over from "D" Coy 6TH SOUTH. Coy HQ near the junction of POSEN ALLEY and TENTH AVENUE
(A Coy will be under the 466TH Coy. REs for work and under O.C. 6TH SOUTH tactically for the defence of the line).

(b) "B" Coy on relief will move to huts in MAZINGARBE

(c) C Coy on relief will move to dugouts in TENTH AVENUE taking over from "A" Coy 6TH SOUTH — Coy HQ will be at OLD BATTN. HQ. (This Coy will be under the Australian Tunnel Coy. for work and under OC. 5TH SOUTH tactically for defence of the line)

(d) "D" Coy on relief will move to dugouts in TENTH AVENUE taking over from "C" Coy 6TH SOUTH. Coy. HQ near junction of LONE TRENCH, VENDIN ALLEY and TENTH AVENUE (This Coy will work under R.E's and be under orders of OC 5TH SOUTH tactically for defence of the line)

(e) Os.C. "A", "C" & "D" Coys will each send one Officer, & two N.C.Os to take over dugouts etc to report to O.C the Coy which they are relieving at 3-0 pm.

(f) "B" Coy will send an Officer, 1 NCO, 1 cook 1 servant. Bde Guard, Bn Quarter Guard & Divl. Bar b Stores Guard (as detailed by R.S.M) to report to Bn H.Q at 2-pm.

(g) Lewis guns and 12 magazines will be carried out by Lewis gun sections 20 magazines per gun in panniers will be handed over to the incoming unit and a like number being taken over from 6TH SOUTH.

CONTINUED

(a) HQ and B Coys stores will be at HAY DUMP by 8.0 pm.

(b) "List of Stores handed over" and "Statement of work done during tour" will be sent to Batt'n H.Q. by 10.0 a.m.

(c) RELIEF COMPLETE to be reported to Batt'n H.Q by B.A.B. Code.

Monday
1st Oct 1917.

E.A. WILSON
Capt and Adjt
1/5th Bn. North Staffs. Regt

Copies issued to at 11 pm.
No. 1. Commanding Officer
2. 2nd in Command
3. O.C. 117th Inf Bde
4. O.C. 1/5th South Staffs Rgt
5. O.C. 16th South Staffs Rgt
6/9. O.C. Companies
10. Lewis Gun Officer
11. T.O and Q.M.
13. Medical Officer
14. R.S.M.
15. Signal Officer
16. File
17/18. Diary

at 11 pm

REPORT ON RAID CARRIED OUT BY
1/5th Battalion North Stafford Regt.
on the night 15th October 1917.

On 14th October 1917, a patrol under 2nd. Lieut. L. STANIFORTH., located an enemy post at H.19.a.65.70.

On the night of the 15th, a patrol consisting of 2nd. Lieut. Staniforth, 2nd. Lieut. J. Oulton and 11 Other Ranks was detailed to attack this post and obtain identification.

The patrol left BOYAU 70 about 10.pm. and proceeded to point H.19.a.60.80 from where they crawled through the enemy wire which was about 40 ft in depth but very broken.

2nd. Lieut. Oulton and 6 O.R.s crossed the enemy's front line trench, and after going North for about 25 yds, turned South and made a detour behind the enemy's front line trench in order to attack the post from the rear.   At the same time 2nd. Lieut. STANIFORTH and 4 O.R·s moved South along enemy's parapet, and one man advanced along the trench.

Patrol was challenged from the enemy's post, and both sides exchanged bombs.   Patrol then lay quiet for about 10 minutes and the enemy were heard coming along the trench.   Then two of the enemy appeared, one of these was at once captured, but the second man following behind, bolted back along the trench and escaped.

Patrol then returned with the prisoner, when the enemy opened fire with prawns and machine guns.

Our casualties were nil.

Prisoner belonged to 5th Company, 2nd Battalion, 26th Regiment.

                                      (sd).   H. Pochin   Major,

16th Oct.17.   Comdg 1/5th Bn. North Stafford Regiment.

SECRET.   COPY No. _____

1/5th Battn. Prince of Wales's (North Staffordshire Regt).

4th October 1917.

Ref. Secret Trench Map,
    LOOS, Sheet 1/10,000

1. A combined gas operation by 46th and 2nd Divisions will take place to-night, 4th/5th October, or first favourable night after this night date.

2. Zero hour will be same for both Divisions.

3. The datum hour will be 11 pm. Zero hour will be notified to units with reference to that hour, i.e.,- if zero hour is 11-40 pm it will be notified as plus 40'; 3-10 am as plus 4 hours 10'.

4. The following code will be used :-

    Operation will take place   SOMERSET.
    Operation cancelled --------   DEVON.
    Discharge complete and all
       clear (cylinders only)   GLAMORGAN.
    Discharge complete and all
       clear (Stokes Mortars).   DIAMOND.

    The code will be sent by wire from Brigade Headquarters at Zero- 2 hours. If weather conditions are unfavourable at Zero-2 hours, DEVON will be sent out and the operation cancelled for the night.

5. Wind limits for discharge will be -WQN.W. through W. to W.S.W., between 3 and 15 miles per hour.

6. The following gas precautions will be taken from Zero-5' till ALL CLEAR.
   HULLUCH SECTION.
    Box respirators will be worn by all troops in front of Reserve Line; gas doors will be lowered on all exits to HULLUCH TUNNEL East of Reserve Line.
    All troops will be withdrawn from the front and support lines between BOYAUX 64 and 75 by ZERO-15', except for Lewis-gun teams in VENDIN POST and at HULLUCH TUNNEL South Posts. These teams will wear box respirators.
    Troops will not return to the front line until Zero plus 60' and then only when "C" Special Coy.R.E.officer reports "ALL CLEAR"

7. Machine guns will co-operate as follows :-

    137th Infantry Brigade will from Zero plus 5' to Zero plus 20' with all available guns concentrate on HULLUCH and approaches to HULLUCH.

8. Watches will be synchronised at 7-0 p.m.
   O.C.Companies will send an Officer to Headquarters in the line at 7-0 p.m.

B.A.WILSON,
Captain & Adjutant,
1/5th Bn.North Staffs Regt

COPY.   Copy. No. 16

1/5TH BATTALION PRINCE OF WALES'S (NORTH STAFFORDSHIRE REGT.)

RELIEF ORDER No. 74.
5th Oct. 1917.

Reference :-
Sheet 36C.N.W.1/20,000.

1. **INTENTION.**
   (a) The Battalion will relieve the 1/6th South Staffordshire Regt., in the HULLUCH Right Subsection on the night of 6th/7th October 1917.
   (b) Dispositions
   - "D" Company ----- Right Coy.
   - "C"   "   ----- Left Coy.
   - "A"   "   ----- Left Support Coy.
   - "B"   "   ----- Right Support Coy.

2. **INSTRUCTIONS.**
   (a). Guides for "B", "C" and "D" Coys will report to their respective Coy.H.Qrs. in TENTH AVENUE at 6-30 pm. "A" Coy and "H.Q" will move from here at 7-0 pm.
   (b). Advance Party
   The usual advance party will proceed to the trenches early during the afternoon.
   (c). Officers valises and mess-boxes of "H.Q" and "A" Coy will be collected at H.Q. and Coy.H.Q at 5-0 p.m. Packs will also be collected from the Coy.H.Q. at the same hour.
   (d). Stores for the trenches will be collected at 6-45 p.m. (6-15 pm)
   (e) Lewis Gun Magazines.
   80 Lewis gun magazines per company will be taken over from the 1/6th South Staffordshire Regt., a similar number being handed over to the 1/5th South Staffordshire Regt.
   (f). Whale Oil will be used by all ranks before proceeding to the trenches.
   (g). Relief complete will be sent to Battn.H.Q., in B.A.B. code.
   (h). Returns :- "Lists of Stores taken over" and "Disposition of posts (with map references)" will be rendered to O.Room as soon as possible after relief.

E.A.WILSON,
Captain & Adjutant
1/5th Bn. North Staffd.
Regt.

Copies issued to :-
- No. 1. ----- Commanding Officer.
- " 2 ------ H.Q., 137th Infantry Brigade.
- " 3 ------ O.C. 1/5th Bn. South Staffordshire Regt.
- " 4 ------ O.C. 1/6th South Staffordshire Regt.
- " 5/8 ----- Os.C. Companies.
- " 9. ------ Transport Officer & Quartermaster
- "10. ------ Lewis Gun Officer.
- "11 ------ Signal Officer.
- 12 ------ Medical Officer.
- "13 ------ R.S.M.
- "14 ------ File.
- "15/16 ---- War Diary.

SECRET.   Copy No. 1.

1/5TH Bn.(Prince of Wales's) North Staffordshire Rgt.

R E L I E F   O R D E R.   No. 73

The following reliefs will be carried out on dates stated :-

Night of 3rd/4th.Oct.1917
"B" Company will relieve "C" Company in TENTH AVENUE.
"C" Coy. moving to huts in MAZINGARBE.

Night of 4th/5th Oct.1917
"C" Company will relieve "D" Company in TENTH AVENUE.
"D" Coy. moving to huts in MAZINGARBE.

Night of 5th/6th.Oct.1917.
"D" Company will relieve "A" Company in TENTH AVENUE.

---------- oOo ----------

RATIONS.
In each case rations for the following day will be carried up.

LEWIS GUN MAGAZINES.
Lewis gun magazines will be handed over but not lewis-gun equipment.

COOKING UTENSILS will be handed over.

RELIEFS WILL NOT INTERFERE WITH WORKING PARTIES.

                                           E.A.WILSON,
                                        Captain & Adjutant.

Copies issued to :-
    No.1. ----- Commanding Officer.
    Nos.2/5. ----Os.C.Companies.
    No.6. ----- Transport   Officer.
    " 7   ----- Quartermaster.
    " 8.   ----- File.

SECRET.   COPY No 16
            1/5th BATTALION PRINCE OF WALES'S (NORTH STAFFS REGT)

RELIEF ORDER
No 75

REFERENCE :- MAPS 36c N.W. 1/20000   Tuesday, 9th Oct. 1917
             and 36a   1/40,000

1. INTENTION

(a) The Battalion will be relieved by the 1/6th Battalion South Staffs Regt on the night of the 10/11th October at about 8 p.m.

(b) On relief the Battalion will be in Divisional Reserve at VERQUIN.

2. INSTRUCTIONS

(a) On relief platoons will move independently to L.23.c.15.70 and march by Companies from that point to VERQUIN.

(b) Route :- Main Road to NOEUX-LES-MINES – K.12.c.85.85 – VERQUIN.

(c) Quartermaster will arrange for tea at L.23.c.15.70 and a hot meal on arrival at VERQUIN.

(d) Lewis guns and 12 magazines per gun will be carried by gun teams to PHILOSOPHE where they will be loaded on Lewis gun limbers. 60 Lewis gun magazines per Company will be handed over.

(e) Advance party consisting of Company Quartermaster, 1 N.C.O., 1 Cook and Officers Servant per Company and the Quarter Guard (as detailed by R.S.M.) will rendezvous at Cross Roads NOYELLES L.11.c.9..25 at 10 a.m. and march under orders of Senior N.C.O. to Q.M. Stores at LABOURSE.

(f) Quartermaster will arrange to take over billets and Lewis gun magazines & maps of training areas from 1/6th Bn. South Staffs. Regt.

(g) Company Officers chargers will be at Brigade H.Qrs. at 9.30 p.m. and Hd. Qrs. Officers chargers at 10.0 p.m.

(h) Lists of stores to be handed over, statement of work done & work proposed, and maps of NO MAN'S LAND will be sent to Headquarters by 10 a.m.

(i) Relief complete will be reported to Hd. Qrs. in B.1.a. both and arrival in billets at VERQUIN by runner.

(k) ACKNOWLEDGE

                                     E.A. WILSON, Capt. & Adjutant
                                     1/5 Bn. Prince of Wales's (North Staffs R)

Issued at 3.30 p.m. by runner to :-
1. Commanding Officer
2. 2nd in Command
3. O.C. 137 Bde.
4. O.C. 1/6 South Staffs.
5. O.C. 1/5 South Staffs.
6. O.C. Companies
7. Medical Officer
8. Transport Offr. & Q.M.
9. Signal Offr.
10. R.S.M.
11. Lewis gun Offr.
12. File

SECRET.   COPY No.

1/5th Battalion Prince of Wales's (North Staffordshire Regt.)

R E L I E F   O R D E R   No. 75.   13th Oct.1917.

Reference :- Sheets 36B 1/40,000 and 36C N.E. 1/20,000

1. INTENTION.
   (a) The Battalion will relieve the 1/6th South Staffordshire Regiment in the Left Subsector on the night of the 14/5th October 1917.
   (b) Dispositions.
       "C" Company ---- Right Coy.
       "D"   "   Centre Coy.
       "B"   "   Outpost Coy.
       "A"   "   Left Coy.

2. INSTRUCTIONS.
   (a) The Battalion will move off by companies at 200 yards distance to Bde.Headqrs.Grounds.
   (b) Time :- 2-0 p.m.
   (c) Meal :- A hot meal will be served on arrival at Bde.H.Q.grounds.
   (d) The Battalion will move off from Bde.H.Q., by Platoons at 200 yards distance.
       Time :- 5-30 p.m.
   (e) Order of march :- "C","D","B", "H.Q" and "A".
   (f) Dress. :- Fighting order - waterproof sheets, greatcoats mess tins, water bottles full and rations for the 15th inst.
   (g) Packs. :- Packs will be collected from company H.Qrs at 12 noon.
   (h) Advance party :- One Officer per company, Lewis gun Sergeant, one N.C.O. per platoon. R.S.M., Pioneer Sgt Signal Officer and Battn.Signal Section also Coy.cooks will proceed to the trenches early to take over commencing to leave here at 12-30 p.m.
   (j) EAST OF PHILOSOPHE parties must not be of more than two at 100 yards distance during daylight.
   (k) Officers valises & mess boxes will be collected from company H.Q., at 12-0 noon.
       Stores for the trenches will be collected from Coy. H.Qrs at 1-30 p.m.
   (l) Transport Officer will detail two water duty men to go up with H.Q., and remain there for the tour.
   (m) Lewis Guns and 12 magazines per gun will be taken to PHILOSOPHE by the Transport and carried from there by the Lewis gun teams to the line.
       Eighty magazines per Coy. will be taken over from the 1/6th South Staffordshire Regt and a like number handed over to the 1/6th South Staffordshire Regt.
   (n) DIXIES. Quartermaster will arrange for two dixies per company to be taken into the line.
   (o) Whale Oil will be used by all ranks before proceeding to the trenches.
   (p) Relief samples will be sent to Battn.H.Q., in B.A.B. Code.
   (q) Returns.. "List of stores taken over" and "Dispositions of Posts (with map references)" will be rendered to Orderly Room as soon as possible after relief.

                                        H.A. HITSON,
                                        Captain & Adjutant,
                                        1/5th Bn.North Staffs Regt.

Copies issued as under :-

```
Copy No. 1.  --------  Commanding Officer.
  "      2   --------  2nd in Command.
  "      3   --------  H.Q., 137th Infantry Brigade.
  "      4.  --------  O.C. 1/6th Bn. South Staffs. Regt.
  "      5.  --------  O.C. 1/5th Bn. South Staffs. Regt.
  "      6/9 --------  O.C. Companies.
  "      10. --------  Transport Officer.
  "      11  --------  Quartermaster.
  "      12  --------  Signal Officer.
  "      13  --------  Medical Officer.
  "      14  --------  R.S.M.
  "      15. --------  L.G.Sergt.
  "      16. --------  File.
  "      17/18. ----  War Diary
```

COPY.
Corps No. 788 (G.S.).
t. Div. G.737/215.
t. Bde. S.25/1917.

46th Division:

The following remarks by the Corps Commander with reference to the report on raid carried out by two Officers and 30 men of the 1/5th North Staffordshire Regt. are forwarded for your information and communication to all concerned :-

"A good enterprise boldly and methodically carried out.
Great credit is due to 2/Lieut. STAFFORTH
2/Lieut. WILDE for their staunchness and enterprise.
The fact that there were no casualties shows how well the whole operation was planned."

19th October 1917.
sd/ -   Major,
for Brigadier General.
General Staff, Corps.

- 2 -

137th Infantry Brigade:

For information.

20th October 1917.
sd/ -   (Captain,
General Staff, 46th Division.

- 3 -

Officer Commanding,
1/5th North Staff. Regt.

Forwarded.

1.10.1917.
sd/ -
137th Infantry Brigade.

SECRET.   Copy No. _____

1/5th Battalion Prince of Wales's (North Staffordshire Regt.).

                                                    17th Oct. 1917.
                    R E L I E F   O R D E R   No. 78.

Reference :- Sheet 36C N.W. 1/20,000

1. INTENTION.
   (a) The Battalion will be relieved by the 1/5th Bn. South
       Staffordshire Regiment on the night of 18th/19th Oct.
       1917 at about 8-0 pm.
   (b) On relief the Battalion will be in Close Support -
       The Battalion (less "B" and "D" Coys.) in MAZINGARBE
       "B" and "D" Coys. in TENTH AVENUE.

2. INSTRUCTIONS.
   (a) On relief Headquarters, "A" and "C" Coys. will move
       into huts in MAZINGARBE.
   (b) "B" Coy. on relief will move into dugouts in TENTH
       AVENUE. Company Headquarters will be in NINTH AVENUE.
       (This Coy. will be under the 3rd Australian Tunnelling
       Coy. for work and under O.C. 1/5th South Staffs. Regt.
       tactically.
   (c) "D" Company on relief will move into dugouts in
       TENTH AVENUE. - (Coy. Headquarters near junction of LONE
       TRENCH and TENTH AVENUE. (This Coy. will be under
       O.C. 466th Field Coy. R.Es for work and under O.C.
       1/5th South Staffs. Regt. tactically.
   (d) Os.C. "D" and "B" Coys will each send an Officer and
       2 N.C.Os to take over dugouts etc., to report to the
       O.C. Coy which they are relieving at 2-0 pm.
   (e) Os.C. "A" and "C" Coys. will each send an Officer, one
       N.C.O., one cook, one servant also Brigade Guard,
       Battn. Quarter Guard and Divl. Bomb-store Guard (as
       detailed by R.S.M.) to report to Battn. H.Q., at 2-0 pm.
   (f) 20 (twenty) magazines per gun (in panniers) will be
       handed over to the incoming companies and a like
       number will be taken over from companies of the 1/5th
       South Staffs. Regt.
   (g) Cooking utensils will be taken out.
   (h) Stores of H.Q., "A" and "C" Coys. will be at HAY DUMP
       by 5-30 pm.
   (j) Rations and blankets for "B" and "D" Coys. will be
       brought up on the tramway to HAY DUMP. Os.C. "B" &
       "D" Coys will each send a N.C.O to meet truck at
       HAY DUMP at 5-45 pm.
   (k) 'List of Stores handed over' and 'Statement of work
       done during tour' will sent to H.Q., by 10-0 am.
   (l) 'Relief complete' will be reported to H.Q., in
       B.A.B. Code.
   (m) Os.C. Companies will report when they have taken up
       their new positions in B.A.B. Code or by runner.

                                    E.A. WILSON,
                                    Captain & Adjutant,
                                    1/5th Bn. North Staffs. Regt.

Copies issued as under at   pm.
       Copy No. 1. ----- Commanding Officer.
         "   " 2. ---- 2nd. in Command.
         "   " 3 ----- H.Q., 137th Infantry Brigade.
         "   " 4 ------ O.C. 1/5th Bn. South Staffs. Regt.
       Copies Nos. 5/8 - Os.C. Companies.
       Copy No. 9. ---- Transport Officer & Quartermaster.
         "   " 10. ---- Medical Officer.
         "   " 11 ----- Signal Officer.
         "   " 12 ----- Lewis Gun Officer.
         "   " 13 ----- R.S.M.
         "   " 14 ----- File.
       Copies Nos 15/16- War Diary.

SECRET   Copy No. 12

1/5th Battalion Prince of Wales's (North Staffordshire Regt).

                                                Friday, 19-10-17
                    R E L I E F   O R D E R. No.79.

1. INTENTION.
   (a). On the night of the 20th/21st October 1917,
        "A" and "C" Companies will relieve "B" and "D"
        Companies respectively in Close Support in
        TENTH AVENUE.

2. INSTRUCTIONS.
   (a). "A" and "C" Coys will commence leaving MAZINGARBE
        at 5-0 pm.
   (b). Cooking utensils, Lewis gun magazines and blankets
        will be taken over.
   (c). Rations for the 21st will be carried on the man.
   (d). "B" and "D" Coys will each send one Officer, 2 N.C.Os
        one cook and one servant during the afternoon of the
        20th inst to take over billets etc.
   (e). Relief Complete will be reported by B.A.B.Code.

3. ACKNOWLEDGE.

                                        E.A.WILSON,
                                    Captain & Adjutant,
                                   1/5th Bn.North Staffs.Regt.

   Copies issued as under :-
            No.1. ----- Commanding Officer.
            " 2 ------ 2nd.in Command.
            " 3 ------ Transport Officer.
            " 4 ------   Quartermaster.
            Nos 5/8 -- Os.C.Companies.
            No.9 ----- R.S.M.
            " 10 ----- O.C.466th Field Coy.R.Es.
            " 11 ----- O.C. 3rd Australian Tunnelling Coy.
            " 12 ----- File.
            Nos.13/14 - War Diary.

SECRET   COPY No.6

1/5th Battalion Prince of Wales's (North Staffordshire Regt.)

21-10-17

RELIEF ORDER No.80

Reference - Sheet 36.C. N..., 1/20,000

1. **INTENTION**
   (a) The Battalion will relieve the 1/5th Bn.South
       Staffordshire Regiment in the HULLUCH Left Subsection
       on the night of the 22nd/23rd October, 1917.
   (b) Dispositions
       "C" Coy.   -   Right Coy.
       "D" Coy.   -   Centre Coy.
       "B" Coy.   -   Left Coy.
       "A" Coy.   -   Outpost Coy

2. **INSTRUCTIONS**
   (a) "A" & "C" Companies will move from TENTH AVENUE
       5.0.p.m.
       "B" & "D" Companies will leave here at 5.0.p.m.
       Order of march - "B" Coy., "D" Coy., Headquarters.
   (b) Advance Party.
       The usual advance party, with Coy. and Headquarter
       Gas N.C.Os. will proceed to the trenches early in
       the afternoon.
   (c) Officers' valises and mess boxes of "B" & "D" Coys
       will be collected from Coy.H.Qrs. at 3.0.p.m.
       Packs will be collected at the same hour.
   (d) Stores for the trenches will be collected at 4.45.p.m.
   (e) Lewis Gun Magazines
       60 Lewis Gun Magazines per Company will be taken
       over from 1/5th Bn.South Staffordshire Regt., a
       similar number being handed over.
   (f) Cooking Utensils
       8 boilers and 4 baking tins will be taken over from
       1/5th Bn.South Staffordshire Regt. and 6 boilers and
       2 baking tins will be handed over to them.
   (g) Whale Oil will be used by all ranks before proceeding
       to the trenches.
   (h) RELIEF COMPLETE will be sent to Bn.H.Qrs. in D.A.D.
       Code.
   (j) Returns.
       Lists of Stores taken over and Dispositions of Posts
       (with map references) will be rendered to H.Qrs. as
       soon as possible after relief.

                                        D. A. WILSON,
                                        Captain & Adjutant,
                                        1/5th Bn.North Staffs.Regt.

Copies issued at   p.m.

No.1   -   Commanding Officer
" 2   -   2nd in Command.
" 3.   -   137th Infantry Brigade
" 4   -   1/5th Bn.South Staffs.Regt.
" 5/8   -   Os.C. Companies.
" 9   -   Transport Officer
" 10   -   Quartermaster
" 11   -   Lewis Gun Officer
" 12   -   Signal Officer
" 13   -   Medical Officer
" 14   -   R.S.M.
" 15   -   File
" 16/17   -   War Diary

SECRET   Copy No...

1/5th Battalion PRINCE OF WALES'S (North Stafford Regt).

RELIEF ORDER No 61.

(Reference Sheet 36.c.N.W. 1/20,000)

1. **INFANTRY.**
   (a). The Battalion will be relieved by the 1/6th Bn. South
       Stafford Regt on the night 26/27th October 1917,
       about 7-30.pm.

   (b). On relief the Battalion will be in close support.
       The Battalion less "A" & "C" Companies in MAZINGARBE.
       "A" & "C" Companies in TENTH AVENUE.

2. **INSTRUCTIONS.**
   (a). On relief, "B" & "D" Coys will move to Huts in
       MAZINGARBE,
   (b). "A" Coy, on relief will move into dugouts in TENTH
       AVENUE, taking over from "C" Coy 1/5th Bn. South
       Staffordshire Regt. (Coy H.Q. in NINTH AVENUE)
       This Company will be under the orders of the O.C.
       3rd Australian Tunnelling Coy for work, and O.C.
       1/6th South Staffordshire Regt tactically.
   (c). "C" Coy on relief will move into dugouts in TENTH
       AVENUE, taking over from "D" Coy, 1/5th Bn. South
       Staffordshire Regt.(Coy H.Q. near junction of TENTH
       AVENUE and LONE TRENCH.) This Company will be under
       O.C. 466th Field Coy. R.E. for work, and O.C. 1/5th
       South Staffordshire Regt tactically.
   (d). O.s.C. "A" & "C" Coys will each send one Officer
       and N.C.O. to take over dugouts &c; to report to
       O.C. Company which they are relieving before 3-30.pm.
   (e). "B" & "D" Coys will each send the following advance
       party to report to H.Qrs at 2.pm. - 1 N.C.O., 1 Cook,
       1 Officer's Servant, Bde Guard, Divl. Bomb Store
       Guard (as detailed by R.S.M.)
   (f). 80 Lewis Gun Magazines (in panniers) per Company
       will be handed over and taken over.
   (g). Stores of H.Qrs and "B" & "D" Coys will be at HAY DUMP
       by 5-45.pm.
   (h). 2 Cooking Boilers per Company will be handed over to
       relieving Companies. Quartermaster will arrange
       for Cooking Utensils for "A" & "C" Coys to come up
       with rations.
   (i). List of Stores to be handed over, Statement of Work
       done, and Maps of N" MAN'S LAND, will be sent to H.Qrs
       by 10.am.
   (k). Relief complete to be reported to Head-qrs in B.A.B.
       Code.

3. ACKNOWLEDGE.   Captain & Adjutant.

                                              1/5th Bn. Prince of Wales's
                                                (North Stafford Regiment)

Copies issued at   pm on 26-10-17.
  No. 1. Copy.   Comdg Officer   Copy No. 10. T.O. & Q.M.
      2   "   2nd. in Command   11. Signals.
      3   "   H.Q. 137th Inf. Bde.   12. Med. Offr.
      4. "   O.C. 1/5th S. Staffs Rgt.   13. L.G. Sgt.
      5. "   O.C. 1/6th S. Staffs Rgt.   14. R.S.M.
      6/9.   Companies   15. File.
                                                          16/17. War Diary.

SECRET.   Copy No. 12

1/5th Bn. Prince of Wales's (North Staffordshire Regiment).

R E L I E F   O R D E R   No 82.
27th October 1917

1. INTENTION.
   (a). On the night of the 28th/29th October 1917, "B" and "D" Companies will relieve "A" and "C" Companies respectively in Close Support in TENTH AVENUE.

2. INSTRUCTIONS.
   (a). "B" & "D" Coys. will commence leaving MAZINGARBE at 5-0 pm.
   (b). Packs and Officers' valises will be collected from the camp and Coy.H.Qs at 4-30 pm.
   (c). Cooking utensils, Lewis-gun magazines and blankets will be taken over.
   (d). Rations for the 29th inst will be carried on the man.
   (e). "A" and "C" Coys. will each send one Officer, 2 N.C.Os, one cook and one servant during the afternoon of the 29th inst to take over billets etc.
   (f). 'Relief Complete' will be reported by B.A.B. code.

3. ACKNOWLEDGE.

                                    E.A.WILSON,
                                    Captain & Adjutant,
                                    1/5th Bn. North Staffs. Regiment.

Copies issued at   pm as under :-

No. 1 ------ Commanding Officer.
 " 2 ------ 2nd.in Command.
 " 3 ------ Transport Officer.
 " 4 ------ Quartermaster.
Nos 5/8 ---- Os.C.Companies.
No.9. ------ R.S.M.
 " 10. ----- O.C. 466th Field Coy.R.Es.
 " 11 ------ O.C. 3rd Australian Tunnelling Coy.
 " 12 ------ X File.
 " 13/14. -- War Diary.

SECRET   Copy No.

1/5th Battalion Prince of Wales's (North Staffordshire Regt.)

                                                                      29-10-17

R E L I E F   O R D E R   No. 83

Reference Sheet 36.c.N.W., 1/20,000

1. **INTENTION**
   (a) The Battalion will relieve the 1/6th Bn. South Staffs. Regt. in the HULLUCH Left Subsection on the night of the 30th/31st October, 1917.
   (b) Dispositions
         "C" Company   -   Right Coy.
         "D"   "   -   Centre Coy.
         "B"   "   -   Left Coy.
         "A"   "   -   Outpost Coy.

2. **INSTRUCTIONS**
   (a) "B" & "D" Companies will move from TENTH AVENUE at 5.0.p.m.
       "A" & "C" Companies will leave here at 4.30.p.m.
       Order of march - "A"Coy., "C"Coy., Headquarters.
   (b) Advance Party, consisting of one officer per Company, Lewis Gun Officer, one N.C.O. per platoon, R.S.M., Pioneer sergeant, Signal Officer and Bn. Signal Section, Headquarter & Coy Gas N.C.Os., and Coy. cooks, will proceed to take over early, those in MAZINGARBE commencing to leave here at 3.0.p.m.
   (c) Officers' valises and mess boxes of "A" & "C" Coys. will be collected from Coy.H.Qrs. at 3.0.p.m. Packs will be collected at the same hour.
   (d) Stores for the trenches will be collected at 4.15.p.m.
   (e) Lewis Gun Magazines.
       80 Lewis Gun Magazines per Company will be taken over from the 1/6th South Staffs. Regt., a similar number being handed over.
   (f) 8 boilers and 8 baking tins will be taken over from the 1/6th South Staffs. Regt, and a like number will be handed over to them.
   (g) Whale Oil will be used by all ranks before proceeding to the trenches.
   (h) RELIEF COMPLETE will be sent to Bn.H.Qrs. in B.A.B. Code.
   (j) Returns.
       Lists of stores taken over and Disposition of Posts (with map references) will be rendered to H.Qrs. as soon as possible after relief.

                                          E. A. WILSON,
                                             Captain & Adjutant,
                                                1/5th Bn. Prince of Wales's
                                                   (North Staffs. Regt.)

Copies issued at   p.m.

   No. 1   -   Commanding Officer
    " 2   -   2nd in Command
    " 3   -   137th Infantry Brigade
    " 4   -   1/6th Bn. South Staffs. Regt.
    " 5/8   -   Os.C. Companies
    " 9   -   Transport Officer
    " 10   -   Quartermaster
    " 11   -   Lewis Gun Officer
    " 12   -   Signal Officer
    " 13   -   Medical Officer
    " 14   -   R.S.M.
    " 15   -   File
    " 16/17 -   War Diary.

Copy No. 14

1/5th Battalion PRINCE OF WALES'S (NORTH STAFFORD REGT)

OPERATION ORDER No. 84.

Reference Sheet 36.c.N.W. 1/20,000.

1. A raid will be carried out by the 1/6th Battalion Prince of Wales's (North Stafford Regiment) on the afternoon of 31st October 1917, on the enemy's first and second line trench, between points H.25.d.76.94 and H.25.b.59.52.

2. ZERO hour will be 4-32 pm.

3. A dummy raid will take place on the front BOYAU 71 to 72.a. at ZERO - 4 minutes.

4. **Artillery and Machine Guns.** The Artillery and Machine Gun Programmes have been issued to all concerned.

5. **Trench Mortars.**

    For Dummy Raid.
    From ZERO - 4 minutes to ZERO. 137th Trench Mortar Battery will engage following points :-
    H.13.d.30.50.
    H.13.c.63.75.
    and from H.13.a.30.42 to H.13.a.35.30.

    X/46th Trench Mortar Battery.
    One 2" Trench Mortar will :- engage Trench Mortar emplacements at H.19.a.85.70. to H.19.a.90.50. and form a flank barrage to the Artillery creeping barrage.

    One 2" Trench Mortar will :- engage enemy T.M.s at H.13.a.93.63.

    One 2" Trench Mortar will :- engage enemy T.M.s at H.13.a.58.35

    One 9.45" T.M. will engage enemy emplacements around H.13.Central.

    For raid.
    137th Trench Mortar Battery. From ZERO onwards, will engage points H.19.d.39.08. and H.19.c.90.60.

    139th Trench Mortar Battery. From Zero to ZERO plus 7 minutes, will barrage enemy's trench H.26.c.72.65. to H.26.c.30.90.

    X/46th Trench Mortar Battery.
    One 2" Trench Mortar will :- engage POSEN CRATER.

    One 6" Trench Mortar will :- Bombard junction of HIVE and HOBART Trenches, and engage T.M. emplacements surrounding this junction

6. No. 4. Special Company R.E. will co-operate as follows :-
    (a). Place a thin screen in front of dummies at ZERO - 4 minutes.
    (b) Smoke barrage just South of HULLUCH to cover left flank of raiding party from ZERO to ZERO plus 1 hour.
    (c). Bombard Southern portion of HULLUCH with Gas bombs at ZERO plus 10 minutes.

    All precautions as detailed in Trench Standing Orders Appendix 11 (Gas Operations) will be carried out.

1/5th Battalion North Stafford Regiment.

NOTES ON DUMMY RAID

ON LEFT BATTALION FRONT.

OF HULLUCH SECTION.   31-10-17.

The barrage put down at 4-28.pm (ZERO - 4 minutes) immediately South of HULLUCH was most effective. It took about one minute before sections of smoke screen joined up, and became a continuous wall. This probable gave sufficient time for the enemy to see the dummy figures in the lanes between through the smoke.
From ZERO to ZERO plus 25 minutes the smoke barrage was very dense. There was a very slight current of air from the South West.
Puffs of magenta coloured smoke appeared in the white smoke cloud. These were 'short' lachrymatory gas bombs from the 4" Stokes Mortars.

Enemy barrage. This appeared to commence on our front and support lines at ZERO plus 6 minutes. A few minutes later it lifted on to our Support lines a line between Reserve and Support lines.
Apparently the feint was extremely successful, as most of the enemy barrage was attracted to the area between VERMELLES - HULLUCH Rd and VENDIN ALLEY, and the real raid front farther South received very little attention from the enemy's guns.
Our tunnel post area was shelled with 77 mm. Front and support line trenches 69 to 72.a received a thin barrage of 77.mm, 4.2 H.E. Shrapnel and 5.9.
Barrage became more dense, and for a few minutes was quite heavy when it lifted on to open ground about 150 yds West of our Support Line. Very few shells came near our Supporting Reserve line.
At ZERO plus 25 minutes, enemy shelling died away and became slight.

At 6.18 pm. a heavy barrage of 77.mm, 4.2"., 5.9" was put down on our tunnel posts, and our Reserve Line also came in for a little attention. The Outpost Company sent through "ATTACK HULLUCH" at 6.22.pm and our artillery who were "standing to" opened up almost immediately. The enemy fire ceased about 6-30.pm. and our barrage was quickly stopped.

DUMMY figures. These appeared to have been much damaged by enemy artillery fire.

Machine Gun Fire. Enemy machine gun fire appeared to be chiefly laid on to front and support lines and tunnel post area.
TENTH AVENUE near junction with ESSEX LANE was enfiladed by M.G. fire and was dangerous to walk along. Fire appeared to come from the QUARRIES in G.12.a.

AEROPLANES. Our areoplanes caused several fire in HULLUCH with their bombs.

Enemy Signals. One White Very light on Dummy raid front, and Red lights behind VENDIN were the only Signals seen.

(sd).   A.E.F. FAWCUS.
Lt-Col.
Comdg 1/5th Battalion North Stafford Regiment.

1-11-17.

1/5th Battalion North Stafford Regiment.

NOTES ON DUMMY RAID

ON LEFT BATTALION FRONT.

OF HULLUCH SECTION.   31-10-17.

The barrage put down at 4-28.pm (ZERO - 4 minutes) immediately South of HULLUCH was most effective. It took about one minute before sections of smoke screen joined up, and became a continuous wall. This probable gave sufficient time for the enemy to see the dummy figures in the lanes between through the smoke.
From ZERO to ZERO plus 25 minutes the smoke barrage was very dense. There was a very slight current of air from the South West.
Puffs of magenta coloured smoke appeared in the white smoke cloud. These were 'short' lachrymatory gas bombs from the 4" Stokes Mortars.

Enemy barrage. This appeared to commence on our front and support lines at ZERO plus 6 minutes. A few minutes later it lifted on to our Support lines a line between Reserve and Support lines.
Apparently the feint was extremely successful, as most of the enemy barrage was attracted to the area between VERMELLES - HULLUCH Rd and VENDIN ALLEY, and the real raid front farther South received very little attention from the enemy's guns.
Our tunnel post area was shelled with 77 mm. Front and support line trenches 69 to 72.a received a thin barrage of 77.mm, 4.2 H.E. Shrapnel and 5.9.
Barrage became more dense, and for a few minutes was quite heavy when it lifted on to open ground about 150 yds West of our Support Line. Very few shells came near our Supporting Reserve line.
At ZERO plus 25 minutes, enemy shelling died away and became slight.

At 6.18 pm. a heavy barrage of 77.mm, 4.2"., 5.9" was put down on our tunnel posts, and our Reserve Line also came in for a little attention. The Outpost Company sent through "ATTACK HULLUCH" at 6.22.pm and our artillery who were "standing to" opened up almost immediately. The enemy fire ceased about 6-30.pm. and our barrage was quickly stopped.

DUMMY figures. These appeared to have been much damaged by enemy artillery fire.

Machine Gun Fire. Enemy machine gun fire appeared to be chiefly laid on to front and support lines and tunnel post area.
TENTH AVENUE near junction with ESSEX LANE was enfiladed by M.G. fire and was dangerous to walk along. Fire appeared to come from the QUARRIES in G.12.a.

AEROPLANES. Our areoplanes caused several fire in HULLUCH with their bombs.

Enemy Signals. One White Very light on Dummy raid front, and Red lights behind VENDIN were the only Signals seen.

(sd). A.E.F. FAWCUS.
Lt-Col.
Comdg 1/5th Battalion North Stafford Regiment.

1-11-17.

ORIGINAL

1/5th BATTALION PRINCE OF WALES'S (NORTH STAFFORDSHIRE REGIMENT).

W A R   D I A R Y

for month of

NOVEMBER 1917.

ooOoo

Army Form C. 2118.

WAR DIARY
or
INTELLIGENCE SUMMARY

1/5th Battalion North Stafford Regiment.

Page 1.

(Erase heading not required.)

Instructions regarding War Diaries and Intelligence Summaries are contained in F.S. Regs., Part II. and the Staff Manual respectively. Title pages will be prepared in manuscript.

Place	Date	Hour	Summary of Events and Information	Remarks and references to Appendices
	November 1917.		Reference Maps. Sheet 36.c. N.W. 1/20,000. & 36.b 1/40,000.	
TRENCHES.	1st.		Quiet day. Gas Operation as per Orders attached. No retaliation.	1
do	2nd.		Quiet day. 2nd. Lieut. Staniforth awarded the MILITARY CROSS for good work on patrol on night of 15/16th October 1917.	2
do	3rd.		Quiet day. Battalion was relieved by the 1/5th South Stafford Regt, and went into Divisional Reserve at VERQUIN. Relief complete 8-30.pm.	3
VERQUIN.	4th.		Battalion in Divisional Reserve. Bathing and cleaning up.	
do	5th.		General and Specialist training. 9.am to 1.pm.	
do	6th.		Battalion on Firing Range. Concert at night. Message received from Division "Be prepared to move at 2 hours notice." Battalion "Stood to" until 1.pm.	
do	7th.		Battalion moved to trenches and relieved the 1/5th South Stafford Regt in the Left Subsection. Relief complete 7.40.pm. Quiet night.	4
TRENCHES.	8th.		Quiet day. A few 4.2.s fell in Reserve Line.	
do	9th.		Reserve and Support Lines shelled intermittently during day. About 200 4.2s and 5.9.s. No casualties.	
do	10th.		Attempted raid made by "D" Coy. 2nd. Lieut. H.F. Evans and 1 O.R. wounded. 2 O.R.s Missing, but one missing man returned after 24 hours. Patrol Report attached.	5
do	11th.		Battalion relieved by 1/6th South Stafford Regiment, and proceed to Support. "B" & "C" Coys in MAZINGARBE, and "A" & "D" Coys in TENTH AVENUE. Relief complete 7-30.pm.	6
MAZINGARBE.	12th.		Cleaning up and Baths. Football Match against 231st Bde R.F.A. Result. Win 4.2.	

WAR DIARY
or
INTELLIGENCE SUMMARY.

(Erase heading not required.)

1/5th Bn. North Stafford Regt Army Form C. 2118.

Page 11.

Place	Date	Hour	Summary of Events and Information	Remarks and references to Appendices
	November 1917.			
MAZINGARBE.	13th.		Parades in the morning for 1 hour. "B" & "C" Companies relieved "A" & "D" Coys respectively. Relief complete 3.pm.	7
do	14th.		Bathing and Cleaning up. Battalion played Football against 137th Bde Headquarters. Result:- Win 7.0.	8
do	15th.		Battalion relieved 1/5th South Stafford Regiment in the Right Subsection. Relief complete by 7.pm.	
TRENCHES.	16th.		Quiet day and night	
do	17th.		Harrassing fire on/roads and tracks by our Artillery and Machine Guns from 9.pm. to 10-30.pm. Very little retaliation. enemy	
do.	18th.		Enemy Artillery fairly active, shelling C.Ts and Reserve Line with 5.9.s., and front and Support Lines with 4.2s and Trench Mortars. No casualties.	
do	19th.		Fairly Quiet day. Battalion relieved by 1/6th South Stafford Regt and moved to billets at VERQUIN (Divisional Reserve) via PHILOSOPHE to SAILLY-LABOURSE Light Railway. All in billets by 10-30.pm.	9.
VERQUIN.	20th.		Baths and cleaning up. Football match against 6th Bn. Sherwood Foresters. Result Win 2. o.	
do	21st.		General and Specialist Training. Casual Visit by G.O.C. Division.	
do	22nd.		General and Specialist Training from from 8-45.am to 1.pm.	
do	23rd.		Battalion relieved 1/5th South Stafford Regiment in the Left Subsector Relief complete 6-30.pm.	10
TRENCHES.	24th.		Quiet day. Tump line and Yukon Pack used for carrying 2' Trench Mortars, proved successful.	
do	25th		Quiet day. Enemy Patrol encountered in NO MANS LAND about 30 strong, but were driven off by one of our Patrols – 8 strong.	

Army Form C. 2118.

WAR DIARY
or
INTELLIGENCE SUMMARY.

1/5th Bn. North Stafford Regt.

Page 111.

(Erase heading not required.)

Place	Date	Hour	Summary of Events and Information	Remarks and references to Appendices
	NOVEMBER 1917.			
TRENCHES.	26th.		Enemy shelled Tunnel Posts and Reserve Line during morning.	
do.	27th.		Battalion relieved by 1/6th South Stafford Regiment, and went into Support. "A" & "D" Coys in NOYELLES and "B" & "C" Coys in TENTH AVENUE. Relief complete 6-40.pm. 2nd. Lieut. A.L. Paget of 3rd Durham Light Infantry joined Battalion from the Base, and posted to "C" Coy. Battalion Officers' Mess commenced.	11
NOYELLES.	28th.		Bathing and Cleaning up. Gas Projectors successfully discharged in Left Subsection. The enemy retaliated on Reserve lines with H.E. & 4.2.s.	
do	29th.		"A" & "D" Companies relieved "B" & "C" Companies respectively. Relief complete 7.pm. Harrassing fire carried out on enemy roads and tracks. He retaliated and village and camp was shelled by 4.2.s. No casualties.	12
do	30th.		Cleaning up and Baths. Battalion played football against 4th Leicesters. Stiff game. Result Draw 1 each. Camp shelled between 8-30.pm. and 9.pm. with H.E. and Gas Shells. One N.C.O. wounded.	

W. Paulson, Major,
Commanding 1/5th Bn. North Stafford Regiment.

Army Form C. 2118.

WAR DIARY
1/5th Bn. North Stafford Regt.
or
INTELLIGENCE SUMMARY.

Page iv.

(Erase heading not required.)

SUMMARY of Strength and Casualties for month of November 1917.

	Casualties.							Strength.	
	Officers.				Other Ranks.				
	K.	W.	M.	Hosp.	K.	W.	M.	Hosp.	Officers.	Other Ranks.
For week ending 2-11-17.	-	-	-	-	-	-	-	6	40.	824.
" " " 9-11-17.	-	-	-	1	-	-	-	8	40.	820.
" " " 16-11-17.	-	1	-	-	1	1	-	8	40	812.
" " " 23-11-17.	-	-	-	1	-	-	-	8	38.	804.
" " " 30-11-17.	-	-	-	-	-	-	-	9.	39	805.
	-	1	-	2	-	1	1	39.		

Major,
Commanding 1/5th Bn. North Stafford Regiment.

SECRET.   Copy No. 12

1/5th Battalion PRINCE OF WALES'S (NORTH STAFFORD REGT).

OPERATION ORDER No. 85.

Reference Sheet 36.c. N.W. 1/20,000.

1. On the night 1/2nd November 1917, if the wind is favourable, or on the first succeeding favourable night, a gas operation will be carried out on HULLUCH & ST ELIE.

2. "K" Special Company R.E. will carry out a projector attack as follows:-
    (a). Position of Projectors :-   G.18.b.3.3.
         Target.   HULLUCH H.13.d.5.8.
         Number of Drums.   300 (C.G.)

    (b). Position of Projectors -   G.18.a.Central.
         Target.   - ST ELIE. G.12.b.8.7.
         Number of Drums.   - 350. (C.G.)

3. Wind Limits :- N.W. through W. to S.

4. Lieut. C.D. STOKES "K" Special Company R.E. will be in command of the firing parties, and will be at Battalion Headquarters at G.18.a.0.2.

5. Special Gas precautions will be taken from ZERO - 5' until Special Company Gas Officer reports "ALL CLEAR", as follows :-
    (a). All personnel will wear Box Respirators, all dug-out entrance blankets will be lowered and all gas doors closed within the triangle G.18.a.Central - G.12.c.5.8. - G.12.d.8.0. and the triangle G.18.b.3.3. - G.19.b.8.8. - H.13.c.3.3.

6. Codes :-
    Operation will take place tonight - First ZERO   - LONDON A.
    Operation will not take place tonight   -do-   - BRIGHTON A.

    Operation will take place tonight - Second ZERO. - LONDON B.
    Operation will not take place tonight   -do-   - BRIGHTON B.

    Operation complete   "ALL CLEAR"   - DOVER.

    ZERO.
7. To allow for any change in the wind two alternative ZEROS have been arranged.
   ZERO hours will be notified later.

8. ACKNOWLEDGE.

                                              E. A. WILSON.
                                              Captain & Adjutant.
                                              1/5th Bn. North Stafford Regt.

Copies issued at   pm. on 30.10.17.
    Copy. No. 1.   Comdg. Officer.
            2.   2nd. in Cmd.
            3.   O.C. "A" Coy.
            4.   O.C. "B" "
            5.   O.C. "C" "
            6.   O.C. "D" "
            7.   Signalling Officer.
            8.   Lewis Gun Offr.
            9.   Medical Offr.
           10.   R.S.M.
           11.   File.
           12/13.   War Diary.

SECRET.
COPY No. 1

1/5th Battalion Prince of Wales's (North Staffs. Regt.).

RELIEF ORDER No. 87.

Reference :- Sheet 36C. NW.1/20,000
" 36B. 1/40,000

Friday - 2.11.17.

1. The Battalion will be relieved by the 1/5th Battalion South Staffs. Regiment on the night of 3/4th November 1917. Relief may be expected about 7.30 p.m..

2. On relief, the Battalion will be in Divisional Reserve at VERQUIN.

3. MOVE. On relief platoons will move independently to L.23.b.10.70 and march from that point to VERQUIN. Route - Main Road to NOEUX-LES-MINES K.12.c.85.85 - VERQUIN.

4. Quartermaster will arrange for tea at L.23.b.10.70 and a hot meal on arrival at VERQUIN.

5. Stores of Headquarters, "A", "B" & "C" Companies, will be at HAY DUMP at 5.45 p.m. and stores of "D" Company at QUARRY DUMP by 5.45 pm..

6. Lewis Guns and 12 magazines per gun will be taken out by gun teams to PHILOSOPHE where they will be loaded on Lewis Gun Limbers. 80 Lewis Gun magazines per Company will be handed over to relieving Battalion and the Quartermaster will arrange to take over a similar quantity at VERQUIN.

7. 8 Cooking Boilers will be handed over to relieving Battalion and Quartermaster will arrange to take over a like quantity at VERQUIN.

8. Advance Party consisting of Company Quartermaster-Sergts., 1 N.C.O., 1 Cook and 1 Officers' Servant per Company, Quarter Guard & R.E. MINX Guard (as detailed by R.S.M.) will report to Headquarters at 10.0 a.m. and march under orders of senior N.C.O. to VERQUIN where they will report to Quartermaster.

9. Quartermaster will arrange to take over billets and maps of training areas from 1/5th Bn. South Staffs. Regiment.

10. Company Officers' Chargers will be at Brigade Headqrs. at 8.0 p.m. and Headqrs. Officers Chargers at 8.30 p.m..

11. Lists of Stores to be handed over, and Statements of work done & Work proposed, and maps of NO MAN'S LAND will be sent to Headqrs. by 10.0 a.m..

12. Relief complete will be reported to Headquarters by B.A.B. Code and arrival in billets at VERQUIN by runner.

13. ACKNOWLEDGE.

E. A. WILSON,
Captain & Adjutant,
1/5th Bn. Prince of Wales's (North Staffs. Regiment).

Copies issued at 7 p.m. on 2.11.17 to :-
Copy No. 1. Commanding Officer.
2. 2nd in Command
3. 137 Brigade H.Q.
4. O.C.1/5 South Staffs.
5/8. Os.C.Companies
9. Medical Officer.
10. Lewis Gun Officer.
11. Signal Officer.
12. Transport Offr.& Q.M.
13. R.S.M.
14. File.
15/16 War Diary.

SECRET.   Copy No.
          1/5th Battalion Prince of Wales's (South Staffs. Regt.)

                                                                   S.11.N.
                    R E L I E F   O R D E R   No. 20.

Reference:- Sheets 550.1/40,000 & 20,000, S.A.1/10,000.

1.   The Battalion will relieve the 1/6th South
    Staffordshire Regiment in the Left Subsection on the night of
    the 7/8th November 1917.

2.   DISPOSITIONS.
                 "D" Coy. .... Right Company.
                 "C" Coy. .... Centre Company.
                 "A" Coy. .... Outpost Company.
                 "B" Coy. .... Left Company.

3. The Battalion will move off by Companies at 200 yards distance
    to Brigade headquarters ground.
                 Time 1.0 p.m..

4.   Tea will be served on arrival at Brigade Headqrs.
    Grounds.

5.   The Battalion will move off from Brigade H.Q. by
    platoons at 200 yards distance.
                 Time - 4.30 p.m..

6. Order of March - "D", "C", "A", Hedqrs, "B" Company.

7. Dress - Fighting Order, rubber mac' sheets, greatcoats, mess tins
    water-bottles full and rations for the 8th inst..

8. Packs will be collected from Company Headqrs. at 11.30 a.m..

9. Advance Party. Consisting of one Officer per Company, Lewis
    Gun Officer, one N.C.O. per platoon, C.S.M., Pioneer Sergt.,
    Signal Officer and Battalion Signal Section, M.G. & Company
    Gas N.C.Os., and Coy. Cooks will proceed to the trenches early
    to take over, marching off from here at 10 a.m. under the senior
    officer.

10. Each of following parties will not have more than 2 at 100
    yards distance during daylight.

11. Officers' kitbags and mess boxes will be collected from Coy.
    Headqrs. at 12 noon.   Stores for the trenches will be
    collected from Coy. Headqrs. at 1.30 p.m.. 4 Leader, Servts,
    and 2 servts. per Coy. under 1/Cpl. Greenhalgh with limber
    taking trench stores. This party will push up the trucks.

12. The Transport Officer will detail two water-duty men to go
    up with rations and remain in the trenches for the tour.

13. Ample supply of ammunition per gun will be taken to
    the line by the machinery and carried from there by the Lewis
    Gun teams in the line.

    6 magazines per gun. will be taken over from the 1/6th
    South Staffs. Regt. and a like number handed over to the 1/6th
    South Staffs. Regt. by the Quartermaster.

14. S.A.A. machinery will be taken over from the 1/6th
    South Staffs. Regiment.

15. Mule it. will be effected as hereunder on proceeding to
    the trenches.

16. O.C. Companies will send in relief report form from the
    trenches in the Battalion T.M. code.

17. Daily reports of all relevant to be submitted to Headquarters
    in B.T.M. code.

18. Lists of stores taken over and dispositions with map
    references will be rendered to Headquarters as soon as possible
    after relief.

                                          Captain   Adjt.
                                    1/5th Bn. Prince of Wales's (South Staffs.Regt.)

Copies Issued to:-   No.
to :-   No. 1. Commanding Officer.
           2. 2nd in Command.
           3. 137 Bde. H.Q.
           4. O.C. 1/5th South Staffs. Regt.
           5. O.C. 1/6th   "   "   "
           6/9. O.Cs. Companies.
           10. Transport Officer & Q.M.
           11. R.S.M.
           12. File.

1/5th Battalion North Staffordshire Regiment.   Date... 10th Nov.1917

PATROL REPORT.

Composition of Patrol	Task.	Time & Point of Departure.	REPORT.	Time & Point of Return.
2nd Lieut. H.F. EVANS and 10. O.R's.	To enter enemy line and obtain identification.	11.45 p.m. H.19.a.35.58.	Patrol proceeded E. for 100 yds. when Leader went forward and remainder formed covering party. Sounds of a wiring party were heard in front and large number of men were distinguished in groups. The enemy opened fire with M.G. from both flanks, and threw about 20 bombs when party tried to move forward. Party then rejoined remainder of patrol and opened rifle fire on enemy party, to which enemy retaliated with Priester bombs. Further progress could not be made.	2.30 a.m. H.19.a.35.58.

Divisional Commander's remarks :- "Good effort."

SECRET. COPY No. 140

1/5th Battalion Prince of Wales's (North Staffs. Regiment).

RELIEF ORDER No. 89. 10/11/17.

Reference :-
Sheet 36C. N.W.1/20,000.

1. The Battalion will be relieved by the 1/6th South Staffs. Regt. on the night of 11/12th November 1917, about 7.0 p.m..

2. On relief, the Battalion will be in close support.
   The Battalion - less "B" & "D" Companies in MAZINGARBE.
   "B" & "D" Companies in TENTH AVENUE.

3. "A" & "C" Companies on relief, will move by platoons to Huts in MAZINGARBE.

4. "B" Company on relief will move into dugouts in TENTH AVENUE taking over from "A" Company 1/6th South Staffs. Regt.. This Company will be under O.C. 3rd Australian Tunnelling Coy. for work and O.C. 1/6th South Staffs. tactically.

5. "D" Company on relief will move into dugouts in TENTH AVENUE taking over from "B" Company 1/5th South Staffs. Regt.. This Company will be under O.C. 466 Field Coy. R.E. for work and O.C. 1/6th South Staffs. Regt. tactically.

6. Os.C. "B" & "D" Companies will each send one Officer and one N.C.O. to take over dugouts &c.to report to O.C. the Company which they are relieving before 2.30 p.m..

7. Os.C. "A" & "C" Companies will each send the following to report to Headquarters at 11.30 a.m. as advance party -
   1 N.C.O., 1 Cook, and 1 Officers' Servant.
   R.S.M. will detail the Brigade Guard and Divisional Bomb Store Guard.

8. 80 Lewis Gun Magazines (in panniers) per Company will be handed over and taken over. 2 Cooking Boilers per Company will be handed over.

9. Stores of Headquarters and "A" & "C" Companies will be at HAY DUMP by 5.45 p.m..

10. Gum Boots will be handed in to Brigade Stores and receipts taken.

11. Quartermaster will arrange for rations, blankets and cooking utensils for "B" & "D" Companies to be brought up. O.C. "B" Company will send a N.C.O. to HAY DUMP at 5.45 p.m. and O.C. "D" Company a N.C.O. to QUARRY DUMP at 5.30 p.m. to meet rations.

12. Lists of Stores to be handed over, statements of work done & work proposed, and NO MAN'S LAND maps, will be sent to Headquarters by 10.0 a.m..

13. RELIEF COMPLETE to be reported to Headquarters by B.A.B. Code.

14. ACKNOWLEDGE.

E. A. WILSON,
Captain & Adjutant,
1/5th Bn.Prince of Wales's (North Staffs.Regt).

ISSUED by runner at 8.0 p.m.
to :- Copy No. 1. Commanding Officer.
" 2. 2nd in Command.
" 3/6. Os.C.Companies.
" 7. Transport Officer & Qmr.
" 8. R.S.M.
" 9. Hqrs.137 Bde.
" 10. O.C. 1/5th South Staffs.Regt..
" 11. O.C. 1/6th South Staffs. Regt..
" 12. File.
" 13/14. War Diary.

SECRET Copy No. ___

1/5th Battalion Prince of Wales's (North Staffs.Regt.)

12th November 1917.

R E L I E F   O R D E R   No.90

1.   On the night of the 13th/14th November, 1917, "B" and "C" Coys. will relieve "A" and "D" Coys. respectively in Close Support in TENTH AVENUE.

2.   "B" and "C" Companies will commence leaving MAZINGARBE at 4.30.p.m.

3.   Packs and Officers' valises will be collected from the Camp and Coy. H.Qrs. at 4.15.p.m.

4.   Cooking utensils, Lewis Gun magazines and blankets will be taken over.

5.   Quartermaster will arrange for rations for the 14th inst to go up on trucks.

6.   "A" and "D" Coys. will each send one officer, 2 N.C.Os. one cook and one servant during the afternoon of the 13th inst. to take over billets, etc. and "B" & "C" Coys. will each send an officer to TENTH AVENUE to take over during the afternoon.

7.   RELIEF COMPLETE will be reported to Headquarters in B.A.B. Code.

8.   "C" Coy. will find a carrying party of 1 N.C.O. and 15 men to report to QUARRY DUMP at 5.0.p.m. to carry Trench Mortars.. This party will go up early under orders from O.C. "C" Coy.

9.   ACKNOWLEDGE.

                            E. A. WILSON,
                              Captain & Adjutant,
                              1/5th Bn.North Staffs.Regt.

Copies issued at   p.m.

No.	
1	Commanding Officer
2	2nd in Command.
3.	Transport Officer and Quartermaster.
4/7	Os.C. Companies
8	R.S.M.
9	O.C. 466th Field Coy.R.E.
10	O.C. 3rd Australian Tunnelling Coy.
11	File
12/13	War Diary.

SECRET.   COPY No. 14?

1/5th Battalion Prince of Wales's (North Staffs. Regiment).

R E L I E F   O R D E R   No 91.

REFERENCE :- Sheet 36C, N.W. 1/20,000.

1. **RELIEF.** The Battalion will relieve the 1/5th Battalion South Staffs. Regiment in the HULLUCH - RIGHT SUBSECTION on the night of 15/16th November 1917.

2. **DISPOSITION.** On relief, Companies will be as under :-

    "A" - Left Support Company.
    "B" - Left Company.
    "C" - Right Company.
    "D" - Right Support Company.

3. **MOVE.** "B" & "C" Companies will move from TENTH AVENUE at 4.0 p.m.
   "A" & "D" Companies will parade in ground behind the huts at 3.45 p.m. Order of march:- "D", "A", Headquarters. Dress:- Fighting Order and greatcoats. Route:- LAMBERTS' TRACK.

4. **ADVANCE PARTY.** An advance party, consisting of 1 Officer per Company, Lewis Gun Sergeant, 1 N.C.O. per platoon, R.S.M., Pioneer Sergeant, Signal Officer and Battalion Signal Section, Headquarters and Company Gas N.C.Os., and Company Cooks, will proceed to take over early, those in MAZINGARBE parading on Camp ground under Senior Officer at 3.0 p.m.

5. **STORES &c.** Officers' valises and mess boxes of "A" and "D" Companies will be collected from Company Headquarters at 2.0 p.m. Packs will be collected at the same hour.
   Stores for the trenches will be collected at 3.45 p.m.

6. **LEWIS GUN MAGAZINES.** 80 Lewis Gun Magazines per Company will be taken over from the 1/5th South Staffs. Regt. and a similar number handed over.

7. **GUM BOOTS.** "B" Company will draw 75 prs. from Brigade Store, LONE TRENCH.
   "C" Company "   "   70 prs. from -do-.
   "A" Company will draw 15 prs. from Quartermaster at 11 a.m. tomorrow.
   "D" Company "   "   20 prs. from   -do-.
   Headquarters "   "   20 prs. from   -do-.

8. **COOKING UTENSILS.** Quartermaster will arrange for 8 Boilers and 4 Bacon Tins to be taken into the trenches.

9. **WHALE OIL,** will be used by all ranks before proceeding to the trenches.

10. BLANKETS of "B" & "C" Companies will be sent back on the empty ration trucks.

11. RELIEF COMPLETE will be wired to Battalion Headquarters in B.A.B. Code.

12. RETURNS.   Lists of Stores taken over, Disposition of Posts giving map references, Distribution of Rifles, will be rendered to Battalion Headquarters as soon as possible after relief.

13. ACKNOWLEDGE.

E. A. WILSON,
Captain & Adjutant,
1/5th Battalion Prince of Wales's (North Staffs.Regiment).

COPIES ISSUED at 8:30 p.m. on 14/11/17.
    to :-
No. 1. Commanding Officer.
"   2. 2nd in Command.
"   3/6. Os.C. Companies.
"   7. Transport Officer and Quartermaster.
"   8. R.S.M.
"   9. Headquarters, 137th Inf.Bde.
"   10. O.C. 1/5th South Staffs. Regt.
"   11. O.C. 1/6th South Staffs. Regt.
"   12. File.
"   13/14. War Diary

SECRET. (9) Copy No. 14

1/5th Battalion Prince Of Wales's (North Staffs.Regt.)
----------oo0Ooo----------

R E L I E F   O R D E R   No.92.
18th November 1917.

Reference Maps :-
Sheet 36 C.N.W.1/20,000
" 36B, 1/40,000
----

1. **Relief** . The Battalion will be relieved in the trenches by the 1/6th Bn.South Staffordshire Regt., at about 6-30 pm on the 19th November 1917.

2. **Disposition** The Battalion on relief will be in Divisional Reserve at VERQUIN.

3. **Move.** Instructions as to route and transport will be issued to all concerned.

4. **Stores.** All stores for companies will be at CHALK PIT DUMP at 5-30 pm, for Headquarters and Canteen at POSEN DUMP at 5-30 pm.
Cooking utensils will be taken out.

5. 80 Lewis-gun magazines (in panniers) per company will be handed over. Quartermaster will take over a like number at VERQUIN.

6. **Gum Boots.** Instructions re gum boots will be issued tomorrow.

7. **Billeting party** consisting of one N.C.O., one cook and one Officer's servant per company, one N.C.O. from Headqrs., and Battn.Quarter Guard will report to Battn., Headqrs. at 10-0 am.

8. **Returns.** 'List of Stores to be handed over', 'Work done and work proposed' and 'No Man's Land maps' will be sent to Orderly Room by 10-0 am.

9. **Relief Complete** will be wired to Headqrs. by sending the word 'PRIMITIVE'.

10. ACKNOWLEDGE.

E.A.WILSON,
Captain & Adjutant,
1/5th Bn.North Staffs.Regt.

Copies issued at 8.0 pm as under :-
No.1........ Commanding Officer.
     2........ 2nd in Command.
     3........ H.Qrs.,137th Infantry Brigade.
     4........ O.C.1/6th Bn.South Staffs.Regt.
Nos 5/8. ....O.C.Companies
No.9........ Transport Officer.
  "10........ Quartermaster.
    11 ...... R.S.M.
    12....... File.
    13/14....War Diary

SECRET.   COPY No. 13

1/5th Battalion Prince of Wales's (North Staffordshire Regiment).

RELIEF ORDER No.93.
Thursday - 22.11.17.

Reference:-
Sheets 36 B. 1/40,000 &
36 C. NW. 1/20,000.

1. The Battalion will relieve the 1/5th Battalion South Staffordshire Regiment in the Left Subsection on the night of the 23rd/24th November 1917.

2. Dispositions :-
    "A" Company......... Left Company.
    "B"   "   .... Outpost Company.
    "C"   "   .... Right Company.
    "D"   "   .... Centre Company.
   The Tump Line Section under 2nd Lieut. Oulton will be at Battalion Headquarters.

3. The Battalion will move off by Companies at 300 yards interval to Brigade Headquarters ground.
    Time :- 12.45 p.m.
    Tea will be served on arrival at Brigade Headquarters grounds.

4. The Battalion will move off from Brigade Headquarters by platoons at 200 yards interval.
    Time :- 3.45 p.m.
    Order of march :- "C", "B", "D" Hqrs., "A" Company.
    Strict march discipline will be observed.

5. Dress :- Fighting Order, waterproof sheets, greatcoats, mess tins and waterbottles full.

6. Packs will be collected from Company Headquarters at 11.30 a.m..

7. Advance Party consisting of one Officer per Company, Lewis Gun Sergeant, one N.C.O. per platoon, R.S.M., Pioneer Sergeant, Signal Officer and Battalion Signal Section, H.Q. and Company Gas N.C.Os. and Company Cooks, will proceed to the trenches early to take over, marching off from here at 12 noon under the Senior Officer.

8. East of PHILOSOPHE parties will not be of more than two at 100 yards distance during daylight.

9. Officers' valises and mess boxes will be collected from Company Headquarters at 12.0 noon.
   Stores for the trenches will be collected from Company Headquarters at 12.45 p.m. Four Headquarters Servants and two servants per Company under L/Cpl. Green will march with limber taking trench stores. This Party will push up the trucks.

10. Transport Officer will detail two water-duty men to go up with Headquarters and remain in the trenches for the tour.

11. Lewis Guns and 12 magazines per gun will be taken to PHILOSOPHE by the Transport and carried from there by the Lewis Gun Teams to the line.
    80 magazines per gun will be taken over from the 1/5th South Staffs. Regiment and a like number handed over to the 1/6th South Staffs. Regiment by the Quartermaster.

12. Two dixies per Company will be taken over from the 1/5th South Staffs. Regiment.

13. Whale oil will be used by all ranks before proceeding to the trenches.

14. O.C. "C" Company will draw 24 pairs Gum Boots from Brigade Gum Boot Store.
R.S.M. will draw 6 pairs.

15. <u>RELIEF COMPLETE</u> will be wired to Battalion Headquarters by the code word 'VANITY'.

16. Lists of Stores taken over, and Dispositions (with map references) will be rendered to Headquarters as soon as possible after relief.

E.A. WILSON,
Captain & Adjutant,
1/5th Bn. Prince of Wales's (North Staffs. Regt).

Copies issued at 7.0 p.m. to:-

No. 1. Commanding Officer.
" 2. 2nd in Command.
" 3. 137th Infantry Brigade.
" 4. O.C. 1/5th Bn. South Staffs. Regt..
" 5. O.C. 1/6th Bn. South Staffs. Regt..
" 6/9. Os.C. Companies.
" 10. Transport Officer.
" 11. Quartermaster.
" 12. File.
" 13/14. War Diary.

SECRET.   COPY No.

1/5th Battalion Prince of Wales's (North Staffordshire Regiment).

R E L I E F   O R D E R No.94.
26.11.17.

Reference :- Sheets
            36C.1N.E.1/20,000.
            36B. 1/40,000.

1. The Battalion will be relieved by the 1/6th Battalion South Staffordshire Regiment on the night of 27th/28th November 1917, at about 6.30 p.m..

2. On relief, the Battalion will be in close support -
   H.Q., "A" & "D" Companies in NOYELLES.
   "B" & "C" Companies in TENTH AVENUE.

3. (a) Headquarters, "A" & "D" Companies, on relief, will move to Huts in NOYELLES, guides meeting platoons at Cross Roads - L.17.B.30.80.
   (b) "B" Company will move into dugouts in TENTH AVENUE, taking over from "D" Company 1/5th Battalion South Stafford Regiment (Company Headquarters in NINTH AVENUE).
   The Company will be under O.C. 1/6th South Staffords Regiment tactically and O.C. 3rd Australian Tunnelling Company for work.
   (c) "C" Company will move into dugouts in TENTH AVENUE taking over from "C" Company 1/5th South Staffordshire Regiment (Company Headquarters near junction of TENTH AVENUE and LONE TRENCH).
   This Company will be under O.C. 1/5th South Staffs. Regiment tactically and O.C. 466th Field Company R.E. for work.

4. Os.C. "B" & "C" Companies will each send one Officer and one N.C.O. to take over dugouts etc. to report to O.C. the Company which they are relieving before 2.30 p.m..

5. The following advance party will report to Headquarters at 10.30 a.m., one N.C.O., one Cook, and one Officers servant from "A" & "D" Companies, Brigade Guard, Divisional Bomb Store Guard and Brigade Quarter Guard,(as detailed by R.S.M.).

6. 80 Lewis Gun Magazines (in panniers) per Company will be handed over and taken over.

7. Stores from Headquarters, "A" & "D" Companies, will be HAY DUMP by 5.15 p.m..

8. 2 Cooking Boilers per Company will be handed over to relieving Companies. Quartermaster will arrange for Cooking utensils for "B" & "C" Companies to come up with rations.

9. Os.C. "B" & "C" Companies will send a N.C.O. to HAY DUMP and QUARRY DUMP respectively at 5.0 p.m. to meet ration trucks.

10. Lists of Stores to be handed over, Statements of work done and work proposed, and No Man's Land Maps will be sent to Headquarters by 10.0 a.m..

11. RELIEF COMPLETE to be 'phoned to Battalion Headquarters by the Code word - NATIONAL.

12. ACKNOWLEDGE.

Captain & Adjutant,
1/5th Battalion Prince of Wales's (North Staffordshire Regiment).

COPIES ISSUED at 6.30 p.m. to :-

```
No. 1.  Commanding Officer.
    2.  2nd in Command.
    3.  137th Infantry Brigade.
    4.  O.C. 1/5th South Staffs. Regt..
    5.  O.C. 1/6th South Staffs. Regt..
  6/9.  Os.C. Companies.
   10.  Transport Officer & Quartermaster.
   11.  R.S.M.
   12.  File.
13/14.  War Diary.
```

SECRET.   COPY No. 12

1/5th Battalion Prince of Wales's (North Staffordshire Regiment).

RELIEF ORDER No. 95.   28/11/17.

1. On the night 29/30th November "A" & "D" Companies will relieve "B" & "C" Companies respectively in TENTH AVENUE.

2. "A" & "D" Companies will parade and move off at 3.45 p.m.

3. Packs and Officers' valises will be collected from the Camp at 3.0 p.m.

4. Cooking utensils, Lewis Gun magazines and blankets will be taken over and handed over.

5. Quartermaster will arrange for the rations for the 30th to go up on trucks.

6. "B" & "C" Companies will send down their Billeting parties during the afternoon of the 29th to take over, and "A" & "D" Companies will each send an Officer to TENTH AVENUE to take over.

7. Stores for the trenches will be ready at the Camp by 3.15 p.m.

8. RELIEF COMPLETE will be reported to Headquarters in B.A.B. Code.

9. ACKNOWLEDGE.

                                                   Captain & Adjutant,
                                          1/5th Bn. North Staffs. Regiment.

Copies issued at 2 p.m.
to :-

No. 1. Commanding Officer.
    2. 2nd in Command.
    3. Transport Officer & Quartermaster.
    4/7. Os.C. Companies.
    8. R.S.M.
    9. O.C. 466th Field Coy. R.E.
    10. O.C. 3rd Aust. Tunnelling Coy.
    11. File.
    12/13. War Diary

SECRET.   Copy No.

1/5th Battalion Prince of Wales's (North Staffordshire Regiment).

R E L I E F   O R D E R   No. 96.

REFERENCE :-   Friday -
Sheet 36C.N.W. 1/20,000.   30.11.17.

1. **RELIEF.** The Battalion will relieve the 1/5th Battalion South Staffordshire Regiment in the HULLUCH RIGHT SUBSECTION on the night of 1/2nd December 1917.

2. **DISPOSITION.** On relief, Companies will be as under :-

    "A" - Left Company.
    "B" - Left Support Company.
    "C" - Right Support Company.
    "D" - Right Company.

3. **MOVE.** "A" & "D" Companies will move from TENTH AVENUE at 3.30 p.m..
    "B" & "C" Companies and Headquarters will parade in ground behind the huts at 3.30 p.m.
    Order of march :- "B", "C", Headquarters.
    Dress :- Fighting Order and greatcoats and leather jerkins.
    Route :- LAMBERT'S TRACK.

4. **ADVANCE PARTY.** An advance party consisting of 1 Officer per Company, Lewis Gun Officer, 1 N.C.O. per platoon, R.S.M., Pioneer Sergeant, Signal Officer and Battalion Signal Section, Headquarters and Company Gas N.C.Os., and Company Cooks, will proceed to take over early, those in NOYELLES parading on Camp ground under Senior Officer at 2.0 p.m..

5. **STORES &c.** Officers' valises and mess boxes of "B" & "C" Companies will be collected from Company Headquarters at 2.0 p.m.. Packs will be collected at the same hour. Stores for the trenches will be collected at 3.15 p.m.

6. **LEWIS GUN MAGAZINES.** 80 Lewis Gun magazines per Company will be taken over from the 1/5th South Staffs. Regiment, and a similar number handed over.

7. **GUM BOOts.** "A" Company will draw 75 pairs gum boots from Brigade Store, LONE TRENCH.
    "D" Company will draw 70 pairs from -do-.
    "B"   "   "   "   15   "   "   "
    "C"   "   "   "   20   "   "   "
    Headquarters "   "   20   "   "   "

8. **COOKING UTENSILS.** Quartermaster will arrange for 12 boilers and 4 bacon tins to be taken into the trenches.

9. **WHALE OIL,** will be used by all ranks before proceeding to the trenches.

10. **BLANKETS** of "B" & "D" Companies will be sent back on the empty ration trucks.

11. **RELIEF COMPLETE** will be wired to Battalion Headquarters in B.A.B. Code.

12. **RETURNS.** Lists of stores taken over, Dispositions of Posts giving map references, Distribution of Rifles, will be rendered to Battalion Headquarters as soon as possible after relief.

13. **TUMP LINE SECTION.** The Tump Line Section will be at Battalion Headqrs..

14. ACKNOWLEDGE.

                              E.A.WILSON,
                                    Captain & Adjutant,
        1/5th Battalion Prince of Wales's (North Staffordshire Regiment)

Copies issued at   5.30 p.m. on 30/11/17.
    to :-   No. 1. Commanding Officer.
                 " 2. 2nd in Command.
                 " 3/6. Os.C. Companies.
                 " 7. Transport Officer & Quartermaster.
                 " 8. R.S.M.
                 " 9. Headquarters, 137 Infantry Bde.
                 " 10. O.C. 1/5th South Staffs. Regt.
                 " 11. O.C. 1/6th South Staffs. Regt.
                 " 12. File.
                 " 13/14. War Diary.

Original

Army Form C. 2118.

WAR DIARY
or
INTELLIGENCE SUMMARY.
(Erase heading not required.)

Vol 35

1/5th Battalion Prince of Wales's
(North Staffordshire Regiment)
War Diary.
for
Month of December 1917

Army Form C. 2118.

WAR DIARY

1/5th Bn. North Staffordshire Regiment.

~~INTELLIGENCE SUMMARY~~

PAGE 1.

(Erase heading not required.)

Instructions regarding War Diaries and Intelligence Summaries are contained in F. S. Regs., Part II. and the Staff Manual respectively. Title pages will be prepared in manuscript.

Reference Maps :- Sheets 36C. N.W. 1/20,000 and 36B. 1/40,000.

Place	Date	Hour	Summary of Events and Information	Remarks and references to Appendices
	December 1917.			
NOYELLES.	1st		"B" & "C" Companies 1½ hours parade. Battalion relieved 1/5th Bn. South Staffs. Regt. in HULLUCH Right Subsection. Relief complete 6.45 p.m. Order No. 96 attached.	
TRENCHES	2nd.		Quiet day. Usual patrolling of front carried out.	
do.	3rd.		Quiet day. Patrolling as usual during night.	
do.	4th.		Quiet day.	
do.	5th.		Battalion relieved by 1/6th Bn. South Staffs. Regt. and went into Divisional Reserve at NOEUX-LES-MINES. Battalion all in camp at 9.0 p.m. Order No. 97. attached.	
NOEUX-LES-MINES.	6th.		Companies at disposal of Company Commanders for bathing and cleaning up.	
do.	7th.		Parades from 9.0 a.m. to 1.0 p.m. Commanding Officer inspected "C" & "D" Companies in Field Service Marching Order at 9.0 a.m. and 10.0 a.m. respectively.	
do.	8th.		Parades from 9.0 a.m. to 1.0 p.m. Commanding Officer inspected "A" & "B" Companies in Field Service Marching Order at 9.0 a.m. and 9.45 a.m. respectively. Battalion Canteen Accounts audited by an Audit Board under the Presidency of Captain G.J.Worthington.	
do.	9th.		Church Parades in morning. Battalion relieved 1/5th Bn. South Staffs. Regiment in HULLUCH Left Subsection. Relief complete 6.30 p.m. Order No. 98 attached.	
TRENCHES.	10th.		Quiet day. Intermittent shelling of Reserve Line.	
do.	11th.		Quiet day. Enemy Machine Guns active at dusk, sweeping dumps &c..	
do.	12th		Quiet day. 2nd Lieut. WINT and 9. O.R's attempted to enter the enemy trenches at night at	

Army Form C. 2118.

WAR DIARY

Intelligence Summary.

1/5th Battalion North Staffs. Regt.

PAGE II.

(Erase heading not required.)

Instructions regarding War Diaries and Intelligence Summaries are contained in F.S. Regs., Part II. and the Staff Manual respectively. Title pages will be prepared in manuscript.

Place	Date	Hour	Summary of Events and Information	Remarks and references to Appendices
	December 1917.			
TRENCHES.	12th contd.		about H.19.a.60.90 but were frustrated by persistent Machine Gun fire from flanks. G.O.C. Division wired his appreciation and remarked ' A bold and Good attempt to carry out the task allotted'.	
	13th.		Battalion relieved by the 1/6th Bn. South Staffs. Regt. and proceeded to close support. "B" & "C" Companies and Headquarters in NOYELLES. "A" Company in TENTH AVENUE, "D" Company in TUNNELS. Relief complete 7.0 p.m. Order No. 99 attached.	
NOYELLES.	14th.		"B" & "C" Companies at the disposal of Company Commanders for cleaning up, bathing and kit inspections.	
do.	15th.		Inter-Company reliefs. Order No. 100 attached. Morning Parades "B" & "C" Companies 1½ hours platoon drill and musketry. Order No. 100 attached.	
do.	16th.		Church Parades. "A" & "D" Companies bathing.	
do.	17th.		1 hours Guards under R.S.M. Battalion relieved 1/5th Bn. South Staffs. Regt. in HULLUCH Right Subsection. Relief complete 6.15 p.m. Order No. 101 attached.	
TRENCHES.	18th.		Very quiet day. Mist prevented activity and allowed movement. Plenty of work done round dumps.	
do.	19th.		Frost & mist. Right Reserve Company shelled - 2 casualties.	
do.	20th.		Very misty. No artillery or aerial activity. Salvage parties in front of Reserve Line.	
do.	21st.		2nd Lieut. WINT and 10 O.R's made a daylight sortie near FOSEN CRATER and inflicted casualties (estimated at 14) on enemy. Our casualties were 2nd Lieut.WINT wounded, 2 O.R's killed, 2 O.Rs wounded and 2 missing. Operation Order No. 103 and report in detail attached. Battalion relieved by 1/6th Bn. South Staffs. Regt. and proceeded to Divisional Reserve in NOEUX-LES-MINES. Relief complete 6.30 p.m. Order No. 102. attached.	

WAR DIARY 1/5th Bn. North Stafford Regiment. Army Form C. 2118.

Page 3.

INTELLIGENCE SUMMARY.

(Erase heading not required.)

Place	Date	Hour	Summary of Events and Information	Remarks and references to Appendices
	December 1917.			
NOEUX-les-MINES	22nd.		Companies at the disposal of Company Commanders for cleaning up, kit inspections &c.	
do.	23rd.		Church Parades. 1 hours Ceremonial. Transport Christmas Dinner.	
do.	24th.		Battalion celebrated Christmas Day. One hours parade followed by Football Match - "A" & "C" Coys -V- "B" & "D" Companies. Result:- Draw. 1 each. Battalion Christmas Dinner at 2.pm. W.O.s and Sergeants at 7-30.pm., followed by Concert in the Sergeants' Mess.	
do.	25th.		Church Parades in the morning. Battalion relieved 1/5th South Stafford Regiment in the HULLUCH LEFT SUBSECTION. Relief complete 6-30.pm. Order. No. 104 attached.	
TRENCHES.	26th.		Quiet day.	
do.	27th.		Quiet day. Enemy fired gas-shells near QUARRY DUMP.	
do.	28th.		Quiet day. Enemy Trench Mortars and Artillery more active than usual.	
do.	29th.		Battalion relieved by 1/6th South Stafford Regiment. Relief complete 6-30.pm. Order No. 105 attached. H.Qrs. "A" & "D" Coys in MAZINGARBE. "B" Coy in HULLUCH TUNNEL. "C" Coy in TENTH AVENUE.	
MAZINGARBE.	30th.		Bathing and Cleaning up. Church Parades.	
do.	31st.		1½ hours parade. Lecture on economy. "D" Coy relieved "B" Coy, and "A" Coy relieved "C" Coy. "B" & "C" Coy back in billets at 7.pm.	

A. Porker
Major,
Commanding 1/5th Bn. North Stafford Regiment.

WAR DIARY or INTELLIGENCE SUMMARY

1/5th Bn. North Stafford Regiment Army Form C. 2118.

Page. 4.

(Erase heading not required.)

Instructions regarding War Diaries and Intelligence Summaries are contained in F. S. Regs., Part II. and the Staff Manual respectively. Title pages will be prepared in manuscript.

SUMMARY OF CASUALTIES AND STRENGTH.

	CASUALTIES							STRENGTH	
	OFFICERS				OTHER RANKS				
	K.	W.	M.	Hosp.	K.	W.	M.	Hosp.	OFFICERS.	OTHER RANKS.
For week ending 7-12-17.	-	-	-	1.	-	1	-	12	39.	799.
" " " 14-12-17.	-	1 H.P.	H.P.	1	-	5	-	10	36.	792.
" " " 21-12-17.	-	-	-	-	3	6	2	6	37.	789.
" " " 28-12-17.	-	1 H.P.	H.P.	-	-	-	-	10.	32	814.
	-	2	-	2	3	12	2	38.		

A. Pocher, Major,
Commanding 1/5th Battalion North Stafford Regiment.

SECRET.   COPY No.

1/5th Battalion Prince of Wales's (North Staffordshire Regiment).

O R D E R No. 97.

4th December 1917.

Reference - Maps :-
    Sheet 36C. NW. 1/20,000.
      "   36B. 1/40,000.

1. **Relief.** The Battalion will be relieved in the trenches by the 1/6th Battalion South Staffordshire Regiment at about 6.0 p.m. on the 5th December 1917.

2. **Disposition.** The Battalion on relief will be in Divisional Reserve at NOEUX-LES-MINES.

3. **Move.** On relief platoons will march independently to Cross Roads L.22.d.85.55, and thence by Companies to NOEUX-LES-MINES. Guides will be at cross roads L.13.c.05.95.

4. **Stores.** All stores of "C" & "D" Companies will be at CHALK PIT DUMP at 5.30 p.m., of "A" & "B" Companies at GUN DUMP at 5.30 p.m. and Headquarters and Canteen at POSEN DUMP at 5.30 p.m..
Cooking utensils will be taken out.

5. 80 Lewis Gun Magazines (in panniers) per Company will be handed over. Quartermaster will take over a similar number at NOEUX-LES-MINES.

6. **Gum Boots.** These will be sent to Brigade Gum Boot Store in LONE TRENCH tomorrow morning, (Support Companies carrying for forward Companies). Receipts will be sent to Orderly Room.

7. **Billeting Party,** consisting of one N.C.O., one cook, and one Officers' servant per Company, one N.C.O. from Headquarters, and Battalion Quarter-Guard will report to Headquarters at 9.0 a.m..

8. **Officers' Chargers** will be at Brigade Headquarters at 7.0 p.m.

9. **Returns.** 'Lists of Stores to be handed over','Work done and work proposed' and 'No Man's Land maps' will be sent to Orderly Room by 10.0 a.m..

10. **Relief Complete** will be wired to Headquarters by the Code - word :-'BELT.'

11. ACKNOWLEDGE.

                                                E. A. WILSON,
                                                    Captain & Adjutant,
    1/5th Battalion Prince of Wales's (North Staffordshire Regiment).

Copies issued at   p.m. as under :-
    No. 1. Commanding Officer.
       2. 2nd in Command.
       3. Headquarters, 137 Infantry Bde.
       4. O.C. 1/6th Bn. South Staffs. Regt..
    5/8. Os.C Companies.
       9. Transport Officer & Quartermaster.
      10. R.S.M.
      11. File.
   12/13. War Diary.

SECRET.   Copy No. __14__

1/5th Battalion Prince of Wales's (North Staffordshire Regiment).

O R D E R   No.98.
8th December 1917.

Reference :-
   Sheets   36 B 1/40,000 &
            36 C.NW. 1/20,000

1. The Battalion will relieve the 1/5th Battalion South Staffordshire Regiment in the Left Subsection on the night of 9th December 1917.

2. Dispositions :-
   "B" Company .... Left Company.
   "A"   "   .... Outpost Company.
   "D"   "   .... Right Company.
   "C"   "   .... Centre Company.
   The Tump Line Section under 2nd.Lieut Oulton will be at Battalion Headquarters.

3. The Battalion will move off by companies at 300 yards interval
      Time :- 2 p.m.
   Companies will proceed by platoons at 200 yards interval for MAZINGARBE commencing at 3-30 p.m.
      Order of march :- "D","A","C", "H.Qrs" and "B" Coy.
   Strict march discipline will be observed.

4. Dress :- Fighting order, waterproof sheets, greatcoats, mess tins and waterbottles full. Leather jerkins will be rolled in greatcoats.

5. Packs and blankets will be collected from Coy.H.Qrs. at 10-30 am

6. Advance Party consisting of one Officer per company, Lewis Gun Sergeant, one N.C.O. per platoon, R.S.M., Pioneer Sergeant, Signal Officer and Battn.Signal Section, H.Q.& Coy.Gas N.C.Os and Company cooks, will proceed to the trenches early to take over, marching off from here at 12 noon under the senior Officer.

7. East of PHILOSOPHE parties will not be of more two at 100 yards distance during daylight.

8. Officers' valises and mess boxes will be collected from the corner near H.Q.Mess at 1-0 pm.
   Stores for the trenches will be collected from Coy.H.Qr. at 12-45 pm. Four H.Q.servants and two servants per company under L/C.Green will march with limber taking trench stores. This party will push up the trucks

9. Transport Officer will detail water-duty men to go up with Headquarters and remain in the trenches for the tour.

10. Lewis Guns and 12 magazines per gun will be taken to PHILOSOPHE by the transport and carried from there by the Lewis gun teams to the line.
    80 magazines per gun will be taken from the 1/5th Bn.South Staffs. and a like number handed over to the 1/6th Bn.South Staffs.Regt by the Quartermaster.

11. The Quartermaster will arrange for 12 boilers and 8 fryers to be taken into the trenches.

12. Whale Oil will be used by all ranks before proceeding to the trenches and a certificate rendered to Orderly Room that this has been done. Whilst in the line feet will be rubbed daily and a certificate rendered.

P.T.O.

13. O.C. "D" Company will draw 24 pairs Gum Boots from the Brigade Gum Boot Store.
    R.S.M. will draw 6 pairs.

14. Relief Complete will be wired to Battalion Headquarters.
    Code word :- 'HUD'.

15. 'List of Stores taken over   'Dispositions of Posts' (giving map references) and 'Dispositions of Rifles' will be rendered to Headquarters as soon as possible after relief.

                           J.MURPHY, 2nd.Lieut
                              A/Adjutant.
             1/5th Bn.Prince of Wales's (North Staffs.Regt

Copies issued at 8¤ pm. to :-

No.1. Commanding Officer.
  2. 2nd. in Command.
  3. 137th Infantry Brigade.
  4. O.C. 1/5th Bn.South Staffs.Regt.
  5. O.C. 1/6th Bn.South Staffs.Regt.
  6/9.Os.C.Companies.
  10. Transport Officer.
  11. Quartermaster.
  12. R.S.M.
  13. File.
  14/15. War Diary

SECRET

1/5th Battalion Prince of Wales's (North Staffs.Regt.)   Copy No. 13

ORDER No. 99   12th December, 1917

Reference Sheet 36.C.N.W. 1/20,000
36.B. 1/40,000

1. The Battalion will be relieved by the 1/6th Battalion South Staffs.Regt. on the night of the 13th/14th December, 1917.
2. On relief the Battalion will be in Close Support. H.Q., "B" & "C" Coys. in NOYELLES, "D" Coy. in Tunnels, "A" Coy. in TENTH AVENUE.
3. (a) On relief guides will meet platoons of "B" & "C" Coys. and Headquarters at Cross Roads, L.17.b.30.80. and conduct them to billets.
   (b) "D" Coy. will move into dugouts in Tunnels, taking over from "B" Coy. 1/5th Battalion South Staffs.Regt. (Coy.H.Q. at bottom of RESERVE SHAFT).
   This Company will be under O.C. 1/6th Battalion South Staffs. Regt. tactically and under O.C. 3rd Australian Tunnelling Coy. for work.
   (c) "A" Coy. will move into dugouts in TENTH AVENUE, taking over from "A" Coy. 1/5th South Staffs.Regt. (Coy.H.Q. near junction of TENTH AVENUE and LONE TRENCH).
   This Coy. will be under O.C. 1/6th Battalion South Staffs. Regt. tactically and under O.C. 466th Field Coy.R.E. for work.
4. Os.C. "A" & "D" Coys. will each send one officer and one N.C.O. to take over dugouts, etc., to report to O.C. the Coy. which they are relieving before 2.30.p.m.
5. The following Advance Party will report to Headquarters at 10.30.a.m. one N.C.O., one cook and one officer's servant per Company from "B" & "C" Coys. Brigade Guard, Divisional Bomb Store Guard and Battalion Quarter Guard (as detailed by R.S.M.)
6. 80 Lewis Gun Magazines (in panniers) per Coy. will be handed over and taken over.
7. Stores from Headquarters, "B" & "C" Coys. will be at HAY DUMP by 4.30.p.m.
8. 2 Boilers and one fryer per Coy. will be handed over to relieving Coy.
   "C" Coy. will hand over remaining boiler and fryer to "A" Coy. and B Coy. to D Coy.
9. Os.C. "A" & "D" Coys. will each send a N.C.O. to HAY DUMP and QUARRY DUMP respectively at 4.30.p.m to meet ration trucks.
10. Lists of Stores to be handed over, Statements of work done and work prepared and No Man's Land Maps will be sent to Headquarters by 10.0.a.m.
11. RELIEF COMPLETE to be 'phoned to Battalion Headquarters by the Code word - 'GRANTHAM'
12. Acknowledge.

J Murphy 2/Lt
A/Adjutant,
1/5th Battalion, Prince of Wales's
(North Staffordshire Regiment.)

Copies issued at 6.0 p.m.

No.1	-	Commanding Officer
2	-	2nd in Command
3	-	137th Infantry Brigade
4	-	O.C. 1/5th Bn.South Staffs.Regt.
5	-	O.C. 1/6th Bn.South Staffs.Regt.
6/9	-	Companies
10	-	T.O. and Q.M.
11	-	R.S.M.
12	-	File
13/14	-	War Diary

SECRET   Copy No. _____

1/5th Battalion Prince of Wales's (North Staffordshire Regiment.)

ORDER No. 101   16-12-17

Reference :- Sheet 36.C. N.W. 1/20,000

1. **RELIEF** — The Battalion will relieve the 1/5th Battalion South Staffs.Regt. in the HULLUCH RIGHT SUBSECTION on the night of the 17th/18th December, 1917.

2. **DISPOSITIONS** — On relief, disposition of Companies will be as under :-
    - "B" Coy.   -   Left Company
    - "A" Coy.   -   Left Support Company
    - "D" Coy.   -   Right Support Company
    - "C" Coy.   -   Right Company

3. **MOVE** — "B" & "C" Companies will move at 3.30.p.m.
    "A" & "D" Companies and Headquarters will parade on ground behind the huts at 3.30.p.m.
    Order of March :- "D" Coy., "A" Coy., Headquarters.
    Dress :- Fighting Order and greatcoats; leather jerkins will be worn over the tunic.
    Route :- LAMBERT'S TRACK.

4. **ADVANCE PARTY** — An Advance Party consisting of one officer per Company, Lewis Gun Sergeant, one N.C.O. per platoon, R.S.M., Pioneer Sergeant, Signal Officer and Bn.Signal Section, H.Q. and Coy. Gas N.C.Os. and Coy. cooks will proceed to take over early, these in NOYELLES parading on Camp Ground under senior officer at 2.0.p.m.

5. **STORES** — Officers' valises and Mess boxes of "A" & "D" Coys. will be collected from Q.M.Stores at 2.0.p.m. Packs will be collected at the same hour from billets. Stores for the trenches will be collected at 3.0.p.m. at Cross Roads.

6. **LEWIS GUN MAGAZINES** — 80 L.G. Magazines per Company will be taken over from the 1/5th South Staffs.Regt. and a similar number handed over.

7. **GUM BOOTS** — Gum boots will be drawn from Brigade Stores LONE TRENCH, as follows :-
    - "B" Coy.   -   75 pairs.
    - "C" "   -   70 pairs.
    - "A" "   -   15 pairs.
    - "D" "   -   20 pairs.
    - Headquarters   -   20 pairs.

8. **COOKING UTENSILS** — Quartermaster will arrange for 7 boilers and 4 biscuit tins to be taken into the trenches.

9. **WHALE OIL** — Whale Oil will be used by all ranks before proceeding to the trenches and certificates rendered. Whale Oil will be used daily in the trenches and certificates given.

10. **BLANKETS** — Blankets of "B"&"C" Coys. will be sent back on the empty ration trucks.

11. **RELIEF COMPLETE** — Relief Complete will be wired to Br.H.Q. in B.A.B. Code.

12. **RETURNS** — Lists of stores taken over, Dispositions of Posts (with map references) Distribution of Rifles will be rendered to Br.H.Q. as soon as possible after relief.

13. **TUMP LINE SECTION** — The Tump Line Section will be at Br.H.Q. and will provide a carrying party for the T.M.Battery to be at CHALK PIT DUMP at 8.0.a.m. each day.
    The R.S.M. will detail 24 Other Ranks to work in shifts of 8 under Tunnelling Coy., commencing at 9.p.m.

14. **ACKNOWLEDGE**

                                            J. MURPHY,
                                            2nd Lieut.& a/Adjutant,
                                            1/5th North Staffs.Regt.

Copies issued at 5.30.p.m.   16-12-17

No.1	-	Commanding Officer
2	-	2nd in Command
3	-	137th Infantry Brigade
4	-	O.C. 1/5th South Staffs.Regt.
5	-	O.C. 1/6th South Staffs.Regt.
6/9	-	Companies
10	-	TO. & Q.M.
11	-	R.S.M.
12	-	File
13/14	-	War Diary

SECRET.

1/5th Battalion Prince of Wales's (North Staffordshire Regiment)

ORDER No. 100

14-12-17

1. On the night 15th/16th December, 1917 "B" & "C" Companies will relieve "A" & "D" Companies in TENTH AVENUE and TUNNELS respectively.

2. "B" & "C" Companies will parade to move off at 3.45.p.m.

3. Packs and Officers' valises will be collected from billets at 3.0.p.m.

4. Cooking utensils, Lewis Gun Magazines and blankets will be taken over and handed over.

5. Quartermaster will arrange for rations for the 16th inst. to go up on trucks.

6. "A" & "D" Companies will send down their billeting parties during the afternoon of the 15th to take over, and "B" & "C" Companies will each send an officer to TENTH AVENUE and TUNNELS respectively to take over.

7. Stores for the trenches will be ready at the Camp by 3.15.p.m.

8. RELIEF COMPLETE will be reported to Headquarters in B.A.B. Code.

9. ACKNOWLEDGE.

J. MURPHY,

2nd Lieut.& A/Adjutant,
1/5th Bn.North Staffs.Regt.

Copies issued at 6.0.p.m.

No. 1   Commanding Officer
    2   2nd in Command
    3   Transport Officer and Quartermaster
    4/7 Companies
    8   R.S.M.
    9   O.C.466th Field Coy.R.E.
    10 O.C. 3rd Australian Tunnelling Coy.
    11 File
    12/13 War Diary

SECRET.   Copy No............

1/5th Battalion Prince of Wales's (North Staffordshire Regiment).

O R D E R   No.   102.   20th December 1917.

Reference Maps:-   Sheet 36.b. 1/40,000.
                      Sheet.36.c.NW. 1/20,000.

1. **Relief.** The Battalion will be relieved in the trenches by the 1/6th Battalion South Staffordshire Regt at about 6.pm. on 21st December 1917.

2. **Disposition.** The Battalion on relief will be in Divisional Reserve at NOEUX-les-MINES.

3. **Move.** On relief platoons will march independantly to Cross Roads L.22.d.85.55., and thence by Companies to NOEUX-les-MINES. Guides will be at Cross Roads L.13.c.05.95.

4. **Stores.** All Stores for "C" & "D" Companies will be at CHALK PIT DUMP at 4-30.pm. of "A" & "B" Companies at GUN DUMP at 4.pm., and Headquarters and Canteen at POSEN DUMP at 4-30.pm.
Two Boilers and 1 Fryer per Company will be handed over. The remainder to be taken out.
The Quartermaster will arrange to take over from 1/6th South Stafford Regt. 8 Boilers and 4 Fryers.

5. **Lewis Guns.** 80 Lewis Gun Magazines (in Panniers) per Company will be handed over. Quartermaster will take over a similiar number at NOEUX-les-MINES.

6. **Gum Boots.** All Gum Boots will be sent to Bde Gum Boot Store in LONE TRENCH tomorrow morning (Tump Line Section carrying for Forward Companies) Receipts will be sent to Orderly Room.

7. **Billeting Party,** consisting of X one N.C.O. per Coy, One Cook and one Officers Servant per Company, One N.C.O. from Headquarters, and Battn Quarter Guard, will report to Headquarters at 9. am. tommorow.

8. **Officers Chargers** will be at Brigade Headquarters at 7.pm.

9. **Returns.** 'Lists of Stores to be handed over" "Work done and Work Proposed, and Maps of NO. MANS' LAND" will be sent to Orderly Room at 10.am.

10. **Relief complete** will be wired to Headquarters; Code Word:- CHITS.

11. **Acknowledge.**

                                                    J. MURPHY. 2nd. Lieut.
               A/Adjt. 1/5th Bn. North Stafford Regiment.

Copies issued at   p.m. on 20th Dec. 1917 as under.
- No. 1.   Commanding Officer.
- " 2.   2nd in Command.
- " 3.   H.Q. 137th Inf. Bde.
- " 4.   O.C. 1/6th South Staffs Regt.
- " 5.   O.C. 1/5th South Stafford Regt.
- " 6/9.   O.C.s All Companies.
- " 10.   T.O. & Q.M.
- " 11.   R.S.M.
- " 12.   File.
- " 13/14.   War Diary.

SECRET.   COPY No.

1/5th Battalion North Staffordshire Regiment.

O P E R A T I O N   O R D E R   No. 103.

Thursday - 20.12.17.

1. **INTENTION.**
   To enter enemy trench between H.19.d.18.30 and H.19.d.12.50 to secure identification.

2. **INSTRUCTIONS.**
   (a) The party will consist of 2nd Lieut. WINT, one sergeant, two corporals, and 7 men.
   (b) The party will assemble in old front line about H.19.c.98.30 tomorrow, 21st inst..
   (c) At 8.5 a.m. the party will move forward and enter enemy's line.
   (d) A Lewis Gun will be placed in front line at H.25.b.00.99 and will be in position not later than 7.45 a.m. O.C."C" Company will be responsible for this.
   (e) Watches will be synchronised at Battalion Headquarters at 6.0 a.m.
   (f) The 137th Stokes Mortar Battery will co-operate as follows :-
   At 8.12 a.m. until 'All Clear' two rounds per minute will be fired on the following targets :-
   (1). POSEN CRATER.
   (2). H.19.d.42.30.
   (3). H.19.d.30.15.
   (g). **ARTILLERY.**
   'GLEAM' will fire 3 minutes intense with 2 guns and then normal until 'all Clear' on enemy front line between H.19.d.c.97.61. and H.19.c.93.80. commencing at 8.12.a.m.

   (h). **Machine Guns.**
   The 137th Machine Gun Company will fire on enemy front line between H.19.a.70.70 and H.19.a.20.20 from 8.12 a.m. until 'All Clear'.

   (j). Signal Officer will be responsible for arranging telephone communication from H.25.b.00.99 to Battalion Headquarters.

3. **ACKNOWLEDGE.**

J. MURPHY,
2nd Lieut.
A/Adjutant,
1/5th Bn. North Staffs. Regt.

Copies issued to :-

No. 1. Commanding Officer.
2. 137th Inf.Bde.
3. O.C. "A" Company.
4. O.C. "C" Company.
5. O.C. 137th T.M.Battery.
6. O.C. 137th Machine Gun Company.
7. O.C. 'GLEAM'
8. File.
9/10.War Diary.

Copy:-

R E P O R T on an attempt to kill enemy and secure identification, carried out in daylight by the 1/5th Battalion North Staffordshire Regiment.

At 8.5. a.m. on the 21st December, a party of 1 Officer (2nd Lieut. WINT) and 10. O.R's. having crept out to the old front line at H.19.c.98.30, made a sudden dash to the enemy line at H.19.d.10.45.

The enemy wire was crossed without difficulty and the party reached the trench and jumped in. Immediately on their right was a hostile party of at least 20 men. Rifle and revolver shots and bombs were exchanged, and the Officer seeing that his party was outnumbered, ordered them to withdraw. He himself was the last to leave trench and at least 3 of the enemy were shot dead and probably others were wounded by bombs. While the party was returning to our lines, heavy rifle fire was opened on them and several were hit. The Officer and a Corporal were caught in the enemy wire but managed to escape, and as many bombs were being thrown at them, they dropped into a shell-hole close to the wire. Here the Corporal bound up the wounds in the Officer's hand and knee.

A party of ten of the enemy then left their line and coming near the shell-hole, shouted "Hands up, we know where you are". At the same moment rifle and Lewis Gun fire from our front line knocked out four of the enemy, and the remainder retired, while the Officer and Corporal made a dash for a ditch, and ultimately succeeded in getting back to our trenches. While they were getting in, three more of the enemy were hit by our snipers. Also at the moment when the party commenced to withdraw, our snipers accounted for 3 of the enemy who got out of the trench.

Two of our men were wounded near our own lines, and after two men had been hit in going to help them, a third man was killed.

Gaps were then cut in our own wire in a disused trench, and the two men were brought in, one of whom died immediately.

Two of the patrol are at present missing.

The enemy suffered at least 13 casualties and probably more.

The enemy were wearing dark grey uniform, 'pork-pie' caps with a red band and a small grenade badge, similar to our Royal Fusiliers, but light in colour.
One man stated that the collars of the tunics were red.

sd/. H. POCHIN,
Major,
21.12.17.   Commanding 1/5th Battalion North Staffs. Regt.

CORPS COMMANDERS REMARKS.

' I consider this a very fine bit of work, and wish 2nd.Lt. WINT and the Members of his patrol congratulated for me, on their dash and enterprise. It is by indivual and collective acts of gallantry such as was shewn by this patrol, that we establish our superiority over the enemy'

SECRET.   COPY No. 14

1/5th Battalion Prince of Wales's (North Staffordshire Regiment).

O R D E R   No. 104.
24th December 1917.

Reference :- Sheets - 36B, 1/40,000 & 36C. N.E. 1/20,000.

1. The Battalion will relieve the 1/5th Battalion South Staffordshire Regiment in the Left Subsection on the night of 25th December 1917.

2. Dispositions :-
   "A" Company .... Left Company.
   "B"   "   .... Outpost Company.
   "C"   "   .... Right Company.
   "D"   "   .... Centre Company.

   The Tump Line Section under 2nd Lieut. Culton will be at Battalion Headquarters.

3. The Battalion will move off by companies at 300 yards interval
   Time :- 2.15 p.m.
   Companies will proceed by platoons at 200 yards interval from MAZINGARBE commencing at 3.30 p.m.
   Order of march :- "C", "B", "D", "Hqrs" and "A" Company. Strict march discipline will be observed.

4. Dress :- Fighting Order, waterproof sheets, greatcoats, mess tins, and waterbottles full. Leather jerkins will be rolled in greatcoats.

5. Packs and blankets will be collected from the camp at 10.30 a.m.

6. Advance Party consisting of one Officer per Company, Lewis Gun Sergeant, one N.C.O. per platoon, R.S.M., Pioneer Sergeant, Signal Officer and Battalion Signal Section, HQrs. and Company Gas N.C.Os, and Company Cooks, will proceed to the trenches early to take over, marching from here at 12 noon under the senior Officer.

7. Last of PHILOSOPHE parties will not be of more than two at 100 yards distance during daylight.

8. Officers' valises and mess boxes will be collected from the corner near Battalion Hqrs at 1.0 p.m.
   Stores for the trenches will be collected from Company Hqrs. at 12.45 p.m. Four H.Q. servants and two servants per company under L/C. Green will march with limber taking trench stores. This party will push up the trucks.

9. Transport Officer will detail water-duty men to go up with Headquarters and remain in the trenches for the tour.

10. Lewis Guns and 12 magazines per gun will be taken to PHILOSOPHE by the transport and will move from the camp at 1.30 p.m., three Lewis Gunners per Company marching with the limbers.
    80 magazines per gun will be taken over from the 1/5th Bn. South Staffs. Regt. and a similar number handed over to the 1/6th Bn. South Staffs. Regt. by the Quartermaster.

11. The Quartermaster will arrange for 12 boilers and 8 fryers to be taken into the trenches.

12. Whale Oil will be used by all ranks before proceeding to the trenches and a certificate rendered to Orderly Room that this has been done. Whilst in the line feet will be rubbed daily and a certificate rendered to Orderly Room to this effect.

13. O.C. "C" Company will draw 24 pairs gum boots from the Brigade Gum Boot Store.
R.S.M. will draw 6 pairs.

14. <u>Relief Complete</u> will be wired to Battalion Headquarters.
Code Word :- ' DIRT '.

15. 'Lists of Stores taken over', 'Dispositions of Posts' (giving map references) and 'Distributions of Rifles' will be rendered to Headquarters as soon as possible after relief.

F.A. WILSON,
Captain & Adjutant,
1/5th Bn. Prince of Wales's (North Staffs. Regt).

Copies issued at   p.m. to :-

No. 1. Commanding Officer.
2. 2nd in Command.
3. 137th Infantry Bde.
4. O.C. 1/5th Bn. South Staffs. Regt.
5. O.C. 1/6th Bn. South Staffs. Regt.
6/9. Os.C. Companies.
10. Transport Officer.
11. Quartermaster.
12. R.S.M.
13. File.
14/15. War Diary.

SECRET.
1/5th Battalion Prince of Wales's (North Staffordshire Regt.)   COPY No.

O R D E R   No. 105

Friday – 28/12/17.

Reference :– Sheets 36C. N.W. 1/20,000 &
36B. 1/40,000.

1. **Relief.** The Battalion will be relieved in the trenches by the 1/6th Battalion South Staffordshire Regiment on the night of 29/30th December 1917, at about 5.30 p.m..

2. **Disposition.** The Battalion, on relief, will be in close support – The Battalion (less "B" & "C" Companies) in MAZINGARBE, "B" Company in HULLUCH TUNNEL and "C" Company in TENTH AVENUE.

3. **Move.** On relief, Headquarters, "A" & "D" Companies will move into huts in MAZINGARBE.
   "B" Company on relief will move into dugouts in HULLUCH TUNNEL. (This Company will be under the 3rd Australian Tunnelling Coy for work and under O.C. 1/6th South Staffs. Regt. tactically).
   "C" Company on relief will move into dugouts in TENTH AVENUE (Company Headquarters near junction of LONE TRENCH and TENTH AVENUE. (This Company will be under O.C. 466th Field Coy. R.E. for work and under O.C. 1/5th South Staffs. Regt. tactically).

4. **Advance party.** Os.C. "B" & "C" Companies will each send an Officer and 2 N.C.Os to take over dugouts &c., to report to the O.C. Company which they are relieving at 2.0 p.m..
   Os. C. "A" & "D" Companies will each send one N.C.O. one cook, one servant, also Brigade Guard, Battalion Quarter Guard, and Divisional Bomb Store Guard (as detailed by R.S.M.) to report at Battalion Headquarters at 10.0 a.m..

P.T.O.

5. **Lewis Guns.** 20 magazines per gun (in panniers) will be handed over to the incoming battalion and a similar number will be taken over from companies of the 1/5th South Staffs. Regt..

6. **Cooking utensils** will be taken out.

7. Stores of Headquarters, "A" & "D" Companies will be at HAY DUMP by 4.30 p.m.

8. **Gum Boots** will be handed into Brigade Gum Boot Store and receipts sent to Battalion Headquarters.

9. **Rations and blankets** for "B" & "C" Companies will be brought up on the tramway to HAY DUMP. Os.C. "B" & "C" Companies will each send a N.C.O. to meet truck at HAY DUMP at 4.30 p.m.

10. **Returns.** 'Lists of Stores handed over', 'Statements of work done & work proposed', and 'No Man's Land Maps' will be sent to Headquarters by 10.0 a.m.

11. **Relief Complete** will be wired to Headquarters; code word 'COPPER'. Os.C. Companies will report when they have taken up their new positions.

12. ACKNOWLEDGE.

             E.A.WILSON,
                Captain & Adjutant,
        1/5th Battalion North Staffordshire Regt.

ORIGINAL

1/5th BATTALION PRINCE of WALES'S

(NORTH STAFFORD REGIMENT).

W A R   D I A R Y

for

month of

J A N U A R Y 1918.

WAR DIARY

1/5th Bn. North Stafford Regt. Army Form C. 2118

INTELLIGENCE SUMMARY

Page 1.

(Erase heading not required.)

Instructions regarding War Diaries and Intelligence Summaries are contained in F.S. Regs., Part II. and the Staff Manual respectively. Title Pages will be prepared in manuscript.

Place	Date	Hour	Summary of Events and Information	Remarks and references to Appendices
			Reference Maps:- Sheet. 36.b. 1/40,000. and 36.c. N.W. 1/20,000.	
	January.1918.			
MAZINGARBE.	1st.		Battalion in Brigade Support. "C" & "D" Companies Bathing and Cleaning up.	
do.	2nd.		do. do. One Hours parade. Battalion relieved 1/5th South Stafford Regiment in the trenches (HULLUCH Right Subsection) Order No. 107 attached. Relief complete about 7.pm. Quiet night.	
TRENCHES.	3rd.		Quiet day.	
do	4th.		"B" & XXX "C" Companies relieved "A" & "D" Companies in the front line. Quiet night.	
do.	5th.		Quiet day.	
do.	6th.		Battalion relieved in the trenches by the 1/6th South Stafford Regiment, and proceeded to billets in NOEUX-les-MINES, arriving about 9-30.pm. The undermentioned Officers and men received Honours and Awards in the Half Yearly Honours List. MILITARY CROSS :- Captain U.U. Millar. (RAMC), Lieut (Act. Capt) W.F. Cowlishaw, 2nd Lieut T. Wint.. DISTINGUISHED CONDUCT MEDAL. :- 201525. Corpl. Johnson. T., MM.	
NOEUX-les -MINES.	7th.		Battalion in Divisional Reserve. Bathing and Cleaning up.	
do.	8th.		do do 3 hours parade including Route March.	
do.	9th.		do. do. 2 hours parade.	
do.	10th.		Battalion relieved 1/5th South Stafford Regiment in the HULLUCH Left Subsection. Order No 110. attached. Relief complete about 7.pm.	
TRENCHES.	11th.		Quiet day and night.	
do.	12th.		do do	

Army Form C. 2118.

WAR DIARY
or
INTELLIGENCE SUMMARY

1/5th Bn. North Stafford Regiment.

Page 2.

(Erase heading not required.)

Place	Date	Hour	Summary of Events and Information	Remarks and references to Appendices
	January, 1918.			
TRENCHES.	13th.		Quiet day.	
do.	14th.		Battalion relieved in the trenches by the 1/6th Bn. South Stafford Regiment. (HULLUCH right Subsection). Relief complete at 7.pm. Order No. 110 attached.	
MAZINGARBE.	15th.		Battalion in Brigade Support. Bathing and Cleaning up.	
do.	16th.		do. do. "B" Coy relieved "C" Coy in HULLUCH Tunnel.	
do.	17th.		do. do. "Bathing and Cleaning up. Kit Inspections.	
do.	18th.		Battalion relieved by the 1/5th South Stafford Regiment in the HULLUCH Right Subsection. Relief complete 6-45.pm.	
TRENCHES.	19th.		Quiet day. Usual patrolling activity.	
do	20th.		do	
do	21st		do	
do	22nd.		Battalion relieved in the trenches by the 1/5th South Stafford Regiment. Relief complete 6-45pm Order No. 116 attached.	
MAZINGARBE.	23rd.		Battalion in Brigade Support. H.Qrs and "D" Coy Bathing.	
do.	24th.		Battalion relieved by 6th Border Regiment. Relief complete 7-30.pm. Order No. 111 attached Battalion marched by Companies to FOUQUEREUIL, arriving about 11. pm.	
FOUQUEREUIL.	25th.		Battalion in G.H.Qrs Reserve. Companies at the disposal of Company Commanders for Cleaning up, kit Inspections and Bathing.	
do.	26th.		General Training and reorganization.	

Army Form C. 2118.

WAR DIARY

1/5th Bn. North Stafford Regt. Page. 3.

(Erase heading not required.)

Place	Date	Hour	Summary of Events and Information	Remarks and references to Appendices
FOUQUEREUIL.	January. 1918. 27th.		Battalion in G.H.Qrs Reserve. Church Parades.	
do.	28th.		do. Physical Training and Bayonet Fighting followed by Route March.	
do.	29th.		4 Officers and 200 Other Ranks posted to 2/6th Bn. North Stafford Regiment. and 4 Officers 190 Other Ranks posted to 9th Bn. North Stafford Regiment	
do.	30th.		5 Officers and 184 Other Ranks posted to 1/6th Bn. North Stafford Regiment, and 10 Officers and 197 Other Ranks posted to 5th Bn.North Stafford Regiment.	
	3-2-18.			

J.E. Wemyss
Captain for O.C.
1/5th Bn. North Stafford Regiment.

1/5th Bn. Prince of Wales's (North Staffordshire Regiment).

ORDER No. 106.

No. 14

1/1/18.

Reference :- Sheets 36 C. N.E. 1/..., &
36 B, 1/4, ...

1. **Relief.** The Battalion will relieve the 1/5th Battalion South Staffs. Regiment in the HULLUCH RIGHT Subsection on the night of the 2/3rd January 1918.

2. **Dispositions.** On relief Companies will be as under :-
   - "A" Company   —   Left Company
   - "B"   "   —   Left Support Company
   - "C"   "   —   Right Support Company
   - "D"   "   —   Right Company

3. **Move.** "A" & "D" Companies will move at 3.30 p.m.
   "B" & "C" Companies and Headquarters will parade in ground behind the huts at 3.45 p.m.
   Order of march :-   "C" Company, "B" Company, Headquarters.
   Dress :-   Fighting Order and greatcoats; Leather jerkins will be worn over the tunics.
   Route :-   LAMBERT'S TRACK.

4. **Advance Party.** An advance party consisting of one Officer per Company, Lewis Gun Sergeant, one N.C.O. per platoon, R.S.M., Pioneer Sergeant, Signal Officer and Battalion Signal Section, HQ. & Coy. N.C.Os. and Company Cooks, will proceed to the trenches to take over early. Those in MAZINGARBE parading on Camp ground under senior Officer at 2.0 p.m.

5. **Stores.** Officers valises and mess boxes, and packs of "B" & "C" Companies will be collected at 2.0 p.m. Stores for the trenches will be collected at 3.0 p.m.

6. **Lewis Gun Magazines.** 80 Lewis Gun Magazines per Company will be taken over from the 1/5th Bn. South Staffs. Regt. and a similar number handed over.

7. **Gum Boots.** Gum Boots will be drawn from Brigade Store, LONE TRENCH as follows :-   "B" Company - 30 pairs.
   "C"   "   - 20 pairs.
   Headquarters - 20 pairs.

8. **Cooking Utensils.** Quartermaster will arrange for 7 boilers and 4 bacon tins to be taken into the trenches.

9. **Whale Oil.** Whale Oil will be used by all ranks before proceeding to the trenches and a certificate that this has been done rendered to Orderly Room. Whale oil will be used daily in the trenches and certificates rendered.

10. **Blankets.** Blankets of "A" & "D" Companies will be sent back on the empty ration trucks.

11. **Relief Complete** will be wired to Battalion Headquarters in B.A.B. Code.

12. **Returns.** Lists of Stores taken over, Dispositions of Posts (with map references) Distribution of rifles; will be rendered to Battalion Headquarters as soon as possible after relief.

13. **Tump Line Section.** The Tump Line Section will be in dugouts in RESERVE LINE N. of POSEN ALLEY and will provide carrying parties for the T.M.Battery to be at CHALK PIT DUMP at 8.30 a.m. each day.
    The R.S.M. will detail 24 O.R's to work in shifts of 8 under Tunnelling Company, commencing at 9.0 p.m.

14. **Acknowledge.**

E.A.WILSON,
Captain & Adjutant,
1/5th Bn. North Staffs. Regiment.

Copies issued at   p.m. to :-
No. 1. Commanding Officer.   4. O.C.1/5th S.Staffs.Regt.   10. T.O. & S.M.
2. 2nd in Command.   5. O.C.1/6th S.Staffs.Regt.   11. R.S.M.
3. 137th Infantry Brigade.   6/9. O.s.C.Companies.   12. File.
13/14. War Diary.

137th Infantry Brigade - PATROL REPORT.   27th/28th December, 1917.

Right Subsection - 1/6th North Staffs Regt.

Sgt. J. Brown & 6 O.R.	To keep No Man's Land clear of the enemy.	4-30 am. H 25 b 16.10.	Party patrolled our front from H 25 b 16.10 to H 25 d 25.80. No enemy patrols or working parties were seen, and no movement was observed. Enemy very quiet.	A.20 am. H 25 d 25.80

Left Subsection - 1/5th North Staffs Regt.

To patrol No Man's Land, & keep it clear of enemy.

Two Officer & one N.C.O. patrols reconnoitred No Man's Land at 6-35 pm., 10 pm., & 1-30 am. respectively; no enemy were encountered. Talking was heard in enemy lines about H 15 a. 30.55., and M.G. fired from H 13 a 20.70. Engine was heard whistling to the East of HULLUCH.

28-12-17.

SECRET.   Copy. No.........

1/5th Battalion Prince of Wales's (North Staffordshire Regiment)

O R D E R   No. 108.

5th January. 1918.
----oO-----

Ref. Maps :- Sheet 36.c.NW. 1/20,000 and 36.b. 1/40,000.

1. RELIEF. The Battalion will be relieved in the trenches by the 1/6th Bn. South Stafford Regt, at about 6.pm. on 6th January 1918.

2. DISPOSITION. The Battalion on relief will be in Divisional Reserve at NOEUX-les-MINES.

3. MOVE On relief platoons will march independently to NOEUX-les-MINES.

4. STORES. All Stores of 'C' and 'D' Companies will be at CHALK PIT DUMP at 5.pm.; of 'A' and 'B' Companies at GUN DUMP at 5.pm. and Headquarters and Canteen at POSEN DUMP at 5.pm.
2 Cooking boilers and one fryer per Company will be handed over.

5. LEWIS GUNS. 80 Lewis Gun Magasines (in panniers) per Company will be handed over. Quartermaster will take over a similiar number at NOEUX-les-MINES.

6. GUM BOOTS. These will be sent to Brigade Gum Boot Store in LONE TRENCH tomorrow morning. (Support Companies carrying for forward Companies) Receipts will be sent to Orderly Room.

7. BILLETING PARTY. A billeting party consisting of One N.C.O., one cook, and one Officer's servant per Company; one N.C.O. from Headquarters, and Battalion Quarterguard will report at Headquarters at 9.am.

8. OFFICERS' CHARGERS. Orders re these will be issued later

9. RETURNS. "Lists of stores to be handed over","Work done and work proposed" and "NO MANS LAND" Maps", will be sent to Orderly Room by 10.am.

10. RELIEF COMPLETE will be wired to Headquarters by the Code word:- "CHEEROH"

11. ACKNOWLEDGE.

E.A. WILSON,
Captain & Adjutant.
1/5th Battalion Prince of Wales's (North Stafford Regiment.

Copies issued at   p.m. as under:-

No. 1. Commanding Officer.
    2. 2nd. in Command.
    3. Headquarters, 137th Infantry Brigade.
    4. Officer Commanding 1/5th South Staffs Rgt.
    5. Officer Commanding. 1/6th South Staffs. Rgt.
  6/9. O.C. Companies.
   10. Transport Officer and Quartermaster.
   11. R.S.M.
   12. File.
13/14. War Diary.

Copy No. 11

1/5th Battalion Prince of Wales's (North Staffordshire Regiment)

O R D E R No.109   9th January, 1918

Reference :-
   Sheets 36 B. 1/40,000
         36 C. N.W., 1/20,000

1. The Battalion will relieve the 1/5th Battalion South Staffordshire Regt. in the Left Subsection on the night of 10th/11th January, 1918.

2. <u>Dispositions</u>   "B" Coy. - Left Company
                     "A" "   - Outpost Company
                     "D" "   - Right Company
                     "C" "   - Centre Company
     The Tump Line Section will be at Battalion Headquarters.

3. The Battalion will move off by Companies at 300yds. interval.
Time - 2.15.p.m.
Companies will proceed by Platoons at 200 yds.interval from MAZINGARBE, commencing at 3.30.p.m.
Order of March - "D", "A", "C", Headquarters, "B" Coy.
Strict march discipline will be observed.

4. Dress - Fighting order, waterproof sheets, greatcoats, mess tins and water bottles full. Leather Jerkins will be worn.

5. Packs and blankets will be collected from Coy.H.Qrs. at 10.30.a.m.

6. <u>Advance Party</u> consisting of one officer per Company, Lewis gun Sergeant, One N.C.O. per platoon, R.S.M. Pioneer Sergeant, Signal Section and Bn.Signal Section, H.Q. & Coy. Gas N.C.Os. and one cook per Coy. will proceed to the trenches early to take over, marching off from here at 12 noon under the Senior Officer.

7. East of PHILOSOPHE parties will not be of more than two at 100 yards distance during daylight.

8. Officers' valises and mess boxes will be collected from the corner near H.Q. Mess at 1.0.p.m.
Stores for the trenches will be collected from Coy.H.Qrs. at 12.45.p.m.
4 H.Q.Servants and 2 servants per Coy under L/C.Green will march with limber taking trench stores. This party will push up trucks.

9. Transport Officer will detail two water duty men to go up with H.Qrs. and remain in the trenches for the tour.

10. Lewis Guns and 12 magazines per gun will be taken to PHILOSOPHE by the Transport and carried from there by the Lewis Gun teams to the line. Lewis gun limbers will move off from here at 1.30.p.m. 3 Lewis Gunners per Coy will proceed with the limbers.
80 magazines per Coy will be taken over from the 1/5th Bn.South Staffs. Regt. and a like number handed over to the 1/6th Bn.South Staffs.Regt. by the Quartermaster.

11. The Quartermaster will arrange for 12 boilers and 8 fryers to be taken into the trenches.

12. Whale Oil will be used by all ranks before proceeding to the trenches and a certificate rendered to Orderly Room that this has been done.
In the line feet will be rubbed daily and a certificate rendered.

13. O.C."D" Coy. will draw 24 pairs Gum Boots from the Brigade Gum Boot Store.

14. <u>Relief Complete</u> will be wired to Bn.H.Q. by the Code Word - FROZEN.

15. List of Stores taken over. Disposition os Posts (with map references) and Distribution of Rifles will be rendered to Headquarters as soon as possible after relief.

                                            E. A. WILSON,
                                               Captain & Adjutant,
                  1/5th Battalion Prince of Wales's (North Staffs.Regt.)

Copies issued as under at   p.m.
    No.1   -   Commanding Officer
    2   -   2nd in Command
    3   -   137th Infantry Brigade
    4   -   O.C.1/5th Bn.South Staffs.Regt.
    5   -   O.C.1/6th Bn.South Staffs.Regt.
    6/9   -   Companies
    10   -   T.O. & Q.M.
    11   -   R.S.M.
    12   -   File
    13/14   -   War Diary

1/5th Bn.Prince of Wales's (North Staffordshire Regiment).

SECRET   Copy No. 14

OPERATION ORDER No.110.
13th January 1918.

Reference :- 36C N.E.3, 1/10,000

1. The Battalion will be relieved by the 1/6th Bn.South Staffordshire Regiment about 6-0 pm. on the 14th inst.

2. Dispositions after relief :-
   "Headquarters and "B" Coy. in MAZINGARBE.
   "D" and "C" Coys. in HULLUCH TUNNEL, relieving "B" & "D" Coys. 1/5th South Staffs.Regt., respectively.
   "A" Coy. in TENTH AVENUE relieving "C" Coy. 1/5th South Staffs. Regt.

3. (a). "C" Coy. will be under orders of O.C. 3rd Australian Coy for work and O.C. 6th South Staffs.Regt., tactically.
   (b). "D" Coy. will be under orders of O.C. 466th Field Coy.R.E's for work and 137th Brigade tactically.
   (c). "A" Coy will be under orders of O.C. 466th Field Coy.R.E's for work and O.C. 5th South tactically.

4. (a). Os.C. "A","C" and "D" Coys. will each send one Officer to take over to report to the O.C.Coy they are relieving before 2-30 pm.
   (b). Advance Party from "B" Coy. and Brigade guard will report to Headquarters at 10-0 am.

5. Stores from Headquarters and "B" Coy. will be on HAY DUMP at 5-15 pm.

6. 'List of Stores to be handed over', 'Statement of work proposed' and 'No Man's Land maps' will be sent to H.Qrs., by 10-0 am.

7. 80 Lewis gun magazines (in panniers) per company will be handed over and taken over.
   1/5th South Staffs Regt., will send up on ration trucks 80 magazines. O.C. "C" Coy will arrange to take these over.

8. Rations and blankets for "C" and "D" Coys will be at HAY DUMP about 5-15 pm and "A" Coy's at QUARRY DUMP about 5-0 pm.
   Each company will detail a N.C.O. to meet their blankets.

9. Tump line Section will rejoin their companies on relief.

10. Relief Complete will be wired to headquarters - code word :- BLIGHTY.

11. ACKNOWLEDGE.

L.A.WILSON,
Captain & Adjutant,
1/5th Bn.North Staffs Regiment.

Copies issued at   pm. to :-
   No.1. ....   Commanding Officer.
   " 2. .... 2nd.in Command.
   " 3. .... 137th Infantry Brigade.
   " 4. .... O.C. 1/5th Bn.South Staffs.Regt.
   " 5. .... O.C. 1/6th Bn.South Staffs Regt.
   " 6/9. .....   Os.C.Companies.
   " 10. ......   Transport Officer & Quartermaster.
   " 11. ......   R.S.M.
   " 12. ......   File.
   " 13/14 ...... War Diary.

FIRST ARMY SUMMARY OF OPERATIONS
for the 24 hours ending in the early morning of 7/1/18.

FIRST ARMY.

Operations. During the afternoon the enemy carried out an unusually heavy trench-mortar bombardment of our lines from MAD POINT to the LA BASSEE Canal. Our artillery bombarded the active trench-mortars and the German trenches opposite.

Artillery. During the day our artillery shelled LOISON Station, the Coke Ovens, and dumps in LENS. Nineteen destructive shoots were carried out and thirteen hostile batteries were neutralised.

Royal Flying Corps. One of our machines over VALENCIENNES was attacked by 5 Albatross scouts from above and below. One of the E.A. was brought down out of control and 2 others were driven down. In combats during the day one E.A. was crashed E. of FRESNES and another near FRESNOY. Another E.A. was brought down out of control near QUIERY-la-MOTTE and one apparently out of control near FAUMONT. One of our machines was forced to land yesterday morning, with engine trouble, in "No Man's Land", S.W. of MERICOURT. The pilot and observer succeeded in reaching our lines. 48 bombs were dropped on points of importance behind the enemy lines.

OTHER ARMIES. Nothing of importance to report.

FRENCH FRONT.
There has been moderate activity of the opposing artilleries in the neighbourhood of CORBENY and in Upper Alsace. No infantry actions have taken place.

ITALIAN FRONT.
The usual reciprocal harassing fire is reported on the whole front.

MISCELLANEOUS.
A Russian Government wireless message says that German deserters state that all soldiers up to the age of 35 are being rapidly drawn upon from different detachments now on the Eastern front to join new units being formed at KOVNO and VILNA, for the purpose of transferring to the Western front, in contravention of the armistice between Russia and Germany. These proceedings are creating unrest among German troops. German soldiers declare that to go to Western front means going to be slaughtered, and they are deserting in large numbers. According to further information from the same source, about 24,000 German soldiers in region E. of KOVNO have revolted and have entrenched themselves with rifles and machine-guns against other units. Military authorities are powerless against them, and are trying to cut off supplies.

R.S.RYAN, Lieut.-Col.,
General Staff, First Army.

7/1/18.

SECRET.   Copy No. 13

1/5th Bn.Prince of Wales's (North Staffordshire Regiment.)

OPERATION ORDER No.111
15th Jany.1918

Reference :- 36B. 1/40,000

1. The 137th Infantry Brigade will be relieved by the 33rd Infantry Brigade on the 16th and 17th inst.

2. This Battalion will be relieved by the 6th BORDER Regt. on the 16th inst. (6th BORDER Regt., will not arrive in MAZINGARBE before 4-0 pm.)

3. On relief the Battalion will march to billets at FOUQUEREUIL.

4. Advance party consisting of 2nd.Lt.J.Murphy, Coy.Q.M.Sergts and one N.C.O. and one Officer's servant per company also one signaller with telephone, will parade at Headquarters MAZINGARBE at 8-0 am and march to FOUQUEREUIL and take over billets from the 9th Bn.SHERWOOD FORESTERS.

5. (a). "B" Coy. and H.Q.details will parade in the camp at 4-30 pm. and on arrival of relief will march under O.C. "B" Coy to FOUQUEREUIL.
   (b). "A", "C" and "D" Coys, on relief, will march independently to L.21.a.05.70 where a hot meal will be ready - after which they will march independently to FOUQUEREUIL.

6. Guides will meet "A", "C" and "D" Coys at Brigade Headquarters.

7. Billeting Party will meet companies at E.14.c.85.30.

8. Transport will move under orders of Transport Officer - instructions will be given to him in detail.

9. The following maps will be retained by Officers :-
   all 1/10,000, 1/20,000, 1/40,000, 1/100,000 and 1/250,000 scale maps.

10. All Trench Stores will be handed over and receipts taken in triplicate.

11. Billets and transport lines will be handed over to the Town Major or Sub-area Commandant concerned and a certificate obtained that same have been left clean and tidy. Certificates to be sent to H.Q.
    Transport Officer will arrange to do this for the transport line and Q.M.Stores.

12. The guard on Bde.Headquarters found by this Battalion will move with Brigade Headquarters on the 17th inst.
    (per company)

13. Four guides/from "A", "C" and "D" Coys will be at MAZINGARBE Bde.Headquarters at 3-30 pm, 16th inst.

14. ACKNOWLEDGE.

                                                E.A.WILSON,
                                                Captain & Adjutant,
                                                1/5th Bn.North Staffs.Regt.

Copies issued at // am as under :-
    No.1.------ Commanding Officer.
    " 2 ..... 137th Inf.Brigade
    " 3 ....   O.C. 6th Border Regt.
    " 4 ....   9th Bn.Sherwood Foresters.
    " 5/8 ... Os.C.Companies.
    " 9 ..... Transport Officer & Q.Master.
    " 10 .... R.S.M.
    " 11 .... File.
    " 12/13 .. War Diary

SECRET. Copy No. _____
1/5th Bn. Prince of Wales's (North Staffordshire Regiment.)

OPERATION ORDER No. 112
16th Jany. 1917.

1. "B" Coy. will relieve "C" Coy. in HULLUCH TUNNEL tonight.
   Details of relief to be arranged between Os.C.Coys. concerned.

2. Men from the Bde. Pioneer Coy of "A" and "D" Coys. will march
   up under orders of O.C. "B" Coy and join their companies on
   TENTH AVENUE.

3. Packs and Officers' valises will be ready in the camp by 3-0 pm.

4. "C" Coy. will send down Bde.H.Q.guard, Divl.Bomb-store guard
   and Battn.Quarter-guard in advance.
   O.C. "B" Coy. will send up a party to take over early.

                                                E.A. WILSON,
                                          Captain & Adjutant.

Copies issued to :-
        No. 1. ...... Commanding Officer.
        Nos. 2/5   Os.C.Companies.
        No. 6. .   T.C. and Q.M.
         " 7.   R.S.M.
         " 8.   File.
         " 9./10.   Diary.

SECRET.   COPY No. /3

1/5th Battalion   Prince of Wales's (North Staffordshire Regiment)

O P E R A T I O N   O R D E R   No. 112.
17th January 1918.

Reference:-
Sheet 36C.N.E. 1/20,000.

1. **Relief.**   The Battalion will relieve the 1/5th Battalion South Staffs. Regiment in the HULLUCH RIGHT Subsection on the night of the 18/19th January 1918.

2. **Dispositions.**   On relief Companies will be as under :-
   "A" Company   -   Left Company
   "B"   "   -   Left Support Company
   "C"   "   -   Right Support Company
   "D"   "   -   Right Company

3. **Move.**   "A" & "B" Companies will move at 3.30 p.m.
   "C" Company and Headquarters will parade on ground outside the huts at 3.45 p.m.
   Order of march - "C" Company, Headquarters.
   Dress - Fighting order and greatcoats; leather jerkins will be worn over the tunics.
   Route - LAMBERT'S TRACK.

4. **Advance Party.**   An advance party consisting of one Officer per Company, Lewis Gun Officer, one N.C.O. per platoon, and the Pioneer Sergeant, Signal Officer and Battalion Signal Section, HQ and Company Gas N.C.Os. and Company Cooks, will proceed to the trenches early to take over, those in MAZINGARBE parading on camp ground under Senior Officer at 2.0 p.m.

5. **Stores.**   Officers valises and mess boxes, and packs of "C" Company will be collected at 2.0 p.m. Stores for the trenches will be collected at 3.0 p.m.

6. **Lewis Gun Magazines.**   30 Lewis Gun Magazines per Company will be taken over from the 1/5th South Staffs. Regt. and a similar number handed over.

7. **Gum Boots.**   Gum Boots will be drawn from Brigade Store LONE TRENCH as follows :-
   "A" Company   -   60 pairs.
   "B"   "   -   30   "
   "C"   "   -   30   "
   "D"   "   -   60   "
   Headquarters -   20   "

8. **Cooking Utensils.**   Quartermaster will arrange for 7 boilers and 4 tins to be taken into the trenches.

9. **Whale Oil.**   Whale oil will be used by all ranks before proceeding to the trenches and a certificate that this has been done rendered to Orderly Room. Whale oil will be used daily in the trenches and certificates rendered.

10. **Blankets.**   Blankets of "A", "B" & "D" Companies will be sent back on empty ration trucks.

11. **Relief Complete.**   Will be wired to Battalion Headquarters in B.A.B.

12. **Returns.**   Lists of stores taken over, Dispositions of posts, (map references) and Distributions of rifles, will be rendered to Battalion Headquarters as soon as possible after relief.

13. **Tump Line Section.**   The Tump Line Section will be in dugouts in the line N of OSSEY ALLEY and will provide carrying parties for T.L. Battery to be at CHALK PIT TRIB at 8.30 a.m. on said day. R.E. will hand 24 O.R's to work in shift of 8 under Tunnelling Company, commencing at 9.0 p.m.

14. ACKNOWLEDGE.
                                              E.A. WILSON,
                                                    Captain & Adjutant,

COPIES ISSUED to :-
at   p.m.

No. 1.   Commanding Officer.
 " 2.   2nd in Command.
 " 3.   137th Infantry Brigade.
2" 4.   O.C. 1/5th South Staffs. Regt..
 " 5.   O.C. 1/6th South Staffs. Regt..
 " 6/9. Os.C. Companies.
 " 10.   Transport Officer & Quartermaster.
 " 11.   R.S.M.
 " 12.   File.
 " 13/14. War Diary.

SECRET   Copy No. 1/14

1/5th Battn. Prince of Wales's (North Staffordshire Regiment).

OPERATION ORDER No. 116.
21st Jany, 1918

Reference :- 36C. N.W.3. 1/10,000

1. The Battalion will be relieved by the 1/5th Bn. South Staffordshire Regiment at about 5-30 pm on the 22nd. inst.

2. Dispositions after relief :-
   "H.Qrs" (including Tump line Section) and "D" Coy. in MAZINGARBE.
   "A" Coy. in HULLUCH TUNNEL.
   "B" Coy in TENTH AVENUE.
   "C" Coy. at POSEN.

3. "A" Coy. will be under orders of O.C. 3rd Australian Coy for work and under O.C. 1/6th Bn. South Staffs. Regt., tactically.
   "B" Coy. will be under orders of O.C. 466th Field Coy. R.E's for work and 137th Brigade tactically.
   "C" Coy. will be under orders of O.C. 466th Coy. REs for work and O.C. 1/6th Bn South Staffs. Regt. tactically.

4. Os.C. "A", "B" and "C" Coys. will each send one Officer to take over to report to the O.C. Coy they are relieving before 2-30 pm.

5. Billeting party consisting of C.Q.M. Sergts., one servant and one runner per company will go out in advance reporting at Bn.H.Q., at 9-0 am.

6. Stores of H.Qrs. will be at POSEN DUMP and of "D" Coy at CHALK PIT DUMP at 5-30 pm.

7. 80 lewis gun magazines (in panniers) per company will be handed over Quartermaster will arrange to take over a similar number from the 1/5th Bn. South Staffs. Regt.

8. Gum boots. The tump line Section will collect these from Coys tomorrow morning and carry to Gum Boot Store in LONE TRENCH receipts being sent to Orderly Room.

9. Cooking utensils will be taken out and none taken over.

10. "List of Stores to be handed over" and "Statement of work done and proposed" will be sent to Orderly Room by 10-0 am.

11. Relief Complete will be wired to "H.Qrs" by B.A.B.

12. ACKNOWLEDGE.

                                          T. MURPHY, 2/Lieut.
                                          A/Adjutant,
                                          1/5th Bn. North Staffs. Regt.

Copies issued at   pm to :-
   No. 1........ Commanding Officer.
   "   2 .... 2nd. in Command.
   "   3 .... 137th Infantry Brigade.
   "   4 .... O.C. 1/5th Bn. South Staffs. Regt.
   "   5 .... O.C. 1/6th Bn. South Staffs Regt.
   "   6/9 ... Os.C. Companies.
   "   10 ..... R Transport Officer & Quartermaster.
   "   11 ..... R.S.M.
   "   12 ..... File.
   "   13/14 ... War Diary.

Army Form C. 2118.

WAR DIARY
or
INTELLIGENCE SUMMARY

1/5th Bn. North Stafford Regiment.

Page. 4.

(Erase heading not required.)

SUMMARY OF CASUALTIES and STRENGTH for month of January 1918.

	Casualties.						Strength.	
	Officers.			Other Ranks.			Officers.	O.Ranks.
	K.	W.	M. Hosp.	K.	W.	M. Hosp.		
For week ending 4-1-18.	-	-	-	-	1	-	9	32	817.
do. 11-1-18.	-	-	-	2	2	-	10	29	819.
do. 18-1-18.	-	-	-	-	2	-	9	29	810
do. 25-1-18.	-	-	-	-	-	-	7	30	808
For period to 31-1-18.	-	-	-	-	-	-	-	2	37
	-	-	-	2	5	-	35.		

J.E. Wragg.
Captain for O.C.
1/5th Bn. North Stafford Regiment.

www.ingramcontent.com/pod-product-compliance
Lightning Source LLC
Chambersburg PA
CBHW080840010526
44114CB00017B/2343